Lecture Notes in Computer Science 9680

Commenced Publication in 1973
Founding and Former Series Editors:
Gerhard Goos, Juris Hartmanis, and Jan van Leeuwen

More information about this series at http://www.springer.com/series/7412

Alamin Mansouri · Fathallah Nouboud
Alain Chalifour · Driss Mammass
Jean Meunier · Abderrahim El Moataz (Eds.)

Image and Signal Processing

7th International Conference, ICISP 2016
Trois-Rivières, QC, Canada, May 30 – June 1, 2016
Proceedings

Springer

Editors

Alamin Mansouri
Université de Bourgogne
Auxerre
France

Fathallah Nouboud
Université du Québec à Trois-Rivières
Trois-Rivières, QC
Canada

Alain Chalifour
Université du Québec à Trois-Rivières
Trois-Rivières, QC
Canada

Driss Mammass
Université Ibn Zohr
Agadir
Morocco

Jean Meunier
Université de Montréal
Montréal, QC
Canada

Abderrahim El Moataz
Universitè de Caen Basse Normandie
Caen
France

ISSN 0302-9743   ISSN 1611-3349   (electronic)
Lecture Notes in Computer Science
ISBN 978-3-319-33617-6   ISBN 978-3-319-33618-3   (eBook)
DOI 10.1007/978-3-319-33618-3

Library of Congress Control Number: 2016937937

LNCS Sublibrary: SL6 – Image Processing, Computer Vision, Pattern Recognition, and Graphics

Printed on acid-free paper

This Springer imprint is published by Springer Nature
The registered company is Springer International Publishing AG Switzerland

Preface

ICISP 2016, the International Conference on Image and Signal Processing, was the seventh ICISP conference, and was held in Trois-Rivières, Québec, Canada. Historically, ICISP is a conference resulting from the actions of researchers from Canada, France, and Morocco. Previous editions of ICISP were held in Cherbourg-Octeville (France, 2014 and 2008), in Trois-Rivières, Québec (Canada, 2010), and in Agadir (Morocco, 2012, 2003, and 2001). ICISP 2016 was sponsored by EURASIP (European Association for Image and Signal Processing) and IAPR (International Association for Pattern Recognition).

The response to the call for papers for ICISP 2016 was encouraging. From 83 recorded submissions, 40 papers were finally accepted. The review process was carried out by the Program Committee members; all are experts in various image and signal processing areas. Each paper was reviewed by at least two reviewers, and also checked by the conference co-chairs. The quality of the papers in these proceedings is attributed first to the authors, and second to the standard of the reviews provided by the experts. We would like to thank the authors for responding to our call, and we thank the reviewers for their excellent work.

For this edition, ICISP was pleased to host the 18th International Symposium on Multispectral Colour Science (MCS 2014) as a special track, as well as the special session Digital Cultural Heritage (scientifically supported by the COST action TD 1201; Colour and Space in Cultural Heritage — COSCH).

We were very pleased to be able to include in the conference program keynote talks by three world-renowned experts: Jocelyn Chanussot (University of Grenoble, France, and currently Guest Researcher at UCLA, USA), Roland Memisevic (University of Montreal, Canada) and Robert Laganiere (University of Ottawa, Canada).

We would also like to thank the members of the local Organizing Committee for their advice and help. We would like to thank Olivier Lézoray for his advice and all the material he provided for preparing this volume of proceedings. The proceedings preparation was also eased thanks to the tools provided by the EasyChair platform.

We are also grateful to Springer's editorial staff for supporting this publication in the LNCS series. Finally, we were very pleased to welcome all the participants to this conference. For those who did not attend, we hope this publication provides a good view into the research presented at the conference, and we look forward to meeting you at the next edition of the ICISP conference.

May 2016

Alamin Mansouri
Fathallah Nouboud
Alain Chalifour
Driss Mammass
Jean Meunier
Abderrahim El Moataz

Organization

General Chairs

Fathallah Nouboud   University of Québec at Trois-Rivières, Québec, Canada
Alain Chalifour   University of Québec at Trois-Rivières, Québec, Canada

Program Committee Chair

Alamin Mansouri   University of Bourgogne, France

Program Committee Co-chairs

Driss Mammass   University Ibn Zohr, Morocco
Jean Meunier   University of Québec at Montréal, Montréal, Canada
Abderrahim El Moataz   University of Caen Basse-Normandie, France

Local Arrangements/Finance Chairs

Fathallah Nouboud   University of Québec at Trois-Rivières, Québec, Canada
Alain Chalifour   University of Québec at Trois-Rivières, Québec, Canada

Website Chair

Alamin Mansouri   University of Bourgogne, France

Proceedings Chair

Alamin Mansouri   University of Bourgogne, France

Program Committee

S. Battiato   University of Catania, Italy
G. Bebis   University of Nevada, USA
Y. Benezeth   Université de Bourgogne, France
Yannick Berthoumieu   IMS, UMR 5218 CNRS, University of Bordeaux, France
G. Boccignone   University of Milano, Italy
F. Boochs   i3mainz, Germany
Saida Bouakaz-B   Université Claude Bernard Lyon 1, France
Aarnaud Boucher   Université de Bourgogne - Le2i, France
S. Bougleux   Université de Caen Basse-Normandie, France
El-Bay Bourennane   Le2i Laboratory, France

Contents

Feature Extraction, Computer Vision and Pattern Recognition

On the Benefit of State Separation for Tracking in Image Space with an
Interacting Multiple Model Filter. 3
  Stefan Becker, Hilke Kieritz, Wolfgang Hübner, and Michael Arens

Feature Asymmetry of the Conformal Monogenic Signal 12
  Ahror Belaid

Edge Detection Based on Riesz Transform. 21
  Ahror Belaid, Soraya Aloui, and Djamal Boukerroui

Otolith Recognition System Using a Normal Angles Contour 30
  El Habouz Youssef, Es-saady Youssef, El Yassa Mostafa,
  Mammass Driss, Nouboud Fathallah, Chalifour Alain,
  and Manchih Khalid

A Hybrid Combination of Multiple SVM Classifiers for Automatic
Recognition of the Damages and Symptoms on Plant Leaves 40
  Ismail El Massi, Youssef Es-saady, Mostafa El Yassa, Driss Mammass,
  and Abdeslam Benazoun

Leaf Classification Using Convexity Measure of Polygons 51
  Jules Raymond Kala, Serestina Viriri, Deshendran Moodley,
  and Jules Raymond Tapamo

Privacy Preserving Dynamic Room Layout Mapping 61
  Xinyu Li, Yanyi Zhang, Ivan Marsic, and Randall S. Burd

Defect Detection on Patterned Fabrics Using Entropy Cues 71
  Maricela Martinez-Leon, Rocio A. Lizarraga-Morales,
  Carlos Rodriguez-Donate, Eduardo Cabal-Yepez,
  and Ruth I. Mata-Chavez

Curve Extraction by Geodesics Fusion: Application to Polymer Reptation
Analysis. 79
  Somia Rahmoun, Fabrice Mairesse, Hiroshi Uji-i, Johan Hofkens,
  and Tadeusz Sliwa

Multispectral and Colour Imaging

A Chaotic Cryptosystem for Color Image with Dynamic Look-Up Table   91
   Med Karim Abdmouleh, Ali Khalfallah, and Med Salim Bouhlel

Nonlinear Estimation of Chromophore Concentrations and Shading from
Hyperspectral Images.   101
   Rina Akaho, Misa Hirose, and Norimichi Tsumura

A Color Image Database for Haze Model and Dehazing Methods
Evaluation   109
   Jessica El Khoury, Jean-Baptiste Thomas, and Alamin Mansouri

Collaborative Unmixing Hyperspectral Imagery via Nonnegative Matrix
Factorization.   118
   Yaser Esmaeili Salehani and Saeed Gazor

A New Method for Arabic Text Detection in Natural Scene Image Based
on the Color Homogeneity   127
   Houda Gaddour, Slim Kanoun, and Nicole Vincent

Measuring Spectral Reflectance and 3D Shape Using Multi-primary Image
Projector   137
   Keita Hirai, Ryosuke Nakahata, and Takahiko Horiuchi

Computer Vision Color Constancy from Maximal Projections Mean
Assumption   148
   Elkhamssa Lakehal and Djemel Ziou

Demosaicking Method for Multispectral Images Based on Spatial Gradient
and Inter-channel Correlation   157
   *Shu Ogawa, Kazuma Shinoda, Madoka Hasegawa, Shigeo Kato,
   Masahiro Ishikawa, Hideki Komagata, and Naoki Kobayashi*

Image Filtering, Segmentation and Super-Resolution

Single Image Super-Resolution Using Sparse Representation on a K-NN
Dictionary   169
   Liu Ning and Liang Shuang

Super-Resolved Enhancement of a Single Image and Its Application
in Cardiac MRI.   179
   *Guang Yang, Xujiong Ye, Greg Slabaugh, Jennifer Keegan,
   Raad Mohiaddin, and David Firmin*

Signal Processing

Speaker Classification via Supervised Hierarchical Clustering Using ICA
Mixture Model 193
  Muhammad Azam and Nizar Bouguila

Speaker Discrimination Using Several Classifiers and a Relativistic Speaker
Characterization 203
  Siham Ouamour, Zohra Hamadache, and Halim Sayoud

Speaker Discrimination Based on a Fusion Between Neural and Statistical
Classifiers 213
  Siham Ouamour and Halim Sayoud

Multiple-Instance Multiple-Label Learning for the Classification of Frog
Calls with Acoustic Event Detection 222
  Jie Xie, Michael Towsey, Liang Zhang, Kiyomi Yasumiba,
  Lin Schwarzkopf, Jinglan Zhang, and Paul Roe

Feature Extraction Based on Bandpass Filtering for Frog Call Classification . . . 231
  Jie Xie, Michael Towsey, Liang Zhang, Jinglan Zhang, and Paul Roe

Biomedical Imaging

Classification of Eukaryotic Organisms Through Cepstral Analysis
of Mitochondrial DNA. 243
  Emmanuel Adetiba and Oludayo O. Olugbara

A Novel Geometrical Approach for a Rapid Estimation of the HARDI
Signal in Diffusion MRI 253
  Ines Ben Alaya, Majdi Jribi, Faouzi Ghorbel, and Tarek Kraiem

Detection of Activities During Newborn Resuscitation Based
on Short-Time Energy of Acceleration Signal 262
  Huyen Vu, Trygve Eftestøl, Kjersti Engan, Joar Eilevstjønn,
  Ladislaus Blacy Yarrot, Jørgen E. Linde, and Hege Ersdal

Geoscience and Remote Sensing

Unsupervised Classification of Synthetic Aperture Radar Imagery Using a
Bootstrap Version of the Generalized Mixture Expectation Maximization
Algorithm 273
  Ahlem Bougarradh, Slim Mhiri, and Faouzi Ghorbel

Palm Trees Detection from High Spatial Resolution Satellite Imagery Using
a New Contextual Classification Method with Constraints   283
  Soufiane Idbraim, Driss Mammass, Lahoucine Bouzalim, Moulid Oudra,
  Mauricio Labrador-Garca, and Manuel Arbelo

Fast Autonomous Crater Detection by Image Analysis–For Unmanned
Landing on Unknown Terrain.   293
  Payel Sadhukhan and Sarbani Palit

Automatic Detection and Classification of Oil Tanks in Optical Satellite
Images Based on Convolutional Neural Network.   304
  Qingquan Wang, Jinfang Zhang, Xiaohui Hu, and Yang Wang

Watermarking, Authentication and Coding

Digital Watermarking Scheme Based on Arnold and Anti-Arnold
Transforms.   317
  M. Abdallah Elayan and M. Omair Ahmad

A JND Model Using a Texture-Edge Selector Based on Faber-Schauder
Wavelet Lifting Scheme.   328
  Meina Amar, Rachid Harba, Hassan Douzi, Frederic Ros,
  Mohamed El Hajji, Rabia Riad, and Khadija Gourrame

A Fragile Watermarking Scheme for Image Authentication Using Wavelet
Transform   337
  Assma Azeroual and Karim Afdel

Single-Loop Architecture for JPEG 2000   346
  David Barina, Ondrej Klima, and Pavel Zemcik

Robust Print-cam Image Watermarking in Fourier Domain.   356
  Khadija Gourrame, Hassan Douzi, Rachid Harba, Frederic Ros,
  Mohamed El Hajji, Rabia Riad, and Meina Amar

3d Acquisition, Processing and Applications

No-Reference 3D Mesh Quality Assessment Based on Dihedral Angles
Model and Support Vector Regression.   369
  Ilyass Abouelaziz, Mohammed El Hassouni, and Hocine Cherifi

Kinect Depth Holes Filling by Similarity and Position Constrained Sparse
Representation   378
  Jinhui Hu, Zhongyuan Wang, and Ruolin Ruan

Color Correction in 3D Digital Documentation: Case Study   388
  Krzysztof Lech, Grzegorz Mączkowski, and Eryk Bunsch

The Traveling Optical Scanner – Case Study on 3D Shape Models of
Ancient Brazilian Skulls.   398
    *Camilla Himmelstrup Trinderup, Vedrana Andersen Dahl,
    Kristian Murphy Gregersen, Ludovic Antoine Alexandre Orlando,
    and Anders Bjorholm Dahl*

Author Index   407

Feature Extraction, Computer Vision and Pattern Recognition

On the Benefit of State Separation
for Tracking in Image Space
with an Interacting Multiple Model Filter

Stefan Becker$^{(\boxtimes)}$, Hilke Kieritz, Wolfgang Hübner, and Michael Arens

Fraunhofer IOSB, Gutleuthausstr. 1, 76275 Ettlingen, Germany
stefan.becker@iosb.fraunhofer.de
http://www.iosb.fraunhofer.de

Abstract. When tracking an object, it is reasonable to assume that the dynamic model can change over time. In practical applications, Interacting Multiple Model (IMM) filter are a popular choice for considering such varying system characteristics. The motion of the object is often modeled using position, velocity, and acceleration. It seems obvious that different image space dimensions can be considered in one overall system state vector. In this paper, the fallacy of simply extending the state vector in case of tracking an object solely in image space is demonstrated. Thereby, we show how under such conditions the effectiveness of an IMM filter can be improved by separating particular states. The proposed approach is evaluated on the VOT 2014 dataset.

Keywords: Interacting Multiple Models · Visual tracking

1 Introduction

An important component of tracking is the filtering problem in which estimates of object's state are computed while observations are progressively received. The estimation process is in general modeled using a Bayesian formulation [2]. For many filters, i.e. the well-known Kalman filter [1] or nonparametric methods such as particle filters [3], the posterior probability can be recursively updated by applying a perception model and a motion model. Under real world conditions, the object motion can change over time and it is impossible to define a unique motion model which captures all different motions the object can execute. An elegant way of dealing with motion uncertainties and capturing the complex dynamics of objects is the Interacting Multiple Model (IMM) filter [4]. It has been successfully employed in several applications [5,6]. The IMM approach can be used to fuse several models in one context by weighting each model from a set of models as possible candidates. Each model contributes to the final distribution depending on its current weight. In most cases, the motion is modeled by a bank of standard Kalman filters per object and the dynamics are described in 3D space. However, there exist several scenarios where objects are solely tracked on directly observed image space information. For example person tracking without

© Springer International Publishing Switzerland 2016
A. Mansouri et al. (Eds.): ICISP 2016, LNCS 9680, pp. 3–11, 2016.
DOI: 10.1007/978-3-319-33618-3_1

available external calibration. The goal of this paper is to reveal some fallacy when applying an IMM filter restricted to such information. We show how a separation of the state space vector improves the overall system accuracy. After some basic concepts of an IMM filter are described in Sect. 2, we show how a basic IMM setup with three standard motion models should be modified for a better image space object tracking. The results achieved on the public available VOT 2014 dataset are presented in Sects. 3 and 4 contains a conclusion.

2   Interacting Multiple Model Filter

In this section the basic concepts of the IMM filter and a reference IMM config-uration for the evaluation are described. For a more detailed description see for example Hartikainen and Särkkä [7] or Bar-Shalom et al. [8]. As mentioned, it is reasonable to assume that the dynamic model of an object can change from time to time. As a solution, a system is considered to be composed of multiple independent models, where the currently active model is one from a discrete set of n candidate models ($M = \{M^1, \ldots, M^n\}$). The IMM filter is a popu-lar choice for practical applications. Some prior probability μ_0^j for each model M^j and the state transition probability between time index $k - 1$ and k from model i to model j (denoted by $p_{ij} = P(M_k^j | M_{k-1}^i)$) are assumed to be known. The transition probability matrix p_{ij} can be interpreted as a first order Markov chain characterizing the mode transitions. Hence systems of this type are com-monly referred to Markovian switching systems (Bar-Shalom et al. [8]). Thus, the model or mode transition can be characterized by a first order Markov chain and described as transition probability matrix p_{ij}. The closed form solution for the state estimation problem of a discrete-time IMM filter can be written as follows:

$$x_k = F_k^j x_{k-1} + w_k^j \tag{1}$$

$$y_k = H_k^j x_k + r_k^j \tag{2}$$

Here, x_k is the state of the object and the effective model in time step $k - 1$ is denoted by j. F_k is the state transition matrix which applies the effect of each system state parameter at time $k - 1$ on the system state at time k. H_k is the measurement model matrix that maps the state parameters into the mea-surement domain. $w_k \sim N(0, Q_k)$ is the process noise and $r_k \sim N(0, R_k)$ is the measurement noise. For our goal to only rely on the directly observed information y_k, we use the image space coordinates and the scale of the object as measure-ment. This information can be obtained from every object detector following the sliding window paradigm. Although the detectors differ in many aspects, the output of such a sliding window based detector is a rectangular bounding box centered at the object location. Here (x, y) is the center position in the image space and s the scale. For describing the overall state of our reference IMM con-figuration the corresponding velocities $(\dot{x}, \dot{y}, \dot{s})$ and acceleration are used $\ddot{x}, \ddot{y}, \ddot{s}$. The most common linear motion models are the constant position model (CP), the constant velocity model (CV), and the constant acceleration model (CA). In our experiments, we choose an IMM filter configuration, which consist of these three basic models. When the object remains at the same position the velocity and acceleration are reduced to zero since the object is not moving. Thus, the transition matrix for a state vector including the 9 mentioned states $(x_k = (x, y, s, \dot{x}, \dot{y}, \dot{s}, \ddot{x}, \ddot{y}, \ddot{s}))$ for the constant position motion model is defined as

$$F_k^{CP} = \begin{bmatrix} I_{3\times3} & 0_{3\times6} \\ 0_{3\times6} & 0_{6\times6} \end{bmatrix}. \tag{3}$$

The constant velocity model is used in most tracking approaches and can be then be defined as

$$F_k^{CV} = \begin{bmatrix} I_{3\times3} & I_{3\times3}T & 0_{3\times3} \\ 0_{3\times3} & I_{3\times3} & 0_{3\times3} \\ 0_{3\times3} & 0_{3\times3} & 0_{3\times3} \end{bmatrix}. \tag{4}$$

Here, T is the number of discrete time steps. In literature, several assumptions on how to model the acceleration process of an object are proposed (see Li and Jilkov [9]). Here, a CA model is considered as

$$F_k^{CA} = \begin{bmatrix} I_{3\times3} & I_{3\times3}T & \frac{1}{2}I_{3\times3}T^2 \\ 0_{3\times3} & I_{3\times3} & I_{3\times3}T \\ 0_{3\times3} & 0_{3\times3} & 0_{3\times3} \end{bmatrix}. \tag{5}$$

The IMM filter basically consists of three major steps: interaction (mixing), filtering and combination. In the interaction stage and under the assumption that a particular model is the right model at the current time step, the initial conditions for this model are obtained by mixing the state estimates produced by all filters. In detail, the mixing probabilities $\mu_k^{i|j}$ for each model M^i and M^j are calculated as $\mu_k^{i|j} = \frac{1}{\bar{c}_j}p_{ij}\mu_{k-1}^i$ with $\bar{c}_j = \sum_{i=1}^{n}p_{ij}\mu_{k-1}^i$. Thereby, μ_{k-1}^i is the probability of model M^i in the time step $k-1$ and $\bar{c}_j$ a normalization factor. For each filter the mixed mean and covariance is computed as follows:

$$m_{k-1}^{0j} = \sum_{i=1}^{n}\frac{1}{\bar{c}_j}\mu_k^{i|j}m_{k-1}^i \tag{6}$$

$$P_{k-1}^{0j} = \sum_{i=1}^{n}\mu_k^{i|j}\left(P_{k-1}^i + (m_{k-1}^i - m_{k-1}^{0j})(m_{k-1}^i - m_{k-1}^{0j})^T\right) \tag{7}$$

Here, m_{k-1}^i and P_{k-1}^i are the updated mean and covariance for model i at time step $k-1$.

Then in the filtering stage, for each individual model conditioned on the current active mode, a standard Kalman filtering (KF) is done. Correspondingly a prediction $\left[m_k^{-,i}, P_k^{-,i}\right] = KF_p(m_{k-1}^{0j}, P_{k-1}^{0j}, F_k^i, Q_k)$ and update step $[m_k^i, P_k^i] = KF_u(m_k^{-,i}, P_k^{-,i}, H_k^i, R_k^i)$ is applied. Initialization is done with m_{k-1}^i and P_{k-1}^i. Then the model probabilities $\mu_k^i = \frac{1}{c}\Lambda_k^i\bar{c}_i$ are adapted according to the likelihood of the measurement for each filter Λ_k^i. Where $c = \sum_{i=1}^n \Lambda_k^i \bar{c}_i$ is a normalizing factor.

The final step of the IMM filter is combination. There, the combined estimate for the state mean and covariance is computed as follows:

$$m_k = \sum_{i=1}^n \mu_k^i m_k^i \tag{8}$$

$$P_k = \sum_{i=1}^n \mu_k^i \left(P_k^i + (m_k^i - m_k)(m_k^i - m_k)^T \right) \tag{9}$$

3   IMM Configuration and Evaluation

In this section, we evaluate the effectiveness of different IMM filter configuration in terms of state separation for the case of tracking the object only with directly observed image space information. The desired states for the IMM filter for tracking were determined in Sect. 2. Besides the center position in the image space (x, y) and the scale (s) of the object, the IMM filter uses the corresponding velocities $(\dot{x}, \dot{y}, \dot{s})$ and acceleration $(\ddot{x}, \ddot{y}, \ddot{s})$. The discrete set of motion models consists of three basic models, in particular CP, CV, and CA. Intuitively, one would simply set the state vector set to

$$x_{k,IMM\,1} = (x, y, s, \dot{x}, \dot{y}, \dot{s}, \ddot{x}, \ddot{y}, \ddot{s}). \tag{10}$$

Thus, only one IMM filter is required for monitoring all desired states. For a standard Kalman filter, a separation of the states and additionally required filter is redundant. Due to the characteristics of an IMM filter, not only a poor choice of single motion model, but in addition a careless extension of the states can lead to a non optimal performance. An optimal filtering behavior using a multiple model system requires an optimal filter for every possible model sequence. Hence, some kind of approximations are needed in practical applications. For an IMM filter, this is done by conditioning all filters on the currently active model and the final state estimate is obtained by merging the results of all elemental filters. Hence, a poor estimate of active model affects the weighting of the mixed inputs. A combining of the image coordinates and the scale in one state vector can thereby result in errors for the calculation of the model probabilities, especially when combining the scale with the image position. For example, the scale change of an object can be constant while the object is moving. Thus the best fitting model for describing the scale is CP, whereas this model is a poor fit for the image position. Therefore, we propose to use an extra IMM-filter instead of one. Hence, the scale and the corresponding velocity and acceleration are estimated independent from the position states and their derivatives. This leads to the following IMM configuration:

$$x_{k,IMM\,2} = (x, y, \dot{x}, \dot{y}, \ddot{x}, \ddot{y}); (s, \dot{s}, \ddot{s}). \tag{11}$$

A separation of the scale with an additional filter seems obvious, but when tracking with directly observed image space data, a split into independent image coordinates may appear to be at first not required. In order to show the benefit of such an IMM set up, we recommend an IMM configuration as follows:

$$x_{k,IMM\ 3} = (x, \dot{x}, \ddot{x}); (y, \dot{y}, \ddot{y}); (s, \dot{s}, \ddot{s}). \tag{12}$$

Here, three IMM filter are used to describe the x position, y position, scale, and the corresponding derivatives. Hence, every motion along the image axes is captured with a separate filter.

Evaluation is done on the VOT 2014 dataset [10]. This dataset is a selection of 25 widely-used object tracking sequences. Although the dataset is originally designed to compare different appearance or visual tracker, it includes a variety of different object motions. Figure 1 shows the first frame of exemplary sequences where the unified bounding box of the object is highlighted in green.

Fig. 1. Example tracking sequences for evaluation from the VOT 2014. The first frame with the unified bounding box of the object is shown for the sequences "bicycle", "jogging", "surfing", "woman". (Color figure online)

The main feature of the IMM filter is the ability to estimate the state of a dynamic system with several behavior modes which can switch from one to another. Besides that, the IMM filter is a good compromise between performance and complexity [11]. The overall performance depends on a number of design parameters. The most critical design parameters are the model set structure, process and measurement noises, initial state, and the jump structure with transition probabilities. Nonetheless, the above described basic IMM setup with 3 standard motion model is suboptimal for some scenarios from the VOT 2014 dataset [10], we keep the combination of one constant position, one constant velocity, and one constant acceleration model fixed. In practice, the transition probability matrix is often assumed known and is chosen a priori. As stated in Bar-Shalom [8], an ad-hoc approach is to fill the diagonals with values close to one. We set the diagonals to 0.99 and the other transition values to 0.005. Because the CV model is the mostly used in tracking approaches, we set the initial model probability μ_0^i in favor of this model to 0.98 and to 0.01 for the other models. The measurement and process noise is modeled as additive white noise. In the experiments the standard deviation of both noises was varied between 1, 2, 5, and 10. Here, only the diagonals of process noise covariance matrix Q and measurement noise covariance R include non-zero values.

For every image sequence, the first 10 frames are excluded and used for initializing of the filters. The update interval t_{update} for getting a new measurement for the filter was varied between every frame, every third frame and fifth frame. Since, the standard output of object detectors are a rectangular bounding box centered at the object location, we use the ground truth bounding boxes from the VOT 2014 dataset to simulate the output of an object detector and for evaluating the prediction accuracy. Performance measures aim at summarizing the extent to which the trackers prediction agrees with the ground truth annotation. In Cehovin et al. [12], a general definition of an object state description in a sequence with length N is established based on the center of the object and the region of the object at time k. In case of tracking an object in image space the region is usually described by a bounding box. From the IMM filter, we use the predicted states center location x, y and scale s to calculate an unified bounding box A_k^O. With this predicted objects region form the tracker and the ground-truth region an overlap can be calculated as $\frac{A_k^O \cap A_k^{GT}}{A_k^O \cup A_k^{GT}}$. For the ground truth area A_k^{GT} also an unified bounding box is considered. In general, the width of the enclosing bounding box is more strongly influenced by the body pose of the objects. Hence, a unified bounding box with a width of $\frac{1}{3}$ scale is used. A property of region overlap measures is that they account for both position and size of the predicted and ground-truth bounding boxes simultaneously, and there is no normalization problem. The overlap measure is summarized over an entire sequence by an average overlap. In addition to the average overlap, the number of frames in which the overlap is below a threshold of 0.5 is recorded and used as a second comparative score.

The overall results for the three different IMM configurations are exemplary summarized for $\sigma_w^2 = 2$, $\sigma_r^2 = 5$, $t_{update} = 3$ in Table 1. Other parameter settings may differ slightly, but are equal at their core. This means that the achieved overlap varies and that for some specific sequences the ranking of the IMM configuration changes, but overall it can clearly be noticed that the IMM configuration, that uses separated image space coordinates and scale, outperforms the other configurations. Due to the fact that the motion of objects in some particular sequence is highly non-linear, the chosen combination of motion model is not optimal. Moreover, this can also result in a changed ranking, but the trend towards the third configuration for achieving superior results is clearly visible for all evaluated parameter settings.

When tracking an object without a mapping between measurement domain and the states, the motion in a particular direction is independent from the other direction. Because the elemental filters are conditioned on the best fitting model the final estimate is negatively influenced by a naive extension of the state vector. For combining the scale and its derived changes with the actual motion states this seems obvious. But the presented results show how crucial this is also for mixing between image coordinates. For the majority of the evaluated sequences the average overlap achieved with the separated IMM states is larger than with the other configuration. An improvement can also be perceived by avoiding a combination between dynamics and scale. Thus the second

Table 1. Performance summary for the different IMM filter configurations.

Settings: $\sigma_w^2 = 2$, $\sigma_r^2 = 5$, $t_{update} = 3$						
	IMM 1		IMM 2		IMM 3	
Sequence	Failure rate	Overlap ratio	Failure rate	Overlap ratio	Failure rate	Overlap ratio
Ball	0.270	0.634	0.191	0.679	0.164	**0.695**
Basketball	0.003	0.863	0.003	0.884	0.004	**0.891**
Bicycle	0.304	0.602	0.233	0.641	0.173	**0.692**
Bolt	0.080	0.774	0.044	0.810	0.027	**0.842**
Car	0.340	0.610	0.261	0.642	0.108	**0.710**
David	0.167	0.697	0.152	0.715	0.141	**0.720**
Diving	0.082	**0.793**	0.135	0.749	0.135	0.736
Drunk	0.000	0.931	0.000	0.929	0.000	**0.931**
Fernando	0.018	0.857	0.021	0.852	0.018	**0.859**
Fish1	0.242	0.663	0.144	**0.726**	0.111	0.725
Fish2	0.107	0.745	0.084	0.769	0.064	**0.775**
Gymnastics	0.107	**0.798**	0.138	0.787	0.138	0.786
Hand1	0.262	0.656	0.232	0.664	0.227	**0.665**
Hand2	0.410	0.542	0.379	0.559	0.359	**0.576**
Jogging	0.047	0.769	0.054	0.776	0.047	**0.777**
Motocross	0.092	0.752	0.188	0.745	0.188	**0.755**
Polarbear	0.011	0.848	0.008	0.849	0.011	**0.852**
Skating	0.000	0.866	0.000	0.881	0.000	**0.898**
Sphere	0.295	0.618	0.300	**0.629**	0.316	0.605
Sunshade	0.559	0.426	0.571	0.442	0.484	**0.488**
Surfing	0.111	0.699	0.081	0.746	0.048	**0.773**
Torus	0.150	0.706	0.146	**0.723**	0.142	0.712
Trellis	0.358	0.579	0.276	0.633	0.238	**0.661**
Tunnel	0.129	0.695	0.078	**0.734**	0.101	0.729
Woman	0.051	0.773	0.053	0.794	0.051	**0.805**

configuration (IMM 2) outperforms the naive state extension from configuration one (IMM 1). This state splitting is also recommend when the actual motion is described in 3D. In summary, when relying on direct observed measurement, which is common for 2D Tracking, a naive extension of the state vector in case of tracking with an IMM filter instead of using single Bayes filter should be avoided. However, the fact that independent states are affected by mixing the inputs from the elemental filters, which is a result of the required approximation for an optimal filtering without keeping every possible model sequence, is easily forgotten when applying IMM filter for direct tracking in 2D. With this simple reminder a better IMM filtering can be achieved. While, the overall performance can be further improved by selecting alternative motion models which better fit to the dynamics of the object in the scene, the awareness of not naively extend the state is also crucial. All states of an IMM state vector should depend on each other and hence each additional independent state and its derivatives should be considered in an additional IMM filter. Hence the conditioning on the current best fitting model can not negatively affects the overall performance. The motion of an object in image space is a very good example where the dynamics along the image axes should be considered independently with an IMM filter.

4   Conclusion

In this paper, we showed how a naive extension of the state space can negatively affect the performance of an IMM filter. The required approximation by merging the output of the elemental filter based on the current best fitting filter affects states which are independent of each other. Especially when tracking an object only based on direct image space measurement, a combination in the state vector of both image coordinates should be avoided. This simple reminder of a common fallacy helps to improve the effectiveness of an IMM filter for considering varying system characteristics. The benefit of this favored design scheme for an IMM filter configuration is shown on the VOT 2014 dataset.

References

1. Kalman, R.E.: A new approach to linear filtering and prediction problems. ASME J. Basic Eng. **82**(1), 35–45 (1960)
2. Thrun, S., Burgard, W., Fox, D.: Probabilistic Robotics. Intelligent Robotics and Autonomous Agents. The MIT Press, Cambridge (2005)
3. Arulampalam, M.S., Maskell, S., Gordon, N., Clapp, T.: A tutorial on particle filters for online nonlinear/non-Gaussian Bayesian tracking. IEEE Trans. Signal Process. **50**(2), 174–188 (2002)
4. Blom, H.A.P., Bar-Shalom, Y.: The interacting multiple model algorithm for systems with Markovian switching coefficients. Trans. Autom. Control **33**, 780–783 (1988)
5. Cooper, D.C.: Multiple target tracking with radar applications. Electron. Power **33**(6), 407 (1987)
6. Blackman, S.S., Popoli, R.: Design and analysis of modern tracking system. Artech House radar library (1999)
7. Hartikainen, J., Särkkä, S.: Optimal filtering with Kalman filters and smoothers a Manual for Matlab toolbox EKF/UKF (2008). http://www.lce.hut.fi/research/mm/ekfukf/
8. Bar-Shalom, Y., Kirubarajan, T., Li, X.-R.: Estimation with Applications to Tracking and Navigation. Wiley, New York (2002)
9. Li, X.R., Jilkov, V.P.: Survey of maneuvering target tracking. Part V. Multiple-model methods. Trans. Aerosp. Electron. Syst. **41**(4), 1255–1321 (2005)

10. VOT: Visual Object Tracking Challenge Dataset. In: European Conference on Computer Vision Workshops (2014). http://www.votchallenge.net/vot2014/
11. Gomes, J.B.B.: An overview on target tracking using multiple model methods, PhD thesis, Technical University of Lisbon (2008)
12. Cehovin, L., Kristan, M., Leonardis, A.: Is my new tracker really better than yours? In: Winter Conference on Applications of Computer Vision (WACV), pp. 540–547 (2014)

Feature Asymmetry of the Conformal Monogenic Signal

Ahror Belaid[✉]

Medical Computing Laboratory (LIMED), University of Abderrahmane Mira,
06000 Bejaia, Algeria
ahror.belaid@univ-bejaia.dz

Abstract. Local properties of image (phase, amplitude and orientation) can be estimated practically using quadrature filters kernel and can be easily represented in two dimensions using the monogenic signal. This powerful feature representation has given rise to robust phase-based edge detection. Nonetheless, it is limited to the class of intrinsically one-dimensional signals, such as lines and edges. All other possible local patterns such as corners and junction are of intrinsic dimension two. Our aim in this paper is to present a new edge detection method for extracting local features of any curved signal. It is based on the conformal monogenic signal which is in practical applications compatible with intrinsically one and two-dimensional signal. Using different filters, our model have been tested and compared with classical models and some recent ones. The preliminary results show that our detection technique is more efficient and more accurate.

Keywords: Conformal monogenic signal · Local phase information · Feature asymmetry · Edge detection

1 Introduction

Interestingly, several physiological experiences have suggested that image structures like lines, edges, junctions and orientations play an important role in the Human Visual System. Consequently, these features have always been considered as central in the analysis since the early days. Their detection has therefore been a fundamental operation that needed to be processed in a reliable and robust way. Feature detection has been extensively studied in the literature and still remains an active field of research [1,6,9–13,16].

Throughout the history of digital image processing, smoothing and differentiation have been subjects of intense study. A variety of optimal differential operators have been proposed to solve different computer vision problems. For instance, edges and lines detection have received a particular attention. Differentiation is highly sensitive to illumination variations and do not localize accurately or consistently. Indeed, the localization of gradient based features varies with scale of analysis. Amplitude-based techniques however are known to be

© Springer International Publishing Switzerland 2016
A. Mansouri et al. (Eds.): ICISP 2016, LNCS 9680, pp. 12–20, 2016.
DOI: 10.1007/978-3-319-33618-3_2

sensitive to smooth shading and lighting variations. Furthermore, edges, corners and other features are not simple step changes in luminance. Hence, recent contributions have reached a high degree of sophistication [13]. These may include, for instance, statistical models based detection [9]; linear and non linear scale space methods and links to regularisation theory [11].

Amplitude-based operators (Gradient) are sensitive to intensity variations and do not localize accurately or consistently. To minimize these problems we need a feature operator that is maximally invariant to intensity and scale. An alternative approach to amplitude based techniques is the use of phase information. Theoretically, it is known that a wide range of feature types gives rise to points of high Phase Congruency (PC). Also,it has been shown that this model successfully explains a number of psychophysical effects on human feature perception. PC is a dimensionless quantity, invariant to contrast and allows to the features to be tracked over extended sequences more reliably. Indeed, phase is an underused local image attribute that can have many applications [3,4,10].

Local properties of image (phase, amplitude and orientation) can be estimated practically using *quadrature filters* kernel [2,5] and can be easily represented in two dimensions using the *monogenic signal* [7]. This powerful feature representation has given rise to robust phase based detectors contours, the most remarkable is the Feature Asymmetry (FA) [3,4,10]. Nonetheless, it is limited to the class of intrinsically one-dimensional signals.

Two dimensional images can be classified into local regions of different intrinsic dimensions as shown in Fig. 1. The intrinsic dimension expresses the number of degrees of freedom necessary to describe local structure. Constant signals are of intrinsic dimension zero (i0D), lines and edges are of intrinsic dimension one (i1D) and all other possible patterns such as corners and junction are of intrinsic dimension two (i2D). For a given two-dimensional signal f and local region $N \subseteq \mathbb{R}^2$:

$$i0D = \{f : f(\mathbf{x}_i) = f(\mathbf{x}_i) \forall \mathbf{x}_i, \mathbf{x}_j \in N\}, \tag{1}$$

$$i1D = \{f : f(\mathbf{x}) = g(\langle \mathbf{x}, \mathbf{y} \rangle) \forall \mathbf{x} \in N, \mathbf{y} \in \mathbb{R}^2 \text{ and } |\mathbf{y}| = 1\} \backslash i0D, \tag{2}$$

$$i2D = f \notin (i0D \cup i1D), \tag{3}$$

Fig. 1. Typical examples of a global intrinsic 2D signals. From left to right: a constant signal (i0D), an arbitrary rotated 1D signal (i1D) and a curved i2D signal. All signals displayed here preserve their intrinsic dimension globally. Figure from [18].

where $\langle \cdot, \cdot \rangle$ denotes the inner product and $g : \mathbb{R} \to \mathbb{R}$ represents the local structural feature function of 1D signal model such as $g(x) = a(x) \cos(\phi(x))$. Note that, in general, i2D signals can only be modeled by an infinite number of superimposed i1D signals [18].

In this paper, we present a novel way to compute the FA. It is based on the *conformal monogenic signal* which is a rotational invariant quadrature filter for extracting local features of any curved signal [18]. The conformal monogenic signal contains the introduced monogenic signal as a special case and combines scale space theory in one unified algebraic framework. The main advantage of the conformal monogenic signal in practical applications is its compatibility with intrinsically one-dimensional (i1D) and special intrinsically two-dimensional signal (i2D).

2   The Conformal Monogenic Signal

The local properties of a given 2D signal $f(\mathbf{x})$ can be estimated by the monogenic signal $f_M(\mathbf{x}) : \mathbb{R}^n \to \mathbb{R}^{n+1}$. It is defined in a space of dimension $n + 1$ with sufficient degrees of freedom to represent the local characteristics of a signal in nD:

$$f_M(\mathbf{x}) = (f, \mathbf{f}_\mathcal{R})(\mathbf{x}). \tag{4}$$

The Riesz transform $\mathbf{f}_\mathcal{R}$ is considered as a generalised 1D Hilbert transform and preserves its most interesting properties, it is written by means of convolution as:

$$\mathbf{f}_\mathcal{R}(\mathbf{x}) = (\mathbf{h} * f)(\mathbf{x}) = \frac{\mathbf{x}}{A_{n+1}|\mathbf{x}|^{n+1}} * f(\mathbf{x}), \text{ with } A_{n+1} = \frac{2\pi^{\frac{n+1}{2}}}{\Gamma(\frac{n+1}{2})}. \tag{5}$$

For the particular case of a two-dimensional signal $(n = 2)$ the generalised Hilbert transform kernel $\mathbf{h}$ is given by:

$$\mathbf{h}(\mathbf{x}) = (h_1, h_2)(\mathbf{x}) \text{ , and } h_i = \frac{x_i}{2\pi|\mathbf{x}|^3}. \tag{6}$$

The local properties turned out to be invariant with respect to rotations and translation, due to the rotational equivalent and the linear shift invariance properties of the Riesz transform. These properties make the monogenic signal as a powerful feature representation. Nonetheless, it is limited to the class of intrinsically one-dimensional signals. Thus, the conformal monogenic signal is considered as a generalisation for analysing i1D and i2D local feature for two-dimensional signal.

2.1   The Conformal Space

As introduced by Wietzke and Sommer [18], the main idea of the conformal monogenic signal is to lift up 2D signals to an appropriate conformal space with more degrees of freedom compared to the 2D monogenic signal. Since, line and circle of the two-dimensional signal domain are mapped to circles on the sphere in conformal space, with center $(0, 0, \frac{1}{2})^T$ and radius $\frac{1}{2}$:

$$\mathbb{S} := \left\{ \xi \in \mathbb{R}^3 : \xi_1^2 + \xi_2^2 + (\xi_3 - \frac{1}{2})^2 = \frac{1}{4} \right\}. \tag{7}$$

The sphere $\mathbb{S}$ touches the Euclidean plan $\mathbb{R}^2$ such that its south-pole coincides with the origin $(0, 0, 0)^T$. This projection is conformal and can be inverted by $\mathcal{C}^{-1}$ for all elements of $\mathbb{S} \in \mathbb{R}^3$:

$$\mathcal{C}^{-1}(\mathbf{x}) = \frac{1}{x_1^2 + x_2^2 + 1} \begin{pmatrix} x_1 \\ x_2 \\ x_1^2 + x_2^2 \end{pmatrix}, \tag{8}$$

for $\mathbf{x} = (x_1, x_2)^T \in \mathbb{R}^2$ whereas the projection from $\mathbb{S}$ to $\mathbb{R}^2$ is given by:

$$\mathcal{C}(\omega) = \frac{1}{1 - \omega_3} \begin{pmatrix} \omega_1 \\ \omega_2 \end{pmatrix}, \text{ with } \omega \in \mathbb{S}. \tag{9}$$

Lines and circles of the 2D signal domain will be mapped to circles on the sphere. All planes corresponding to circles remain unchanged. That is the reason why the conformal monogenic signal models i1D line and all kinds of curved i2D signals which can be locally approximated by circles.

The spherical embedding f_c of the circular signal f with respect to a point on interest $\mathbf{x} \in \mathbb{R}^2$ is given by:

$$f_c(\mathbf{x}; \xi) = \begin{cases} f(\mathcal{C}(\xi) + \mathbf{x}) & \text{for } \xi \in \mathbb{S}, \\ 0 & \text{else}. \end{cases} \tag{10}$$

Now the conformal monogenic signal can be introduced by:

$$\begin{aligned} f_{CM}(\mathbf{x}) &= (f_c, \mathbf{f}_C)(\mathbf{x}; 0), \\ &= (f_c, h_1 * f_c, h_2 * f_c, h_3 * f_c)(\mathbf{x}; 0). \end{aligned} \tag{11}$$

We are now able to estimate the i1D and i2D local amplitude, orientation and phase of curved 2D signal respectively by:

$$a(\mathbf{x}) = \sqrt{f_c^2(\mathbf{x}; 0) + \sum_{i=1}^{3} (h_i * f_c)^2(\mathbf{x}; 0)}, \tag{12}$$

$$\theta(\mathbf{x}) = \arctan 2 \left(h_2 * f_c, h_1 * f_c \right)(\mathbf{x}; 0), \tag{13}$$

and

$$\phi(\mathbf{x}) = \arctan 2 \left(\sqrt{\sum_{i=1}^{3} (h_i * f_c)^2(\mathbf{x}; 0)}, f_c(\mathbf{x}; 0) \right). \tag{14}$$

3   Feature Asymmetry

In practical applications, the local properties are estimated using a pair of bandpass quadrature filters. Indeed, the detection of local properties by the conformal monogenic signal assumes that the signal consists of few frequencies, that is bandlimited. A real image consist of a wide range of frequencies, therefore a set of bandpass filters needs to be combined with the conformal monogenic signal. Equation (11) becomes:

$$f_{CM}^s(\mathbf{x}) = (\mathcal{Q} * f_c, \mathcal{Q} * \mathbf{f}_C)(\mathbf{x}; 0), \tag{15}$$

where $\mathcal{Q}(\mathbf{x}; s)$ is the spatial domain representation of an isotropic bandpass filter and $s > 0$ is a scaling parameter. Thus, the monogenic signal can be represented by a scalar valued even and vector valued odd filtered responses, with the following simple tick:

$$even = (\mathcal{Q} * f_c)(\mathbf{x}; 0),$$
$$\mathbf{odd} = (\mathcal{Q} * h_1 * f_c, \mathcal{Q} * h_2 * f_c, \mathcal{Q} * h_3 * f_c)(\mathbf{x}; 0).$$

Several families of quadrature pairs have been proposed and applied in the literature. Most authors have not provided a reasonable justification for the use of a particular family apart from simplicity of use or the satisfaction of the zero DC condition. In [2], the authors introduce a new generalised pairs of quadrature filters, and after comparison, they concluded that the widely used log-Gabor kernels are probably not a very good choice in the case of feature detection. They showed that Derivative of Derivative/Difference of α scale space family (ASSD and DoSS respectively) has better properties. (see Fig. 2). A 2D isotropic ASSD kernel is defined in Fourier domain by

$$\mathcal{Q}_{ASSD}(\mathbf{u}) = \begin{cases} n_c \mathbf{u}^a \exp\left(-(s\mathbf{u})^{2\alpha}\right) & \text{if} \quad \mathbf{u} \geq 0 \\ 0 & \text{otherwise} \end{cases} \tag{16}$$

where the frequency coordinate $\mathbf{u} = (u_1, u_2)$, $\alpha \in {]}0, 1]$, n_c is a normalisation constant. The derivative parameter $a \in \mathbb{R}^+$ meaning we are using fractional order derivatives.

3.1   The Edge Detection Measure

Step edge detection is performed using the *feature asymmetry* measure (FA) of Kovesi [10] redefined using the conformal monogenic signal presented previously. To identify step edges essentially involves finding points where the absolute value of the local phase is $0°$ at a positive edge and $180°$ at a negative edge. In other words, the difference between the odd and the even filter responses is large. We define the new multiple scales feature asymmetry by:

$$FA_{CM} = \frac{\sum_s \lfloor |\mathbf{odd}_s| - |even_s| - T_s \rfloor}{\sum_s \sqrt{even_s^2 + |\mathbf{odd}_s|^2 + \varepsilon}}. \tag{17}$$

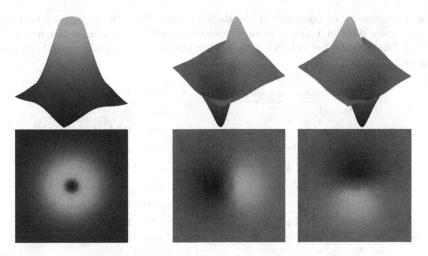

Fig. 2. 2D DoSS kernels in Fourier domain for certain parameters. From left to right: the isotropic even part and the pair composing the odd part.

where $\lfloor \cdot \rfloor$ denotes zeroing of negative values and T is a noise threshold estimate [10]. Here, ε is used to avoid zero division. The FA_{CM} takes values in $[0, 1]$, close to zero in smooth regions and close to one near boundaries.

4   Results and Discussion

To evaluate the performance of the proposed approach, we made comparisons between manual delineation of Berkeley Segmentation Database [1] and the automatic results. One band-pass filter has been chosen for these tests, namely the α-Scale Spaces Derivative filter [2] (ASSD). This filter was chosen for its parametric nature of $\alpha \in]0, 1]$ which makes it possible to find the classic filters like the Derivative (Difference) of Gaussian ($\alpha = 1$) and Poisson filter ($\alpha = 0.5$).

The evaluation of this method is carried out by Precision-Recall curves which are obtained by varying the detection threshold. There is however, an interesting point on the curves defined by the measure $F = 2\frac{Precision \cdot Recall}{Precision + Recall}$. Thus, the location of the maximum of this measure along the curve defines the optimum threshold and provides a summary score. Table 1 reports a summary of results obtained on the database of 500 images of Berkeley. It should be noted that the most interesting measure is the F-measure (ODS), the other ones are involved only to bring more precision. Table 1 summarises the comparison results between the proposed method FA_{CM} and the classical models as well as some newer and more sophisticated models [1,8,16]. An overview of these results is illustrated in Fig. 3. It is easy to see that the FA_{CM} approach significantly exceeds, in terms of performance, the remaining methods, irrespective of the selected filter (Gaussian or Poisson). Since the FA_{CM} detector performed by conformal monogenic signal combines all intrinsic dimensions in one framework, including curved edges

18   A. Belaid

Table 1. Summary of comparison results. Represented on the table, the best score over the image dataset ODS (Optimal Dataset Scale), the best score per image OIS (Optimal Image Scale), as well as the area below the precision-recall curve AR (Average Precision).

Edge detection method	ODS	OIS	AR
Manual	0.80	0.80	–
FA_{CM}	0.61	0.64	0.54
Felzenszwalb and Huttenlocher [8]	0.61	0.64	0.65
Arbelaez et al. [1]	0.60	0.64	0.58
Sharon et al. [16]	0.56	0.59	0.54
Canny [6]	0.60	0.63	0.58
Marr and Hildreth [12]	0.57	0.59	0.21
Prewitt [14]	0.51	0.54	0.38
Sobel and Feldman [17]	0.51	0.53	0.38
Roberts [15]	0.50	0.53	0.73

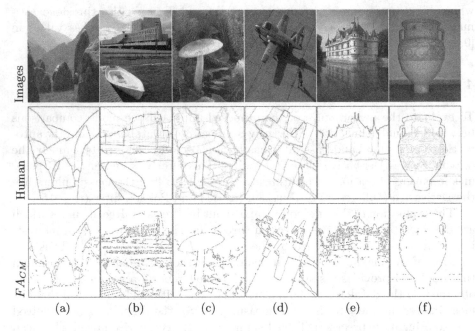

(a)   (b)   (c)   (d)   (e)   (f)

Fig. 3. Edge detection results on the BSDS500 benchmark. From top to bottom: original images, corresponding manual segmentations, results obtained by the FA_{CM} method.

and lines. It could be an interesting alternative for the gradient or the Laplace operator.

The FA_{CM} can be computed efficiently and easily implemented into existing low level image processing steps of Computer Vision applications. Furthermore, it can be calculated with all the advantages of rotationally invariant local phase based approaches, robustness against brightness and contrast changes, and without the need of any partial derivatives. Hence, lots of numerical problems of partial derivatives on discrete grids can be avoided.

It is natural to think tackle the proposed approach with more recent and efficient ones, such as the model called GPB-owt-ucm of [1]. However, such methods are in a quite developed and sophisticated level, and take into account the texture, the multi-scale framework and the presence of noise in images. To be at the same level and get better detection, it is interesting to include a component for treating texture. We can note also that according to the experiments carried out on the Berkeley database, the measure F depends on the size and type of the selected images sample. Thus, we plan to experiment our approach by other publicly available datasets.

5   Conclusion

We proposed in this paper a new idea in isotropic 2D phase based edge detection. This new Conformal Monogenic Feature Asymmetry detector combines all intrinsic dimensions in one framework, including curved edges and lines. Using different filters, we tested and compared our approach with conventional models and some newer models. It appears that our results are in the same order as those of the state of the art. Although these results are introductory, they seem to be promising. Indeed, this method, simple to implement and easily expandable to higher dimensions, opens up new perspectives. Furthermore, it can be computed efficiently and easily implemented with all the advantages of rotationally invariant local phase based approaches, robustness against brightness and contrast changes, and without the need of any partial derivatives. Hence, lots of numerical problems of partial derivatives on discrete grids can be avoided. In short, it could be an interesting alternative for the gradient based method. More applications of the FA_{CM} such as edge detection on three-dimensional data will be part of our future work.

References

1. Arbelaez, P., Maire, M., Fowlkes, C., Malik, J.: Contour detection and hierarchical image segmentation. IEEE Trans. Pattern Anal. Mach. Intell. **33**(5), 898–916 (2011)
2. Belaid, A., Boukerroui, D.: A new generalised α scale spaces quadrature filters. Pattern Recognit. **47**(10), 3209–3224 (2014)
3. Belaid, A., Boukerroui, D., Maingourd, Y., Lerallut, J.F.: Implicit active contours for ultrasound images segmentation driven by phase information and local maximum likelihood. In: Proceedings of the IEEE International Symposium on Biomedical Imaging, pp. 630–635. Chicago, April 2011

4. Belaid, A., Boukerroui, D., Maingourd, Y., Lerallut, J.F.: Phase based level set segmentation of ultrasound images. IEEE Trans. Inf. Technol. Biomed. **15**(1), 138–147 (2011)
5. Boukerroui, D., Noble, J.A., Brady, M.: On the choice of band-pass quadrature filters. J. Math. Imag. Vis. **21**(1), 53–80 (2004)
6. Canny, J.: A computational approach to edge detection. IEEE Trans. Pattern Anal. Mach. Intell. **8**(6), 679–698 (1986)
7. Felsberg, M., Sommer, G.: The monogenic signal. IEEE Trans. Signal Process. **49**(12), 3136–3144 (2001)
8. Felzenszwalb, P.F., Huttenlocher, D.P.: Efficient graph-based image segmentation. Int. J. Comput. Vis. **59**(2), 167–181 (2004)
9. Konishi, S., Yuille, A.L., Coughlan, J.M., Zhu, S.C.: Statistical edge detection: learning and evaluating edge cues. IEEE Trans. Pattern Anal. Mach. Intell. **25**, 57–74 (2003)
10. Kovesi, P.: Image features from phase congruency. Videre: J. Comput. Vis. Res. **1**(3), 1–26 (1999)
11. Lindeberg, T.: Generalized Gaussian scale-space axiomatics comprising linear scale-space, affine scale-space and spatio-temporal scale-space. J. Math. Imag. Vis. **40**(1), 36–81 (2011)
12. Marr, D., Hildreth, E.: Theory of edge detection. Proc. R. Soc. Lond. B **207**, 187–217 (1980)
13. Papari, G., Petkov, N.: Edge and line oriented contour detection: state of the art. Image Vis. Comput. **29**(2–3), 79–103 (2011)
14. Prewitt, J.M.S.: Object enhancement and extraction. In: Lipkin, B., Rosenfeld, A. (eds.) Picture Processing and Psychopictorics, pp. 75–149. Academic Press, New York (1970)
15. Roberts, L.G.: Machine Perception of Three-Dimensional Solids (1963)
16. Sharon, E., Galun, M., Sharon, D., Basri, R., Brandt, A.: Hierarchy and adaptivity in segmenting visual scenes. Nature **442**, 810–813 (2006)
17. Sobel, I., Feldman, G.: A 3x3 isotropic gradient operator for image processing. In: Pattern Classification and Scene Analysis (1968)
18. Wietzke, L., Sommer, G.: The conformal monogenic signal. In: Rigoll, G. (ed.) DAGM 2008. LNCS, vol. 5096, pp. 527–536. Springer, Heidelberg (2008)

Edge Detection Based on Riesz Transform

Ahror Belaid[1]([⊠]), Soraya Aloui[1], and Djamal Boukerroui[2]

[1] Medical Computing Laboratory (LIMED),
University of Abderrahmane Mira, 06000 Bejaia, Algeria
{ahror.belaid,soraya.aloui}@univ-bejaia.dz
[2] Mirada Medical, Oxford Centre for Innovation New Road, Oxford OX1 1BY, UK
djamal.boukerroui@mirada-medical.com

Abstract. In this paper, we present a new way of 2D feature extraction. We start by showing the direct link that exist between the Riesz Transform (RT) and the gradient and Laplacian operators. This formulation allows us to interpret the RT as a gradient of a smoothed image. Thus, by analogy with the classical models, the maximum gradient and the zero crossings of the divergence of the TR provide information about the position of contours. The interest of the RT is its representation that naturally sweeps the whole area of the image and allows a correct description of structures. Using different filters, our models have been tested and compared with classical models and some recent ones. The results show that our detection technique is more efficient and more accurate.

Keywords: Riesz transform · Edge detection · Laplacian zero crossings · Monogenic signal · α scale space filter

1 Introduction

The derivative of intensity method has been widely used in various fields of image processing for detecting the change of intensity as contours. Indeed, the maximum of the first derivative (or the zero crossing of the second derivative) is used to locate the changes and discontinuities of intensity in the form of *stair* [4,9,10]. These changes and discontinuities are generally associated with contours of objects present in the image. Although very significant progress has been made in the area of edge detection, the empirical estimation of the gradient techniques proposed in the 70s to 80s are often still used in competition with more modern techniques. Indeed, the gradient operator used for the edge detection is formal, but sterile unfortunately.

In the last few years, some authors have shown that local phase information of image is more robust than the intensity gradient [3]. Measuring the local phase in several scales, otherwise the *phase congruency*, is a way of characterising the differences of intensities in terms of shape of intensity. Local phase information is estimated practically using *quadrature filters* kernel [2] and can be easily extended to higher dimensions using the representation of the *monogenic signal* [6].

© Springer International Publishing Switzerland 2016
A. Mansouri et al. (Eds.): ICISP 2016, LNCS 9680, pp. 21–29, 2016.
DOI: 10.1007/978-3-319-33618-3_3

The *monogenic* signal is considered as a natural extension of 2D analytic signal. In fact, this signal is derived from the generalisation of the Hilbert transform known as the Riesz transform. The appearance of this generalisation has opened up new perspectives in image processing. We cite in a non-exhaustive manner, the works on the optical flow of Zang et al. [16], wavelets of Unser et al. [15] and a recent work on segmentation by Belaid et al. [3].

It is in this double context of edge detection and the Riesz transform that our contribution lies. We will proceed by recalling the link that connects the Riesz transform and the gradient and Laplacian operators. Specifically, we will find the *equivalent* of the Canny detector and the Laplacian zero crossings in monogenic field. This view allows us to highlight new perspectives on the edge detection models.

This article is organised as follows: first, a simple background note is desirable to understand the proposed approach, and subsequently, we will develop the details associated with it. Finally, some preliminary comparison results and a conclusion will be presented.

2   Monogenic Signal and Riesz Transform

From the Hilbert transform concept, it is possible to introduce the analytic signal $f_A(x)$ corresponding to the original 1D signal $f(x)$. This concept is a widely used tool in signal processing and it is given by:

$$f_A(x) = f(x) + if_{\mathcal{H}}(x). \tag{1}$$

Applying this signal to the image processing requires the generalisation of the Hilbert transform to the multidimensional signals. A direct generalisation thereof in higher dimensions is not obvious. Indeed, the concept of positive and negative frequencies is not clear in this case. Several attempts of 1D analytic signal generalisation can be found in the literature. However, the monogenic signal, introduced by Felsberg and Sommer [6], is considered as a *natural* 2D extension of the analytic signal. It is derived from the generalisation of Hilbert transform known as the Riesz transform.

It should be noted that this nD generalisation approach is based on the conservation of the 1D local phase information by adding the information of the local orientation. Both features are integrated into a larger space. Thus, for a real signal nD, the extension is represented by an analytic signal of dimension $(n + 1)$. The combination of the pair of the Riesz transform and the original signal forms the new generalised nD analytic signal [6]. The Riesz transform in the spatial domain is given by:

$$\mathbf{f}_{\mathcal{R}}(\mathbf{x}) = \frac{\mathbf{x}}{A_{n+1}|\mathbf{x}|^{n+1}} * f(\mathbf{x}) = (\mathbf{h} * f)(\mathbf{x}), \ \text{with} \ A_{n+1} = \frac{2\pi^{\frac{n+1}{2}}}{\Gamma(\frac{n+1}{2})}. \tag{2}$$

For the particular case of a two-dimensional signal ($n = 2$) the generalised Hilbert transform is written as:

$$\mathbf{h}(\mathbf{x}) = \frac{\mathbf{x}}{2\pi|\mathbf{x}|^3} = (h_x, h_y)(\mathbf{x}) = \left(\frac{x}{2\pi(x^2 + y^2)^{3/2}}, \frac{y}{2\pi(x^2 + y^2)^{3/2}} \right). \tag{3}$$

Once the nD generalisation of the Hilbert transform is defined, it is then easy to introduce the generalisation of the analytic signal. The new signal $f_M(\mathbf{x})$: $\mathbb{R}^n \to \mathbb{R}^{n+1}$, called the monogenic signal, is defined in a space of dimension $n+1$ with sufficient degrees of freedom to represent the local characteristics of a signal in nD:

$$f_M(\mathbf{x}) = (\mathbf{f}_{\mathcal{R}}, f)(\mathbf{x}). \tag{4}$$

The Riesz transform preserves the most interesting properties of the 1D Hilbert transform.

3 Link Between the Differential Operators and the Riesz Transform

Felsberg and Sommer [7] and Unster et al. [15] in their very recent works have shown the existence of a direct link between the Riesz transform $\mathbf{f}_{\mathcal{R}}(\mathbf{x})$ and the *complex gradient* (also called *Wirtinger operator*):

$$\mathbf{f}_{\mathcal{R}}(\mathbf{x}) = -\left(\frac{\partial}{\partial x} + i\frac{\partial}{\partial y} \right) \left(\frac{1}{2\pi|\mathbf{x}|} * f(\mathbf{x}) \right), \tag{5}$$

which means that:

$$|\mathbf{f}_{\mathcal{R}}(\mathbf{x})| = \left| \nabla \left(f(\mathbf{x}) * \frac{1}{2\pi|\mathbf{x}|} \right) \right|. \tag{6}$$

This formulation allows us to interpret the Riesz transform as the gradient of a smoothed image. Thus, two models can be derived from this interpretation; the maximum of $\mathbf{f}_{\mathcal{R}}$ which is similar to the Canny edge detector, and the zero crossing of the derivative of $\mathbf{f}_{\mathcal{R}}$ which is analogous to the Laplacian model.

The first method based on the maximum of the Riesz transform, denoted Max_TR, consists in applying a convolution between the image f and the band-stop filter kernel ψ_s (see Fig. 1):

$$f * \nabla(\psi_s), \tag{7}$$

with $\psi_s = h * c_s$, $h = -\frac{1}{2\pi|\mathbf{x}|}$ and c_s a low-pass filter at a given scale $s > 0$. Thus the equivalent of function h in the Fourier domain is given by $H(\mathbf{u}) = -|\mathbf{u}|$.

This new detector expresses that an image contour is obtained by filtering the image by the first derivative of a band-stop filter (see Fig. 1), and then detecting the maximum of the function obtained thereby.

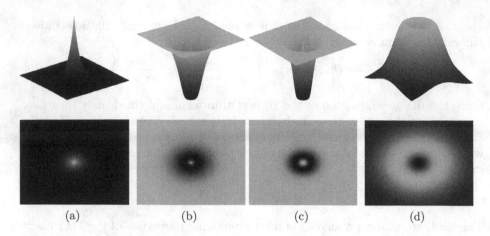

Fig. 1. Shape of the used filters. From left to right, the filters c_s (a), ψ_s (b), $\nabla\psi_s$ (c) and $\Delta\psi_s$ (d) in the Fourier domain at a given scale $s > 0$.

Based on the same interpretation, the second method denoted PZ_DTR consists in following the same development as the one used by the Haralick-Canny detector of the Laplacian zero crossings [4,9].

In order to achieve this, we associate to f an image of the directions[1] of the Riesz-transform:

$$\mathbf{r} = \frac{\mathbf{q}}{|\mathbf{q}|}. \tag{8}$$

A contour point is then defined as the place of the standard maximum of the Riesz transform in the direction specified by $\mathbf{r} = (q_1/|\mathbf{q}|, q_2/|\mathbf{q}|)$. Thus, a contour point satisfies:

$$\frac{\partial|f_{\mathcal{R}}(\mathbf{x})|}{\partial\mathbf{r}} = 0, \quad \text{and} \quad \frac{\partial^2|f_{\mathcal{R}}(\mathbf{x})|}{\partial\mathbf{r}^2} \leq 0. \tag{9}$$

The development of this property leads to

$$\frac{\partial|f_{\mathcal{R}}(\mathbf{x})|}{\partial\mathbf{r}} = \mathbf{r}^t\ \nabla|f_{\mathcal{R}}(\mathbf{x})| = \frac{\mathbf{q}^t}{|\mathbf{q}|}\nabla|\mathbf{q}| \tag{10}$$

$$= \frac{\mathbf{q}^t}{|\mathbf{q}|}\left(\begin{array}{c}\frac{\partial}{\partial x}\sqrt{q_1^2 + q_2^2} \\ \frac{\partial}{\partial y}\sqrt{q_1^2 + q_2^2}\end{array}\right) = \frac{\mathbf{q}^t}{|\mathbf{q}|}\left(\begin{array}{c}\frac{q_1 q_{1x}+q_2 q_{2x}}{|\mathbf{q}|} \\ \frac{q_1 q_{1y}+q_2 q_{2y}}{|\mathbf{q}|}\end{array}\right)$$

$$= \frac{\mathbf{q}^t}{|\mathbf{q}|}\left(\begin{array}{cc}q_{1x} & q_{2x} \\ q_{1y} & q_{2y}\end{array}\right)\frac{\mathbf{q}}{|\mathbf{q}|} = \mathbf{r}^t H \mathbf{r},$$

where $H = \begin{pmatrix} q_{1x} & q_{2x} \\ q_{1y} & q_{2y} \end{pmatrix}$ represents a symmetric matrix similar to the Hessian matrix. The symmetry is due to certain properties of the Riesz transform (see [7],

---

[1] For some formulations, we prefer the simplified vector notation $\mathbf{q}$ which represents the Riesz transform.

Eq. (9)). In addition, if we assume that the image f is locally coherent, that means it has a one-dimensional structure along the direction of $\mathbf{r}$, then the matrix H is of rank 1, and $\mathbf{r}^t H \mathbf{r} = trace(H) = q_{1x} + q_{2y}$.

Finally, we obtain the following equation:

$$\frac{\partial |\mathbf{f}_\mathcal{R}(\mathbf{x})|}{\partial \mathbf{r}} = q_{1x} + q_{2y} \tag{11}$$

$$= \frac{\partial}{\partial x}(f * h_x * c_s) + \frac{\partial}{\partial y}(f * h_y * c_s)$$

$$= 0.$$

Equation (11) shows that the points which maximise $|\mathbf{f}_\mathcal{R}(\mathbf{x})|$ are those representing the zero crossing of the divergence of the Riesz transform div($\mathbf{q}$). Thus, by analogy with the Marr detector [10], the zero crossing of the divergence of the Riesz transform (DTR) provides information about the position of the contour.

Using the convolution product properties, Eq. (11) can be rewritten as follows:

$$f * \left(\frac{\partial^2}{\partial x^2} + \frac{\partial^2}{\partial y^2} \right) \left(h * c_s \right), \tag{12}$$

the symbolic writing of our detector will be given by:

$$Image\ contours = Zero\ crossings\left(f * \Delta \psi_s\right). \tag{13}$$

This shows that a contour image is obtained by filtering the image by the second derivative of a band-stop filter (see Fig. 1), and then detecting the zeros of the function thus obtained. Figure 1 shows the shape of c_s filter and the band-stop filter kernel ψ_s and its Laplacian used for edge detection.

4   Results and Discussion

To evaluate the performance of the proposed approach, we made comparisons between manual delineation of Berkeley Segmentation Database [1] and the automatic results. One filter has been chosen for these tests, namely the α-scale-space filter [5]. This filter was chosen for its parametric nature of $\alpha \in]0,1]$ which makes it possible to find the classic filters like the Gaussian filters ($\alpha = 1$) and the Poisson filter ($\alpha = 0.5$).

The evaluation of these methods is carried out by Precision-Recall curves which are obtained by varying the detection threshold. For this purpose, three performance measures were selected, the best score over the image dataset ODS (Optimal Dataset Scale), the best score per image OIS (Optimal Image Scale), as well as the area below the precision-recall curve AR (Average Precision). There is however, an interesting point on the curves defined by the measure $F = 2\frac{Precision \cdot Recall}{Precision + Recall}$. Thus, the location of the maximum of this measure along the curve defines the optimum threshold and provides a summary score.

Table 1. Summary of comparison results. Represented on the table, the F measure (ODS) of the best score over the entire image database, the OIS measure of the best score by image and the AR measure representing the area below the Precision-Recall curve.

Detector	ODS	OIS	AR
Manual	0.80	0.80	–
Max_TR	0.62	0.64	0.54
PZ_DTR	0.57	0.59	0.50
Felzenszwalb and Huttenlocher [8]	0.61	0.64	0.65
Arbelaez et al. [1]	0.60	0.64	0.58
Sharon et al. [13]	0.56	0.59	0.54
Canny [4]	0.60	0.63	0.58
Marr and Hildreth [10]	0.57	0.59	0.21
Prewitt [11]	0.51	0.54	0.38
Sobel and Feldman [14]	0.51	0.53	0.38
Roberts [12]	0.50	0.53	0.73

Table 1 reports a summary of results obtained on the database of 500 images of Berkeley. It should be noted that the most interesting measure is the F measure (ODS), the other ones are involved only to bring more precision.

Table 1 summarises the comparison results between the proposed methods -Max_TR and PZ_DTR- and the classical models as well as some newer and more sophisticated models [1,8,13]. An overview of these results is illustrated in Fig. 2. It is easy to see that the Max_TR approach significantly exceeds, in terms of performance, the remaining methods, irrespective of the selected filter (Gaussian or Poisson). However, the PZ_DTR approach is less efficient in comparison to other more recent approaches. Indeed, the last ones use in practice a fairly elaborate techniques, that motivate us to improve this detector involving for example the principle of multiscale.

Experimental tests have shown that the Poisson filter gives better results than the Gaussian one. Moreover, the best result is obtained for $\alpha = 0.27$. Thus, we can recognise that the Gaussian filter often used is probably not the best choice. Indeed, since the recent appearance of the α scale-space theory [5], other kernel filters having the same properties as the Gaussian filter are put forward [2,7].

Before the emergence of the Riesz transform, a combination of different directions was necessary to describe correctly a structure. Using six directions was a good compromise for edge detection applications. Using henceforth the monogenic signal, the filter is composed of three components which can be seen as three directions. These three directions: a pair of *even* component and two *odd* components are enough to naturally and correctly sweep the whole area of the image. Indeed, the odd part of the filter is treated as a natural extension of the two-dimensional representation of the anisotropic filter. After development, this

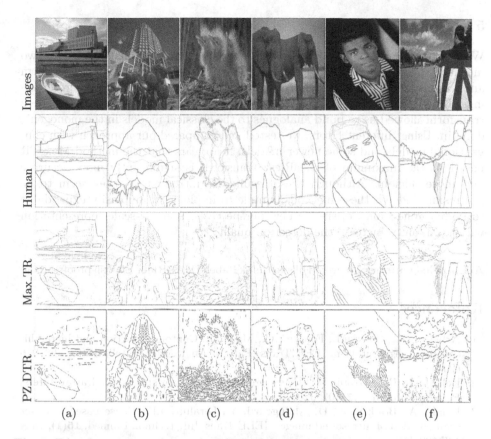

Fig. 2. Edge detection results on the BSDS500 benchmark. From top to bottom: original images, corresponding manual segmentations, results obtained by the methods Max_TR, PZ_DTR.

part is reduced to a single component capable of detecting structures of stair type. Therefore, compared to the case of steerable filters, there is a reduction in the number of the directions used. All these reasons justify the performance of suggested approach compared with the gradient based approaches.

It is natural to think tackle the proposed approach with more recent and efficient ones, such as the model called GPB-owt-ucm of [1]. However, such methods are in a quite developed and sophisticated level, and take into account the texture, the multi-scale framework and the presence of noise in images. To be at the same level and get better detection, it is interesting to develop our approach to multiscale framework and include a component for treating texture. We can note also that according to the experiments carried out on the Berkeley database, the measure F depends on the size and type of the selected images sample. Thus, we plan to experiment our approach by other publicly available datasets.

5   Conclusion

We proposed in this paper a new edge detection technique that has led to two methods called Max_TR and PZ_DTR. These are based on the Riesz transform and are inspired by the model of maximum gradient and Laplacian zero crossings. Indeed, the recent generalisation of the analytic signal, based on the Riesz transform allowed us to build analogues to the classical models in the monogenic domain. Using different filters, we tested and compared our approach with conventional models and some newer models. It appears that the method Max_TR based on the maximum of the Riesz transform is significantly more accurate and more efficient. Although these results are introductory, they seem to be promising. Indeed, these methods, simple to implement and easily expandable to higher dimensions, opens up new perspectives. A multi-scale representation will significantly increase the detection quality.

Acknowledgement. We would like to thank Rabeh DJABRI for English proofreading.

References

1. Arbelaez, P., Maire, M., Fowlkes, C., Malik, J.: Contour detection and hierarchical image segmentation. IEEE Trans. Pattern Anal. Mach. Intell. **33**(5), 898–916 (2011)
2. Belaid, A., Boukerroui, D.: A new generalised α scale spaces quadrature filters. Pattern Recognit. **47**(10), 3209–3224 (2014)
3. Belaid, A., Boukerroui, D., Maingourd, Y., Lerallut, J.F.: Phase based level set segmentation of ultrasound images. IEEE Trans. Inf. Technol. Biomed. **15**(1), 138–147 (2011)
4. Canny, J.: A computational approach to edge detection. IEEE Trans. Pattern Anal. Mach. Intell. **8**(6), 679–698 (1986)
5. Duits, R., Felsberg, M., Florack, L., Platel, B.: α scale spaces on a bounded domain. In: Griffin, Lewis D., Lillholm, Martin (eds.) Scale-Space 2003. LNCS, vol. 2695. Springer, Heidelberg (2003)
6. Felsberg, M., Sommer, G.: The monogenic signal. IEEE Trans. Signal Process. **49**(12), 3136–3144 (2001)
7. Felsberg, M., Sommer, G.: The monogenic scale-space: a unifying approach to phase-based image processing in scale-space. J. Math. Imag. Vis. **21**(1), 5–26 (2004)
8. Felzenszwalb, P.F., Huttenlocher, D.P.: Efficient graph-based image segmentation. Int. J. Comput. Vis. **59**(2), 167–181 (2004)
9. Haralick, R.M.: Digital step edges from zero crossing of second directional derivatives. IEEE Trans. Pattern Anal. Mach. Intell. **6**(1), 58–68 (1984)
10. Marr, D., Hildreth, E.: Theory of edge detection. Proc. R. Soc. Lond. B **207**, 187–217 (1980)
11. Prewitt, J.M.S.: Object enhancement and extraction. In: Lipkin, B., Rosenfeld, A. (eds.) Picture Processing and Psychopictorics. Academic, New York (1970)
12. Roberts, L.G.: Machine Perception of Three-Dimensional Solids. Outstanding Dissertations in the Computer Sciences. Garland Publishing, New York (1963)
13. Sharon, E., Galun, M., Sharon, D., Basri, R., Brandt, A.: Hierarchy and adaptivity in segmenting visual scenes. Nature **442**, 810–813 (2006)

14. Sobel, I., Feldman, G.: A 3 × 3 isotropic gradient operator for image processing. In: Pattern Classification and Scene Analysis (1968)
15. Unser, M., Sage, D., Ville, D.V.D.: Multiresolution monogenic signal analysis using the Riesz-Laplace wavelet transform. IEEE Trans. Image Process. **18**(11), 2402–2418 (2009)
16. Zang, D., Wietzke, L., Schmaltz, C., Sommer, G.: Dense optical flow estimation from the monogenic curvature tensor (2007)

Otolith Recognition System Using a Normal Angles Contour

El Habouz Youssef[1(✉)], Es-saady Youssef[1], El Yassa Mostafa[1],
Mammass Driss[1], Nouboud Fathallah[2], Chalifour Alain[2], and Manchih Khalid[3]

[1] IRF-SIC Laboratory, University Ibn Zohr, Agadir, Morocco
elhabouzyoussef@gmail.com
[2] LIRIC, Université du Québec à Trois-Rivières, Québec, Canada
[3] Laboratory of Biology and Ecology of the National Fisheries Research Institute,
Casablanca, Morocco

Abstract. The proposed approach aims to develop an automatic recognition system of fish species based on otolith shape analysis. From the 8-connected external contour of each otolith we extract the normal angles contour and then we represent it with Fourier coefficients. These coefficients are used to identify the classes of the otoliths using a neural network classification method. The approach was tested over 450 otolith images belonging to 15 species originated from a Moroccan Atlantic Ocean area. This database was collected and prepared in collaboration with the National Institute of Fisheries Research (INRH, Morocco). The experimental results showed a promising approach to classify otoliths.

Keywords: Otoliths · Shape analysis · Otolith recognition and classification · Neural network · Normal angles · Fourier descriptors · 8-connected contour

1 Introduction

The bony fishes have calcified structures called otoliths. They are located in the inner ear of fish species, and are composed of calcium carbonate crystals and organic materials (Fig. 1). Among fish species, otoliths have various shapes and are characteristic features for fish species classification [1–4]. Since otoliths are resistant to degradation they are often the only identifiable structures that can be recovered from the stomach and feces of fish specimen. In this context, the shape analysis of otolith is largely used to identify food web of fish species, but also in taxonomy, phylogenetic, paleontology and stock discrimination [2,5]. The classical approach for identification of fish species using otoliths is based on natural observation from experts using a naked eye approach. However, this technique is quite expensive and time consuming [6,7]. Accordingly, looking for a more accurate, automatic, inexpensive and faster methodology to recognize fish species using otoliths is relevant for marine biologists [8]. In this field, a variety of results have been reported [9–12], usually by applying classical complex Fourier descriptors (CFD) or elliptical Fourier descriptors (EFD) [13].

© Springer International Publishing Switzerland 2016
A. Mansouri et al. (Eds.): ICISP 2016, LNCS 9680, pp. 30–39, 2016.
DOI: 10.1007/978-3-319-33618-3_4

The EFD method decomposes in harmonic series the contour of an otolith, otherwise EFD outperforms CFD in the classification of otoliths when otoliths have complex shapes. In this paper, we present an automatic classification method of otoliths based on a representation by the normal angles of the counter-clockwise 8-connected contour [14] of the otolith. Finally, the Fourier descriptors of the curve of the normal angles along the contour are used in a neural network classification method.

Fig. 1. Otolith fish species of Engraulis encrasicolus.

The paper is structured as follows: the Sect. 2 describes the architecture of the proposed approach. In this section, we present the algorithm to approximate the contour by a discrete polygonal in order to avoid discontinuities along the contour obtained from the acquisition of images. Then, we describe the extraction of a counterclockwise 8-connected otoliths contour and the calculation of normal angles of the contour. At the end of this section, we present the extraction of the characteristic parameters (Fourier descriptors) and the classification method. Section 3 is devoted to experimental tests. Finally, a conclusion and future works are discussed in Sect. 4.

2 System Design

The aim of the proposed approach is to design an automatic recognition and classification system of otolith images. This approach is based on shape analysis

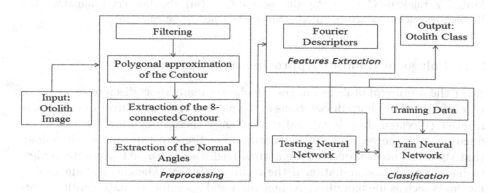

Fig. 2. Design of proposed system.

of otolith in order to manage marine resources. The system design is showed in Fig. 2.

2.1 Image Acquisition

The first step is to collect the sample images for building the database in order to train and test the classification system. The otoliths dataset (DB) used in this study derived from the Moroccan Atlantic area between Larache and Dakhla. The otoliths were collected by scientists of the National Institute of Fisheries Research (INRH) during sampling campaigns, spread over year 2002 to 2014, on research vessels and trawlers commercial landing. After the collection operation, we proceed to otolith acquisition using a stereo microscope Leica S8 APO, a Leica camera EC3 connected to a PC and Leica LAS EZ software (Version 3.0.0 for windows). The database contains 450 images from 15 different species, with 30 images by species. In Fig. 3, we illustrate examples of otolith images in the database.

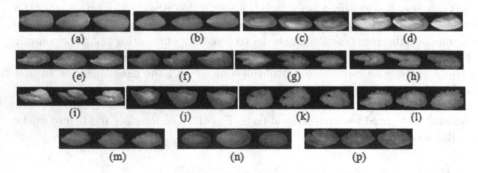

Fig. 3. (a) Micromesitius poutassou(C2), (b) Merluccius merluccis(C3), (c) Merluccius polli(C12), (d) Merluccius senegalensis(C13), (e) Helicolenus dactylopterus(C8), (f) Trachurus trachurus(C9), (g) Engraulis encrasicolus(C10), (h) Sardina pilchardus(C11), (i) Trachyscorpia cristulata(C14), (j) Argentina sphyraena(C1), (k) Mullus surmuletus(C4), (l) Pagellus acarne(C5), (m) Pagellus erythrinus(C6), (n) Dicologoglossa cuneata(C7), (p) Plectorhynchus mediterraneus(C15).

2.2 Polygonal Contour Approximation

After the capture of otoliths images, we observe many short discrete segments of pixels followed by sharp fluctuations in the pattern of normal directions along the frontier (Freeman directions) and consequently these discontinuities will introduce noise in the sequence of the normal directions to the contour. It follows that the curve of variations of the normal angles seems to be inaccurate in view to have a good discrimination if the contour is noisy. The classical smoothing methods such as median filter, average filter and operators of mathematical morphology are not satisfactory to smooth the contours of our images. In order to overcome this difficulty, we first approximate the contour by a polygonal contour to obtain a more compact description of the contour suitable for further processing and shape classification [15]. Several polygonal approximation methods have been proposed in recent years. We used the algorithm proposed by HUANG and WANG [16]. In general, the pixels on the 8-connected initial contour (see Sect. 2.3) are successively examined in order to determine a sequence of longest segments that satisfy a predefined threshold. Basically, let P0 and P1 the two pixels on the frontier of the otolith such that the segment [P0, P1] is the longest secant on the otolith itself. This secant divides the otolith into two regions R0 and R1 with contours C0 and C1 respectively. In each region, we look for the pixel P2 on the contour, one pixel P2 in each region, such that the distance to its projection P on the segment [P0, P1] is maximal. If the length of the segment [P, P2] is less than $\epsilon > 0$ (threshold) we retain P2 as a summit of the polygon. This process is repeated on each successive sub region obtained as long as the criterion is respected. Figure 4 below illustrates the result of this method.

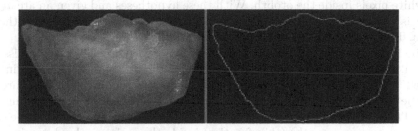

Fig. 4. Original image (left) and the polygonal approximation (right).

2.3   Counterclockwise 8-Connected Contour and Normal Angles Contour

In this section we present a method to extract the counterclockwise 8-connected contour of an otolith image. This contour has a minimum length and is characterized by an ordered sequence of Freeman chain codes [17] associated to the successive displacements between pixels along the contour.

Extraction of the Counterclockwise 8-Connected Contour: After the polygonal approximation, which is not necessarily 8-connected, we consider the binary image of the otolith (white pixels inside and black pixels outside). Each black pixel is indexed by the value 0 and each white pixel by the value 255 (Fig. 5). Our objective is to construct a counterclockwise 8-connected contour and from this contour we calculate the normal angles contour. For this, we applied an algorithm proposed by Chalifour et al. [14]. As a result, the contour of an otolith will be a closed, simple or weakly simple path, positively oriented (counterclockwise) with a thickness equal to one pixel. The contour of black pixels $C = [P_1, P_2, , P_i, , P_L, P_{L+1} = P_1]$ have a minimum chain length L, with

Fig. 5. Binary images of two different species.

regard to the 8-connectivity. The pixel P_1 is called the starting pixel of C and this unique pixel is located at the upper left corner with a Freeman direction $\alpha = 5$ between P_1 and P_2.

From that first displacement, we construct successively, and unequivocally, the arcs between pixels of the otolith contour, such that the arc $a_k = [P_k, P_{k+1}]$, for $k \geq 2$ is constructed from the previous arc a_{k-1}, respecting hypotheses [14,18] : the choice of P_{k+1} minimizes the contour length with regard to the 8-connectivity, the chain is counterclockwise, the extremity of each arc is a black pixel, and the pixels at the left of the arc, compared to the oriented displacement, are white pixels inside the otolith. With these hypotheses and given an arc a_{k-1}, there is the only oriented arc a_k, that simultaneously verifies the hypotheses above. The choice of the pixel P_{k+2} is performed according to the pixel P_{k+1}. We use the Freeman indices to indicate the direction of each arc. The only admissible pairs (i, j) of successive displacements (Freeman directions) are presented in the Table 1 below, where the first index i (line) indicates the direction of an arc a_k and the index j (column) indicates the admissible direction of the following arc a_{k+1}. The configurations can have two opposite successive directions in the case where the contour growths (thin frontier) inside the region with white pixels.

We associate to the contour C, the oriented chain of Freeman directions $[\alpha_1, \alpha_2, ..., \alpha_k, ..., \alpha_L]$ where ak is the direction of the arc $[P_k, P_{k+1}]$, for $k = 1, ..., L$. These sequences of pixels and directions allow us to compute the normal angles on the contour. We associate a normal angle θ_k to each pixel $P_k, 1 \leq k \leq L$, along the contour. For this, we consider two successive displacements between the pixels $[P_{k-1}, P_k, P_{k+1}]$ for $2 \leq k \leq L$ and the pixels

Table 1. Pairs of admissible successive directions.

i/j	0	1	2	3	4	5	6	7
0	x	x			x	x	x	x
1	x	x	x	x		x	x	x
2	x	x	x	x			x	x
3	x	x	x	x	x	x		x
4	x	x	x	x	x	x		x
5		x	x	x	x	x	x	x
6			x	x	x	x	x	x
7	x	x		x	x	x	x	x

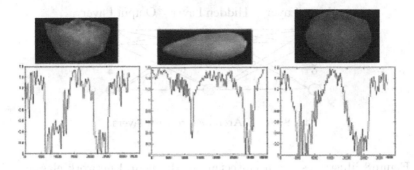

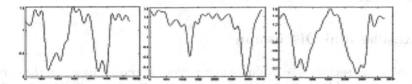

Fig. 6. Patterns of normal angles along the contour of three otoliths.

Fig. 7. Patterns of normal angles after Fourier approximation of the otoliths in Fig. 6.

$[P_L, P_1, P_2]$ for $k = 1$. The normal angle associated to P_k is the average value (in radians), of the perpendicular directions of the directions α_{k-1} and α_k. For the allowable displacements presented in Table 1, the only possible angles are in the set $\{0, arctan(0.5), \frac{\pi}{4}, arctan(2)\}$ and their appropriate rotations. We note $C_a = [\theta_1, \theta_2, ..., \theta_{i-1}, \theta_i, ..., \theta_L, \theta_{L+1} = \theta_1]$ the set of normal directions associated to the pixels of the contour. We obtain a discrete function of the normal angles along the contour, each angle being dependant of the position of pixels in the chain of the contour (Fig. 6). In order to get a standardized representation of the functions of normal angles, independent of the length of the otolith contour, we brought back by contraction, the definition interval of these functions to the interval $[0, 1]$. We approximate C_a by a periodical function using the classical discrete Fourier transform (Fig. 7). We only kept the first fifteen coefficients that multiply each cosine or sine base function in the Fourier development (a_k, b_k $k = 1, ..., 15$). Among the properties of the Fourier descriptors we cite its invariance to translation, rotation, and scale change.

2.4 Classification Method

In this section we describe the classification system based on the extracted features from the otolith images as input in view to associate each image to a class. This system is based on a neural networks classifier. This classifier consists of three layers of processing nodes (neurons) [19], an input layer, a hidden layer and an output layer. Only one hidden layer is used in order to restrict the calculation

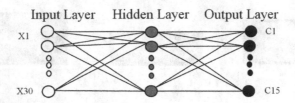

Fig. 8. ANN Architecture with layers.

time. Figure 8 illustrates the architecture of the neural network classifier. The input layer consists of the Fourier coefficients (n = 30). The hidden layer contains thirty two neurons (H = 32), and the output layer contains the 15 classes (species) tested.

3   Results and Discussion

The goal of this section is to evaluate and test our approach based on the normal angles contour (NAC method). We compare the quality of the classification of the specimen obtained with our approach and the methods using complex Fourier descriptors (CFD) and Elliptic Fourier descriptors (EFD). Table 2 presents the classification rates obtained with the three methods applied over all otoliths (450 specimens) in the database. With the NAC method, we obtained the better classification rate (94.7 %) with 426 otoliths well identified against 320 otoliths using CFD and 361 otoliths using EFD.

The improvement of the classification provided by the NAC method, in comparison with other approaches, is statistically significant and is confirmed by statistical tests (T-test, McNemar test, Odds ratio). These tests demonstrated that the proposed method correctly identify otolith specimens which are not recognized by the other methods (Table 3). This shows that the classification features proposed offer a significant improvement of the recognition performance.

The details of the classification are reported in the table (confusion matrix) in Fig. 9 (15 classes or species). The confusion matrix summarizes the reclassification of the specimens using NAC approach and a total of 426 otolith images are correctly recognized, 24 are misclassified. We used 70 % of the images for the training of the neural network, 15 % for testing and 15 % for the validation. The validation data serves to avoid the overlearning (to determine a stopping point of the neural network learning). Figure 10 shows an efficient validation results.

Table 2. Classification rate: CFD, EFD, NAC.

Methods	CFD	EFD	NAC
Well classified	320/450	361/450	426/450
Classification rate	71.1 %	80.2 %	94.7 %

Table 3. Classification with CFD and EFD methods revisited by NAC method.

	Well classified by CFD	Misclassified by CFD
Well classified by NAC	320	106
Misclassified by NAC	0	24
	Well classified by EFD	Misclassified by EFD
Well classified by NAC	361	65
Misclassified by NAC	0	24

Actual Class	Estimated Class														
	C1	C2	C3	C4	C5	C6	C7	C8	C9	C10	C11	C12	C13	C14	C15
C1	30	0	0	0	0	0	0	0	0	0	0	0	0	0	0
C2	0	30	0	0	0	0	0	0	0	0	0	0	0	0	0
C3	0	0	29	0	0	0	0	0	0	0	0	1	0	0	0
C4	0	0	0	28	0	2	0	0	0	0	0	0	0	0	0
C5	0	1	0	1	26	2	0	0	1	0	0	0	0	0	0
C6	0	0	0	0	1	28	0	0	0	0	0	0	0	0	1
C7	0	0	0	0	0	0	30	0	0	0	0	0	0	0	0
C8	0	0	0	0	0	0	0	30	0	0	0	0	0	0	0
C9	0	0	0	0	0	0	0	0	29	0	0	0	0	1	0
C10	0	0	0	0	0	0	0	0	0	30	0	0	0	0	0
C11	0	2	0	0	0	0	0	0	0	1	27	0	0	0	0
C12	0	1	0	0	0	0	0	0	0	2	0	27	0	0	1
C13	0	0	3	0	0	0	0	0	0	0	0	0	27	0	0
C14	0	1	0	0	0	0	0	0	1	0	0	1	0	26	1
C15	0	0	0	0	0	0	0	0	0	0	0	0	1	0	29

Fig. 9. Confusion matrix.

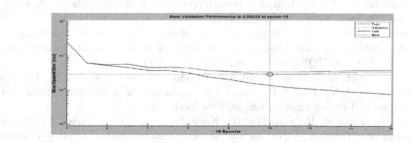

Fig. 10. Validation after training.

The classification errors are mainly caused by the similarity of the shapes of some classes. For example, 3 otoliths images of Merluccius senegalensis (C13) are classified as Merluccius merluccius (C3), and 2 otolith images of Pagellus acarne (C5) are classified as Pagellus erythrinus (C6). In fact, this resemblance of otolith shapes, for species in that case lying in the same genus, occurs at a specific age for these species. To solve this problem we need to increase the number of otoliths in the training phase of the multi-layer neural networks.

4   Conclusion and Future Work

Recognition of otolith images is the aim of the current study. The approach aimed to design an automatic classification system based on the Fourier descriptors of the normal angles of the contour. The developed system was tested successfully on a national otoliths database collected in collaboration with INRH (Morocco). The experimental results indicate that the proposed approach is promising. Future works will focus on the rising of the number of images in the training phase and the addition of other features in order to improve the discriminating power and the recognition rate. In addition, our approach will be to the stocks discrimination of fishes.

Acknowledgments. We would like to thank Hammou El Habouz and Khalid Manchich, scientists at INRH (Morocco), for their contribution to the data sampling and the identification of the otolith images.

References

1. El habouz, Y., Es-saady, Y., Elyassa, M., Mammass, D., Nouboud, F., Chalifour, A., El habouz, H., Manchih, K.A.: A new otolith recognition system based on image contour analysis. J. Entomol. Zool. Stud. **4**(1), 580–590 (2016)
2. Schmidt, W.: The otoliths as a means for differentiation between species of fish of very similar appearance. In: Proceedings of the Symposium Oceanog, Fish. Res. Trop. Atl., UNESCO, FAO, OAU, pp. 393–396 (1969)
3. El habouz, Y., Es-saady, Y., Elyassa, M., Mammass, D., Nouboud, F., Chalifour, A., Manchihn, K.: Recognition of otoliths having a high shape similarity. J. Theor. Appl. Inf. Technol. **84**(1), 19–23 (2016)
4. El habouz, Y., Es-saady, Y., Elyassa, M., Mammass, D., Nouboud, F., Chalifour, A. Otolith identification system based on image contour analysis. In: 5th International Otolith Symposium (IOS 2014), Mallorca, Spain (2014)
5. Platt, C., Popper, A.N.: Hearing and Sound Communication in Fishes. In: Tavolga, A.N., Popper, A.N., Fay, R.R. (eds.) Fine structure and function of the ear. Proceedings in Life Sciences. Springer, New York (1981)
6. Denison, R., Zangerl, R., Capetta, H., Norlf, D., Stahl, B. J, Mrss, T., Turner, S., Karatajute-Talimaa, V.N.: Handbook of Paleoichthyology: Otolith piscium, vol. 10. Verlag Dr. F. Pfeil ed., p. 145 (2007)
7. Frost, K.J., Lowry, L.F.: Trophic importance of some marine gadids in Northern Alaska and their body-otolith size relationships. Fish. Bull. **79**(1), 87–192 (1981)

8. Lombarte, A., Chic, Ó., Parisi-Baradad, V., Olivella, R., Piera, J., Garcia-Ladona, E.: A web-based environment for shape analysis of fish otoliths. The AFORO database. Scientia **70**, 147–152 (2006)
9. Harbitz, A., Albert, O.T.: Pitfalls in stock discrimination by shape analysis of otolith contours. ICES J. Mar., Sci. **72**(7), 2090–2097 (2015)
10. Reig-Bola, R., Marti-Puig, P., Rodrguez, S., Bajo, J., Parisi-Baradad, V., Lombarte, A.: Otoliths Identifiers Using Image Contours EFD. In: de Leon F. de Carvalho, A.P., Rodríguez-González, S., De Paz Santana, J.F., Corchado Rodríguez, J.M. (eds.) Distributed Computing and Artificial Intelligence. Advances in Intelligent and Soft Computing, vol. 79, pp. 9–16. Springer, Heidelberg (2010)
11. Keating, J.P., Brophy, D., Officer, R.A., Mullins, E.: Otolith shape analysis of blue whiting suggests a complex stock structure at their spawning grounds in the Northeast Atlantic. Fish. Res. **157**, 16 (2014)
12. Jonsdottir, I.G., Campana, S.E., Marteinsdottir, G.: Otolith shape and temporal stability of spawning groups of Icelandic cod (Gadusmorhua L.). ICES J. Mar. Sci. **63**, 1501–1512 (2006)
13. Kuhl, F.P., Giardina, C.R.: Elliptic features of a closed contour. Comput. Graph. Image Process. **18**, 237–258 (1982)
14. Chalifour, A., Beauchemin, S., Bose, P., Nouboud, F.: Analyse morphologique des filets de tricoptres: un problme dcotoxicologie et de gomtrie discrte. Vision Interface 1998, Van-couver, pp. 479–486 (1998)
15. Perez, J., Vidal, E.: Optimum polygonal approximation of digitized curves. Pattern Recogn. Lett. **15**(8), 743–750 (1994)
16. Huang, L.K., Wang, M.J.J.: Efficient shape matching through model-based shape recognition. Pattern Recogn. **29**(2), 207–215 (1996)
17. Freeman, H.: On the encoding of arbitrary geometric configurations. Electron. Comput. IEEE Trans. Comput. **10**(2), 260–268 (1961)
18. Siddour, A., Nouboud, F., Mammass, D., Chalifour, A. et Campeau, S.: Classification des diatomes par les descripteurs de Fourier du contour. e-TI La revue lectronique des technologies d'information, numro 4 (2007)
19. Basheer, I.A., Hajmeer, M.: Artificial neural networks: fundamentals, computing, design, and application. J. Microbiol. Methods **43**(1), 3–31 (2000)

A Hybrid Combination of Multiple SVM Classifiers for Automatic Recognition of the Damages and Symptoms on Plant Leaves

Ismail El Massi[1]([✉]), Youssef Es-saady[1], Mostafa El Yassa[1], Driss Mammass[1], and Abdeslam Benazoun[2]

[1] IRF-SIC Laboratory, Ibn Zohr University, B.P. 80 000 Agadir, Morocco
ismail.elmassi@gmail.com, melyass@gmail.com,
{y.essaady,mammass}@uiz.ac.ma
[2] Department of Plant Protection, Hassan II Institute of Agronomy and Veterinary,
Complex of Agadir, Temara, Morocco
abbenazoun@gmail.com

Abstract. A machine vision system is reported in this study for automatic recognition of the damages and symptoms on plant leaves from images. The system is based on a hybrid combination of three SVM classifiers including an individual classifier, which is used in parallel with a serial combination of two classifiers. The individual classifier adopts two types of features (texture and shape) to discriminate between the damages and symptoms. In serial architecture, the first classifier adopts the color features to classify the images; it considers the damages and/or symptoms that have a similar or nearest color belonging to the same class. Then, the second classifier is used to differentiate between the classes with similar color depending on the shape and texture features. A combination function is provided for comparing the decision of the individual classifier and of the serial architecture in order to achieve the final decision that represents the class of the form to be recognized. The tests of this study are carried out on six classes including three types of pest insects damages and three forms of fungal diseases symptoms. The results, with an overall recognition rate of 93.9 %, show the advantages of the proposed method compared to the other existing methods.

Keywords: Hybrid combination of classifiers · Automatic recognition · SVM · Damages · Symptoms · Plant leaves · Image

1 Introduction

The agriculture in Morocco has several issues. The damages of pest insects and symptoms of fungal diseases are among the major problems. They cause the diminution of the quality and quantity of the agricultural products. Therefore, significant economic losses can be result to farmers. In this context, the pattern recognition and machine vision methods can be used to reduce the losses.

© Springer International Publishing Switzerland 2016
A. Mansouri et al. (Eds.): ICISP 2016, LNCS 9680, pp. 40–50, 2016.
DOI: 10.1007/978-3-319-33618-3_5

These methods provide support decision systems that are used as means of diagnosis and recognition of a phytosanitary problem from images of the infected plant [11]. In recent years, several approaches have been proposed in the literature concerning the recognition of the damages and symptoms [7]. Some of the principal approaches are published in [1–6,11]. However, there is no satisfactory solution available with the existing methods, because the complexity of the studied system in which some damages and/or symptoms can have similar characteristics (Color, texture, shape). This similarity, in characteristics, between classes makes the classification more difficult.

In the present study, a method is proposed to reduce the problems that experienced by the previous approaches. The suggested method is based on a hybrid combination of classifiers technique [8] that consists on combining an individual classifier in parallel with a serial architecture of two classifiers. In that case, a combination function is proposed to compare the decision of the individual classifier and of the serial architecture in order to obtain the final decision which represents the class of the form (damages or symptoms) in the input image. The main objective of the adopted technique is to improve our previous method [3] that based only on a serial combination of two classifiers, and to reduce its classification errors, which are occurred especially by the first classifier that uses only the color in the classification of the images. The errors of our previous method are reduced, in fact, by the individual classifier, used in parallel with the sequential architecture, which does not adopt color features, and on the other hand it uses only texture and shape features. The improvement of our previous method includes also the features extraction step, in which in the proposed method we adopt more attributes in texture, shape and color features. Moreover, we use SVM method [12] for classification instead neural networks, because of its simplicity, and it also gives significant results.

This study focuses on six classes including, on the one hand, the damages of three pest insects (Leaf miners, Thrips and Tuta absoluta), and on the other hand, the symptoms of three fungal diseases (Early blight, Late blight and Powdery mildew), which are among the major challenges of the vegetables crops in Souss Massa region (located in the south of Morocco).

2   Related Works

In this section, we present some existing works in automatic recognition of the damages and symptoms on plant leaves, which are used in this study to contribute to the realization of our proposed method.

In [1], Camargo et al. implemented a machine vision system for automatic recognition of three classes including one class represented by the damages of a type of pest insect (Green stink), and two classes represented by two forms of fungal diseases (Bacteria angular and Ascochyta blight). Their approach is based on a set of features including color, texture, shape, lacunarity, fractal dimension and Fourier descriptors, which are needed to achieve the classification by SVM method. They are tested their method on 117 images, in which the recognition rate was 93 %.

In [2], Wang et al. proposed an approach for automatic recognition of two fungal diseases symptoms (Downy mildew and Powdery mildew), based on neural networks in classification and on four sorts of features including fractal dimension, texture, color and shape. The recognition rate was 97 % on a database of 83 images (50 of Downy mildew and 35 of Powdery mildew).

In [3], we proposed an approach for automatic recognition of four classes including the damages of two pest insects (Leaf miners and Tuta absoluta) and symptoms of two fungal diseases (Downy mildew and internal Powdery mildew). This method is based on a serial combination of two neural networks classifiers. The tests were carried out on a database of 200 images including 50 images in each class of the four adopted classes.

In [4], Al Bashish et al. introduced a system for the recognition of five diseases including Early scorch, Cottony mold, Ashen mold, Late scorch and Tiny whiteness, which mainly attack the cotton. Their system is based on the Haralick texture features and neural networks for classification. They tested the system on a database of 192 images of six classes (5 of diseases symptoms and one class represents the normal leaves). The global recognition rate was 93 %.

3   Proposed System Design

The proposed system is based on hybrid combination of three SVM classifiers: A serial combination of two classifiers, which is used in parallel with an individual classifier. The system was preliminary designed as follow (Fig. 1).

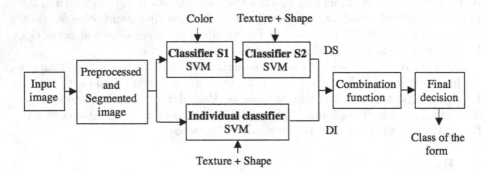

Fig. 1. Design of proposed system.

3.1   Image acquisition

As a first step in our work, the collection of the images in order to build the database. These images are needed to train and test the system. They are captured using a digital camera in several farms with the help of an expert in the agricultural field. Other images are downloaded from the Internet in order to increase the database size and to have diverse environments. Figure 2 shows some images of the database.

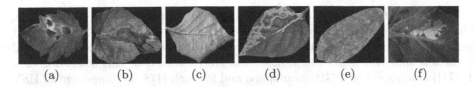

(a)   (b)   (c)   (d)   (e)   (f)

Fig. 2. Some images of the database. The symptoms: (a) Early blight, (b) Late blight, (c) Powdery mildew. The damages: (d) Leaf miners, (e) Thrips, (f) Tuta abosluta.

3.2 Preprocessing and Segmentation

The input image should to be preprocessed in order to improve its quality and to facilitate the segmentation and analysis steps. The adopted preprocessing methods in this work include resizing and filtering. At first, the image is resized with a standard size. Then, a filter median is applied as filtering method to reduce the noise in the image. The noise is generally due to acquisition process.

After preprocessing, the image is segmented in order to extract the infected area from leaf area. K-means clustering method [9] is used in this context for segmentation of the input image. This method is the most known and the most used in the previous works, since it gives good results in segmentation of the colored images (see [3,4,11] for more detail about segmentation with k-means clustering method). In this study, the k-means clustering algorithm segments the input image into k clusters (k=5 in our case) in which one of them containing the majority of the infected area. Figure 3 shows the segmentation results of two images of two infected leaves with Leaf miners damages and Late blight symptoms using the k-means clustering technique.

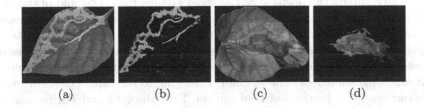

(a)   (b)   (c)   (d)

Fig. 3. Segmentation result of two images of two leaves infected by damages and symptoms. (a) Leaf infected by Leaf miners damages and (b) cluster containing the damages area. (c) Leaf infected by Late blight symptoms and (d) cluster containing symptoms area.

3.3 Features Extraction and Selection

The features extraction is the next necessary step to carry out. It consists of representing the segmented image on a vector of fixed features that should be distinct and relevant for the classifier performance. The selected features in this study include color, texture and shape features.

Color moments [10] method is used in this work for color features extraction. This method is adopted because of its ease of use and it provides important results. Color moment method is defined by three moments: Mean, Standard deviation and Skewness. These moments are extracted in this study for each R/G/B component of RGB color space and for each H/S/V component of HSV color space. In total, 18 color features are calculated.

For texture, we adopted Grey Level Co-occurrence Matrix (GLCM) [11] method. This method is the most adopted for texture features in the majority of previous works, since it gives extra informations for dictimination between the damages and symptoms. GLCM is a statistical analysis tool of an image in gray levels, which measures the distribution of gray levels in the image based on the spatial relations of pixels. Haralick introduces 14 attributes of texture based on GLCM. Five attributes were only used in this study including Contrast, Energy, Entropy, Homogeneity and Correlation. These five attributes are the most used in previous works, because they are relevant and distinct. In this work, these five attributes are calculated for each component R/G/B and for each component H/S/V, in which 30 texture features are extracted in total.

Twelve shape features are adpted in this study including Area, Perimeter, Circularity, Complexity, Solidity, Extent, Major axis length, Minor axis length, Eccentricity, Centroid and Diameter. We associate in this work the most used shape attributes in previous works, and then the results are significant.

3.4   Classification

The adopted classifiers in this study are based on SVM method [12]. They are used in a hybrid combination, in which a serial architecture of two classifiers is used in parallel with an individual classifier. Then, a combination function is provided to compare the decision of the serial architecture (DS) and of the individual classifier (DI) in order to achieve the final decision (FD) that represents the class of the damages or symptoms in the input image. Figure 4 demonstrates the architecture of the serial combination of two classifiers: The first classifier S1 uses the color to classify the images; it considers that the damages and/or symptoms, with similar or nearest color, belonging to the same class. For example, in our case, the damages of Leaf miners, Tuta absoluta and Thrips, and the symptoms of Powdery mildew are placed in the same class that is named class of

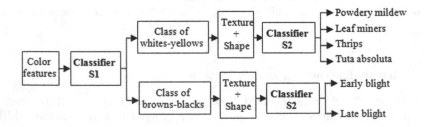

Fig. 4. Architecture of the serial combination

whites-yellows. Also, the symptoms of Early blight and of Late blight are placed in the same class which is named class of browns-blacks. Then, the second classifier S2 is used to differentiate between the classes with similar color depending on the texture and shape features. It has two cases: the first one consists of discriminating between the classes within the whites-yellows class; then, in the other case, the second classifier differentiates between the classes that belong to the browns-blacks class.

The individual classifier adopts texture and shape features, and based on the one-against-one strategy [13] of SVM for the classification of the six chosen classes. The color features have not been used in the individual classifier. This is because of the similarity between some classes in their color. Moreover, the objective of this classifier consists of reducing the errors occurred by the serial combination, especially by its first classifier that adopts only the color in classification of the images. Therfore, the individual classifier is used here to correct the incorrectly classified images in serial combination (Fig. 5).

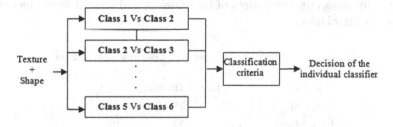

Fig. 5. Architecture of the individual classifier based on the one-against-one strategy of SVM.

The choice of the combination function plays an important role to obtain good results, and therefore having a more efficient system. Figure 6 shows the algorithm of the proposed combination function. When the decisions DS (Decision of serial architecture) and DI (Decision of individual classifier) are equal, then the final decision FD is the same. In the other case, when they are different, FD is obtained by applying a binary classification, based on SVM with the texture and color features, for discriminating between the two decisions DS and DI. This proposed algorihm which gives the good results in this study in the case where one of the two decisions DS and DI is incorrect and the other is correct.

```
If (DS==DI) then
    FD=DS=DI;
Else
    FD= ({Texture + Color} + Binary SVM (DS, DI));
```

Fig. 6. Algorithm of the combination function

It is used to correct the wrongly classified instance of the two decisions. The limitations of this combination function are when the two decisions are incorrect then the final decision is also incorrect.

4 Experimental Results

In order to test and evaluate our method, a comparison is carried out with the three existing methods [1–3] (see Sect. 2). For that, experiments are carried out on 284 images of the six chosen classes (48 Early blight, 41 Late blight, 46 Powdery mildew, 58 Leaf miners, 38 Thrips, 53 Tuta absoluta).

As a first step, the three previous methods are implemented and tested on our database of images. Then, the obtained results are compared and analyzed for designing our proposed approach that gives the highest recognition rate.

In this experiment, the dataset is divided into two subsets: a set of 202 images (70 %) used for training, and a set of 82 images (30 %) for the test (Table 1). For dividing the dataset, we used the hold-out cross validation technique [14] that automatically generates the indices of the training and test set from the outputs vector of the six classes.

Table 1. Dividing the dataset into training and test set

Classes	Dataset	Training	Test
Early blight	48	34	14
Late blight	41	29	12
Powdery mildew	46	33	13
Leaf miner	58	41	17
Thrips	38	27	11
Tuta absoluta	53	38	15
Total	**284**	**202**(70 %)	**82**(30 %)

Table 2 demonstrates the results of the individual classifier and the serial architecture compared to the global result of the hybrid combination. The results are represented by the recognition rate, which is expressed in percentage with the ratio between the number of correctly classified images and the total images used for test. In this table, we see that the two decisions of individual classifier and serial architecture have the same recogntion rate which is 87,80 %, since the two decisions have the same number of correctly classified images (72 images from 82). The global recognition rate of the hybrid combination using the proposed function combination is 93,90 %.

Table 3 illustrates the results of the indivdiual classifier and serial architecture depending on the number of classified images used for test. From this table, we notice that there are some coincident errors but the majority is always correct and there exists one of the two decisions that produces the correct answer.

Table 2. Results of the individual classifier, serial architecture and hybrid combination.

Individual classifier	Serial architecture	Hybrid combination
87,80 %	87,80 %	93,90 %

Table 3. Decision result of the individual classifier and serial architecture for 82 testing images.

Decision of the individual classifier and serial architecture	Number
Two are correct	67
One is correct	10
Two are incorrect	5
Total	82

Table 4. Results of proposed method compared to the three existing methods [1–3]

Approach	Classification	Rate of recognition
Camargo et al. [1]	SVM	82,93 %
Wang et al. [2]	Neural network	79,27 %
El Massi et al. [3]	Neural network	85,36 %
Proposed method	SVM	93,90 %

Table 5. Comparison between the proposed method and the three existing methods depending on the correctly (CC) and incorrectly (IC) classified images

		El Massi [3]		Wang [2]		Camargo [1]		$\sum$	%
		CC	IC	CC	IC	CC	IC		
Proposed	CC	68	9	63	14	67	10	77	**93,90%**
method	IC	2	3	2	3	1	4	5	6,10%
	$\sum$	70	12	65	17	68	14		
	%	85,37%	14,63%	79,27%	20,73%	82,93%	17,07%		

Table 4 shows the comparison between the proposed method and the three existing methods depending on the adopted classification method and the obtained recognition rate.

In Table 5, we demonstrate the comparison between the proposed method and the thee existing methods depending on the correctly and incorrectly classified images. The examination of this table shows that the difference between our method and the three methods is statistically significant.

Figure 7 demonstrates the results per class. The recognition rate is labeled for each class above the black curve that represents the proposed method. This figure shows that the three classes Powdery mildew, Leaf miners and Tuta absoluta

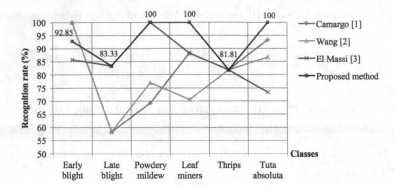

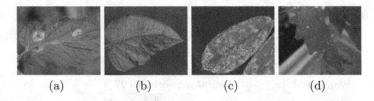

Fig. 7. Results per class of the proposed method compared to the three previous methods.

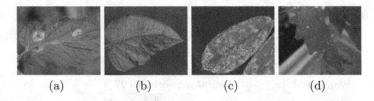

(a)   (b)   (c)   (d)

Fig. 8. Difference, in characteristics, between forms of the same class. (a) and (b): Two forms of Late blight symptoms. (c) and (d): Two forms of Thrips damages.

are totally classified (100 %) by the proposed method. In the case of Early blight class, the rate is 92,85 %, which is less than that of Camargo [1] and Wang [2].

The comparison, carried out in this study, indicate that the results obtained by our method, based on the hybrid combination of classifiers, are significant and encouraging. The examination of Fig. 7 demonstrates that the two classes Late blight and Thrips, with the recognition rate of 83,33 % and 81,81 % respectively, cause the diminution of the global accuracy of the proposed method. This diminution is due to, on the one hand, the number of images, used in these two classes, that are less than those used in the others, and on the other hand, to their complexity, in which it is difficult to discriminate between forms of the same class. Also, the complexity of these two classes is shown in similarity of the recognition rate, which is the same in the proposed method and our previous method [3]. Figure 8 shows two forms of Late blight symptoms and two forms of Thrips damages in two different stages of development. It appears, through the images, the difference, in the characteristics, between forms of the same class.

5   Conclusion and Future Work

Automatic recognition of the damages and symptoms on plant leaves is the aim of this study. The proposed system is based on a hybrid combination of classifiers technique, with the goal of reducing the classification problems that experienced by the previous methods. These problems are generally due to the complexity of the system of damages and symptoms. The results of this study show that the proposed method would be of importance to use as tool of diagnosis and phytosanitary problem recognition from images of the infected plant.

In future work, we plan to improve the proposed method with the use of other features in order to reduce the classification errors, and therefore obtaining more efficient system. We are also looking for increasing the database of images with the use of other damages and symptoms that attack the entire plant.

References

1. Camargo, A., Smith, J.S.: An image pattern classification for the identification of disease causing agents in plants. Comput. Electron. Agric. **66**(2), 121–125 (2009)
2. Wang, H., Li, G., Ma, Z., Li, X.: Image recognition of plant diseases based on back propagation networks. In: IEEE International Congress Image and Signal Processing (CISP), pp. 894–900. IEEE (2012)
3. El Massi, I., Es-Saady, Y., El Yassa, M., Mammass, D., Benazoun, A.: Serial combination of two classifiers for automatic recognition of the damages and symptoms on plant leaves. In: 3th IEEE World Conference on Complex System (WCCS). IEEE, Marrakech (2015)
4. Al Bashish, D., Braik, M., Bani-Ahmad, S.: Detection and classification of leaf diseases using k-means clustering based segmentation and neural networks based classification. Inf. Technol. J. **10**(2), 267–275 (2011)
5. Tian, Y., Zhao, C., Lu, S., Guo, X.: SVM-based multiple classifier system for recognition of wheat leaf diseases. In: IEEE Conference on Dependable Computing (CDC), pp. 189–193. IEEE (2010)
6. El Massi, I., Es-saady, Y., El Yassa, M., Mammass, D., Benazoun, A.: Automatic recognition of the damages and symptoms on plants leaves using parallel combination of two classifiers. In: 13th IEEE International Conference Computer Graphics, Imaging and Visualization (CGIV). IEEE, Beni Mellal (2016)
7. Vipinadas, M.J., Thamizharasi, A.: A survey on plant disease identification. Int. J. Comput. Sci. Trends Technol. **3**(6), 129–135 (2015)
8. Woniak, M., Graa, M., Corchado, E.: A survey of multiple classifier systems as hybrid systems. Inf. Fusion **16**, 3–17 (2014)
9. MacQueenn, J.B.: Some methods for classification and analysis of multivariate observations. In: Proceedings of 5th Berkeley Symposium on Mathematical Statistics and Probability, vol. 1, no.14, pp. 281–297 (1967)
10. Patil, J.K., Kumar, R.: Color feature extraction of tomato leaf diseases. Int. J. Eng. Trends Technol. **2**(2), 72–74 (2011)
11. Sannakki, S.S., Rajpurohit, V.S., Nargund, V.B., Kulkarni, P.: Diagnosis and classification of grape leaf diseases using neural network. In: 4th IEEE International Conference on Computing, Communications and Networking Technologies (ICC-CNT), pp. 1–5. IEEE (2013)

12. Bekkari, A., Idbraim, S., Elhassouny, A., Mammass, D., El yassa, M., Ducrot, D.: SVM and haralick features for classification of high resolution satellite images from urban areas. In: Elmoataz, A., Mammass, D., Lezoray, O., Nouboud, F., Aboutajdine, D. (eds.) ICISP 2012. LNCS, vol. 7340, pp. 17–26. Springer, Heidelberg (2012)
13. Hsu, C.W., Lin, C.J.: A comparison of methods for multi-class support vector machines. IEEE Trans. Neural Netw. 13(2), 415–425 (2002)
14. Sylvain, A.: A survey of cross-validation procedures for model selection. Stat. Surv. 4, 40–79 (2010)

Leaf Classification Using Convexity Measure of Polygons

Jules Raymond Kala(✉), Serestina Viriri, Deshendran Moodley,
and Jules Raymond Tapamo

University of Kwazulu-Natal, Durban, South Africa
raymondkala1@gmail.com
http://www.ukzn.ac.za

Abstract. Plant taxonomy is a long-standing practice in botany. It uses
the morphology of plant leaves to make categories. Leaf shape is one of
the physical characteristics used to discriminate between plant species.
This paper presents the characterisation of a leaf shape using the Convexity Measure of Polygons and the seven invariant moments in combination
with other morphological features to improve leaf classification. The Convexity Measure of Polygons used in this paper is based on the minimum
ratio obtained by dividing the rotated leaf-bounding perimeter of the
associate bounding rectangle of the leaf shape. The proposed model is
rotation, translation and scale invariant. It achieves a classification rate
of 92 % on 400 leaves of 20 species, 99 % on 100 leaves of 4 species and
95 % on 1600 leaves of 32 species using a Multilayer Perceptron classifier. The proposed method out-performs several state-of-the-art methods
when tested under the similar conditions, even with deformed leaves.

Keywords: Shape · Minimum Bounding Rectange (MBR) · Feature
extraction · Convexity measure

1 Introduction

Life on earth depends on plants and the life cycle of human beings is dependent
on them as they have the ability to transform light into food [14]. Plants were
initially organised as useful and not useful. This can be considered as the first
method of plant classification. The science of botany was then created and its
main objectives were to create rules for the classification of plants.

In the 18th century, Linnaeus [11] developed the systematic classification
of plants based on plant morphology. Given the number of rules used in the
systematic classification of plants, it is a difficult task even for a trained botanist,
because it is possible to find two different plants species with almost the same
physical appearance.

The difficulties encountered in manual classification have prompted the neces-
sity of computer vision to automate the process. The classification of plants is
important for botanists and environmentalists who are interested in obtaining an

© Springer International Publishing Switzerland 2016
A. Mansouri et al. (Eds.): ICISP 2016, LNCS 9680, pp. 51–60, 2016.
DOI: 10.1007/978-3-319-33618-3_6

organised series of descriptors or features that describe plant structures. These can be used to determine the properties of plants, prevent their extinction and the spread of diseases caused by plant pollen [6]. Leaf features include texture, vein, shape and water retention capacity. These are important components to take into consideration during leaf studies.

This research proposes a leaf feature extraction model that combines the Convexity Measure with geometrical and morphological features to improve the classification rate of plant leaves.

The Convexity Measure of Polygons is a shape characteriser used to describe the overall structure of a given shape. The New Convexity Measure of Polygons was created to provide solutions to the problems observed when using the Convex Hull polygon when evaluating the convexity measure of a given shape. These problems were the detection of small variations on the shape and the calculation of the convexity measurements of shapes with holes.

The rest of the paper is organised as follows: Sect. 2 discusses some related works; Sect. 3 presents the methods and techniques used; experimental results and discussion are discussed in Sect. 4 and the conclusion and future work are presented in Sect. 5.

2 Related Work

Many approaches have been used to perform plant classification. The following sections explore and discuss the different approaches used in the literature.

2.1 Morphological Based Approach

Panagiotis et al. [12] proposed one of the morphological approaches used for plant classification based on leaf analysis. The goal of this approach was the design of a system that is able to extract specific morphological and geometrical features from a plant leaf. They further use fuzzy surface selection to select the relevant features. This approach reduces the dimensionality of the feature space leading to a very simplified model that is more adapted to real time classification application. The model obtained is scale and orientation invariant and yields to a system that achieved a classification rate of 99 %, even with deformed leaves. The main drawbacks of this approach are the size (less than 5 species) and the system is not translation invariant.

Stephen et al. [13] presented a method based on the combination of the Probalistic Neural Network (PNN) and image processing techniques to construct general purpose semi-automatic leaf recognition for accurate plant classification. This method achieved 90 % accuracy, and is good in running time. However, it is not rotation invariant and requires human intervention during the process of feature extraction.

2.2 Texture Based Approaches

Esma et al. [8] proposed a system based on Dendritic Cell Algorithms derived from the Danger Theory [4], as a classifier. The wavelet transformed is used to extract the leaf features for the classification algorithm. This approach achieved a classification accuracy of 94 %.

Ahmed et al. [3] developed an approach that combines texture features based on Discrete wavelet transformation with an entropy measurement to construct an efficient leaf identifier. An accuracy of 92 % was achieved. The main advantage of this approach is noise removal from the image background. The drawback of the method is the size of the data set as it is based on less than 10 species.

2.3 Hybrid Approaches

Anant et al. [5], presented an approach based on the shape features combined with texture features to generate a feature set that will be used by the nearest neighbour classifier for the classification process. The method achieved a classification rate of 91.5 % for 14 plant species.

3 Materials and Methods

In many applications it is always important to enhance the quality of the captured image before any real processing can start. Particularly, in leaf classification the process we used will be run using four steps - input, preprocessing, feature extraction and classification.

3.1 Image Preprocessing and Leaves Data Set

Figure 1 presents samples of the categories of leaves randomly selected for the experimentation. Figure 2 shows the transformations performed on leaf image before extracting features.

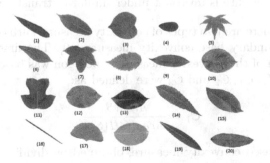

Fig. 1. Leaves selected for the classification

Original Image   Grey level Image   Binary Image   Boundary Image   MBR

Fig. 2. Leaf image processing (Minimum Bounding Rectangle (MBR))

Image Preprocessing

- All images are transformed from a colour image into a grey level image using Eq. (1). In fact, converting the image into grey level will preserve the shape of the leaf; thereby not impacting negatively on the end result.

$$l = 0.2989 * R + 0.5870 * G + 0.1140 * B \qquad (1)$$

- Leaf boundary is extracted by applying the Sobel filter on the leaf binary image.
- Thinning operation is then used to have leaf contours that are one pixel thick.

3.2   Features Extraction

The Convexity Measure of Polygons: A set of points A is said to be convex if the straight line segment joining any two points in A is contained in A [10]. The Convexity Measure of Polygons is a numerical value used to represent the probability that a straight line joining two points in A lies entirely in A.

   The Convexity Measure of Polygons has the following properties as defined in [10]:

- The value of the convexity measure is in (0,1].
- For a given shape, the convexity measure can be arbitrarily close to 0.
- The convexity measure of a convex set is equal to 1.
- The convexity measure is invariant under similarity transformation.

In the literature there are two types of convexity measure: surface base convexity measures and boundary base convexity measure [10]. The first approaches for the determination of the convexity measure of polygon was based on the convex Hull polygon (CH). C_1, C_2 and C_3 were defined as:

$$C_1 = \frac{Area(S)}{Area(CH(S))}. \qquad (2)$$

C_1 is a surface based convexity measure, obtained by dividing the area of the shape with the surface of the associate convex hull polygon.

$$C_2 = \frac{Area(MCS(S))}{Area(S)}. \qquad (3)$$

C_2 is a surface based convexity measure, obtained by dividing the area of the minimum convex set (MCS) of shape S with the surface of shape S.

$$C_3 = \frac{Per(CH(S))}{Per(S)}. \tag{4}$$

C_3 is a boundary based convexity measure, obtained by dividing the perimeter of the convex hull of shape S with the perimeter of shape S.

The Convexity Measure of Polygons New Definition: The new definition of the Convexity Measure of Polygons introduced by J. Zunic et al. [10] was designed because of the incapacity of other convexity measure's to include huge defects. In addition, it can evaluate small variations on a shape. It is the first element in the leaf feature vector. It is the only convexity measure used in this paper. The Convexity Measure of Polygons defined by J. Zunic et al. [10] is evaluated as:

$$C\left(P\right) = \min_{\alpha \in [0,2\pi]} \frac{Per_2\left(R\left(P,\alpha\right)\right)}{Per_1\left(P,\alpha\right)}, \tag{5}$$

where:
α = Rotation angle
P = Shape Parameter
R = The optimal rectangle
Per_2 = Perimeter by projection on axis
Per_1 = Euclidian perimeter
     In this equation the perimeter of the polygon P is fixed and the perimeter of the bounding rectangle note $R(P, \alpha)$ depends on the value of α. $C(P)$ is equivalent to the following equation.

$$C(P) = \min \left\{ \frac{Per_2(R(P,\alpha_i))}{Per_1(P,\alpha_i)} \middle| \; i = 1, 2, ..., n \right\}$$

Where
$$Per_2(R(P, \alpha_i)) = g_i * \cos(\alpha_i) + f_i * \sin(\alpha_i),$$
$$Per_1(P, \alpha_i) = c_j * \cos(\alpha_i) + d_j * \sin(\alpha_i).$$

g_i, f_i, c_j, d_j are the constants associated to the Euclidian length of the rectangle edge and the polygon edges.
     This equation represent the computation process of $C(P)$.
     The Convexity Measure of Polygons (J. Zunic et al. [10]) in order to be used for shape characterisation has to be combined to other convexity measure to increase the recognition rate [10]. The Convexity Measure of Polygons only expresses how convex or concave a given shape is, but it is also important to have another descriptor for the surface.

The Seven Invariant Moments. Hu's seven invariant moments are computed from the central moments. They are very useful for shape description and classification [9]. The discrete form of the geometrical moment of order $p+q$ is defined as:

$$M_{pq} = \sum_{x=1}^{N} \sum_{y=1}^{M} x^p y^q. \tag{6}$$

where:
p,q　　$= 0,1,2,....$
$N \times M =$ the image size.

Consequently, a set of seven invariant moments $(Ph_1, Ph_2, ..., Ph_7)$ can be derived from the normalized central moments as in [13].

Geometrical Features. The *rectangularity* (R) represents the ratio between the leaf area (A_{leaf}) and the area of the minimum bounding rectangle. It evaluate how the leaf shape is close to a rectangle shape.

$$R = \frac{A_{leaf}}{D_{max} \times D_{min}} \tag{7}$$

The *aspect ratio* (A) is the ratio between the maximum length (D_{max}) and the minimum length (D_{min}) of the minimum bounding rectangle

$$A = \frac{D_{max}}{D_{min}} \tag{8}$$

The *sphericity* (S) is express by the following equation.

$$S = \frac{r_i}{r_c} \tag{9}$$

where:
$r_i =$ represents the radius of the in cycle of the leaf.
$r_c =$ the radius of the ex-circle of the leaf.

The ratio between the length of the main inertia axis and the minor inertia axis of the leaf, determines the accent of the leaf. It evaluates how much an iconic section deviates from being circular [2].

$$E = \frac{E_A}{E_B} \tag{10}$$

The *circularity* (C) is defined by all the contour points of the leaf image.

$$C = \frac{\mu_R}{\sigma_R} \tag{11}$$

where

$$\mu_R = \frac{1}{N} \sum_{i=0}^{N-1} \|(x_i, y_i) - (\bar{x}, \bar{y})\|$$

and

$$\sigma_R = \frac{1}{N} \sum_{i=0}^{N-1} (\|(x_i, y_i) - (\bar{x}, \bar{y})\| - \mu_R)^2$$

Form Factor (F) compares the perimeter of the equivalent circle to the perimeter of the leaf shape. It is also used to describe surface irregularity. It is given by the following equation:

$$F = \frac{4\pi A_{leaf}}{P_{leaf}^2} \tag{12}$$

Area ratio of convex hull (CA) is defined as the ratio between the leaf area and the area of it's associated convex Hull polygon (equivalent to the surface based convexity measure). It is expressed by the following equation:

$$CA = \frac{A_C}{A_{ROI}} \tag{13}$$

4 Experimental Result and Discussion

4.1 Experimental Results

The experiments were conducted using FLAVIA. The leaf database is composed of more than 2500 plants leaves of more than 30 species [13]. We randomly chose 400 leaves of 20 species, 1600 leaves of 32 species and 100 leaves of 5 species (the 1600 leaves of 32 species represent all the available species in FLAVIA). The experiments are organized in two phases. First the leaves are characterized using the geometrical features and the seven invariants moments. Secondly the seven invariants moments and the geometrical features are combined to the New Convexity measure of polygones to characterized a leaf image.

Table 1 presents the accuracy of the proposed method with and without the Convexity Measure of Polygon (J. Zunic et al.) in the feature vector. In the first row with the Convexity Measure of Polygons, the Multi Layer Perceptron (MLP) achieved an average of 92 % of well classified leaves with an area under Received Operating Characteristics curve (ROC) equaled 0.993. Without the Convexity Measurement of Polygons, 86 % of well classified leaves with the area under the ROC curve equaled 0.98.

4.2 Discussion

We decided to organise our experiment using three processes to show how efficient our model is when used in various conditions. As Panagiotis et al. in [12] we used 100 images of leaves to illustrate how the proposed method is more efficient when applied to a small number of leaves. We obtained a classification rate of 99 % with the Convexity Measure of Polygons (J. Zunic et al.) in the feature set it shows that the Convexity Measure of Polygon contributed significantly in the discrimination process of leaf shapes even with a small dataset.

Table 1. Comparative study of classifiers

	With the convexity measure		Without the convexity measure	
	% of good classify	AUC average	% of good classify	AUC average
Multilayer Perceptron (400)	92 %	0.993	86 %	0.98
K-Nearest Neighbour (400)	87.5 %	0.971	85 %	0.921
Naive Bayes (400)	80.94 %	0.969	79.2 %	0.966
Multilayer Perceptron (100)	99 %	0.993	97 %	0.97
K-Nearest Neighbour (100)	99 %	0.971	97 %	0.9
Naive Bayes (100)	90 %	0.969	80.2 %	0.95
Multilayer Perceptron (1600)	95 %	0.993	92 %	0.99
K-Nearest Neighbour (1600)	92 %	0.971	89.5 %	0.95
Naive Bayes (1600)	89 %	0.969	80.2 %	0.98

We then applied the proposed method to a medium dataset which had 400 leaves. In this case, a classification rate of 92 % shows again how efficient the proposed method is when applied to a medium size dataset when the Convexity Measure of Polygons (J. Zunic et al.) is used. Finally, to complete our experiment we applied the proposed to a large dataset with 1600 leaves and the classification rate obtained was 96 %. This classification rate shows that the proposed method remains consistent even with a larger dataset. The classification rate and the Area Under the ROC Curve (AUC) clearly shows that the Convexity Measure of Polygons (J. Zunic et al.) contributes to the improvement of the classification rate and to the efficiency of the proposed model.

5   Comparative Study of the Proposed Method with the Available Method in the Literature

In Table 1 some methods of plant classification using leaves are presented. In Table 2 in the first row is - the authors name; the title of the article; the nature of the features; the number of leaves used for the experimentation; the number of species; the classification rate; the classification algorithm; drawbacks of the method and advantages. On the second row of Table 2, Jixian et al. [9] proposed leaf shape based plant species recognition. This approach is shape based as 400 leaves of 20 species of plant were used and a classification rate of 91 % was achieved with the MMC. This was after reduction of the feature space in order to obtain a fast classification method. In the last row the method use in this paper is present. This method is based on the introduction of the Convexity Measure of Polygons to boost the leaf recognition rate. 400 leaves of 20 different species are used for the experiment, and the MLP achieved a classification rate of 92 %. The drawback of this method is time taken to calculate the convexity measure (using J. Zunic et al. [10] definition) of a big leaf image shapes. Despite this, the method is very accurate and fast during the classification and achieved better results even with deformed leaves.

Table 2. Table of some of the methods of plants classification using leaves

Authors	Method	Feature	Nb Leaves	Nb species	Rate	Algorithm	Drawback	Advantages in classification
Panagiotis et al [14]	Plants leaves classification based on morphological feature	Shape	100	4	99%	NN Fuzzy	incomplete experiment	Fast classification
Jixian et al [10]	Leaf shape based plant species recognition	Shape	400	20	91%	MMC	Model evaluation	Fast with the MMC
Stephen et al [15]	A leaf recognition Algorithm for plant classification using PNN	Shape	1800	32	90%	PNN	the method is not completely automatic	Fast classification
Benoit et al [7]	Weed leaf recognition in complex natural scene by model guided edge pairing	Shape	10	1	60%	rating process	incomplete methode	Adaptative method
A. H. Kulkarni al [1]	A Leaf Recognition System for Classifying Plants Using RBPNN and pseudo Zernike Moments	Shape, colour, texture, vein,	1600	32	94.52%	RBPNN	-	Fast
Proposed approach	Leaf Classification using Convexity Measure of Polygons	Shape	400	20	92%	MLP	Convexity measure time complexity with big images	Accurate
Proposed approach	Leaf Classification using Convexity Measure of Polygons	Shape	1600	32	95%	MLP	Convexity measure time complexity with big images	Accurate
Proposed approach	Leaf Classification using Convexity Measure of Polygons	Shape	100	4	99%	MLP	Convexity measure time complexity with big images	Accurate

6 Conclusion

This paper presented the classification of leaf images using shape analysis. Here the investigation of the use of the Convexity Measure of Polygons in the process of leaf shape characterisation is performed. The result obtained is a method with the following properties: rotation, translation and scale invariance. Experiments show that the use of the Convexity Measure of Polygons, combined with classical shape features used for leaf shape characterisation, increases the success rate of leaf shape classification. An average classification rate greater than 95 % was achieved using the multilayer perceptron for all the species in the FLAVIA data set. Good results were also obtained with other classifiers like KNN (90.5 %) and Naive Bayes (88 %). The proposed method outperforms some methods found in the literature. Proposed future works include the design of a new approach for the characterisation of the convexity of object shape inspired by the Convexity Measure of Polygons, as well as the analysis of the shape of colour images using the new design shape characteriser.

References

1. Kulkarni, A.H., Rai, H.M., Jahagirdar, K.A., Upparamani, P.S.: A leaf recognition technique for plant classification using RBPNN and Zernike moments. Int. J. Adv. Res. Comput. Commun. Eng. **2**(1), 984–988 (2013)
2. Ayoub, A.B.: The eccentricity of a conic section. Coll. Math. J. **34**(2), 116–121 (2003)
3. Hussein, A.N., Mashohor, S., Iqbal, M.: A texture based approach for content based image retrieval system for plant leaves images. In: IEEE 7th International Colloquium on Signal Processing and its Applications, pp. 11–14 (2011)
4. Aickelin, U., Bentley, P.J., Cayzer, S., Kim, J., McLeod, J.: Danger theory: the link between AIS and IDS? In: Timmis, J., Bentley, P.J., Hart, E. (eds.) ICARIS 2003. LNCS, vol. 2787, pp. 147–155. Springer, Heidelberg (2003)
5. Anant, B., Manpree, K., Anupam, K.: Recognition of plants by leaf image using moment invariant and texture analysis. Int. J. Innov. Appl. Stud. **3**(1), 375–382 (2013)
6. Babu, M., Prasad, S., Rao, B.S.: Leaves Recognition Using Back Propagation Neural Network-Advice For Pest and Disease Control On Crops. IndiaKisan.Net: Expert Advisory System (2007)
7. Mezo, B.D., Rabatel, G., Forio, C.: Weed leaf recognition in complex natural scenes by model-guided pairing. In: 4th European Conference on Precision Agriculture (2007)
8. Bendiab, E., Kheirreddine, M.: Recognition of plant leaves using the dendritic cell algorithm. Int. J. Digital Inf. Wireless Commun. (IJDIWC) **1**(1), 284–292 (2011)
9. Ji-Xiang, D., Xiao-Feng, W., Guo-Jun, Z.: Leaf shape based plant species recognition. Appl. Math. Comput. **185**(2), 883–893 (2007)
10. Zunic, J., Rosin, P.: A new convexity measure for polygons. IEEE Trans. Pattern Anal. Mach. Intell. **26**(7), 923–934 (2004)
11. Linnus, C.: Systema natur, sive regna tria natur systematice proposita per classes, ordines, genera, and species. Lugduni Batavorum (Haak) (1735)
12. Panagiotis, T., Stelios, P., Dimitris, M.: Plant leaves classification based on morphological features and a fuzzy surface selection technique. In: Fifth International Conference on Technology, pp. 365–370 (2005)
13. Stephen, G., Forrest, S., Eric, Y., Yu-Xuan, W., Yi-Fang, C., Qiao-Liang, X.: A leaf recognition algorithm for plant classification using probalistic neural network. Comput. Sci. Artif. Intell., 11–16 (2007)
14. Beghin, T., Cope, J.S., Remagnino, P., Barman, S.: Shape and texture based plant leaf classification. In: Blanc-Talon, J., Bone, D., Philips, W., Popescu, D., Scheunders, P. (eds.) ACIVS 2010, Part II. LNCS, vol. 6475, pp. 345–353. Springer, Heidelberg (2010)

Privacy Preserving Dynamic Room Layout Mapping

Xinyu Li[1(✉)], Yanyi Zhang[1], Ivan Marsic[1], and Randall S. Burd[2]

[1] Department of Electrical and Computer Engineering, Rutgers University,
New Brunswick, NJ, USA
{xinyu.li1118,yz593,marsic}@rutgers.edu
[2] Division of Trauma and Burns, Children's National Medical Center,
Washington, D.C., USA
RBurd@childrensnational.org

Abstract. We present a novel and efficient room layout mapping strategy that does not reveal people's identity. The system uses only a Kinect depth sensor instead of RGB cameras or a high-resolution depth sensor. The users' facial details will neither be captured nor recognized by the system. The system recognizes and localizes 3D objects in an indoor environment, that includes the furniture and equipment, and generates a 2D map of room layout. Our system accomplishes layout mapping in three steps. First, it converts a depth image from the Kinect into a top-view image. Second, our system processes the top-view image by restoring the missing information from occlusion caused by moving people and random noise from Kinect depth sensor. Third, it recognizes and localizes different objects based on their shape and height for a given top-view image. We evaluated this system in two challenging real-world application scenarios: a laboratory room with four people present and a trauma room with up to 10 people during actual trauma resuscitations. The system achieved 80 % object recognition accuracy with 9.25 cm average layout mapping error for the laboratory furniture scenario and 82 % object recognition accuracy for the trauma resuscitation scenario during six actual trauma cases.

Keywords: Depth sensor · Occlusion compensation · Object recognition · Privacy preserving · Room layout mapping

1 Introduction

Dynamic room layout mapping is useful and critical to many applications such as activity recognition, virtual reality and home automation. The goal of room layout mapping is to identify and localize objects (furniture, equipment, etc.) in an indoor environment and generate a 2D map with their locations. It is also critical that the room layout mapping system be able to work with people moving in the room. Traditional room layout modeling strategies are usually based on RGB cameras or RGBD cameras [1, 2]. Although many systems have been proposed, these systems are not widely used in real-world applications for several reasons. First, RGB camera raises privacy concerns, especially in privacy-sensitive domains such as medical settings. Second, some previous approaches have made use of multiple cameras or a moving robot to better observe the

© Springer International Publishing Switzerland 2016
A. Mansouri et al. (Eds.): ICISP 2016, LNCS 9680, pp. 61–70, 2016.
DOI: 10.1007/978-3-319-33618-3_7

environment, an approach that may not be cost-efficient and may potentially interfere with the work. In addition, most existing research uses 3D models for template matching for indoor 3D object recognition. The 3D model matching yields good performance in some daily-living scenarios with large furniture, such as beds or dining tables. It does not, however, perform well for furniture or equipment with irregular shapes, such as chairs or medical equipment like a fluid-bag stand. In addition, most template matching methods require an unobstructed view of the environment, which is often not the case because people cause view occlusion. The multi-camera based solution [3] is not cost-efficient and aligning the views from different cameras is difficult and slow. We present a system that uses only Kinect V2 depth sensor. Because we do not use RGB cameras and the depth sensor built in the Kinect V2 cannot capture facial details, user's identity cannot be revealed.

To recognize and track 3D objects, such as furniture pieces or equipment in the room, our system first converts the 3D depth-point-cloud taken by the Kinect depth sensor into a 2D top-view image. The furniture mapping and recognition are based on the pixels in the top-view image. The challenge is that the top-view image is not always clear and representative: people walking in the room may cause view occlusion, which leads to undefined pixels in the top-view image that will cause problems with recognition. In addition, the Kinect depth sensing system also generates random noise, which affects the performance of mapping and recognition system. To restore the occluded view, our system tracks people positions in the room and dynamically updates the top-view image based on their location. We also apply filtering to the top-view images to minimize the influence of random noise caused by the Kinect depth sensor.

We evaluated the system performance in two challenging real-world applications: a laboratory room with four people work in it and an actual trauma room of a level 1 trauma center. We tracked six types of furniture pieces in a laboratory room and achieved average 80 % object recognition accuracy with average layout mapping error of 9.25 cm over a 48 h testing period with four people working in the room. For the trauma room application, we were able to keep tracking and recognize eight medical instrument and furniture sets in the room with an average object recognition accuracy rate of 82 %. The contributions of this paper are:

1. A novel dynamic, privacy-preserving room layout mapping strategy using only a commercial depth sensor.
2. A strategy to restore the missing information in Kinect depth-maps caused by random noise or view occlusion by moving people.
3. The implementation and evaluation of the system in two challenging real-world applications.

2   Related Works

Room layout mapping or indoor 3D objects recognition is a widely used method for applications such as activity recognition, 3D object modeling and virtual reality [2, 4]. Early layout mapping strategies used 2D-image features such as SIFT to map indoor furniture [2]. Solutions based on 2D RGB camera, however, are not feasible for complex and dynamic environments because camera angles, lighting, and distance between the object and camera may change rapidly and may be difficult to control in real-world implementations.

With the recent development of commercial depth sensors, researchers have started using RGB-D camera or depth sensor for room layout modeling and furniture recognition. A common approach is to compare the reconstructed 3D environment with the pre-established 3D CAD models [5–7]. Although approaches based on 3D-model matching achieve good performance, their application is limited because some systems require views from different angles or additional cameras [3] which is not cost effective and may hard to implement in real-world applications. In addition, for systems that require known 3D models of objects as templates [8, 9], it may be impractical to build a 3D CAD model for every object used in real-world applications. Another common approach for recognizing and mapping 3D objects is projecting 3D data onto 2D space [10, 11]. Our method builds on this approach by converting a 3D point-cloud into 2D space, and then performing object mapping and recognition based on 2D top-view image. Rather than using a roaming robot equipped with cameras, which is expensive and potentially unfeasible in a crowded setting, we used a fixed commercial depth sensor.

Most prior work in 3D object recognition does not include people. This omission is problematic for many applications because the information loss due to view occlusion caused by people moving will significantly influence the system's performance. To address this issue, we restore and enhance the images based on people locations in the room. People tracking has attracted a great deal of research and has become more manageable with recent hardware, such as Kinect [12, 13]. Our system achieves comparable layout mapping performance in both stationary environments with no people, and in the dynamic real-world scenarios with multiple moving people.

3 Room Layout Mapping

3.1 Room Layout Mapping Model

A key challenge for room layout mapping is that view occlusion caused by people moving in the room results in the captured image partially missing information. Created by the need to avoid compromising user's privacy, an additional challenge, is to use only depth sensor built in the Kinect, which provides low-resolution depth image without detailed texture information. Both view occlusion and low-resolution depth image makes indoor objects recognition difficult. We designed the system to accomplish room layout mapping in dynamic environment through three steps:

Step1: Generate a point-cloud map of the 3D environment based on the depth sensor and converts it into top-view image.

Step2: Process the top-view image by first restoring the part of view occluded by people in the room and then enhancing the top-view image to eliminate the undefined pixels caused by Kinect sensor's random noise.

Step3: Recognize 3D objects (equipment, furniture, etc.) based on shape and height using 2D template matching and then layout mapping based on recognition results.

3.2 From Point-Cloud to Top View

To have a clear view of the room, we mounted the Kinect *H* meters above the ground with a tilt angle α so that people and objects in the room are more likely to be seen in camera view (in our application, $H = 2.5$ m and $\alpha = 7'$). Before converting the 3D point-cloud into a 2D top view, each point in the point-cloud needs to be adjusted for the tilt angle α so that the camera space of the Kinect is aligned with the actual setting. The camera space refers to the 3D coordinate system used by the Kinect (Fig. 1), where the x axis grows to the sensor's left, the y-axis grows up and the z axis grows out in the direction the sensor is facing.

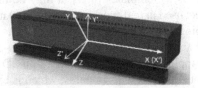

Fig. 1. Coordinate system of Kinect camera space.

If we use *(X, Y, Z)* for each point in the point-cloud in camera space and use *(X', Y', Z')* for the corresponding point in the room, given the tilt angle α, the rotation matrix can be applied as follows:

$$\begin{bmatrix} X' \\ Y' \\ Z' \end{bmatrix} = \begin{bmatrix} 1 & 0 & 0 \\ 0 & \cos(\alpha) & \sin(\alpha) \\ 0 & -\sin(\alpha) & \cos(\alpha) \end{bmatrix} \times \begin{bmatrix} X \\ Y \\ Z \end{bmatrix} + \begin{bmatrix} 0 \\ H \\ 0 \end{bmatrix} \tag{1}$$

For objects below the Kinect sensor, the measured y coordinate in camera space is negative. We add *H* (height of Kinect sensor) to the converted y coordinates to calculate the actual height. By visualizing the point-cloud (Fig. 2) we confirmed that before the tilt-angle adjustment, the ceiling surface (purple pixels) and floor surface (blue pixels) in the point-cloud are not parallel with actual ground due to the tilt angle of Kinect (Fig. 2(b)) After the tilt angle is adjusted, the surfaces are parallel with the actual ground (Fig. 2(c)). Once the tilt angle is adjusted, the top-view image can be generated by

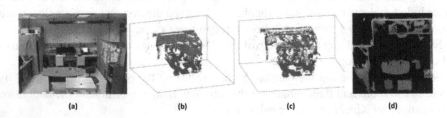

(a)   (b)   (c)   (d)

Fig. 2. (a) The picture of the laboratory. (b) The point cloud of the room before tilt angle adjustment. (c) The point cloud of the room after tilt angle adjustment. (d) The top view image of the room. (Color figure online)

projecting all the points in the point-cloud down to the floor plane using the height of the highest pixel at each position in 2D plane as follows:

$$topView(x, z) = max_{Depth}(Y' | X' = x, Z' = z) \qquad (2)$$

Where $topView(x, z)$ denotes the value of pixels in the top-view image and $max_{Depth}(Y' | X' = x, Z' = z)$ represents the highest point in point-cloud at position (x, z). Because objects are present that we do not want to track, such as lights hanging from the ceiling, we ignore all the points in point-cloud above certain height range to avoid possible confusion. Because the top-view image generated from the adjusted depth image captured by the Kinect, where each pixel represents 1 cm, the pixels in the top-view image reveal the physical dimensions where each pixel represents a 1 cm length in the room. The correlation between pixels and actual distance makes precise room layout mapping possible.

3.3 Top-View Image Enhancement

View occlusion leads to information loss and makes it difficult to recognize 3D objects in top-view images. To address this issue, we restore the missing information in top-view images.

First, the system maintains a dynamic top-view image by selectively updating its pixels. We require that the system start when no people are in the room, which guarantees the initial top-view image free of view occlusion caused by people. The Kinect is set to capture a depth image of the room every 100 ms, which is converted into a top-view image. When a new depth image is captured, the top-view image will not be directly updated unless the room remains empty of people. If a person is detected by the Kinect, the view will be occluded, resulting in information loss in the area of occlusion. Our system only updates the pixels outside the occluded area based on the top-view image and keeps the pixels in the occluded area unchanged from the previous top-view image (Fig. 3).

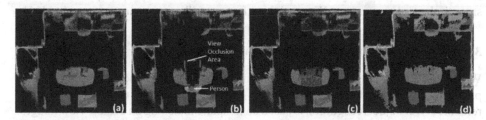

Fig. 3. (a) Top view image with no people. (b) View occlusion caused by people in the room. (c) Compensating for the information loss. (d) Top view image after image enhancement.

Because people blocking the camera view cause view occlusion, occluded areas are defined as rectangular areas behind each person in the room. We used a fixed width for each rectangle (50 cm) based on the average body width of a male adult. The height d

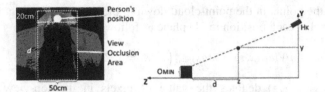

Fig. 4. Left: A person's figure in top view image (red rectangle) and view occlusion area caused by the person (white rectangle). Right: Estimate the length of view occlusion area *d* based on person's position *z* and height *y*. (Color figure online)

of the rectangle is determined from person's location in the room and their estimated height (Fig. 4):

$$d = \frac{(y - O_{min}) \cdot z}{H_k - O_{min}} \tag{3}$$

Here *y* denotes the height of a person's head-joint provided by the Kinect and *z* denotes the horizontal distance between a person's head and the Kinect sensor. The height H_k of the Kinect sensor is fixed once it is installed and O_{min} represents the minimum height of tracked objects. Because the top-view of people will act as outliers to the object recognition system, to have a clear top view image, we replaced the rectangle area (in this paper 20 cm × 50 cm) containing the top view of a person with the pixels in previous top view, so that the figure of person will be "erased" in top-view image (Fig. 3(c)).

In addition to restoring the occluded view, we used filtering to eliminate the random noise caused by the Kinect sensor. We used a buffer to store n previous top-view images and calculate the value of each pixel in current top-view image based on both the current top-view image and n previous top-view images. If a pixel *topView*(x, y) is undefined in current top view image, the system will look back n (n = 5 in our experiments) to previous top view images and assign the value of that pixels using the average value of same pixel in n previous top View images. The image dilate [14] is applied at last to smooth the top-view image. We used the Aforge.net library in our programming [15].

3.4 Object Recognition and Room Layout Mapping

We focused on small furniture and equipment that can be relocated, such as chair, patient-bed or a cart, while large furniture, e.g. metal cabinet, is not likely to be often relocated. Our object recognition is based on template matching on 2D top-view images. We chose template-matching strategy among other pattern recognition approaches for two reasons. First, template matching is fast compared with other strategies, a requirement for real-time room layout mapping because small objects may be frequently relocated. Second, because we are working with top-view images, which are derived from the Kinect depth images, detailed texture information is not available to extract image features.

We generated templates for objects by manually selecting examples of each object from 10 top-view images and averaging them for the template. In practice, the template matching was done using *Aforge.net* library [15], the system will take the area that has maximum matching score with certain template as the location of object. Because, equipment or small furniture pieces might be moved out of the room in real-world applications, we defined a threshold to determine if an object exists in the room. If the maximum matching score of a template is lower than the threshold, the system will decide the certain object is not in the room. The threshold was tuned based on 100 random selected sample images using object recognition accuracy as indicator.

4   Experimental Results

We applied our system in two different application scenarios to test the system performance for normal application and extremely complex and dynamic environment. We first set up the system in a typical laboratory room with four people work in and kept it running for 48 h. None of the individuals were told the system was working in the room in advance so their behavior was not altered by this experiment. We kept tracking six different furniture pieces (Table 1) in the room with very different size and shape, four of the objects were relocated during the experiment. We programmed the system to save a top-view image and a room layout image every minute and later evaluate the system's performance by manually reviewing the top-view image as ground truth and compare it with generated room layout map for evaluation.

The laboratory application scenarios were not crowded and people were working at different place of the room most of time. To further test our system performance, we also applied the system in an actual trauma room in a level 1 trauma center. Deployment and evaluation of the system was approved by the institutional review board (IRB) and was considered do not compromise users' privacy of medical personnel and patients. In this setting, up to 10 people are working simultaneously, an aspect of this setting that leads to view occlusion and increase the difficulty of room layout mapping. We kept tracking eight different piece of medical equipment and furniture sets (Table 1) that varies in shape and size during six trauma resuscitations. Five pieces of medical equipment were relocated. Similar to the experiments we performed in the laboratory, we programmed the system to save a top-view image and a room layout image every minute (Fig. 5). The object recognition accuracy was calculated as follows (Table 1):

$$Accuracy = \frac{number\ of\ images\ that\ an\ object\ is\ correctly\ recognized}{total\ number\ of\ images}$$

We find that the large furniture pieces are easier to track and map in the room: even if few pixels are significantly influenced by the noise or blocked, most of pixels stay similar with template. For smaller objects mapping accuracy is lower because small objects result in few pixels that are easier corrupted by noise. Besides, for objects with irregular shapes, it is hard to generate a representative template for objects with irregular shape. For example, the blood pressure stand has a relatively low tracking accuracy due to its small size and irregular shape (Table 1). Our system is able to achieve performance

Fig. 5. The photo and room layout mapping results of laboratory and trauma room.

Table 1. Objects used for experiments in laboratory room and trauma room with their dimensions and recognition accuracy. The Grey shaded objects were relocated during the experiments. For the objects with irregular shape, height (H) is measured.

Objects(lab)	Size (inch)	Accuracy (0/4 people)	Objects (Trauma room)	Size (inch)	Accuracy (up to 10 people)
Dinning Table	58×28×30	100%/100%	Patient Bed	31×32×80	92.3%
Cart	28×18×36	100%/87.5%	Shelf	57×42×20	100%
Chair	H=31", irregular shape	100%/42.8%	IV Stand	H=68", irregular shape	67.8%
Box	15×13×19	100%/67.1%	BP Stand	H=43", irregular shape	46.1%
Book Shelf	12×14×16	98.0%/89.1%	Cardiac Monitor Adapter	30×28×17	62.5%
Desk	91×30×29	99.1%/90.2%	Bio-Trash Bin	19×32×16	93.2%
			Pyxis	82×27×78	100%
			Sheet Warmer	30×29×72	99.8%

comparable to previous research [1, 8], however, considering that previous approaches [1, 8] were designed for scenarios with no people moves, our system is considered to more suitable for many real-world scenarios.

When no people are moving, the overall system performance in the laboratory room is around 15 % better than it is when four people are moving in the room. This finding may be because Kinect might not be able to continuously track of people in a crowded and dynamic environment. Loss of tracking of people did not necessarily lead to object detection failure, because it is also depending on the whether the people is standing in front of an objects and the size of view occlusion area caused by people. In the medical application, our system was able to maintain similar performance to laboratory room implementation when number of people doubled. We noticed that the patient bed is blocked by personnel most of the time during the trauma resuscitation, because doctors and nurses usually stand around the patient bed when performing their tasks. Our system is able to make compensation and recognize patient bed with 92.3 % accuracy of patient bed with proposed strategy that is satisfied.

In addition to object recognition accuracy, we evaluated the object mapping error in our laboratory environment without people. Because the time of patient arrival is not predictable, staying in actual trauma room and manually measuring the room layout mapping error may potentially interfere with the room's normal usage. For this reason, we did not perform layout mapping error evaluation. We applied the rotation matrix to the Kinect camera space and used the coordinate system after tilt angle adjustment for mapping error evaluation. The Kinect sensor is used as origin of the coordinate system, the x-axis grows to the Kinect's left, z-axis grows out of the Kinect and parallel with ground. We manually measured the distance of each object in the room to Kinect in both x-axis and z-axis direction and compared the measured distance with generated room layout map. The objects were relocated after each experiment and the entire process was repeated 10 times. We averaged the errors in 10 measurements for each object in the room as room layout mapping error (Table 2).

Table 2. Room layout mapping error in X-axis and Z-axis in cm.

Objects	Dinning table	Cart	Chair	Box	Book Shelf	Desk
Error in X-axis (cm)	13	9.7	20.0	13.0	11.6	11.6
Error in Z-axis (cm)	2.7	13.2	5.5	1.6	2.7	6.4

Our research achieves decimeter-level layout mapping error which is similar to previous research [8]. A difference is that our approach uses only a fixed depth sensor which does not compromise user's privacy. In addition, our approach does not rely on pre-defined 3D CAD models for object recognition, a more practical and convenient for real-world applications. Previous research [10] achieves around 3 cm layout mapping error using laser depth sensor, which is considered to be one of the best indoor layout mapping system. The limitation of this type of system is that the system requires a clear view of the room, view occlusion caused by moving people will significantly influence system performance. The indoor layout mapping strategy proposed in this paper works well with people moving in the room, though the system works with slightly higher layout mapping error, it is considered to be more useful and practical for some dynamic applications.

5   Conclusion and Future Work

We developed a novel room layout mapping system that works in crowded real-world applications that does not compromise the privacy of the people in the view area. Its key feature is eliminating the view occlusion caused by people moving in the room. Due to Kinect limitation, Kinect can track no more than 6 people. If more than six people are in the room, the information lost due to view occlusion might not be restored. In addition, it is possible for Kinect to lose track of people in complex and crowded environments. The system may lose track of some objects or make layout-mapping errors in very crowded environments. Also, template matching will not work well if a small object is blocked or partially blocked by larger objects.

Our future work will use multiple Kinect sensors [16] in different view angles to allow tracking more than six people and restore missing information caused by view occlusion from both people and objects. We will also perform more extensive evaluation of our system in different real-world application scenarios.

References

1. Tomono, M.: 3-D object map building using dense object models with SIFT-based recognition features. In: 2006 IEEE/RSJ International Conference on Intelligent Robots and Systems. IEEE (2006)
2. Rusu, R.B., et al.: Functional object mapping of kitchen environments. In: IROS 2008 IEEE/RSJ International Conference on Intelligent Robots and Systems, 2008. IEEE (2008)
3. Susanto, W., Rohrbach, M., Schiele, B.: 3D object detection with multiple kinects. In: Fusiello, A., Murino, V., Cucchiara, R. (eds.) ECCV 2012 Ws/Demos, Part II. LNCS, vol. 7584, pp. 93–102. Springer, Heidelberg (2012)
4. Varvadoukas, T., et al.: Indoor furniture and room recognition for a robot using internet-derived models and object context. In: 2012 10th International Conference on Frontiers of Information Technology (FIT). IEEE (2012)
5. Lin, D., Fidler, S., Urtasun, R.: Holistic scene understanding for 3d object detection with rgbd cameras. In: IEEE International Conference on Computer Vision (ICCV), 2013. IEEE (2013)
6. Camplani, M., Mantecon, T., Salgado, L.: Depth-color fusion strategy for 3-d scene modeling with kinect. IEEE Trans. Cybern. **43**(6), 1560–1571 (2013)
7. Du, H., et al.: Interactive 3D modeling of indoor environments with a consumer depth camera. In: Proceedings of the 13th International Conference on Ubiquitous Computing. ACM (2011)
8. Wittrowski, J., Ziegler, L., Swadzba, A.: 3d implicit shape models using ray based hough voting for furniture recognition. In: 2013 International Conference on 3D Vision-3DV 2013. IEEE (2013)
9. Günther, M., et al.: Model-based furniture recognition for building semantic object maps. Artif. Intell. (2015)
10. Valero, E., Adán, A., Bosché, F.: Semantic 3D reconstruction of furnished interiors using laser scanning and RFID technology. J. Comput. Civil Eng. 04015053 (2015)
11. Salas-Moreno, R.F., et al.: Slam ++: simultaneous localisation and mapping at the level of objects. In: 2013 IEEE Conference on Computer Vision and Pattern Recognition (CVPR). IEEE (2013)
12. Zhang, Z.: Microsoft kinect sensor and its effect. IEEE MultiMedia **19**(2), 4–10 (2012)
13. Munaro, M., Menegatti, E.: Fast RGB-D people tracking for service robots. Auton. Robots **37**(3), 227–242 (2014)
14. Chen, S., Haralick, R.M.: Recursive erosion, dilation, opening, and closing transforms. IEEE Trans. Image Process. **4**(3), 335–345 (1995)
15. AForge.Net Library. http://www.aforgenet.com/framework
16. Asteriadis S, Chatzitofis A, Zarpalas D, et al.: Estimating human motion from multiple kinect sensors. In: Proceedings of the 6th International Conference on Computer Vision/Computer Graphics Collaboration Techniques and Applications, p. 3. ACM (2013)

Defect Detection on Patterned Fabrics Using Entropy Cues

Maricela Martinez-Leon, Rocio A. Lizarraga-Morales(✉),
Carlos Rodriguez-Donate, Eduardo Cabal-Yepez, and Ruth I. Mata-Chavez

Departamento de Estudios Multidisciplinarios, Division de Ingenierias,
Universidad de Guanajauto, Yuriria, Guanajuato, Mexico
{m.martinezleon,ra.lizarragamorales,
c.rodriguezdonate,educabal,ruth}@ugto.mx

Abstract. Quality control is an essential step in the textile manufacturing industry. There is a growing interest in the field of automation using computer vision for freeing human beings from the inspection task. In this paper, patterned fabric images are analyzed using entropy cues in order to detect different kinds of defects. In our proposal, we transform the test image to an entropy image in which the defects show low values and can be easily separated by a simple thresholding. Our method is evaluated and compared with previously proposed approaches, showing better results on an extensive database of real defective and non-defective fabrics.

Keywords: Defect detection · Fabric · Entropy · Texture analysis

1 Introduction

In recent years, computer vision has played an important role in the textile industry. The contribution in this field has been through developing solutions for the automation of production processes. One of the main processes where computer vision has had a major role is in the fabric quality assessment. In this step, fabric is examined for unacceptable defects such as knots, holes or surface blemishes. Traditionally, the quality control is carried out by human visual inspection. However, it is well-known that human-based inspection is imprecise and has disadvantages due to fatigue, visual range, and rate of detection. Therefore, the development of an accurate and robust automatic visual inspection system for quality analysis is a fundamental issue in the modern textile industry [7].

Visual texture analysis applications are of great interest in the automation of textile inspection. Texture is an important feature for the characterization of surfaces of natural and man-made objects. In particular, the analysis of periodic textures, also called patterned textures, is commonly considered in a wide range of applications because of its presence on an assortment of daily-use products such as clothes, shoes, handbags, bed sheets, among others. In order to attend the defect detection problem, researchers in the texture analysis field are actively

© Springer International Publishing Switzerland 2016
A. Mansouri et al. (Eds.): ICISP 2016, LNCS 9680, pp. 71–78, 2016.
DOI: 10.1007/978-3-319-33618-3_8

pursuing new methods to achieve an acceptable detection rate for a variety of defects on different patterned fabrics [13].

A considerable number of methods has been proposed in order to detect defects on different patterned fabrics. These methods can be separated into three categories: spectral, model-based and statistical. Spectral approaches are mainly based on the analysis of the fabric images using tools such as Fourier Transform (FT) [17], wavelet transform (WT) [18], Gabor transform (GT)[2] and filtering [11]. Since the spatial domain is usually noise sensitive, spectral approaches utilize a different domain to characterize defects. The main disadvantage of these approaches is that they cannot detect small defects. Model-based methods characterize fabric patterns with auto-regressive models [1] and Markov random fields [3]. These methods can detect defects by comparing new test fabrics with the corresponding models. A drawback of model-based approximations is that the estimation of the parameters may not be straightforward. Statistical approaches are the most popular because of their simplicity and good performance. In this category, spatial distribution of gray values is defined by different representations such as auto-correlation function [17] and co-occurrence matrix [8,9]. Auto-correlation functions measure spatial frequency and depicts maxima at multiple locations corresponding to the repetitive primitive on an image. If the intensity of maxima stays constant, the repetitive primitive is perfectly replicated, otherwise, a defect is detected. Gray level co-occurrence matrix (GLCM), originally proposed by Haralick [6], characterizes texture features as second-order statistics by measuring spatial dependence of the gray levels of 2 pixels. Much research has been developed using GLCM-based methods [16], however, the main drawbacks are poor performance and the computational requirements needed for the GLCM calculation.

In this paper, defects on patterned fabrics are detected using the property of entropy computed from the sum and difference histograms (SDH). The SDH were introduced by Unser [16] as an alternative to the GLCM in order to simplify the computation and memory requirements. In our proposal, we transform the test image to an entropy image in which the defects show low values and can be easily separated by a simple thresholding. From now on, we call our method as EDD for Entropy-based Defect Detection. The EDD is evaluated and compared with previously proposed approaches, showing better results on an extensive database of real defective fabric images.

This paper is structured as follows: in Sect. 2, the SDH and the computation of entropy are defined. The proposed EDD is presented in Sect. 3. In Sect. 4, we present the experimental setup and the results performed to validate or method. Finally, Sect. 5 presents a summary of this work and our concluding remarks.

2   Entropy Cues

In order to obtain the entropy cus, let us define an image I of $M \times N$ pixels size, which has K gray levels $k = 0, 1, \ldots, K - 1$. Consider a pixel positioned in the coordinates (m, n) with intensity $I_{m,n}$ and a second pixel in the relative position $(m + v_m, n + v_n)$ with intensity $I_{m+v_m,n+v_n}$. The non-normalized sum and differences, of two pixels associated with the relative displacement vector $V = (v_m, v_n)$, are defined as:

$$s_{m,n} = I_{m,n} + I_{m+v_m,n+v_n} \tag{1}$$

$$d_{m,n} = I_{m,n} - I_{m+v_m,n+v_n}. \tag{2}$$

Sum and Difference Histograms h_s and h_d, with displacement vector $V = (v_m, v_n)$ over the image domain D, are defined as:

$$h_s(i) = Card\{(m, n) \in D, s_{m,n} = i\} \tag{3}$$

$$h_d(j) = Card\{(m, n) \in D, d_{m,n} = j\}. \tag{4}$$

The total number of counts in each histogram is

$$A = \sum_i h_s(i) = \sum_j h_d(j). \tag{5}$$

The normalized sum and difference histograms are estimates of the sum and difference probability functions defined by

$$P_s(i) = \frac{h_o(i)}{A}; \qquad\qquad (i = 0, 1, \ldots, 2K - 2), \tag{6}$$

$$P_d(j) = \frac{h_d(j)}{A}; \qquad\qquad (j = -K + 1, -K + 2, \ldots, K - 1). \tag{7}$$

A number of features computed from the sum and difference probability functions have been proposed to be used as textural features like homogeneity, contrast, entropy, etc. and these features were simplified by Unser. Entropy, is defined as:

$$entropy = E = -\sum_i P_s(i) log\left(P_s(i)\right) - \sum_j P_d(j) log\left(P_d(j)\right). \tag{8}$$

3   Defect Detection Using Entropy Cues

In this section, the use of entropy cues for defect detection on patterned fabrics is presented. The proposed framework (EDD) is illustrated in Fig. 1, where it can be seen that it is performed in four steps: histogram equalization, entropy computation, filtering and thresholding.

The pre-processing step is executed to accentuate the defects on the test images. In this step, a histogram equalization was performed. Concerning this task, we have found that this pre-processing offers better results in terms of detection accuracy, in comparison to without any adjustment. After that, the extraction of entropy cues is accomplished. The original Unser proposal is to obtain a unique entropy value for each image. However, in this paper we propose to compute the local entropy of each image, in such a way that entropy may

Fig. 1. Diagram of the proposed approach.

provide information about the uniformity of the analyzed fabric. In the entropy image, each pixel contains the entropy value of a $P \times Q$ neighborhood around the corresponding pixel in the input image. In the EDD method, the size of the neighborhood is fixed according the size of the repetitive primitive of the patterned fabric. The size of the repetitive pattern can be estimated automatically using different methods. In our approach, the neighborhood size is estimated using the algorithm presented by Lizarraga-Morales et al. [10]. Such method is completely automatic, robust, accurate and computationally efficient.

As we can see in the entropy image (presented in Fig. 2), the defects get lower values than the rest of the image, therefore it is possible to separate them from the healthy part of the fabric. This behavior is due to the fact that the defects occurring in the analyzed fabrics are more uniform in terms of the gray levels than the rest of the image. Before the thresholding, an adaptive noise reduction filtering [5] of 5×5 pixels size is performed, in order to diminish the variations of the entropy values. The final thresholding is accomplished using the Otsu method [15]. The resulting images from each step of the defect detection procedure are depicted in Fig. 2. It is important to mention that all the parameters used in our experiments (displacement vector and filter size) were empirically estimated.

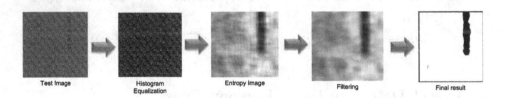

Fig. 2. Resulting images of each step of the EDD.

4   Experimental Setup

In order to study the performance of the proposed algorithm, images of patterned fabrics with defects are analyzed. Although there is an innumerable amount of different designs, it has been proven that all patterned fabrics can be classified into only 17 groups [4]. Each group is defined by the shape of its primitive and its inner symmetry. For these experiments, we have used the database of fabrics provided by Henry Y.T. Ngan from the Industrial Automation Research Laboratory in the Department of Electrical and Electronic Engineering at the University of Hong Kong. Such database is a widely used empirical basis for algorithms of defect detection on patterned fabrics. It consists of 3 different fabrics belonging to the 3 major groups of patterns: p4m (box-patterned), pmm (dot-patterned) and p2 (star-patterned). The groups pmm, p2 and p4m are called major due to the fact that all the other 14 groups can be transformed into these 3, via geometric transformation [12]. Defective samples previously labeled with five of the most common defects are provided: Broken End, Thick Bar, Thin Bar, Hole and Multiple Netting. Furthermore, for each defective image, a ground truth is available and can be used to quantify the reliability of a given method. This database contains 30 healthy samples and 5 samples of each defect for each fabric pattern, giving a total of 165 images of both defective and non-defective images. Examples of the patterned fabrics used for experiments are shown in Fig. 3.

Fig. 3. Patterned fabrics used for experiments: p4m (box-patterned), pmm (dot-patterned) and p2 (star-patterned), respectively.

For a quantitative evaluation, we have adopted the evaluation setup mentioned by Ngan et al. [13] in order to measure the accuracy of detection. Specifically, we have measured the accuracy of our method using the Detection Success Rate (DSR) also known as detection accuracy, which is defined in Eq. 9.

$$DSR = \frac{TP + TN}{TS},\tag{9}$$

where TP stands for True Positives, which are the defective samples classified as defective, TN are the True Negatives: non-defective samples that are correctly classified. TS is the total number of samples.

5   Results

Samples of the resulting images of each test pattern with different defects are presented in Fig. 4. In this figure we can see that with the DEE approach, it is possible to detect both small and big defects occurring among different fabric patterns. Quantitative results are provided in Table 1, where the DSR is presented for each defect type occurring in each patterned fabric. From this table, the DSR is 95.7 %, 95.8 % and 97 % for the p4m (box-patterned), pmm (dot-patterned) and p2 (star-patterned), respectively.

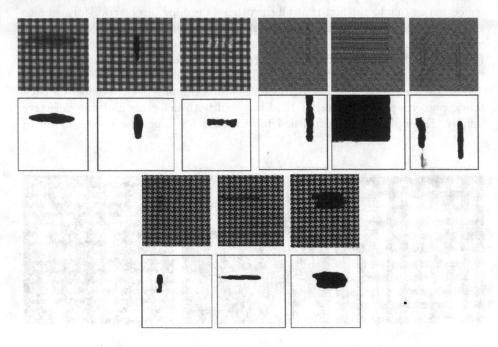

Fig. 4. Samples of defect detection on the p4m, pmm and p2 patterns.

Table 1. EDD Detection success rate for each defect in each fabric pattern.

Pattern	Broken End	Thick Bar	Thin Bar	Hole	Multiple Netting	Average
p4m	96.3	95.3	95.0	97.3	94.8	95.7
pmm	98.7	94.6	92.0	96.5	97.4	95.8
p2	96.3	97.6	95.7	97.4	97.0	96.8

A comparison with other state-of-the-art methods can be consulted in Table 2. For the comparison, methods belonging to the spectral and statistical categories, were selected. From this table it can be seen that our EDD attains a 96.16 % of average performance accuracy for the complete database. In contrast, the previously proposed methods are considerably below this performance with 82.8 %, 88.3 %, 90.7 %, 93.3 %, and 96 % of average detection rate.

Table 2. Comparison chart of the proposed method against previously proposed methods.

Method	Approach	Overall Accuracy
Badnarova et al. [2]	Gabor transform	82.8%
Ngan et al. [14]	Image Subtraction	88.3%
Latif-Amet et al. [9]	Statistical	90.7%
Yang et al. [18]	Wavelet transform	93.3%
Kuo and Su [8]	Statistical	96.0%
Proposed Methodology	**Statistical (Entropy)**	**96.1%**

Regarding the computation time of the EDD approach, the processing time required for analyzing one image is of 120 ms using a non-optimized MATLAB implementation in an ordinary CPU.

6   Conclusions

In this paper, defect detection problem on patterned fabrics is approached using entropy cues, which are computed from the sum and difference histograms. The proposed procedure is conformed by simple, yet effective, steps in order to determine if there is a defect on the image. From the experiments, it has proven to be robust to detect five of the most common defects, regardless of its shape or size. In comparison with other approaches, the EDD has attained the higher accuracy when testing it on a standard database. Such attributes, which overtake different drawbacks of previously proposed methods, make the proposed methodology a good option for defect detection on patterned fabrics.

Acknowledgments. The authors would like to thank Henry Y.T. Ngan from the Industrial Automation Research Laboratory in the Department of Electrical and Electronic Engineering at the University of Hong Kong, for providing the database of fabrics. Martinez-Leon would like to acknowledge for the grant provided by the Mexican National Council of Science and Technology (CONACyT). This research was supported by the PRODEP through the NPTC project with number DSA/103.5/15/7007.

References

1. Alata, O., Ramananjarasoa, C.: Unsupervised texture image segmentation using 2-D quarter plan autorregresive model with four prediction supports. Pattern Recogn. Lett. **26**(8), 1069–1081 (2005)
2. Badnarova, A., Bennamoun, M., Latham, S.: Optimal gabor filter for textile flaw detection. Pattern Recogn. **35**, 2973–2991 (2002)
3. Chan, H.-Y., Raju, C., Sari-Sarraf, H., Hequet, E.F.: A general approach to defect detection in textured materials using wavelet domain model and level sets. In: Proceedings of SPIE 60010D, pp. 1–6 (2005)

4. Conway, J.H., Burgiel, H., Goodman-Strauss, C.: The Symmetries of Things. AK Peters/CRC Press, Taylor and Francis, Boca Raton (2008)
5. Gonzalez, R.C., Woods, R.E.: Digital Image Processing. Prentice-Hall, Upper Saddle River (2002)
6. Haralick, R.M., Shanmugan, K., Dinstein, I.: Textural features for image classification. IEEE Trans. Syst. Man Cybern. **3**(6), 610–621 (1973)
7. Kumar, A.: Computer-vision-based fabric defect detection: a survey. IEEE Trans. Ind. Electron. **55**(1), 348–363 (2011)
8. Kuo, C.J., Su, T.: Gray relational analysis for recognizing fabric defects. Text. Res. J. **73**(5), 461–465 (2003)
9. Latif-Amet, A., Ertuzun, A., Ercil, A.: An efficient method for texture defect detection: sub-band domain co-occurrence matrices. Image Vis. Comput. **18**(6–7), 543–553 (2000)
10. Lizarraga-Morales, R.A., Sanchez-Yanez, R.E., Ayala-Ramirez, V.: Fast texel size estimation in visual texture using homogeneity cues. Pattern Recogn. Lett. **34**(4), 414–422 (2013)
11. Neubauer, C.: Segmentation of defects in textile fabric. In: Proceedings of IEEE 11th International Conference on Pattern Recognition, vol. 1, pp. 688–691, September 1992
12. Ngan, H.Y.T., Pang, G.K.H.: Regularity analysis for patterned texture inspection. IEEE Trans. Autom. Sci. Eng. **6**(1), 131–144 (2009)
13. Ngan, H.Y.T., Pang, G.K.H., Yung, N.H.C.: Automated fabric defect detection - a review. Image Vis. Comput. **29**(7), 442–458 (2011)
14. Ngan, H.Y.T., Pang, G.K.H., Yung, S.P., Ng, M.K.: Wavelet based methods on patterned fabric defect detection. Pattern Recogn. **38**(4), 559–576 (2005)
15. Otsu, N.: A threshold selection method from gray-level histograms. Automatica **11**(285–296), 23–27 (1975)
16. Unser, M.: Sum and difference histograms for texture classification. IEEE Trans. Pattern Anal. Mach. Intell. **8**(1), 118–125 (1986)
17. Wood, E.J.: Applying fourier, associated transforms to pattern characterization in textiles. Text. Res. J. **60**, 212–220 (1990)
18. Yang, X.Z., Pang, G.K.H., Yung, N.H.C.: Discriminative fabric defect detection using adaptive wavelets. Opt. Eng. **41**(12), 3116–3126 (2002)

Curve Extraction by Geodesics Fusion: Application to Polymer Reptation Analysis

Somia Rahmoun[1]([✉]), Fabrice Mairesse[1], Hiroshi Uji-i[2], Johan Hofkens[2], and Tadeusz Sliwa[1]

[1] Le2i - UMR CNRS 6306, Université de Bourgogne Franche-Comté,
BP 16, 89010 Auxerre Cedex, France
`somia.rahmoun@u-bourgogne.fr`
[2] Department of Chemistry, Katholieke University of Leuven,
3001 Heverlee, Belgium

Abstract. In the molecular field, researchers analyze dynamics of polymers by microscopy: several measurements such as length and curvature are performed in their studies. To achieve correct analysis they need to extract the curve representing as good as possible the observed polymer shape which is a grayscale thick curve with noise and blur. We propose, in this paper, a method to extract such a curve. A polymer chain moves in a snake-like fashion (Reptation): it can self-intersect and form several complex geometries. To efficiently extract the different geometries, we generate the curve by computing a piecewise centerline browsing the shape by geodesics: each shape gives a set of separate geodesics. By fusion, we obtain the complete curve traveling the shape. To keep the correct curve orientation, the fusion is considered as a graph traversal problem. Promising results show that the extracted curve properly represents the shape and can be used for polymer study.

Keywords: Shape analysis · Grayscale curves · Morphological operations · Shape extraction · Geodesics fusion · Molecular image analysis

1 Introduction

In the molecular field, polymer chains [17] are observed and studied by microscopy imaging techniques [5,10,14]. The obtained shapes are often corrupted due to convolution effect and/or diffraction of microscopic acquisition [17]. Consequently, the observed polymer chain appears like a thick curve with noise and blur. The shape analysis become problematic and chemist and biologist researchers need dedicated image processing methods. In this paper, the term "Shape" denotes the thick curve representing the studied polymer chain acquired by microscopy. Polymers are widely studied and scientists still have many questions about their organization, structure and dynamics [17]. For example, several properties strongly depend on the polymer length [9]. To be able to effectively deal with this material, we quote its principal characteristics [5,17]:

© Springer International Publishing Switzerland 2016
A. Mansouri et al. (Eds.): ICISP 2016, LNCS 9680, pp. 79–88, 2016.
DOI: 10.1007/978-3-319-33618-3_9

(i) a polymer chain have a constant width and moves in a snake-like fashion (Reptation), it can self-intersect and forms complex geometries including loops,

(ii) the studied images are two dimensional projections of three dimensional motions,

(iii) a higher intensity occurs near to the centerline of the shape with noise and blur around, which is typically obtained by microscopic acquisition.

To study the polymer chains dynamics, scientists reduce the shape acquired by microscope to its minimal representation which is a curve [5]. The extracted curve allows shape measurements, dynamic analysis, motion tracking ... These analysis strongly depend on the extracted curve which must represent properly the shape to achieve accurate analysis. In this paper we propose a method for curve extraction to help polymer chains reptation studies. This curve has to be near to the centerline of the shape and keeps its motion direction.

In the current studies, the curve is typically performed using manual or semi-automated methods. Maximum intensity near to the centerline of the shape is often exploited: several points are selected and the curve is extracted by interpolation [5,6]. The curve can be approximated by computing a skeleton [13,14,16] in order to get the axial shape representation but gives rough boundary [7]. In order to avoid this problem, pruning process can be considered or the skeleton can be combined with other processing methods such as active contour [14]. These methods, however, do not always explicitly model the curve orientation and do not deal with self-intersecting geometries. We propose to extract an oriented curve dealing with such geometries by computing geodesics.

Geodesic is a shortest path connecting two points. When the two points are located at the shape extremities, and the geodesic is near to the shape centerline, this geodesic can give a good shape representation. A geodesic can be extracted by propagation from a point to the other, which allows keeping the curve orientation. This characteristic is not present on classical curve extraction methods and it is important for polymer studying. Moreover, comparing to medial axis, the use of geodesic avoids the problem of spurious branches. As polymer chains can self-intersect, three-dimensional interpretation of the shape [7] is considered. Then, one geodesic cannot travel the entire polymer chain relying its ends because of wave propagation on bifurcation and wave collision (Fig. 1 (a)). We propose to extract a piecewise curve browsing the shape by computing several geodesics each one browsing a part of the shape. By fusion, we obtain the complete curve representing the polymer chain reptation. The fusion is performed in order to keep the natural curve orientation (Sect. 4).

In Sect. 2, we give geodesic definition, present the problematic and explain the proposed method. We present the first part of the algorithm (Separate geodesics extraction) in Sect. 3 and the second part (Separate geodesics fusion) in Sect. 4. Evaluations are done in Sect. 5, and finally conclusions and perspectives follow in Sect. 6.

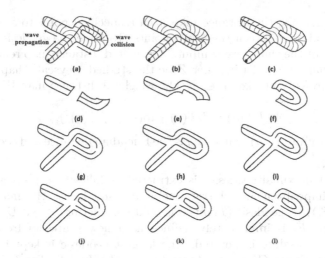

Fig. 1. Geodesics propagation and extraction. (a)...(c): equivalent maximal geodesics according to the same propagation. (g)...(i): maximal geodesics. (j)...(l): geodesic segments after considering bifurcations

2 Methodology

Considering a shape Z, and two points s and e within Z. A shortest path in Z linking s and e is called *Geodesic*. In [7] authors show that the length of an open thick curve is defined as the length of its longest geodesic. To be representative, the geodesic must have a maximal length within the shape. We call it in this paper *Maximal Geodesic*, then it connects the two most distant points in this shape. For an open thick curve, these two points are located at shape extremities.

Considering closed and/or self-intersected shapes, a maximal geodesic cannot travel the entire shape because of the front propagation: on the intersection the front will go in all directions (Fig. 1 (a)) and the geodesic extraction becomes ambiguous. Closed shapes cause front collision stopping the geodesic propagation (Fig. 1 (a)). Considering such geometries, a shape returns a set of maximal geodesics (Sect. 3), where each one travels a specific part of the shape.

To extract a curve traveling the entire shape, we propose to generate it by fusing all the extracted maximal geodesics (Sect. 4). The fusion is performed in order to keep the natural orientation of polymer motion. Two steps perform our algorithm: the separate geodesics extraction (Sect. 3) and the separate geodesics fusion (Sect. 4).

3 Separate Geodesics Extraction

Since a geodesic is a shortest path between two points in the shape, its extraction can be seen as a front propagation problem [11] from one point to the other. The distance transform maps each image pixel into its smallest distance to regions of interest [15]. Tracing the distance map from a specified point to a referred one will give a geodesic between these two points. To force the geodesic to be near the centerline of the shape, we compute a weighted distance map related to grey level of the shape (Sect. 1 (iii)). Let Z be the studied greyscale shape, $Z(a)$ the normalized intensity at pixel $a \in Z$. The weighted distance map WDT of Z is given by:

$$WDT(a) = DT(a).\exp(-coef.Z(a)^2), \tag{1}$$

with $DT(a) = \min_{p \in Z}(d(p, a))$ where $d()$ is the Euclidian distance and $coef$ a weighting coefficient.

The set of maximal geodesics is extracted as follow: we propagate a front within the shape from an arbitrary point S_i, and locate the maxima $E_i = \max(WDT(S_i))$. A geodesic $(TemG_i)$ is built considering S_i and E_i. The newly detected point E_i is immediately defined as a new source of front propagation and the procedure is iterated. The longest geodesic is kept between two successive iterations: $G_i = \max(Length(TemG_i), Length(TemG_{i-1}))$. When $Length(TemG_i) = Length(TemG_{i-1})$, the maximal length is reached and a maximal geodesic is obtained. Then it is subtracted from the shape $Z_{i+1} = Z_i - Dil_B(G_i)$ where $Dil_B(G_i)$ is the morphological dilation operation and B a disk of radius b corresponding to the observed shape width. If Z_{i+1} is empty, the process is stopped. This means that the set of the extracted maximal geodesics (here $\{G_i\}$) covers the entire shape. If Z_{i+1} is not empty, maximal geodesics are iteratively extracted from the remaining shape. G_{i+1} is then computed from the remaining shape Z_{i+1}.

For complex geometries, several equivalent maximal geodesics can exist notably due to intersections (Fig. 1 (a), (b) and (c)). Avoiding intersections leads to a partial shape covering (Fig. 1 (g), (h) and (i)). To manage this point, we decided to split maximal geodesics at each intersection in order to obtain a set of distinct geodesic segments (Fig. 1 (j), (k) and (l)).

Once the geodesic segments set obtained, a complete curve is computed by fusing those elements (Sect. 4).

4   Separate Geodesics Fusion

The goal is to follow the reptation keeping its orientation; we trace the curve unicursally following the less curvature variation at junctions. The geodesic segments previously extracted have to be fused following the correct order to generate the desired curve. We solve the problem by graph theory, and identify the fusion order by finding the optimal path traversing the graph.

According to the studied shape, the modeling graph can be Eulerian (Sect. 4.1) or non Eulerian (Sect. 4.2). A non Eulerian graph is generated when overlapping problem occurs: a polymer chain moves in a snake-like fashion and can self-intersect, as the studied images are two dimensional projections of three dimensional motions (Sect. 1 (ii)), overlapping problem can occurs at intersections (Fig. 2 (c) and (d)).

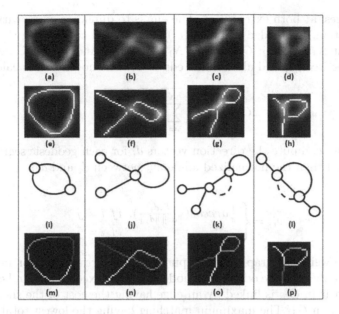

Fig. 2. Algorithm steps. (e)... (h): geodesics segments before fusion. (i)... (l): graph representation. (i)-(j): Eulerian graphs. (k)-(l): non Eulerian graphs become Eulerian after edges duplication. (m)... (p): oriented curves after fusion

4.1 Eulerian Graph

We define an undirected graph $G = (V, E)$, where $V = \{v_1, v_2, ..., v_i\}$ is a set of vertices modeling junctions and $E = \{e_1, e_2, ..., e_j\}$ a set of edges modeling geodesic segments. The fusion order search can be seen as the Königsberg bridge problem [8] which can be solved by finding Eulerian path. We consider undirected graph G whose edges are visited only one time. An Eulerian path exists over these graphs if all nodes got even degree except for start and end nodes (Fig. 2 (j)). A cycle can be considered if the start and the end belong to the same node (Fig. 2 (i)). If a graph G has one or more odd degree edges (except start and end ones), it is needed to consider double pass edges. Regarding Eulerian path, it is more adequate to duplicate specific edges (Fig. 2 (k) and (l)).

4.2 Non Eulerian Graph Consideration

In the Chinese Postman Problem [3], double traced edges are identified by maximum matching. A matching in a graph is a set of edges without common nodes. A maximum matching [2] tries to find the maximum matching that has the highest or lowest total weight. Each edge belonging to the maximal matching is duplicated to allow double pass. For duplication, we build another weighted graph $G_1 = (V, E, C_1)$ from G with same nodes and edges (Algorithm 1. Step 2), C_1 corresponds to edges costs. The edge weight is computed using angles between adjacent edges, at both extremities. The aim is to duplicate edges with less curvature variation. Each edge weight $C(e_i)$ is calculated considering the attached nodes weight N_1 and N_2: $C(e_i) = C(N_1) + C(N_2)$. At a node N, we compute angles w_{ij} between e_i and all incident edges[1] e_j. The nodes cost is calculated as follow:

$$C(N_i) = \sqrt{\sum_{j=1}^{K}(\pi - w_{ij})^2}. \tag{2}$$

For angles, we compute the direction vectors d_i for each geodesic segment at an extremity and then the normalized angle w_{ij} between d_i and d_j:

$$w_{ij} = \begin{cases} \frac{1}{\pi}arccos(\frac{|d_i.d_j|}{\|d_i\|\|d_j\|}), & if \; i \neq j \\ 1 & , \; if \; i = j \end{cases} \tag{3}$$

Once the weighted graph G_1 computed, a third graph G_m for matching is constructed only with the odd degree nodes from G_1, except start and end nodes. Each node pair in G_m is linked by an edge having the cost of the shortest path between them in G_1. The maximum matching having the lowest total weight in G_m is identified. Each matching edge corresponds to a double-traced segment. Theses edges are duplicated in G where the Eulerian path can be extracted.

4.3 Eulerian Path

Two incident edges e_i and e_j connected to a node are referred as a fusion pair (e_i, e_j). The fusion cost $C(e_i, e_j)$ is given for each fusion pair in G. The path $P = e_1, e_2, .., e_n$ cost is defined as the sum of the fusion costs of every two adjacent edges along P. The fusion cost of a pair $c(e_i, e_j)$ is set as the deviation angle from the tangent:

$$C(e_i, e_j) = \pi - w_{ij}. \tag{4}$$

The optimal Euler path is the one minimizing deviations at junctions (Algorithm 1. Step 3).

4.4 Geodesics Fusion

Geodesics fusion is performed according to the optimal path selected. Fusion consists in locally pairing geodesic segments extremities. To keep the curve chaining, attention is made on the pixels order of geodesic segments before fusion. To ensure the continuity along two geodesic segments, the fusion links the ending point of G_i to the starting one of G_j. Inversing pixels order is considered if necessary.

---

[1] let be K the number of incident edges e_j to e_i.

Algorithm 1. The Eulerian path finding algorithm

Input: Undirected connected graph $G = (V, E)$
Output: A cycle or path, optimal solution of the problem
Step 1: Set $G' = G$. If G' has at most two odd degree nodes, go to step 3
Step 2: build $G1 = (V, E, C_1)$

1. V_m the set of vertices of odd degree in G_1.
2. Build the complete graph $G_m = (V_m, E_m)$ where the cost of an edge (v_i, v_j) belongs to E_m is equal to the length of the shortest path S_{ij} between v_i and v_j in G_1
3. Find a maximum matching in G_m having the lowest cost.
4. For each edges (v_i, v_j) belonging to the optimal coupling, add to G' a copy of each edges belonging to S_{ij}.

Step 3: If all the nodes are of even degree, build an Eulerian cycle starting from any node. Otherwise, build an Eulerian path starting from one even degree node.

---

5   Experimental Results

The polymer considered in our study is a polyisocyanopeptide [5]. Visual validation of our method by experts on real polymer images has been done. Ground truth isn't available to validate quantitatively our method (MGF). To confirm the results we simulated polymer reptations by computing several kind of curves, convoluted with Gaussian distribution (the diffraction pattern is commonly modeled by Gaussian distribution [9]) and realistic amount of Poissonian noises was added to images. The simulated polymers were validated by experts (Fig. 3).

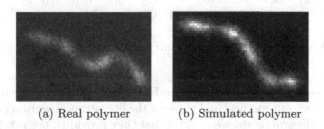

(a) Real polymer   (b) Simulated polymer

Fig. 3. Visual comparison between real and simulated polymer

50 curves for each kind provide the simulated database: open (Fig. 3), closed (Fig. 2 (a)) and self-intersected (Fig. 2 (b), (c) and (d)). We compare our algorithm to classical skeletonization methods: Skeleton (Skel) [4] and a thinning method (Thin) [12]. For quantitative evaluations, distances between the computed curves and the extracted ones are calculated. The comparison criterions used are Hausdorff distance (HD), Dice coefficient (D), Mean Absolute Distance (MAD) and the Mean Sum of Squared Distance (MSSD), equations can be found in [1,18]. Our proposed method aims to approach a continuous representation of the curve by designing it with few pixels. This way, a fine representation

is more effective for measurement and tracking applications. To quantify the method ability to extract a fine curve, we introduce the following coefficient: $TH = \frac{R \cap S}{S}$, Where R and S the reference curve and the calculated one. Dice and TH coefficient measure the correspondence between the two curves. They vary from 0 to 1: 1 corresponds to identical curves. The TH coefficient represents the percentage of S covered by R. While the MAD and MSSD measure a global correspondence between the two curves, the Hausdorff distance evaluates the local behavior of the algorithm.

We start by removing the blur accumulated around the shape, which is typical of microscopy acquisition (Sect. 1): a residual image R is built with the result of a mean filter and a median one: $R = MeanFilter(Z) - MedianFilter(Z)$, where Z is the initial shape. The residual image R is after deconvoluted by two successive kernels having the same size but two different amplitudes and standard deviations, using Lucy-Richardson operation. The size of kernel corresponds to the observed width of the shape, the amplitude and standard deviations to the observed intensity distribution. Curves are extracted from the deconvoluted shapes. Comparison results between the extracted curves and the ground truths are summarized in Table 1.

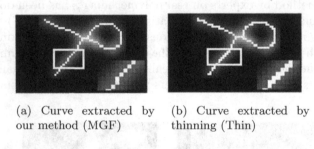

(a) Curve extracted by   (b) Curve extracted by
our method (MGF)   thinning (Thin)

Fig. 4. Visual comparison between our method and the thinning method

Observing overall results according to HD, MAD, and MSSD we note a slight difference between our method and those of the literature. Regarding curves produced by literature methods, we noticed that they provide more pixels representation than our method (Fig. 4): These criterions compute the global distances selecting the maximal of minimal local distances: small variations adversely affect our results unlike the literature methods where their produced curve totally covers the reference one. This is quantitatively expressed regarding results according to TH, we note that best performances are obtained with our method (MGF) (TH= 0.84). These results prove that our extracted curve fits the reference better than the literature methods (Skel: 0.75, Thin: 0.77, Thin_prun1: 0.80). With pruning, the results according to the TH criterion are improved (Thin_prun1: 0.80), but curve behavior gets worse (HD: 3.84, MAD: 1.16, MSSD: 1.83): we noticed that the pruning distorts the curve losing information at extremities.

Generally observing, our method performs promising results compared to the classical methods of the literature, while providing better results with complex

Table 1. Results of curves extraction.

	Methods	TH		HD		MAD		MSSD		D	
		Mean	SD	Mean	SD	Mean	SD	Mean	SD	Mean	SD
Open	MGF	**0.85**	0.05	2.74	1.22	1.06	0.06	1.25	0.33	**0.79**	0.04
	Skel	0.74	0.05	2.08	0.74	**1.02**	0.02	**1.09**	0.10	0.79	0.04
	Thin	0.76	0.06	**2.08**	0.74	**1.02**	0.02	**1.09**	0.10	0.79	0.05
	Thin_prun1	0.79	0.06	4.36	1.63	1.19	0.17	2.01	1.34	0.78	0.05
Closed	MGF	**0.88**	0.04	**1.33**	0.53	**1.00**	0.01	**1.01**	0.05	0.75	0.03
	Skel	0.80	0.05	1.63	1.04	**1.00**	0.01	1.02	0.05	**0.80**	0.04
	Thin	0.83	0.05	1.57	1.05	**1.00**	0.01	1.02	0.06	**0.80**	0.05
	Thin_prun1	0.84	0.05	1.47	0.78	1.01	0.02	1.03	0.08	**0.80**	0.05
Self-inter	MGF	**0.81**	0.05	**2.25**	0.73	**1.02**	0.01	**1.08**	0.08	0.69	0.05
	Skel	0.77	0.05	3.02	1.06	1.06	0.04	1.24	0.18	**0.73**	0.04
	Thin	0.77	0.06	3.16	1.00	1.07	0.04	1.27	0.20	0.72	0.05
	Thin_prun1	0.79	0.06	4.66	1.07	1.24	0.14	2.11	0.77	0.69	0.06
Overall	MGF	**0.84**	0.04	2.36	0.98	1.03	0.04	1.16	0.22	0.76	0.04
	Skel	0.75	0.05	**2.18**	0.86	**1.02**	0.02	**1.10**	0.10	**0.78**	0.03
	Thin	0.77	0.05	2.19	0.85	**1.02**	0.02	1.11	0.11	0.77	0.05
	Thin_prun1	0.80	0.05	3.84	1.34	1.16	0.13	1.83	0.97	0.76	0.05

geometries (closed and self-intersected). Figure 2 presents all the steps of the algorithm. The ordering feature of our extracted curve is shown in the last row: the grayscale gradient shows the curves orientation.

6 Conclusion

We proposed in this paper a method for curve extraction to help polymer analysis. This curve is performed by geodesics extraction and fusion. An important feature is its ability to keep the curve orientation following the natural polymer motion. We simulated polymer reptation to estimate the extracted curve by comparison with ground truth. Obtained results show that the extracted curve represents correctly the shape, and is comparable to the classical skeletonization methods. The method can therefore be used for polymers chemical and physical analysis. In future works, more comparisons will be performed considering real polymers.

References

1. Dietenbeck, T., Alessandrini, M., Barbosa, D., Dhooge, J., Friboulet, D., Bernard, O.: Detection of the whole myocardium in 2D-echocardiography for multiple orientations using a geometrically constrained level-set. Med. Image Anal. **16**(2), 386–401 (2012)

2. Edmonds, J.: Maximum matching and a polyhedron with (0,1) vertices. J. Res. Natl. Bur. Stand. **69B**, 125–130 (1965)
3. Edmonds, J., Johnson, E.: Matching, euler tours and the chinese postman. Math. Program. **5**(1), 88–124 (1973)
4. Gonzalez, R.C., Woods, R.E., Eddins, S.L.: Digital Image Processing using MAT-LAB. Pearson Education India, London (2004)
5. Keshavarz, M., Engelkamp, H., Xu, J., Braeken, E., Otten, M.B., Uji-i, H., Schwartz, E., Koepf, M., Vananroye, A., Vermant, J., et al.: Nanoscale study of polymer dynamics. ACS Nano **10**, 1434–1441 (2015)
6. Kuhn, J.R., Pollard, T.D.: Real-time measurements of actin filament polymerization by total internal reflection fluorescence microscopy. Biophys. J. **88**(2), 1387–1402 (2005)
7. Lantuéjoul, C., Beucher, S.: On the use of the geodesic metric in image analysis. J. Microsc. **121**(1), 39–49 (1981)
8. Leonhard, E.: Solutio problematis ad geometriam situs pertinentis. Commentarii Academiae Scientiarum Petropolitanae **8**, 128–140 (1741)
9. Muls, B., Uji-i, H., Melnikov, S., Moussa, A., Verheijen, W., Soumillion, J.P., Josemon, J., Müllen, K., Hofkens, J.: Direct measurement of the end-to-end distance of individual polyfluorene polymer chains. ChemPhysChem **6**(11), 2286–2294 (2005)
10. Perkins, T.T., Smith, D., Chu, S., et al.: Relaxation of a single DNA molecule observed by optical microscopy. Science **264**(5160), 822–826 (1994)
11. Peyré, G., Cohen, L.: Heuristically driven front propagation for geodesic paths extraction. In: Paragios, N., Faugeras, O., Chan, T., Schnörr, C. (eds.) VLSM 2005. LNCS, vol. 3752, pp. 173–185. Springer, Heidelberg (2005)
12. Pudney, C.: Distance-ordered homotopic thinning: a skeletonization algorithm for 3D digital images. Comput. Vis. Image Underst. **72**(3), 404–413 (1998)
13. Rivetti, C.: A simple and optimized length estimator for digitized DNA contours. Cytometry Part A **75**(10), 854–861 (2009)
14. Romanowska, M., Hinsch, H., Kirchgeßner, N., Giesen, M., Degawa, M., Hoffmann, B., Frey, E., Merkel, R.: Direct observation of the tube model in f-actin solutions: tube dimensions and curvatures. EPL (Europhys. Lett.) **86**(2), 26003 (2009)
15. Rosenfeld, A., Pfaltz, J.: Distance functions on digital pictures. Pattern Recognit. **1**(1), 33–61 (1968)
16. Sanchez, H., Wyman, C.: Sfmetrics: an analysis tool for scanning force microscopy images of biomolecules. BMC Bioinform. **16**(1), 1 (2015)
17. Woll, D., Braeken, E., Deres, A., De Schryver, F.C., Uji-i, H., Hofkens, J.: Polymers and single molecule fluorescence spectroscopy, what can we learn? Chem. Soc. Rev. **38**, 313–328 (2009)
18. Zhou, X.S., Comaniciu, D., Gupta, A.: An information fusion framework for robust shape tracking. IEEE Trans. Pattern Anal. Mach. Intell. **27**(1), 115–129 (2005)

Multispectral and Colour Imaging

A Chaotic Cryptosystem for Color Image with Dynamic Look-Up Table

Med Karim Abdmouleh$^{(\boxtimes)}$, Ali Khalfallah, and Med Salim Bouhlel

University of Sfax,
Research Unit: Sciences and Technologies of Image and Telecommunications
Higher Institute of Biotechnology, Sfax, Tunisia
medkarim.abdmouleh@isggb.rnu.tn, ali.khalfallah@enetcom.rnu.tn,
medsalim.bouhlel@enis.rnu.tn

Abstract. The chaotic cryptosystems have been widely investigated to provide fast and highly secure image encryption. In this paper, we introduce a novel cryptosystem for color image based on chaos by using a dynamic Look-Up Table (LUT). We utilized the Logistic Map chaotic system in order to benefit from its sensitivity to initial conditions.

The result shows that the proposed cryptosystem have many characteristics such as high security, high sensitivity and high speed that can be applied in the encryption of color images. It is demonstrated that the NPCR = 99.6140 %, the UACI = 33.5448 % and entropy = 7.9984 can satisfy security and performance requirements. Simulations show that the proposed cryptosystem has high security and resist various typical attacks.

Keywords: Color image encryption · Chaotic system · Look-Up Table · Logistic map

1 Introduction

In recent years, with the fast exchange and transmission of digital images over the internet, researchers have focused on the image encryption [1]. Chaotic systems have been widely used in the image encryption algorithms [2–22]. Chaotic systems have many particular properties, such ergodicity, sensitivity to initial conditions and to control parameters and randomness [23]. These properties are very important in cryptography. Recently, a variety of chaotic cryptosystem for gray-scale image have been proposed [2–13]. However, a few researches have focused on color image [14–22].

In [15], a novel color image encryption algorithm based on chaos was proposed. The authors used a chaotic system to encrypt the R, G, B components of a color image at the same time and make these three components affect one other. Therefore, the correlations between the R, G, B components can be reduced and the security of algorithm is increased. Wang et al. [16] introduced a new image encryption algorithm based on iterating the chaotic maps. Using the pseudorandom sequence generated by a group of one-dimensional chaotic

© Springer International Publishing Switzerland 2016
A. Mansouri et al. (Eds.): ICISP 2016, LNCS 9680, pp. 91–100, 2016.
DOI: 10.1007/978-3-319-33618-3_10

maps, the proposed algorithm realizes fast encryption and decryption of both a gray-scale image and a true color image. Moreover, the rounds of encryption could be set by the user. In [19] the authors designed a stream-cipher algorithm based on one-time keys and robust chaotic maps, in order to get high security and improve the dynamical degradation. We utilized the piecewise linear chaotic map as the generator of a pseudo-random key stream sequence. The initial conditions were generated by the true random number of generators and the MD5 of the mouse positions. We applied the algorithm to encrypt the color image. In [20], Benjeddou et al. proposed a new color image encryption technique using two multidimensional chaotic maps: a three dimensional chaotic map for the key expansion and a two dimensional chaotic map for the generation of two chaotic Look-Up Tables.

The rest of this paper is organized as follows. Section 2 describes the cryptosystem for color image. Section 3 presents the simulation and the experimental results to prove the performance of encryption algorithm. Finally, Sect. 4 concludes the paper.

2   Color Image Encryption Scheme Based on Chaos

We convert every image I with size (M × N) in 24-bit true color into its 3 components (R, G and B). The size of each color's (R, G or B) matrix is (M × N) and contains integers between 0 and 255, then each matrix will be encrypted. In this paper, we use the Logistic Map as the chaotic system which is widely used in chaotic cryptosystem for its simplicity and high sensitivity to initial conditions. It is defined by:

$$X_{n+1} = \mu \, X_n \, (1 - X_n) \tag{1}$$

where μ is a control parameter, X_n is a real number in the range [0, 1] and X_0 is an initial condition. When $3.569955672 < \mu \leq 4$, the system becomes chaotic [24].

In the rest of this section we provide the process of encryption algorithm.

Step 1. The RGB color image I with size (M × N) is divided into three separate images I_R, I_G and I_B (i.e., every image represents one of the three color components (red, green and blue)) as follows:

$$I_R(x,y) = I(x,y,1); \; I_G(x,y) = I(x,y,2);$$
$$I_B(x,y) = I(x,y,3) \tag{2}$$
$$where \; 1 \leq x \leq M \; and \; 1 \leq y \leq N$$

Step 2. Firstly, we generate a chaotic matrix using the Logistic Map function LM_1 with the parameters (x_{0XOR} and μ_{0XOR}). We mix the obtained chaotic matrix with the original image (I_R, I_G or I_B) using the logical function XOR $\oplus$ to obtain the initial encrypted image I_1 (Fig. 1(a)).

Then, for each pixel P_1 from I_1, we generate a chaotic LUT using the second Logistic Map function (LM_2) having as parameters $(x_0(P_c)$ and $\mu_0)$. Where P_c is the value of the previous encrypted pixel by our cryptosystem. The initial condition $x_0(P_c)$ depends on the previous value of the ciphered pixel and x_0 with $x_0(P_c) \in [0.1, 0.9]$ (Fig. 1(b)).

Finally, we apply the New LUT to P_i to obtain the final encrypted pixel. We repeat this process for each pixel from the initial encrypted image to get the final encrypted one (Fig. 1(c)).

Step 3. We apply the steps in **Step 2** for each component (R, G and B) of the original image I. We obtain three encrypted images (I_{CR} is the encrypted image of I_R, I_{CG} is the encrypted image of I_G and I_{CB} is the encrypted image of I_B).

Step 4. Grouping the three encrypted images (I_{CR}, I_{CG} and I_{CB}) in order to have the encrypted image I_C.

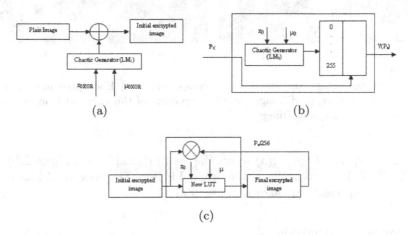

Fig. 1. Architecture of the proposed method: (a) XOR Chaotic encryption (b), Chaotic Dynamic Look-Up Table (c), Chaotic Look-Up Table encryption.

The decryption procedure is identical to that of the encryption algorithm except that the order is reversed.

3   Experimental Results

An image cryptosystem should be robust against all types of attacks (cryptanalytic and statistical attacks). In what follows, we present the different results obtained by statistical analysis of our cryptosystem [25]. These experiments include key space analysis, sensitivity analysis, histogram analysis of the original and the encrypted images, information entropy analysis, correlation coefficient analysis and differential analysis. The Lena color image of size (256×256) is

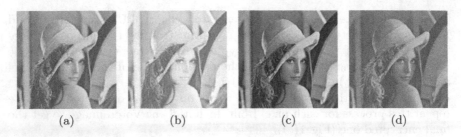

(a)   (b)   (c)   (d)

Fig. 2. Original color image and its R, G, B components: (a) Original image, (b) R component of the original image, (c) G component of the original image, (d) B component of the original image.

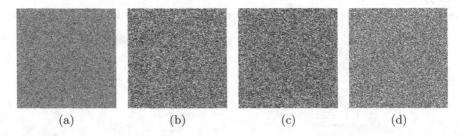

(a)   (b)   (c)   (d)

Fig. 3. Encrypted image and its R, G, B components: (a) Encrypted image, (b) R component of the encrypted image, (c) G component of the encrypted image, (d) B component of the encrypted image.

opted for encryption. Figure 2(a) shows the color original image. Figure 2(b)–(d) show the R, G, B components of the original image. The encrypted image and its R, G, B components are shown in Fig. 3(a)–(d).

3.1   Key Space Analysis

A good encryption algorithm should not only be sensitive to the secret key, but also the key space should be large enough to make brute-force attacks infeasible. In this cryptosystem, the initial conditions and parameters $\{x_0, \mu_0, x_{0XOR}, \mu_{0XOR}\}$ can be used as key. In our simulations we use MATLAB 8.3. This mathematical tool codes real in 8 bytes. Therefore, all the parameters are presented in 64 bits. Then, for each component of the color image we have $\{2^{64} \times 2^{64} \times 2^{64} \times 2^{64}\} = 2^{256}$ combinations. Our secret key has 2^{256} different combinations.

3.2   Sensitivity Analysis

1. **Key Sensitivity Analysis in the Encryption Phase**
   Figure 4(a) shows the original Lena image. Figure 4(b) shows the encrypted image of Lena with the correct encryption key $k_0 = \{0.25, 3.8701, 0.4, 3.9\}$. We change key k_0 by adding 10^{-15} for real x_0, then, the difference between the

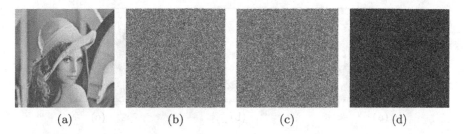

Fig. 4. Key sensitivity analysis in encryption phase: (a) Original image of Lena, (b) Encrypted image with key k_0, (c) Encrypted image with key k_1, (d) Difference between (b) and (c).

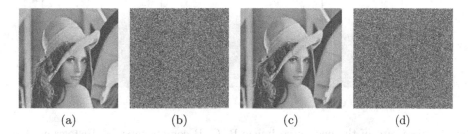

Fig. 5. Key sensitivity analysis in decryption phase: (a) Original image of Lena, (b) Encrypted image with key k_0, (c) Decrypted image with key k_0, (d) Decrypted image with key k_1.

two corresponding encrypted images is calculated. The encrypted Lena image with key $k_1 = \{0.250000000000001, 3.8701, 0.4, 3.9\}$ is shown in Fig. 4(c). Figure 4(d) is a plot of the difference between the two encrypted images.

2. **Key Sensitivity Analysis in the Decryption Phase**

   In addition, decryption using key with slight change above is also performed so as to evaluate the key sensitivity. The original image is encrypted with the original key $k_0 = \{0.25, 3.8701, 0.4, 3.9\}$, and the encrypted image is obtained, it shown in Fig. 5(b). The original key is modified slightly (order of 10^{-15} for real x_0). The encrypted image obtained by key k_0 is decrypted with the modified key $k_1 = \{0.250000000000001, 3.8701, 0.4, 3.9\}$. The results are plotted in Fig. 5. Figure 5(d) shows that the reconstructed image is noisy even when the key has only a tiny modification.

   Therefore, it can be concluded that the proposed algorithm is sensitive to the key, a small change of the key will generate a completely different decryption result and cannot get the correct original image.

3.3 Histogram Analysis

The histograms of the original and the encrypted image are shown in Figs. 6 and 7. Referring to the obtained results, we can see that histogram of the

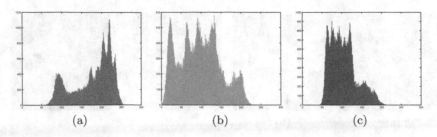

Fig. 6. Histogram of the original image R, G, B components: (a) Histogram of R component, (b) Histogram of G component, (c) Histogram of B component.

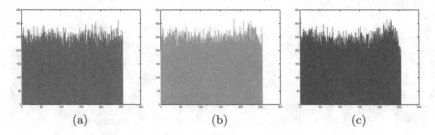

Fig. 7. Histogram of the encrypted image R, G, B components: (a) Histogram of R component, (b) Histogram of G component, (c) Histogram of B component.

encrypted image Fig. 7(a)–(c) is fairly uniform and is significantly different from that of the original image.

3.4   Information Entropy Analysis

The entropy, which was proposed by Shannon in 1948 [26], is defined as:

$$H(m) = - \sum_i^{2^M-1} P(m_i) \ \log_2 P(m_i) \qquad (3)$$

Here, $P(m_i)$ represents the probability of symbol m_i. The entropy H(m) is expressed in bits.

For a purely random source emitting 2^M symbols, the entropy is H(m) = M.

Table 1 shows the entropy of the three color components R, G and B. The values obtained are very close to the theoretical value H(m) = 8 bits/pixel. From this result, it is clear that our encryption image scheme is robust against the entropy attack.

3.5   Correlation Between Neighboring Pixels

It is well known that adjacent image pixels are highly correlated in the original image. In order to resist a statistical attack, we must decrease the correlation of

Table 1. Results of information entropy.

Component	R	G	B
Entropy	7.9945	7.9956	7.9954

two adjacent pixels in the encrypted image [27]. We calculate the correlation for a sequence of adjacent pixels using the following formula:

$$r_{xy} = \frac{\text{cov}(x,y)}{\sqrt{D(x)}\sqrt{D(y)}} \tag{4}$$

Here, x and y are the intensity values of two adjacent pixels in the image. r_{xy} is the correlation coefficient. The cov(x,y), E(x) and D(x) are given as follows:

$$E(x) = \frac{1}{N}\sum_{i=1}^{N} x_i \tag{5}$$

$$D(x) = \frac{1}{N}\sum_{i=1}^{N} [x_i - E(x_i)] \tag{6}$$

$$\text{cov}(x,y) = \frac{1}{N}\sum_{i=1}^{N} [(x_i - E(x_i))(y_i - E(y_i))] \tag{7}$$

N is the number of adjacent pixels selected from the image to calculate the correlation.

To calculate the correlation coefficient, we have randomly chosen 2500 pairs of two adjacent pixels from the original image and the encrypted image.

It's clear from Fig. 8 and Tables 2 and 3 that the correlation between two adjacent pixels for the encrypted Lena image is much smaller than that of the original image. This little correlation between two neighboring pixels in the encrypted image makes the brook of our cryptosystem difficult.

Table 2. Correlation coefficients of two adjacent pixels in the original image.

Correlation direction	Original image		
	R Component	G Component	B Component
Horizontal	0.9523	0.9355	0.9175
Vertical	0.9759	0.9665	0.9478
Diagonal	0.9278	0.9102	0.8883

Table 3. Correlation coefficients of two adjacent pixels in the encrypted image.

Correlation direction	Encrypted image		
	R Component	G Component	B Component
Horizontal	0.0014	0.0003	0.0003
Vertical	0.0015	−0.0044	0.0032
Diagonal	0.0034	0.0024	−0.0067

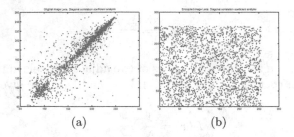

(a)   (b)

Fig. 8. Correlation of diagonal adjacent two pixels: (a) R component of the original image, (b) R component of the encrypted image.

3.6   Differential Analysis

The objective of this analysis is to prove that a small change in the original image introduces a major change to the encrypted image. This difference can be measured by means of two criteria namely, the number of pixel change rate (NPCR) and the unified average changing intensity (UACI). The theoretical values for an ideal cryptosystem are close to 100 % to the value of NPCR while the value of UACI must be very close to 33 %.

Let I_2 be the changed original image on one pixel. C_1 and C_2 are the ciphered images of the original images I and I_2. D is a matrix having the same size as the image figures C_1 and C_2. D(i,j) is determined as follows:

$$D(i,j) = \begin{cases} 1 \; if \; C_1(i,j) \neq C_2(i,j) \\ 0 \; else \end{cases} \tag{8}$$

The NPCR is defined by:

$$NPCR = \frac{\sum\limits_{i=0}^{M-1} \sum\limits_{j=0}^{N-1} D(i,j)}{M \times N} \times 100 \tag{9}$$

M and N are the height and width of encrypted images C_1 and C_2. The UACI is defined by:

$$UACI = \frac{1}{M \times N} \sum\limits_{i=0}^{M-1} \sum\limits_{j=0}^{N-1} \frac{|C_1(i,j) - C_2(i,j)|}{255} \times 100 \tag{10}$$

Two images are used in the tests. The first image is the original image, and the other is obtained by changing the first pixel value of R component from '224' to '225'. Then the two images are encrypted with the same key k_0 to generate the corresponding encrypted images C_1 and C_2.

The results obtained are NPCR = 99.6140 % and UACI = 33.5448 %. The results show that a small change in the plain image introduces a high alteration on the encrypted one. Hence, the proposed cryptosystem is robust against the differential attacks.

4 Conclusion

In this paper, we introduced a new color image encryption algorithm based on chaotic systems called Look-Up Table. This new cryptosystem uses the "Logistic Map" function to generate a dynamic LUT. The performance of this LUT is introduced to the cryptosystem feedback because this LUT depends on the encrypted previous pixel.

Simulation results demonstrate that satisfactory performance (sensitivity and security) is achievable in our proposed cryptosystem. The results show that the cryptosystem can encrypt the color image effectively.

References

1. Uhl, A., Pommer, A.: Image And Video Encryption: From Digital Rights Management To Secured Personal Communication (Advances in Information Security). Springer-Verlag TELOS, Santa Clara (2004)
2. Chen, J.X., Zhu, Z.L., Fu, C., Zhang, L.B., Zhang, Y.: An efficient image encryption scheme using lookup table-based confusion and diffusion. Nonlinear Dyn. **81**(3), 1151–1166 (2015)
3. Abdmouleh, M.K., Khalfallah, A., Bouhlel, M.S.: A new watermarking technique for medical image using hierarchical encryption. Int. J. Comput. Sc. Issues (IJCSI) **11**(4), 27–32 (2014)
4. Abdmouleh, M.K., Khalfallah, A., Bouhlel, M.S.: Dynamic chaotic Look-Up Table for MRI medical image encryption. In: International Conference on Systems, Control, Signal Processing And Informatics (SCSI), pp. 241–246 (2013)
5. Chen, J.X., Zhu, Z.L., Fu, C., Yu, H.: An improved permutation-diffusion type image cipher with a chaotic orbit perturbing mechanism. Opt. Express **21**(23), 27873–27890 (2013)
6. Abdmouleh, M.K., Khalfallah, A., Bouhlel, M.S.: Image encryption with dynamic chaotic Look-Up Table. In: 6th International Conference on Sciences of Electronics, Technologies of Information and Telecommunications (SETIT), pp. 331–337 (2012)
7. Liao, X., Lai, S., Zhou, Q.: A novel image encryption algorithm based on self-adaptive wave transmission. Signal Process. **90**(9), 2714–2722 (2010)
8. Masmoudi, A., Bouhlel, M.S., Puech, W.: A new image cryptosystem based on chaotic map and continued fractions. In: 18th European Signal Processing Conference (EUSIPCO), pp. 1504–1508 (2010)
9. Wang, X.Y., Yang, L., Liu, R., Kadir, A.: A chaotic image encryption algorithm based on perceptron model. Nonlinear Dyn. **62**(3), 615–621 (2010)

10. He, B., Zhang, F., Luo, L., Du, M., Wang, Y.: An image encryption algorithm based on spatiotemporal chaos. In: 2nd International Congress on Image and Signal Processing (CISP), pp. 1–5 (2009)
11. Gao, T., Chen, Z.: A new image encryption algorithm based on hyper-chaos. Phys. Lett. A **372**(4), 394–400 (2008)
12. Sun, F., Liu, S., Li, Z., Lu, Z.: A novel image encryption scheme based on spatial chaos map. Chaos, Solitons Fractals **38**(3), 631–640 (2008)
13. Xiang, T., Wong, K.W., Liao, X.: Selective image encryption using a spatiotemporal chaotic system. Chaos: Interdisc. J. Nonlinear Sci. **17**(2), 023115 (2007)
14. Abu Zaid, O.M., Demba, M.: A proposed cryptosystem algorithm based on two different chaotic systems (PCA2CS) for securing the colored images. Int. J. Comput. Sci. Issues (IJCSI) **11**(2), 159–166 (2014)
15. Wang, X., Teng, L., Qin, X.: A novel colour image encryption algorithm based on chaos. Signal Process. **92**(4), 1101–1108 (2012)
16. Wang, X., Zhao, J., Liu, H.: A new image encryption algorithm based on chaos. Optics Commun. **285**(5), 562–566 (2012)
17. Gupta, K., Silakari, S.: New approach for fast color image encryption using chaotic map. J. Inf. Secur. **2**(4), 139–150 (2011)
18. Mazloom, S., Eftekhari-Moghadam, A.M.: Color image cryptosystem using chaotic maps. In: IEEE Symposium on Computational Intelligence for Multimedia, Signal and Vision Processing (CIMSIVP), pp. 142–147 (2011)
19. Liu, H., Wang, X.: Color image encryption based on one-time keys and robust chaotic maps. Comput. Math. Appl. **59**(10), 3320–3327 (2010)
20. Benjeddou, A., Taha, A.K., Fournier-Prunaret, D., Bouallegue, R.: A fast color image encryption scheme based on multidimensional chaotic maps. In: Global Information Infrastructure Symposium (GIIS), pp. 1–4 (2009)
21. Rhouma, R., Meherzi, S., Belghith, S.: OCML-based colour image encryption. Chaos, Solitons Fractals **40**(1), 309–318 (2009)
22. Pareek, N., Patidar, V., Sud, K.: Image encryption using chaotic logistic map. Image Vis. Comput. **24**(9), 926–934 (2006)
23. Kocarev, L.: Chaos-based cryptography: a brief overview. IEEE Circuits Syst. Mag. **1**(3), 6–21 (2001)
24. Li, J., Feng, Y., Yang, X.: Discrete chaotic based 3D image encryption scheme. In: Symposium on Photonics and Optoelectronics (SOPO), pp. 1–4 (2009)
25. Abdmouleh, M.K., Khalfallah, A., Bouhlel, M.S.: An overview on cryptography and watermarking. In: International Conference on Computers, Automatic Control, Signal Processing and Systems Science, pp. 99–104 (2014)
26. Shannon, C.E.: A mathematical theory of communication. Bell Syst. Tech. J. **27**(3), 379–423 (1948)
27. Behnia, S., Akhshani, A., Mahmodi, H., Akhavan, A.: A novel algorithm for image encryption based on mixture of chaoticmaps. Chaos, Solitons Fractals **35**(2), 408–419 (2008)

Nonlinear Estimation of Chromophore Concentrations and Shading from Hyperspectral Images

Rina Akaho[1(✉)], Misa Hirose[2], and Norimichi Tsumura[2]

[1] Department of Informatics and Imaging Systems, Chiba University, Chiba, Japan
akasanmail.com@gmail.com
[2] Graduate School of Advanced Integration Science, Chiba University, Chiba, Japan

Abstract. This paper aims to apply nonlinear estimation of chromophore concentrations: melanin, oxy-hemoglobin, deoxy-hemoglobin and shading to the real hyperspectral image of skin. Skin reflectance is captured in the wavelengths between 400 nm and 700 nm by hyperspectral scanner. Five-band wavelengths data are selected from skin reflectance. By using the cubic function which obtained by Monte Carlo simulation of light transport in multi-layered tissue, chromophore concentration is determined by minimizing residual sum of squares of reflectance.

Keywords: Melanin volume · Blood volume · Monte Carlo simulation · Spectral reflectance

1 Introduction

Multispectral imaging has generated growing interest in various fields, such as biomedical imaging, recording for digital archives, and sensing and controlling systems in the last few decades [1–9]. The main aim of image sensing is to provide non-contact and non-invasive sensing techniques.

Skin is a multi-layered tissue composed of the epidermis, dermis and subcutaneous tissues and contains chromophores such as melanin, oxy-hemoglobin and deoxy-hemoglobin. Since diffuse reflectance of human skin is changed depending on the concentration of these chromophores, the analysis of diffuse reflectance can provide information about tissue activities related to these chromophores. This information is useful to be applied for early detection of skin disease and monitoring health.

Tsumura *et al.* discussed a method of extracting melanin and hemoglobin information by applying Independent Component Analysis (ICA) to skin color images [1,5]. Kikuchi *et al.* proposed imaging of a hemoglobin oxygen saturation ratio of the face with a spectral camera based on the multi regression analysis [10]. There are many discussions about estimating chromophore concentrations linearly from skin color images and spectral images.

© Springer International Publishing Switzerland 2016
A. Mansouri et al. (Eds.): ICISP 2016, LNCS 9680, pp. 101–108, 2016.
DOI: 10.1007/978-3-319-33618-3_11

On the other hand, Kobayashi *et al.* analyzed the nonlinear relation between absorbance and chromophores of skin based on Monte Carlo simulation and the modified Lambert-Beer's law [11]. Kobayashi *et al.* reported a method of estimating the optical path length of each layer from absorbance and the quantity of chromophores. By using the estimated optical path length, the concentration of chromophores can be analysed based on the modified Lambert-Beer's law. However, this method cannot estimate the optical path length if the concentration of chromophores is not provided. Even if the concentration is supplied, the estimation accuracy is not sufficient because the concentration is derived linearly by multiple regression analysis. Hirose *et al.* calculated the relationship between chromophore concentration and absorbance by creating the combination of a chromophore concentration on the simulation [12]. Estimation accuracy of the method by Hirose *et al.* was evaluated by numerical skin phantom, they concluded that their method performed high accurate estimation. However it was expected to be evaluated by real skin images.

In this paper, therefore, we apply a nonlinear estimation method to the real skin spectral image for chromophore concentration estimation.

2   Nonlinear Estimation of Chromophore Concentrations, Shading and Surface Reflectance from Five Band Images

2.1   Analysis of the Relation Between Absorbance and Chromophore Concentration

First, we analyze the relation between absorbance and chromophore concentration by Monte Carlo simulation and define the absorbance as the cubic functions of chromophore concentration as it was previously performed by minimizing [11].

Diffuse reflectance data for skin is obtained by Monte Carlo simulation of light transport in multi-layered tissue (MCML) [9]. MCML follows the propagation of photons in tissue. As shown in Fig. 1, the two-layered skin model is used and is composed of the epidermis and dermis.

Five optical parameters are set at each layer: thickness t, reflectance index n, anisotropy factor g, scattering coefficient μ_s and absorption coefficient μ_a. The thickness t of epidermis and dermis are 0.006 and 0.40 cm respectively in this basic model [13]. The reflectance index n, scattering coefficient μ_s and anisotropy factor g of two layers are the same value, $n = 1.4$, μ_s and g are based on previously used data [4]. The absorption coefficient μ_a is calculated by the absorption coefficients of chromophores such as melanin, oxy-hemoglobin and deoxy-hemoglobin as follows.

$$
\begin{aligned}
\mu_{a.epi}(\lambda) &= [Mel]\,\mu_{a.mel}(\lambda), \\
\mu_{a.der}(\lambda) &= [Ohb]\,\mu_{a.ohb}(\lambda) + [Hb]\,\mu_{a.hb}(\lambda) \\
&= [Thb]\,[StO]\,\mu_{a.ohb}(\lambda) \\
&\quad + [Thb]\,(1 - [StO])\mu_{a.hb}(\lambda),
\end{aligned}
\tag{1}
$$

where λ is wavelength and the subscript of absorption coefficient *epi*, *der*, *mel*, *ohb* and *hb* indicate epidermis, dermis, melanin, oxy-hemoglobin and deoxy-hemoglobin respectively.

Chromophore concentrations are input to MCML to acquire diffuse reflectance of skin. Set of melanin concentration $[Mel] = 1, 2, 3, 4, 5, 6, 7, 8, 9, 10\%$; blood volume $[Thb] = 0.2, 0.4, 0.6, 0.8, 1.0\%$; and oxygen saturations $[StO] = 0, 20, 40, 60, 80, 100\%$. 300 reflectance data are obtained from their combinations.

The diffuse reflectance obtained by MCML is converted to absorbance with logarithmic transformation, and the absorbance for each wavelength is defined by a cubic function of chromophore concentration. The chromophore concentration is determined to minimize the residual sum of squares of the reflectance as is described in the next section.

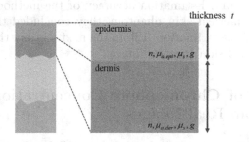

Fig. 1. Two-layered skin model is composed of the epidermis and dermis.

2.2 Estimation of Chromophore Concentrations and Shading from Five Band Images

Four components, melanin, oxy-hemoglobin, deoxy-hemoglobin and shading, are extracted from five band images of the skin by using cubic functions. For this purpose, these four components are determined to minimize the residual sum of squares RSS_{est} as follows.

$$RSS_{est} = \sum_{\lambda} [R(\lambda) - (exp(-(Z(\lambda) + k)))]^2, \tag{2}$$

where $R(\lambda)$ is spectral reflectance of human skin and k indicate bias value which is shading component. $Z(\lambda)$ is absorbance defined by the cubic function of melanin concentration and absorption coefficient of dermis.

$$Z(\lambda) = aX^3 + bX^2Y + cXY^2 + dY^3 \\ - eX^2 - fXY - gY^2 + hX + iY + j, \tag{3}$$

where $a \sim j$ are coefficients optimized at each wavelenght. X is absorption coefficient of dermis and Y is percentage of melanin. Figure 2 shows $Z(\lambda)$ where

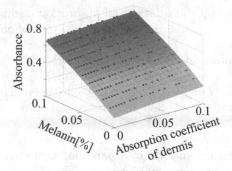

Fig. 2. Skin absorbance $Z(\lambda)$ in 700 nm.

the wavelength is 700 nm. Estimation accuracy of the method by Hirose *et al.* was evaluated by numerical skin phantom, they concluded that their method performed high accurate estimation [12]. In the next section, therefore, we apply this method to the real skin spectral image.

3   Estimation of Chromophore Concentrations, Shading from Real Images

3.1   Experiment Setup and Selected Set of Wavelengths

Figure 3 shows experimental set-up to capture hyperspectral images of skin. Hyperspectral images were captured using a hyperspectral scanner (JFE ImSpector) in every 10 nm between 400 nm and 700 nm and using artificial solar (Seric Ltd.) as a light source in a dark room. First, we captured hyperspectral image of white checker. Reflected spectral power of skin is divided by reflected spectral power of white checker to obtain spectral reflectance of skin. Figure 4 shows the RGB images which is converted from spectral reflectance of skin. We used 10-degree color-matching function and standard illumination light D65 as a light source for conversion to RGB image. We empirically selected 5 wavelengths from the obtained 31 wavelengths data, and estimate chromophore concentrations by using the method describe in Sect. 2.2. Appropriate wavelengths set are determined to minimize the residual sum of squares RSS_{wav} as follows.

$$RSS_{wav} = \sum_{c=1}^{N} \sum_{\lambda} [R_{est}(\lambda) - R_{real}(\lambda)]^2, \tag{4}$$

where $R_{est}(\lambda)$ is spectral reflectance calculated from estimated five compornents and $R_{real}(\lambda)$ is spectral reflectance captured using a hyperspectral scanner. N is the number of pixels in the image.

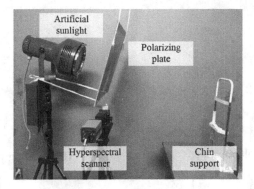

Fig. 3. Experimental set-up.

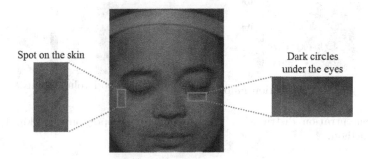

Fig. 4. RGB image of skin.

3.2   Results and Discussion

Appropriate wavelengths set were 470, 510, 570, 630, 700 nm from our results of evaluating using Eq. (3). Figure 5 shows results of estimation at images including pigmented spot on the skin. Melanin concentration map is shown in Fig. 5(a). It is estimated that melanin concentration is high density at pigmented spot area on the skin. Figure 7 shows the result of estimation on dark circles under the eyes. It is also estimated that melanin concentration is high density at the freckle area and the area of dark circles. Shading map is shown in Fig. 7(b). From this result, it is observed that the shading components are estimated appropriately on the aspect of the shape trend in the area. Figure 7(c) shows oxygen saturation map. From this result, it is observed that oxygen saturation is low at dark circles area under the eyes. Figures 6 and 8 show the result of estimation by using conventional multiple regression analysis. Results of both areas show appropriate trend of estimation, however, melanin concentration and blood volume are very low and oxygen saturation are very noisy. From the results, we can see that melanin concentration and blood volume are very low compared to the proposed method, and the spatial distributions are different in some components, and are not valid physiologically valid. It is noted that oxygen saturation are very noisy in the conventional method.

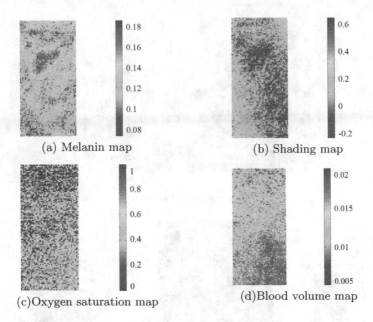

Fig. 5. Concentration distribution of chromophore at spot on the skin by using proposed method.

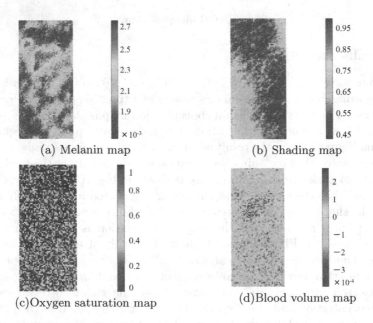

Fig. 6. Concentration distribution of chromophore at spot on the skin by using conventional multiple regression analysis.

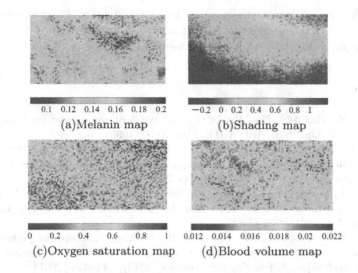

(a)Melanin map   (b)Shading map

(c)Oxygen saturation map   (d)Blood volume map

Fig. 7. Concentration distribution of chromophore at dark circles under the eyes by using proposed method.

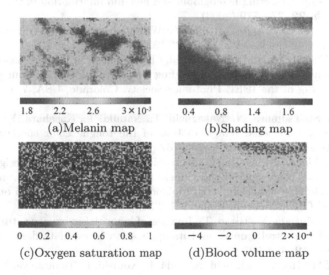

(a)Melanin map   (b)Shading map

(c)Oxygen saturation map   (d)Blood volume map

Fig. 8. Concentration distribution of chromophore at dark circles under the eyes by using conventional multiple regression analysis.

4   Conclusion

We estimated chromophore concentrations from hyperspectral image of skin by using nonlinear estimation method. As a result of melanin concentration map, melanin was high concentration at pigmented spot, freckle and dark circles.

At dark circle area, oxygen saturation was low concentration. From these results, we can conclude that the method by Hirose *et al.* can be applied to real skin images since physiologically valid results were obtained by our study.

References

1. Tsumura, N., Haneishi, H., Miyake, Y.: Independent-component analysis of skin color image. J. Opt. Soc. Am. A. **16**, 2169–2176 (1999)
2. Miyake, Y., Yokoyama, Y., Tsumura, N., Haneishi, H., Miyata, K., Hayashi, J.: Development of multiband color imaging systems for recordings of art paintings. In: Proceeding of the SPIE, vol. 3648, pp. 218–225 (1999)
3. Haneishi, H., Hasegawa, T., Hosoi, A., Yokoyama, Y., Tsumura, N., Miyake, Y.: System design for accurately estimating the spectral reflectance of art paintings. Appl. Opt. **39**, 6621–6632 (2000)
4. Tsumura, N., Kawabuchi, M., Haneishi, H., Miyake, Y.: Mapping pigmentation in human skin from a multi-channel visible spectrum image by inverse optical scattering technique. J. Imaging Sci. Technol. **45**(5), 444–450 (2001)
5. Tsumura, N., Ojima, N., Sato, K., Shiraishi, M., Shimizu, H., Nabeshima, H., Akazaki, S., Hori, K., Miyake, Y.: Image-based skin color and texture analysis/synthesis by extracting hemoglobin and melanin information in the skin. ACM Trans. Graph. **22**, 770–779 (2003)
6. Nishibori, M., Tsumura, N., Miyake, Y.: Why multispectral imaging in medicine? J. Imaging Sci. Technol. **48**(2), 125–129 (2004)
7. Tsumura, N.: Physics and physiologically based image processing based on separation of hemoglobin, melanin and shading information in the skin image. In: 23rd Annual Meeting of the IEEE Photonics Society, Colorado, USA, 7–11 November 2010
8. Yamamoto, S., Tsumura, N., Nakaguchi, T., Namiki, T., Kasahara, Y., Terasawa, K., Miyake, Y.: Regional image analysis of the tongue color spectrum. Int. J. Comput. Assist. Radiol. Surg. **6**, 143–152 (2011)
9. Hirose, M., Akaho, R., Maita, C., Kuroshima, M., Tsumura, N.: Designing spectral sensitivities of mosaic 5-band camera for separating reflectance and pigment components in skin image. In: 11th Finland-Japan Joint Symposium on Optics in Engineering (OIE), Joensuu, Finland, 1–3 September 2015
10. Kikuchi, K., Masuda, Y., Hirao, T.: Imaging of hemoglobin oxygen saturation ratio in the face by spectral camera and its application to evaluate dark circles. Skin Res. Technol. **19**, 499–507 (2013)
11. Kobayashi, M., Ito, Y., Sakauchi, N., Oda, I., Konishi, I., Tsunazawa, Y.: Analysis of nonlinear relation for skin hemoglobin imaging. Opt. Exp. **9**, 802–812 (2001)
12. Hirose, M., Kuroshima, M., Tsumura, N.: Nonlinear estimation of chromophore concentrations, shading and surface reflectance from five band images. In: 23rd Color and Imaging Conference (CIC 23), Darmstadt, Germany, 19–23 October 2015
13. Poirier, G.: Human skin modelling and rendering, Master's thesis (University of Waterloo, 2004) (2004)

A Color Image Database for Haze Model and Dehazing Methods Evaluation

Jessica El Khoury[✉], Jean-Baptiste Thomas, and Alamin Mansouri

Le2i, Université de Bourgogne, Bâtiment Mirande - UFR Sciences and Techniques,
B.P. 47870, 21078 Dijon Cedex, France
jessica.el-khoury@u-bourgogne.fr

Abstract. One of the major issues related to dehazing methods (single or multiple image based) evaluation is the absence of the haze-free image (ground-truth). This is also a problem when it concerns the validation of Koschmieder model or its subsequent dehazing methods. To overcome this problem, we created a database called CHIC (Color Hazy Image for Comparison), consisting of two scenes in controlled environment. In addition to the haze-free image, we provide 9 images of different fog densities. Moreover, for each scene, we provide a number of parameters such as local scene depth, distance from the camera of known objects such as Macbeth Color Checkers, their radiance, and the haze level through transmittance. All of these features allow the possibility to evaluate and compare between dehazing methods by using full-reference image quality metrics regarding the haze-free image, and also to evaluate the accuracy of the Koschmieder hazy image formation model.

1 Introduction

When taking a picture in presence of dust, smoke or water particles hanging in the air, the light emanating from the scene and reaching the camera's sensor is scattered and attenuated. Similarly, the light coming from the light source is scattered by these particles, thus forming the so-called *airlight* [11] and resulting in an undesirable veil that reduces contrast and chroma in the picture [12]. In this context, the image formation can be modeled as the sum of the scene's radiance and the airlight, weighted by a transmission factor $t(x)$ as in Eq. 1:

$$I(x) = J(x)t(x) + A_\infty(1 - t(x)) \tag{1}$$

where x denotes the pixel location. $I(x)$ is the image formed on the camera's sensor. $J(x)$ is the scene radiance. The transmission factor $t(x)$ depends on scene depth d (distance to the sensor) and on the scattering coefficient β of the haze, such that $t(x) = e^{-\beta.d(x)}$ [11]. Unlike more traditional image degradations, haze is a natural, depth-dependent noise that spans non-uniformly over the whole image. The degradation and the loss of information increases with depth, as the amount of fog between the imaged surface and the sensor increases. Hazy and foggy images have also different prevailing color, which depends on the scattering

© Springer International Publishing Switzerland 2016
A. Mansouri et al. (Eds.): ICISP 2016, LNCS 9680, pp. 109–117, 2016.
DOI: 10.1007/978-3-319-33618-3_12

particles density and the ambient light [15]. The process to recover $I(x)$ from $J(x)$ by estimating first, the atmospheric light A_∞ and $t(x)$, is known as dehazing or defogging.

Many dehazing methods have been proposed and compared to each other. Although, there exist a variety of dehazing algorithms for color images, not a single of them is usually accepted to work perfectly neither to work good enough. In addition, the resulting output of these algorithms is highly correlated to the concentration of scattering particles [7].

Image dehazing and its quality evaluation remain difficult processes. Image dehazing is a transdisciplinary challenge, as it requires knowledge from different fields: meteorology to model the fog, optical physics to understand how light is affected by this fog and computer vision, as well as image and signal processing to recover the parameters of the scene. Image quality assessment (IQA) of dehazed images may requires the hazy and the haze-free images of the same real scene to use full-reference image quality metrics, which are captured under the same conditions such as illuminant, viewing geometry and resolution. Existing databases do not meet this feature (cf. Sect. 2). For this reason, we introduce in Sect. 3 an original new color image database devoted to both haze model assessment and dehazing methods evaluation. We then discuss, in Sect. 4, the limitations to invert the haze model without considering the physical aspect of hazy image formation before to conclude.

2   Existing Hazy Image Databases

Several hazy image databases may be used for dehazing investigation. Hazy images databases including the haze-free reference image and other databases without reference. In the first category we find FRIDA (Foggy Road Image DAtabase) [10,18] and FRIDA2 [10,17] that represent evaluation databases for visibility and contrast restoration algorithms. These databases comprise a number of synthetic images with reference of urban road scenes and diverse road scenes, respectively. The view point is close to the one of the vehicle?s driver. The software $SiVIC^{TM}$ was used to build physically-based road environments from a realistic complex urban model and to generate a moving vehicle with a physically-driven model of its dynamic behavior, and virtual embedded sensors. To each image without fog, four foggy images and a depth map are associated. The depth map is required to be able to add fog consistently in the images. Different kinds of fog are added to each of the four associated images: uniform fog, heterogeneous fog, cloudy fog, and cloudy heterogeneous fog. These four types of fog were inserted by applying the Koschmieder's law [11] by weighting differently the attenuation coefficient and/or the atmospheric light with respect to the pixel position. Despite the different aspects that are addressed in this database, simulated images fail to represent accurately the natural phenomena effects [8]. The physical interaction of light with atmospheric particles modifies the perceived colors, while colors in the simulated image maintain their hue information and only their saturation component shifts between the original color (saturated), and the haze color (unsaturated).

WILD (Weather and Illumination Database) [6,14] is an outdoor urban scene database, acquired every hour over seasons. These images are taken under different weather and illumination conditions. Atmospheric conditions, scene distances and temporal data are also associated to images. First, this database cannot be used to compare one dehazed image with a reference due to the variation of illuminant. Second, small changes that could occur would bias a pixel by pixel comparison. Therefore, it appears important to us to build a new database, which does not suffer from these problems and more adequate for such evaluation.

On the other hand, developers often use hazy images of natural scenes, with no reference, which have usually a small size to evaluate dehazing methods within a short time using the minimum amount of resources [2,5]. However, the lack of the haze-free reference image makes the evaluation challenging and less reliable.

3   Proposed Database

In the CHIC database [1], we consider two indoor scenes, Scene A and Scene B. Scenes were set up in a closed rectangular room, which is large enough to simulate the effect of the distance and the fog density on the objects radiance (length = 6.35 m, width = 6.29 m, height = 3.20 m) with a large window (length = 5,54 m, width = 1.5 m) that allows a large amount of omnidirectional outdoor light to get in. It laterally covers the camera and the scenes. The photo session of each scene lasted 20 min. During this limited time, daylight is assumed to remain steady. This experiment was set up on February, from 1:00 to 4:00 p.m. when sunlight was not directly coming in through the window. Thus, the global light is close to the airlight in a cloudy day. Five Macbeth Color Checkers (MCCs) are placed in the scene at different distances to the camera. The farthest one serves to estimate the atmospheric light. This can be useful to follow up the color alteration when haze covers a scene. The scenes components present various colored surfaces types (reflective and glossy surfaces, rough surfaces, etc.).

A fog machine (FOGBURST 1500), which emits a dense vapor that appears similar to fog was used. A large quantity of fog is initially emitted until it is evenly distributed in the room and forms an opaque layer. Fog is then progressively evacuated through the window. This machine operates by evaporation. The vaporization of therein water-based liquid mixed with glycol, is done by heating. The particles of the ejected fog are water droplets, which have approximately the same radius size of the atmospheric fog (1 - 10 μm).

Thereby, in addition to the haze-free image, nine images of different fog levels images of different levels of fog are captured (Table 1), from level 1, the highest fog density, to level 9, the lowest density. This set of images are captured under two illuminants: outdoor daylight and a compound light (outdoor light + ceiling lamp light (fluorescent tube)). For each level, an RGB image was acquired using the color camera Nikon D7100 [4] providing NEF (RAW) and JPEG 6000×4000 images. We used also the spectroradiometer Konica Minolta CS-2000 [3] to measure the transmission of the fog on a white patch of the MCC placed at the back of the scene for each fog density, perpendicularly to the optical path. It was calibrated focusing on the same patch without fog.

3.1 Scenes

- Scene A: The shoot session of this scene was performed around 2:00 p.m. This scene shows a typical indoor view. We put on the table that is placed in the middle, a number of items with different characteristics such as shapes, colors, positions, surface types (glossy or rough surfaces) and textures. The wall behind the scene is half white and the top half with the white lines and the black holes represent distinctive elements to study algorithms handling near edges.
- Scene B: The shoot session of scene B was done two hours later. During this time the temperature of the illuminant significantly changed. Unlike the first one, the distance from the camera to the farthest point is smaller. It contains bigger geometric shapes. The fog densities which are randomly determined are characterized by the transmittance spectrum of each fog level.

The camera stayed still over the shoot session of each scene. However, the illuminant is not the same for both scenes, nor the distance to the camera and the density of fog for the correspondent levels (Table 1).

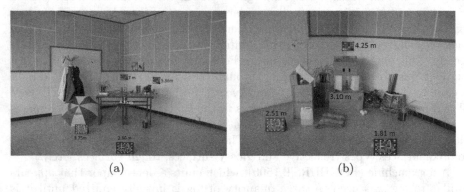

(a)   (b)

Fig. 1. Scene A (a) and Scene B (b). The distances of different MCCs to the camera are shown. The resolution of the image is 6000×4000.

In Table 1, the relative transmittance of fog is calculated with respect to airlight at a given distance over the black patch of original hazy images, as follows:

$$T = 1 - \frac{S_{levelx} - S_{airlight}}{S_{haze-free} - S_{airlight}} \qquad (2)$$

where S_{levelx}, $S_{airlight}$ and $S_{haze-free}$ are the spectral values of green in images of different fog levels, of the airlight image of our database where the scene is completely covered by fog and the haze-free image.

Comparing to outdoor scenes, the light source is located at infinity and the particles forming the synthetic fog are water particles fall in the same range of particles' size, therefore the same scattering law is applied. Since the room where

Table 1. Relative transmittance T of fog in original hazy images of scene A and scene B. Level 1: highest fog density. Level 9: lowest fog density.

T	Level 1	Level 2	Level 3	Level 4	Level 5	Level 6	Level 7	Level 8	Level 9
Scene A	100 %	92 %	90 %	91 %	84 %	71 %	75 %	52 %	28 %
Scene B	100 %	97 %	89 %	91 %	74 %	64 %	55 %	30 %	15 %

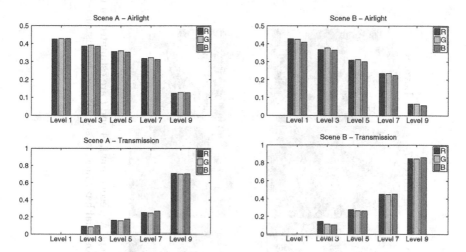

Fig. 2. Estimated A and t obtained for each level of haze for a given distance of the MCC placed at the back of the scene. First row: airlight, second row: transmission. First column: scene A, second column: scene B.

the shoot session was running is not an open place, the airlight color seems to be close to dark gray. According to Fig. 2, the calculated values of A and t are almost the same over channels at all fog levels. All of these facts prove that, the outside conditions are almost fulfilled in our database.

4   Limitation of Koschmieder Model for Image Recovery

Single image dehazing methods, which consider the haze model given in Eq. 1, are usually based on strong assumptions to estimate A_∞ and $t(x)$ from the single RGB hazy image [9,16]. However, the only way to verify these assumptions and the model as well, is to have the haze-free image.

Consequently, A_∞ is the R, G and B values of the fog layer calculated from image level 1, which is uniformly covered by fog. For each level, the airlight $A = A_\infty(1 - t(x))$ is similarly calculated over the black patch of MCC placed at the scene's back (color patch within the red surrounding in Figs. 3 and 4). We subtracted from it the offset values of R, G, and B of a patch of 20×20 pixels of the same black patch from the original image without fog.

Once A_∞ and A are estimated, $t(x)$ of a given scene depth is deduced from the second part of Eq. 1 over the same color chart. Since the distance of each chart

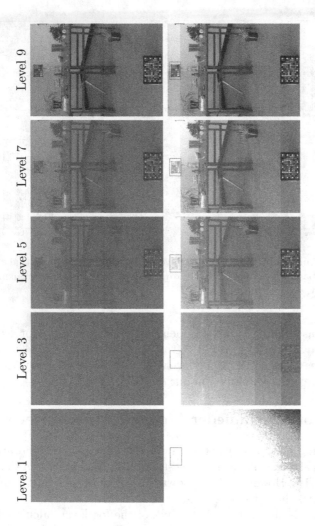

Fig. 3. The original hazy (first row) and the reconstructed images of Scene A (second row). A and t are estimated on the surrounded red color patch. The distance between it and the camera is 7 m. First row: original hazy images, second row: reconstructed images. Cropped image size is 1537×2049.

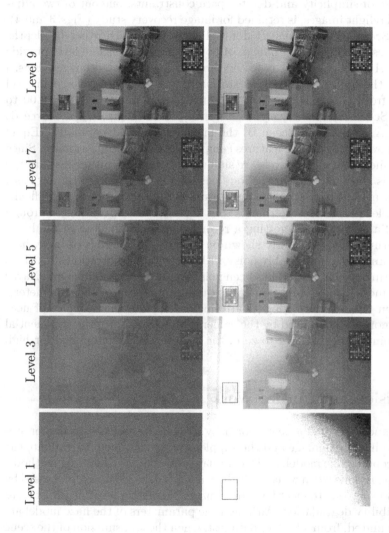

Fig. 4. The original hazy (first row) and the reconstructed images of Scene B (second row). A and t are estimated on the surrounded red color patch. The distance between it and the camera is 4.25 m. First row: original hazy images, second row: reconstructed images. Cropped image size is 1537×3073.

is known, the scattering coefficient is deduced and the transmission matrix is then calculated over the entire image, using approximative depths of secondary objects. Based on the known distances of MCCs, images have been split into four zones. Particular focus should be given to the color patch within the red surrounding, which has an accurate known distance to the camera, and has also the lowest object's transmission.

For the sake of simplicity and due to space constraints, one out of two adjacent levels of daylight images, is retained for image recovery study (Figs. 3 and 4).

Although Scene A and Scene B differ slightly from each other by depths and fog densities, corresponding images of both scenes of the same level provide close values of A and t. This gets reflected through reconstructed images (Figs. 3 and 4), where the area within the red surrounding is poorly recovered in level 1 and level 3 from $t_1 = 0.00$ to $t_2 = 0.09$ in Scene A and from $t_1 = 0.00$ to $t_2 = 0.12$ in Scene B, respectively. From level 5 and on up, when t exceeds 0.17 in Scene A and 0.27 in Scene B, the inversion of the haze model (Eq. 1) succeeds to recover recognizable features comparing to the haze-free image. Since unknown parameters of all fog levels are similarly estimated, this means that the induced error is the same. When the fog density is relatively high (in our case, below level 5), even if the estimation is reasonably accurate, it seems difficult, if not impossible, to compensate thanks to it the lost transmitted light through scattering and absorption and getting a reconstructed image close to the haze-free image features. This is clearly shown on images of low levels of fog, where reconstructed images are noticeably noisy with perceptible saturation shift. This comes to confirm once more what has been pointed out by Narasimhan and Nayar [13], that this model is not valid for depths that are more than a few kilometers. Similarly, when the amount of fog greatly increases, even the radiance of near objects is no more well captured by the camera. Moreover, since the exponential attenuation comes quickly down to zero, the noise is greatly amplified for high fog densities.

5   Conclusion and Future Work

We proposed and described a new color hazy image database of two indoor static scenes. The haze-free image and the supplementary data help to evaluate the commonly accepted haze model, and to evaluate and compare dehazing methods. Such evaluation is done when we consider how much a dehazed image processed by a given method succeeds to meet haze-free image. No matter what circumstances lead up to visibility degradation. Although the parameters of the haze model are accurately estimated, from a level of data lost, when the transmission of the scene is very low, the haze-free image is no longer properly recovered. Koschmieder's model is therefore considered to be not valid for high densities of fog.

Our future work will use this database for an objective assessment of several dehazing methods using IQA indices including full-reference metrics. We will study also the correlation of these metrics with the perceptual judgments as an efficient attempt to develop a proper haze-dedicated evaluating metric.

Acknowledgment. The authors thanks the Open Food System project for funding. This project is a part of The Investments for the Future Programme managed by Bpifrance, www.openfoodsystem.fr.

References

1. CHIC (Color Hazy Image for Comparison). http://chic.u-bourgogne.fr
2. Image dehazing. http://ivrl.epfl.ch/supplementary_material/SFS_ICIP09. Accessed 1 Mar 2016
3. Konica minolta, cs-2000 spectroradiometer. http://sensing.konicaminolta.us/products/cs-2000-spectroradiometer/. Accessed 1 April 2015
4. Users manual, nikon d7100. http://cdn-10.nikoncdn.com/pdf/manuals/dslr/D7100EN.pdf. Accessed 1 April 2015
5. Waterloo ivc dehazed image database. http://ivc.uwaterloo.ca/database/Dehaze/Dehaze-Database.php. Accessed 1 Mar 2016
6. Wild (weather and illumination database). http://www.cs.columbia.edu/CAVE/software/wild/index.php. Accessed 1 April 2015
7. El Khoury, J., Thomas, J.-B., Mansouri, A.: Does dehazing model preserve color information? In: Tenth International Conference on Signal-Image Technology and Internet-Based Systems (SITIS), pp. 606–613. IEEE (2014)
8. El Khoury, J., Thomas, J.-B., Mansouri, A.: Haze and convergence models: experimental comparison. In: AIC 2015 (2015)
9. He, K., Sun, J., Tang, X.: Single image haze removal using dark channel prior. IEEE Trans. Pattern Anal. Mach. Intell. **33**(12), 2341–2353 (2011)
10. IFSTTAR.Frida (foggy road image database). http://www.sciweavers.org/read/frida-foggy-road-imagedatabase-evaluation-database-for-visibility-restoration-algorithms-184350. Accessed 1 April 2015
11. Koschmieder, H.: Theorie der horizontalen Sichtweite: Kontrast und Sichtweite. Keim & Nemnich, Munich (1925)
12. Narasimhan, S.G., Nayar, S.K.: Chromatic framework for vision in bad weather. In: Proceedings of the IEEE Conference on Computer Vision and Pattern Recognition, vol. 1, pp. 598–605. IEEE (2000)
13. Narasimhan, S.G., Nayar, S.K.: Contrast restoration of weather degraded images. IEEE Trans. Pattern Anal. Mach. Intell. **25**(6), 713–724 (2003)
14. Narasimhan, S.G., Wang, C., Nayar, S.K.: All the images of an outdoor scene. In: Heyden, A., Sparr, G., Nielsen, M., Johansen, P. (eds.) ECCV 2002, Part III. LNCS, vol. 2352, pp. 148–162. Springer, Heidelberg (2002)
15. Nayar, S.K., Narasimhan, S.G.: Vision in bad weather. In: The Proceedings of the Seventh IEEE International Conference on Computer Vision, vol. 2, pp. 820–827. IEEE (1999)
16. Tarel, J.-P., Hautière, N.: Fast visibility restoration from a single color or gray level image. In: IEEE 12th International Conference on Computer Vision, pp. 2201–2208. IEEE (2009)
17. Tarel, J.-P., Hautière, N., Caraffa, L., Cord, A., Halmaoui, H., Gruyer, D.: Vision enhancement in homogeneous and heterogeneous fog. IEEE Intell. Transp. Syst. Mag. **4**(2), 6–20 (2012)
18. Tarel, J.-P., Hautière, N., Cord, A., Gruyer, D., Halmaoui, H.: Improved visibility of road scene images under heterogeneous fog. In: IEEE Intelligent Vehicles Symposium (IV), pp. 478–485. IEEE (2010)

Collaborative Unmixing Hyperspectral Imagery via Nonnegative Matrix Factorization

Yaser Esmaeili Salehani[(⊠)] and Saeed Gazor[(⊠)]

Department of Electrical and Computer Engineering,
Queen's University, Kingston, Canada
yaser.esmaeili@gmail.com, gazor@queensu.ca

Abstract. We propose a method of hyperspectral unmixing for the linear mixing model (LMM) while both the spectral signatures of endmembers and their fractional abundances are unknown. The proposed algorithm employs the *non-negative matrix factorization* (NMF) method as well as simultaneous (collaborative) sparse regression model. We formulate the NMF problem along with an averaging over the ℓ_2-norm of the fractional abundances so-called $\ell_{2,q}$-norm term. We show that this problem can be efficiently solved by using the *Karush-Kuhn-Tucker* (KKT) conditions. Our simulations show that the proposed algorithm outperforms the state-of-the-art methods in terms of *spectral angle distance* (SAD) and *abundance angle distance* (AAD).

Keywords: Hyperspectral images · Unmixing · Nonnegative matrix factorization (NMF) · ℓ_0-norm · Collaborative sparse recovery

1 Introduction

Hyperspectral Unmixing methods have been recently developed as the powerful techniques to characterize mixed pixels of the hyperspectral spectrum into a set of constituent spectral signatures called *endmembers*, and the corresponding set of fraction of these endmembers, called *abundances* [2,3,16]. In a linear spectral mixture analysis fashion, we can first identify a collection of pure constituent spectra and then represent the measured spectrum of each mixed pixel with a linear combination of endmembers weighted by their fractional abundances. Using spectral unmixing approach aims to extract endmembers from the hyperspectral image and to compute the corresponding abundances under certain constrains.

In spite of two stages-based unmixing methods that employ both the endmember extraction methods (e.g., N-FINDR [25] and *vertex component analysis* (VCA) [17]) and mixed pixels decomposition methods (i.e., ℓ_2-norm, ℓ_1-norm, and ℓ_0-norm approximation e.g., [5–7]), one-step methods such as *nonnegative matrix factorization* (NMF) [14,19] based approach is highly interested because of its noticeable supports. First of all, the nonnegativity constraints for both spectral signatures and their fractional abundances (called the *abundance nonnegativity constraint* (ANC)) due to the physical consideration are automatically

© Springer International Publishing Switzerland 2016
A. Mansouri et al. (Eds.): ICISP 2016, LNCS 9680, pp. 118–126, 2016.
DOI: 10.1007/978-3-319-33618-3_13

included in the NMF-based methods. Furthermore, it can make decomposition matrices to be more intractable because of a part-based representation of the data, see [4,21] and references therein. The classical NMF problem is a NP-hard optimization problem [24] beyond the very large feasible set of solution without any further constraints over that. Due to the nonconvexity of the corresponding cost function, the algorithm prone to noise corruption and computationally demanding [21]. Although there are various proposed methods based on the NMF approach for unmixing purpose such as $\ell_{1/2}$-norm sparsity constrained [21], substance dependence constrained [26] and manifold regularization into the sparsity constraint [15], they have their own drawbacks and the researches are still working to introduce better (sparser) constrained terms into the cost function in order to improve the current methods.

In this paper, we are initiated to achieve the fact that the fractional abundances of endmembers can be effected by imposing sparsity among the endmembers collaboratively for all hyperspectral pixels. In fact, in hyperspectral images, all the pixels share the same set of spectral signatures of materials lying into a lower dimensional subspace [12]. Although the motivation of simultaneous sparse technique [23] is used in [12] for the unmixing purpose, the spectral library was assumed to be known. Besides, the averaging is applied as an ℓ_1-norm term. Inspired by this motivation, we introduce a new minimization problem that considers the collaborative $\ell_{2,q}$-norm term along with a sparse approximation term for the abundances when the spectral library is also unknown. To solve the acquired minimization problem, we apply the multiplicative updating rule used for the standard NMF problem [13]. We also show that the updating rules will be guarantee to reach a local minimum. The simulation results demonstrate the effectiveness of our proposed method and outperform the other state-of-the-art methods for both metrics of *spectral angle distance* (SAD) and *abundance angle distance* (AAD).

The rest of the paper is organized as follows. Problem formulation for the *linear mixing model* (LMM) and NMF method are briefly described in Sect. 2. Our proposed method for the spectral unmixing is presented in Sect. 3 and we evaluate it by the simulations in Sect. 4. Section 5 concludes the paper.

2   Problem Formulation

In the LMM, the received spectral signature of a pixel in any given spectral band is assumed to be a linear combination of all of the endmembers' spectra present in the pixel at the respective spectral band. The measured reflectance values of the pixel can be provided by a L-dimensional vector $\mathbf{y}$ and can be expressed as $\mathbf{y} = \mathbf{A}\mathbf{x} + \mathbf{e}$, where $\mathbf{y}$ is an $L \times 1$ column vector, $\mathbf{A} = [\mathbf{a}_1, \mathbf{a}_2, ..., \mathbf{a}_N] \in \mathbb{R}_+^{L \times N}$ is the mixing matrix contains N pure spectral signatures (endmembers) with $L >> N$, $\mathbf{x}$ is a $N \times 1$ vector with the corresponding fractional abundances of the endmembers and $\mathbf{e}$ is an $L \times 1$ additive noise vector due to the errors affecting the measurements at each spectral band. The fractional abundances vector $\mathbf{x}$ must satisfy two additional constraints because of the physical considerations as the *abundance nonnegativity constraint* (ANC), $\mathbf{x} \geq 0$, and the *abundance sum-to-one constraint* (ASC), $\mathbf{1}^T\mathbf{x} = 1$. Matrix representation for M pixels can be considered as

$$\mathbf{Y} = \mathbf{AX} + \mathbf{E}, \tag{1}$$

where, $\mathbf{Y} \in \mathbb{R}^{L \times M}$, $\mathbf{X} = [\mathbf{x}_1, \mathbf{x}_2, ..., \mathbf{x}_M] \in \mathbb{R}_+^{N \times M}$ and $\mathbf{E} \in \mathbb{R}^{L \times M}$.

2.1 NMF-Based Methods: An Overview

The goal of NMF is to find two nonnegative matrices $\mathbf{A}$ and $\mathbf{X}$ to approximate a matrix $\mathbf{Y}$ with the size of $L \times M$ as $\mathbf{Y} \approx \mathbf{AX}$, where $N < \min(L, M)$. Then, the loss function for the classic NMF problem can be represented by $\frac{1}{2}\|\mathbf{Y} - \mathbf{AX}\|_2^2$. Finding the global optimal solution for the corresponding minimization problem is difficult due to the nonconvexity of the problem with respect to both $\mathbf{A}$ and $\mathbf{X}$. The regularization method is the natural approach to tackle this problem and to promote the constraints into the cost function. Hence, the ℓ_2-norm regularizer (e.g., [20]) and the ℓ_1-norm regularizer (e.g., [10,11]) are the most common choices in which the former focuses the smooth solution rather than the sparse result and the latter one achieves the sparsity of the spectral signatures dictionary matrix and/or the fractional abundances matrix.

Thinking about the ℓ_0-norm regularizer as the sparsest preference is always challenging since it is an NP-hard optimization problem and cannot be achieved in practice. Thus, some $\ell_p(0 < p < 1)$ regularization methods specifically when $p = \frac{1}{2}$ are the recent interests for unmixing purpose [21]. Accordingly, the cost function can be considered as follows:

$$c(\mathbf{A}, \mathbf{X}) = \frac{1}{2}\|\mathbf{Y} - \mathbf{AX}\|_2^2 + \alpha\|\mathbf{X}\|_{\frac{1}{2}}, \tag{2}$$

where $\|\mathbf{X}\|_{\frac{1}{2}} = \sum_{i=1}^N \sum_{j=1}^M x_{ij}^{\frac{1}{2}}$ and x_{ij} is the corresponding abundance for the i-th endmember at the j-th pixel and $\alpha > 0$ is the Lagrangian parameter. More $\ell_{\frac{1}{2}}$-based methods are also studied for hyperspectral unmixing, e.g., [15,22,26].

The multiplicative updating rules proposed for the standard NMF is used to solve the corresponding minimization problem (2) as follows [21]:

$$\mathbf{A} \leftarrow \mathbf{A}. * \mathbf{YX}^T./\mathbf{AXX}^T \tag{3}$$

$$\mathbf{X} \leftarrow \mathbf{X}. * \mathbf{A}^T\mathbf{Y}./(\mathbf{A}^T\mathbf{AX} + \frac{\alpha}{2}\mathbf{X}^{-\frac{1}{2}}) \tag{4}$$

where $.*$ and $./$ are the element-wise multiplication and division, respectively.

3   Our Proposed Method

The idea of collaborative sparse technique was already used for the unmixing approach in [12] by assuming that the spectral library is known. However, this assumption is not reliable in many application as a blind source separation.

On the other hand, using NMF-based methods are fairly attractive because of their obvious superiorities e.g., [15,21,26] as mentioned earlier.

Here, we first define the following $\ell_{2,q}$-norm based cost function along with the sparsity of the element-wisely fractional abundances term of $\ell_{\frac{1}{2}}$-norm

$$f(\mathbf{A}, \mathbf{X}) = \frac{1}{2}||\mathbf{Y} - \mathbf{A}\mathbf{X}||_2^2 + \alpha||\mathbf{X}||_{\frac{1}{2}} + \beta||\mathbf{X}||_{2,q}^q, \tag{5}$$

where

$$||\mathbf{X}||_{2,q} = \left(\sum_{i=1}^{N} ||\mathbf{x}^i||_2^q \right)^{\frac{1}{q}}, \tag{6}$$

and $||\mathbf{x}^i||_2^q = \left(\sum_{j=1}^{M} |x_{ij}|^2 \right)^{\frac{q}{2}}$ with the similar definition in [18] and $\alpha > 0$ and $\beta > 0$ are the Lagrangian regularizes. In fact, the term of $||\mathbf{X}||_{2,q}^q$ in (5) is the q-th power of $||\mathbf{X}||_{2,q}$ and results in the sum of $||\mathbf{x}^i||_2^q$ over i's. It is obvious that we have the exact averaging of the ℓ_2-norm of vectors $\{\mathbf{x}^i\}$ when $q = 1$, i.e., $\ell_{2,1}$-norm.

The updating rule for the spectral signatures $\mathbf{A}$ keeps the same with (3). To find the updating rule for $\mathbf{X}$, we first take the partial derivative of (5) with respect to $\mathbf{X}$ which gives the following result:

$$\frac{\partial f(\mathbf{A}, \mathbf{X})}{\partial \mathbf{A}} = \mathbf{A}^T \mathbf{A} \mathbf{X} - \mathbf{A}^T \mathbf{Y} + \frac{\alpha}{2} \mathbf{X}^{-\frac{1}{2}} + \beta \mathbf{F}. * |\mathbf{X}|, \tag{7}$$

where

$$\mathbf{F} = q \begin{pmatrix} (||\mathbf{x}^1||_2^2)^{\frac{q}{2}-1} & (||\mathbf{x}^1||_2^2)^{\frac{q}{2}-1} & \cdots & (||\mathbf{x}^1||_2^2)^{\frac{q}{2}-1} \\ (||\mathbf{x}^2||_2^2)^{\frac{q}{2}-1} & (||\mathbf{x}^2||_2^2)^{\frac{q}{2}-1} & \cdots & (||\mathbf{x}^2||_2^2)^{\frac{q}{2}-1} \\ \vdots & \vdots & \ddots & \vdots \\ (||\mathbf{x}^N||_2^2)^{\frac{q}{2}-1} & (||\mathbf{x}^N||_2^2)^{\frac{q}{2}-1} & \cdots & (||\mathbf{x}^N||_2^2)^{\frac{q}{2}-1} \end{pmatrix} . * \text{sign}(\mathbf{X}) \tag{8}$$

and sign function operates element-wisely over $\mathbf{X}$.

Following the *Karush-Kuhn-Tucker* (KKT) conditions and applying the transposition and division, the updating rule can be determined as follows:

$$\mathbf{X} \leftarrow \mathbf{X}. * \mathbf{A}^T \mathbf{Y}./(\mathbf{A}^T \mathbf{A} \mathbf{X} + \frac{\alpha}{2} \mathbf{X}^{-\frac{1}{2}} + \beta \mathbf{F}. * |\mathbf{X}|). \tag{9}$$

The value of Lagrangian parameter α depends on the degree of sparseness for the fractional abundances of endmembers and it can be estimated based on the proportion of ℓ_1-norm of the observed signals to the corresponding ℓ_2-norm as the similar way in [11]. In our simulations, we set a fraction of the value defined in [11] for our proposed method as follows:

$$\alpha = \frac{\eta}{\sqrt{L}} \sum_{k=1}^{L} \frac{\sqrt{M} - \frac{||\mathbf{y}_k||_1}{||\mathbf{y}_k||_2}}{\sqrt{M} - 1}, \tag{10}$$

where $\mathbf{y}_k$ is the k-th band of the observed hyperspectral images and $0 < \eta \le 1$ is a known constant value.

To impose the ASC over the fractional abundances, we append $\delta 1^T$ to $\mathbf{Y}$ and $\mathbf{A}$, respectively, during the iterative process as the same way used in [9] and many literatures afterwards, e.g., [15, 21, 22, 26]. Then, the matrices $\bar{\mathbf{Y}}$ and $\bar{\mathbf{A}}$ take the place of $\mathbf{Y}$ and $\mathbf{A}$ as follows:

$$\bar{\mathbf{Y}} = \begin{bmatrix} \mathbf{Y} \\ \delta 1_M^T \end{bmatrix}, \bar{\mathbf{A}} = \begin{bmatrix} \mathbf{A} \\ \delta 1_N^T \end{bmatrix} \tag{11}$$

where δ is a known constant value that controls the effect of ASC and 1_l is the $l \times 1$ column vector with all elements equal to one.

Now, we show that our proposed method is converging.

Proposition 1. *The loss function in (5) is nonincreasing under (3) and (9).*

Proof. The convergence of the method under the updating rule for $\mathbf{A}$ in (3) can be shown similar to [13]. For the updating rule of $\mathbf{X}$ in (9), we can follow up the same procedure in [21] and shows the cost function in (5) is nonincreasing function under (9).

Our proposed $\ell_{2,q}$-NMF based unmixing method is summarized as the following algorithm.

Algorithm 1. Pseudocode of the collaborative NMF-based unmixing method

INPUT   : The observed matrix data $\mathbf{Y}$
- Set parameters α, β, and δ.
OUTPUT: Spectral signature matrix of endmembers $\mathbf{A}$ and their fractional
             abundances matrix $\mathbf{X}$
- Initialize $\mathbf{A}$ using VCA [17] or randomly from interval $[0, 1]$.
- Initialize $\mathbf{X}$ using $(\mathbf{A}^T\mathbf{A})^{-1}\mathbf{A}^T\mathbf{Y}$.
REPEAT :
- Replace $\mathbf{A}$ and $\mathbf{Y}$ by (11).
- Compute $f_{old} = f(\bar{\mathbf{A}}, \mathbf{X})$ using (5).
- Update $\mathbf{A}$ using (3).
- Update $\mathbf{X}$ using (9).
- Replace $\mathbf{A}$ and $\mathbf{Y}$ by (11).
- Compute $f_{new} = f(\bar{\mathbf{A}}, \mathbf{X})$ using (5).
- Continue if the iteration number is less than I_{max} or $|f_{new} - f_{old}| > \varepsilon$.

---

4   Experimental Results

In this section, we evaluate our proposed method through different experiments. First, we use the USGS library [1] to generate the synthetic data as follows.

We select n_N random spectral signatures from [1] for all of the following experiments. It should be noted that these signatures must be linearly independent. Then, we consider $M = r^2 \times r^2$ pixels of entire image to produce linear mixtures where r is an integer known value. In fact, these pixels are divided into $r \times r$ patches. Each patch is assigned randomly by an integer value, say n_E that is between 2 (to avoid to generate the pure pixels) and m_E shows the maximum number of endmember for pixels involved in the patch. Moreover, the fractional abundances for these spectral signatures are generated randomly with the Dirichlet distribution [8] based on the assigned number of materials for each patch, i.e., n_E. In order to make sure that the number of spectral signatures constructs a mixed pixel has enough contribution to build such pixel, we replace the abundances of all pixels whose their fractional abundances are larger than a threshold, say n_T, with the equal contributions, i.e., $\frac{1}{n_E}$.

Afterwards, we passed the generated pixels through the Additive White Gaussian Noise (AWGN) and observed the outputs. For the evaluation purpose, we use the SAD metric to measure the similarity between the recovered spectral signatures and the ground-truth samples. Besides, we use the AAD metric to find the similarity of the estimated fractional abundances with their ground-truth values. They are defined as follows:

$$\text{SAD}_i = \arccos\left(\frac{\hat{\mathbf{a}}_i^T \mathbf{a}_i}{||\hat{\mathbf{a}}_i|| ||\mathbf{a}_i||}\right), \tag{12}$$

$$\text{AAD}_i = \arccos\left(\frac{\hat{\mathbf{x}}_i^T \mathbf{x}_i}{||\hat{\mathbf{x}}_i|| ||\mathbf{x}_i||}\right), \tag{13}$$

where $\hat{\mathbf{a}}_i$ and $\hat{\mathbf{x}}_i$ represent the estimated spectral signature of i-th material and the corresponding estimated fractional abundances.

Implementation Setting: In our simulations, we set $q = 0.01$ in (5). Also, we set $\eta = 0.5$ and $\beta = 0.2\alpha$ in (10) due to the performance consideration and set $\eta = 1$ for $\ell_\frac{1}{2}$-NMF method as recommended in [21]. Selecting the larger value of δ gives the closer the columns of $\mathbf{X}$ to the full additivity constraint e.g., [21, 26] which leads to more time for unmixing process in simulations. We choose $\delta = 5$ for our experiments over all unmixing methods. Moreover, we set $r = 8$, $n_N = 12$, $m_E = 5$ and $n_T = 0.7$ to generate $M = 4096$ pixels from 12 spectral signatures chosen from [1] with $L = 224$ spectral bands. Thus, each pixel has at most 5 mixed materials where the maximum purity is set to 0.7. Finally, we set $I_{max} = 1000$ and $\varepsilon = 10^{-4}$ in Algorithm 1 as well as $\ell_\frac{1}{2}$-NMF method proposed in [21].

We did several and different experiments and we only report some of the simulation results due to the space limit. First, the unmixing results for a fixed value of *signal-to-noise-ratio* (SNR) is given. Hence, Fig. 1 compares the estimated spectral signatures by our proposed method and the other state-of-the-art methods for 4 sample materials out of 12 while the SNR is set to 25 dB. We can observe that our proposed method gives the closest results to the original spectral signatures of materials compared with the other two unmixing methods.

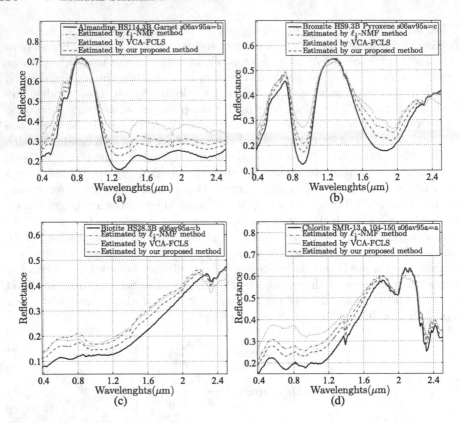

Fig. 1. Comparison of the estimated spectral signatures of four sample materials with the corresponding ground-truth values (SNR = 25 dB) (a) Almandine (b) Bronzite (c) Biotite (d) Chlorite

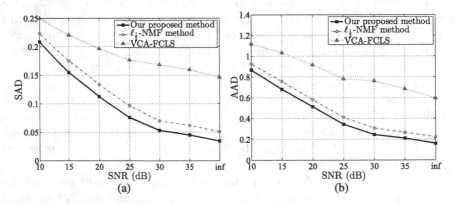

Fig. 2. Simulation results of unmixing methods of (a) SAD (b) AAD as functions of SNRs.

We also evaluate the performance of our proposed method for different values of the noise power. Figure 2 shows the values of SAD and AAD as the functions of SNRs for our proposed method as well as the other two state-of-the-art- methods. The value of inf represents noise-free observation. Our proposed method outperforms the other methods form lower SNRs to the noise-free environments.

5   Conclusion

In this paper, we proposed a method of unmixing hyperspectral images based on the collaborative property of the fractional abundances of endmembers through the NMF problem. We introduced a new cost function based on the NMF and $\ell_{2,q}$-norm to formulate our minimization problem. Then, we applied the multiplicative updating rules to solve the desire objective function. We showed that our proposed method converges and evaluated it by different experiments over the USGS spectral library. Our simulation results illustrated that the proposed method outperformed the other state-of-the-art methods in terms of SAD and AAD metrics. Although the experimental results obtained for the synthetic data analysis are promising, more experiments with real hyperspectral data are also interesting to fully support our contributions.

References

1. http://speclab.cr.usgs.gov/spectral.lib06
2. Bioucas-Dias, J., Plaza, A., Camps-Valls, G., Scheunders, P., Nasrabadi, N., Chanussot, J.: Hyperspectral remote sensing data analysis and future challenges. IEEE Geosci. Remote Sens. Mag. 1(2), 6–36 (2013)
3. Bioucas-Dias, J., Plaza, A., Dobigeon, N., Parente, M., Du, Q., Gader, P.J.C.: Hyperspectral unmixing overview: geometrical, statistical, and sparse regression-based approaches. IEEE J. Sel. Top. Appl. Earth Obs. Remote Sens. 5(2), 354–379 (2012)
4. Cichocki, A., Zdunek, R., Phan, A.H., Amari, S.: Nonnegative matrix and tensor factorizations applications to exploratory multiway data analysis and blind source separation. The Atrium, Chichester (2009)
5. Esmaeili Salehani, Y., Gazor, S., Kim, I.M., Yousefi, S.: Sparse hyperspectral unmixing via arctan approximation of ℓ_0 norm. In: IEEE International Geoscience and Remote Sensing Symposium (IGARSS). pp. 2930–2933, July 2014
6. Esmaeili Salehani, Y., Gazor, S., Yousefi, S., Kim, I.M.: Adaptive lasso hyperspectral unmixing using admm. In: The 27th Biennial Symposium on Communications (QBSC 2014) pp. 159–163, June 2014
7. Esmaeili Salehani, Y., Gazor, S., Kim, I.M., Yousefi, S.: ℓ_0-norm sparse hyperspectral unmixing using arctan smoothing. Remote Sens. 8(3), 187 (2016). http://www.mdpi.com/2072-4292/8/3/187
8. Gelman, A., Carlin, J.B., Stern, H.S., Rubin, D.B.: Bayesian Data Analysis, 2nd edn. Taylor & Francis, Boca Raton (2014)
9. Heinz, D.C., Chang, C.I.: Fully constrained least squares linear mixture analysis for material quantification in hyperspectral imagery. IEEE Trans. Geosci. Remote Sens. 39(3), 529–545 (2001)

10. Hoyer, P.O.: Non-negative sparse coding. In: Proceedings of the IEEE Workshop Neural Networks for Signal Processing XII, Martigny pp. 557–565 (2002)
11. Hoyer, P.O.: Non-negative matrix factorization with sparseness constraints. J. Mach. Learn. Res. **5**, 1457–1469 (2004)
12. Iordache, M.D., Bioucas-Dias, J., Plaza, A.: Collaborative sparse regression for hyperspectral unmixing. IEEE Trans. Geosci. Remote Sens. **52**(1), 341–354 (2014)
13. Lee, D.D., Seung, H.S.: Algorithms for non-negative matrix factorization. In: Advances in Neural Information Processing Systems pp. 556–562 (2001)
14. Lee, D.D., Seung, H.: Learning the parts of objects with nonnegative matrix factorization. Nature **401**(6755), 788–791 (1999)
15. Lu, X., Wu, H., Yuan, Y., Yan, P., Li, X.: Manifold regularized sparse NMF for hyperspectral unmixing. IEEE Trans. Geosci. Remote Sens. **51**(5), 2815–2826 (2013)
16. Ma, W.K., Bioucas-Dias, J., Chan, T.H., Gillis, N., Gader, P., Plaza, A., Ambikapathi, A., Chi, C.Y.: A signal processing perspective on hyperspectral unmixing: insights from remote sensing. IEEE Sig. Process. Mag. **31**(1), 67–81 (2014)
17. Nascimento, J., Bioucas-Dias, J.: Vertex component analysis: a fast algorithm to unmix hyperspectral data. IEEE Trans. Geosci. Remote Sens. **43**(8), 898–910 (2005)
18. Nie, F., Huang, H., Cai, X., Ding, C.: Efficient and robust feature selection via joint $\ell_{2,1}$-norms minimization. Adv. Neural Inf. Process. Syst. **23**, 1813–1821 (2010)
19. Paatero, P., Tapper, U.: Positive matrix factorization: a non-negative factor model with optimal utilization of error estimates of data values. Environmetrics **5**(2), 111–126 (1994)
20. Pauca, V.P., Piper, J., Plemmons, R.J.: Nonnegative matrix factorization for spectral data analysis. Linear Algebra Appl. **416**(1), 29–47 (2006)
21. Qian, Y., Jia, S., Zhou, J., Robles-Kelly, A.: Hyperspectral unmixing via $l_{\frac{1}{2}}$ sparsity-constrained nonnegative matrix factorization. IEEE Trans. Geosci. Remote Sens. **49**(11), 4282–4297 (2011)
22. Rajabi, R., Ghassemian, H.: Spectral unmixing of hyperspectral imagery using multilayer NMF. IEEE Geosci. Remote Sens. Lett. **12**(1), 38–42 (2015)
23. Tropp, J.A.: Algorithms for simultaneous sparse approximation. part II: Convex relaxation. Sig. Process. **86**(3), 589–602 (2006)
24. Vavasis, S.A.: On the complexity of nonnegative matrix factorization. SIAM J. Optim. **20**(3), 1364–1377 (2009)
25. Winter, M.E.: N-findr: an algorithm for fast autonomous spectral end-member determination in hyperspectral data. In: Proceedings of theStorage and Retrieval for Image and Video Databases (SPIE). vol. 3753, pp. 266–275 (1999)
26. Yuan, Y.: Fu, m. abd Lu, X.: Substance dependence constrained sparse nmf for hyperspectral unmixing. IEEE Trans. Geosci. Remote Sens. **53**(6), 2975–2986 (2015)

A New Method for Arabic Text Detection in Natural Scene Image Based on the Color Homogeneity

Houda Gaddour[1(✉)], Slim Kanoun[1], and Nicole Vincent[2]

[1] Miracl Laboratory, Sfax University, Sfax, Tunisia
houda.gaddour@yahoo.fr, slim.kanoun@gmail.com
[2] Lipade Laboratory, Paris Descartes University, Paris, France
Nicole.Vincent@mi.parisdescartes.fr

Abstract. Text detection in natural scene image is still open research topics. Particularly, for Arabic text, a very few studies have been proposed. In this paper, we propose a method for Arabic text detection in natural scene image based on the color homogeneity. Starting from the MSER idea and instead of relying on a range of unique thresholds we calculate a range of pairs of thresholds for each channel in the RGB space in order to generate a set of binary maps. Following extraction of connected components of each binary map we apply a first filtering according to a stability criterion of the written texts to extract candidate components regardless of the language. Then, through the characteristics of the Arabic script we make a second screening to found candidates to keep only those that define a text in the Arabic language.

Keywords: Natural scene image · Arabic text detection · Color homogeneity

1 Introduction

Text detection in natural scene images is an important research subject for content based image analysis field. In this framework, several research works are proposed in lasts years. Nevertheless, we can notice generally several restrictions have been made in the studies. In fact, the type of the text can influence the choice of the used method. Text can be incrusted in the image or natural text written on flat surfaces or on any surface in scene images. Furthermore, the alphabet used for the text gives different aspects that cannot be handled in the same way. Unlike artificial or encrusted text, the natural text can be small and sometimes not readable because it is not intended to be. Then, natural text is difficult to detect and less work has been made in this direction. In the following, we will focus our study on text detection in natural scene image. Existing methods for scene text detection can roughly be categorized into two approaches: approach based on regions segmentation and approach based on texture and learning text properties.

The first approach makes image segmentation into regions and groups them in regions of characters and words. It is based on the color characteristics or on the pixel gray level areas or on the high contrast with the background through the binary information or the properties of the region contours. In [1] three specific text characteristics are applied to generate three contour maps as the Canny filter. For each candidate text

© Springer International Publishing Switzerland 2016
A. Mansouri et al. (Eds.): ICISP 2016, LNCS 9680, pp. 127–136, 2016.
DOI: 10.1007/978-3-319-33618-3_14

boundary, one or more candidate characters are then segmented with a local threshold based on the neighboring pixels. In [2], Sobel filter is used to create a contour map combining four contour maps according to the four directions i.e. horizontal, vertical, oblique top right and top left oblique. A model of scale space with N-levels is constructed and spatial responses to the Laplace Gauss filters are computed to generate a set of text candidates based on the character stroke width. A distribution of the strongest responses from the space scale model is used to check whether a candidate is a text area or not.

In some works, the color information is the basis of its proposed method. In [3], after color constancy and a noise reduction stage, the output image is passed through a color quantization step made by the minimum-variance method proposed in [4]. Indeed, pixels are grouped on the difference basis between their values. N binary maps are generated to retrieve a set of connected components (CCs). These CCs are passed through an initial screening where the regions are analyzed on the basis of geometric properties. A second screening based on the characteristics of the HOG descriptor is achieved. Park et al. [5] consider that the texts are homogeneous in space and use a labeling process that divides roughly an image into multiple layers. Noise pixels are then removed thanks to a median filter. Finally, chromatic and achromatic components are separated by a K-means segmentation method [6]. MSER technical [7] is the most used technique for reliable extraction of CCs. Moreover, the MSER was used as the pretreatment step for detection methods in [8–11], where the authors showed that this method is able to detect text characters as homogeneous components. The Stroke Width Transform (SWT) was their filtering method.

The second approach is based on the assumption that text is characterized by a dense area. This can be equated with a more or less regular pattern texture that enables to distinguish text from background. These texture properties are characterized by techniques based on the Gabor filter [12], the spatial variance, the wavelet [13], the Fourier transform, etc. Yi describes a method in [14] to locate text regions. First, adjacent characters [14] are grouped as candidate patch images. Then, features are extracted using Haar gradient maps. In [15] a texture-based approach is applied based on two characteristics namely contrast and color homogeneity applied on a segmentation of textured pattern using the EM segmentation method.

Most of the proposed works are based on binary or grayscale images through morphological operators, a contour analysis, gradients or wavelets. However, in case of noisy or poorly contrasted images, a detection system will be less efficient. Indeed, the color helps in complex environments. Some works based on color assume that text characters are monochrome and propose color-based methods founded on the dominant color of text through a color quantized histogram. In this case, the text boxes are assumed to have the same color index [16, 17]. This method works well when the text characters are perfectly monochromatic. However, it is not reliable if the processed image has low contrast between the foreground and background. Often it is useful to examine more than a color space [18]. To be able to touch all zones of different intensities (light or dark), the MSERs based methods, have become the focus of several recent works [10, 19] in order to detect all components having a stable uniform color. In this sense we note that the detection of a homogeneous area is not suitable with the search for pixels below or above a given threshold on the opposite it is more significant if the search is between two thresholds interval defining.

In the following, we will focus our study on the natural Arabic text in scene images. Besides the lack of work for the Arabic language has motivated this study. We exploit effectively the color information for the text regions identification in the presence of surrounding noise, complex backgrounds and lighting problems which can degrade the color contrast of the text relative to the background. We propose a method based on the color homogeneity of the text regions and on some Arabic language characteristics to detect the text boxes contained in natural scene images. We prove, through various experiments, the contribution of this method in detecting Arabic texts regions appearing in a scene image.

2 Proposed Method

Text in a scene image generally has a homogeneous color with respect to that of the background. We present here two main steps of the process. First, text candidate regions are extracted and selected in any language with readability criteria and then they are filtered according to the Arabic alphabet characteristics.

2.1 Text Candidates Extraction

In most studies, text candidates extraction is based on a single threshold of a gray level image either a global [20] or a local [21] threshold. However, the use of a single threshold binarization opposes the search for a uniform color. Also, we can see in the real scenes images, it is not easy to know the precise zone of the text color and the approach even can fall in case when the text is polychrome. In our case, we consider homogeneity property in a more strict sense. Indeed, a double dynamic thresholding extracts color uniformity, more accurately than light or dark. This makes more sense in a color context. For this, a range of threshold pairs is applied to the image.

Binary Maps Generation. To fix these pairs of thresholds, we start by clustering the colors in the image to generate the most representative colors in the image. The k-means algorithm classifies the color pixels and creates clusters. In the RGB color space, each channel R, G, or B varies from 0 to 255. To each channel corresponds a grayscale image I_c (c = R or G or B). For each image I_c we apply a k-means to pixel color for dividing the color space into N zones, each of which defines a set of colors considered as similar in the image.

- Input of k-means: As the results of k-means clustering algorithm is depending on the initialization of the class centers, we have chosen to fix them in a deterministic way. N initial centers are uniformly distributed as:

$$C_k = min + k * ((max - min)/(N))$$ (1)

min and max respectively represents the minimum and maximum value of gray levels in the image I_c and $k \in [0, N-1]$.

- Iterations: at each iteration, we evaluate the membership of each pixel to N clusters and we associate it with the class with minimum Euclidean distance. Thereafter new centers are calculated from the clusters as:

$$C_k = \sum (x_{jk})/p_k \tag{2}$$

x_{jk}: is the value of a pixel j associated with the class k the cardinal of which is p_k when $k \in [0, N-1]$ and $j \in [1, p_k]$.

- Output of k-means: final clusters are characterized by their centers, they form different colors defined by a value interval with extremity $S1$ and $S2$ that are used as a pair of thresholds. The thresholds are calculated as follows:

$$\left. \begin{array}{l} S1_k = \left\{ \begin{array}{ll} min & \text{for } k = 0 \\ S2_{k-1} & \text{for } 1 <= k < N \end{array} \right. \\ S2_k = \left\{ \begin{array}{ll} (C_k + C_{k+1})/2 & \text{for } 0 <= k < N-1 \\ max & \text{for } k = N-1 \end{array} \right. \end{array} \right\} k \in [0, N-1] \tag{3}$$

Therefore, the found thresholds divide the axis of the gray levels into N distinct intervals for which $S1_k$ and $S2_k$ are the two extremities of the kth interval. Following a series of experiments made, we empirically have chosen a value of N equal to 8 for our experiments corresponding to the number of colors that the human eye can easily distinguish. Therefore, 8 pairs of thresholds to 8 intervals, so 8 binary maps are found after binarization with two thresholds.

The binary map of each Ik_c interval is generated by assigning the value '1' for the pixels belonging to the interval while fixing the remaining pixel values to '0'. This processing function is reflected as follows:

$$IK_c(x_i) = \left\{ \begin{array}{l} 1 \text{ if } S1_k <= x_i <= S2_k \ (x_i \text{ is the pixel number of the image } I_c) \\ 0 \ Otherwise \end{array} \right. \tag{4}$$

The above process is repeated for each image I_c linked to the three channels R, G and B. Finally, $3N$ binary maps are generated. The Fig. 1 shows the output of this step on a real scene image with '$N = 8$'. We can notice that irrespective of its color in the image, the text must necessarily appear at least in one of 24 (8*3) binary maps which guarantees us both a good extractor of connected components and that all text zones in the picture will be detected.

We will later extract the connected components from each of binary map and filter them in several stages to retain only the text candidates. These steps will be explained below.

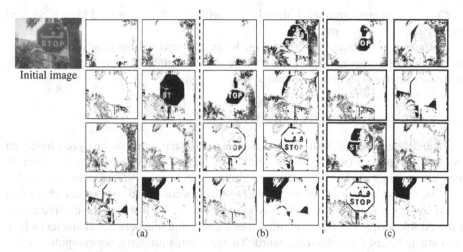

Initial image

(a)   (b)   (c)

Fig. 1. All binary Maps for $N = 8$ (a) for I_R (b) for I_G (c) for I_B

Text Candidates Filtering According to Area Stability. In the binary maps we have defined the CCs that can be considered as text candidate regions. The MSER technique is based on the idea of taking the regions which remain nearly the same throughout a wide range of thresholds. We cannot use the same process because our CCs are not characterized in the same way, then we operate our first contribution, to have split color space into zones across a range of pairs thresholds, to test stability of candidate regions by varying the color areas intervals.

Indeed, we propose a new elimination criterion called double stability test. This criterion tests the stability of the regions through a range of thresholds pairs. In this sense, for each connected component CC_i looking at its evolution by varying the two extremities of the grayscale interval [$S1$, $S2$] either increasing (decreasing $S1$ and increase $S2$) or reducing it (increasing $S1$ and decreasing $S2$). For a text component, surface remains relatively stable since the writing is sharp and is contrasted with respect to the rest of the image. For a non-text component, in most cases there will be a greater variation in the surface of the component. This processing function is reflected as follows:

$$\text{Surface}(CC_i) - \text{Surface}(CC_{1i}) < \varepsilon \qquad (5)$$

and

$$\text{Surface}(CC_i) - \text{Surface}(CC_{2i}) < \varepsilon \qquad (6)$$

Where:

ε: is the area stability threshold.

CC_i: is extracted from the binary image defined by two threshold [$S1$, $S2$].

CC_{1i}: is extracted from the binary image defined by two threshold [$S1 + y$, $S2 - y$] where y it's a level for reducing.

CC_{2i}: is extracted from the binary image defined by two threshold $[S1- y, S2 + y]$ where y it's a level for increasing.

At the end of this step, we see in Fig. 3-b that all text written in any language was selected but also other non-text areas that we need to further filter according to specific characteristics for a particular language.

2.2 Arabic Text Candidates Extraction

Text candidates regions, extracted in the previous step, are first analyzed based on geometric properties (width, height, area). The regions that do not respect geometric lines are eliminated. The remaining candidates are mainly filtered with two Arabic features. Firstly, an entity in an Arabic text is usually a combination of several characters linked by ligatures to form a pseudo-word or a word. This is due to the cursive nature of the Arabic script. The ligature introduces a horizontal line between characters which has a stable height throughout the word. To exploit this property, we compute vertical projection profiles histogram of the CCs. On this histogram, ligatures appear with a constant height. Figure 2-a shows that the criterion of the existence of ligatures in Arabic words is very remarkable while for Latin words it does not appear. Secondly, the baseline corresponds to the line of pixels having the maximum value. If the word or pseudo-word has a single dominant peak in this case we can assume that it is an Arabic word. The vertical projection in Fig. 2-b illustrates the existence of the lonely peak that corresponds

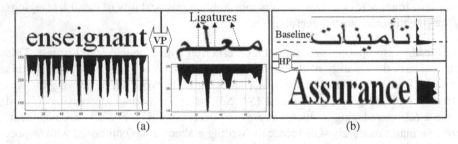
(a) (b)

Fig. 2. Arabic text characteristics (a) Vertical projection (VP) on Latin and Arabic word (b) Horizontal projection (HP) on Latin and Arabic word.

(a)   (b)   (c)

Fig. 3. Text regions detected (a) All of the regions found in the extraction step, regions number = 329 (b) after filtering by color stability, text candidates number = 21 (c) after filtering according to Arabic features, Arabic text regions number = 1.

to the baseline in Arabic word. We note that for a Latin word, histogram is very different, but in Arabic word a second significant maximum is present.

Note that these two features are effective only for horizontal text regions. We notice in Fig. 3-c that we could eliminate false positive candidate region by such a process and only Arabic horizontal text regions are selected.

3 Experiments Results

The proposed method has been evaluated by using our dataset. Experimental results are then presented and discussed.

3.1 Evaluation of Arabic Text Extraction

As there is no public database of natural scene images designed for the detection of Arabic text, the proposed method was evaluated on our own database. To initiate it, we collected 50 images each containing written text areas together with the Latin and Arabic alphabet. All images in our database are captured natural scene images using a digital camera at 92 dpi resolution.

We manually built ground truth associated with this base in which we edited the coordinates of the bounding box of each pseudo-word in the image as well as its width and height. An entity is considered detected if its bounding box has a sufficient common surface in relation to that existing in the ground truth. The results for the experiments on text extraction are summarized in Table 1 where the number of existing pseudo-words, the number of detected pseudo-words, the number of false alarms and the corresponding values for recall and precision are listed.

Table 1. Experimental results for text extraction.

Number of images	50
Number of pseudo-words	307
Number of correct detected pseudo-words	274
Number of false positives detected pseudo-words	33
Recall rate	0.89
Precision rate	0.78

The algorithm of Arabic text detection gives a recall of 0.89 and an accuracy of 0.78. Thus, we conclude that our method achieves promising results. However, the accuracy is relatively low, which explains that the false positive rate is quite high. The detection of these non-text regions can be improved by adding other Arabic alphabet characteristics analysis.

3.2 Evaluation of Text Candidate Extraction

In order to show the contribution of our method we compare our text candidates' extraction algorithm based on a range of two thresholds to MSER algorithm based on a unique thresholds range. To the output of the system, we applied the same stages of selections to generate Arab text candidates. The precision and recall of our system is relatively better with our proposed algorithm than with MSER algorithm for Arabic text candidates extracted as shown in Table 2.

Table 2. Comparaison of our text candidates extraction algorithm to MSER algorithm.

	with MSER algorithm	with our text candidates extraction algorithm
Recall	0.63	**0.89**
Precision	0.57	**0.78**

These encouraging results can be improved by incorporating other descriptors of Arabic texts to detect the variability of orientations and distortion of perspective to more robustly detect all type of text before being recognized and retrieved.

3.3   Discussion

The proposed method still has several limitations that appear either after the filtering step depending on color stability criterion or after the filtering step as characteristics of Arabic illustrated in the examples listed in Table 3 below. Several reasons are discussed in the following.

Table 3. Final results of detection on some other sample images.

Original image	All CCs	CCs detected after filtering by color stability	CCs detected after filtering according to the characteristics of the Arabic language
	(a)	(b)	(c)
	(d)	(e)	(f)

On the one hand, we notice the existence of false positives detected which has an influence on the accuracy rate. The detection of these non-text CCs can be improved by adding the analysis of other characteristics associated with the Arabic alphabet. In addition, some CCs texts, particularly Latin characters are not detected at the first screening (Table 3-b and e). For this, an improvement in the color quantization step is suggested either by using a three-dimensional k-means or a transition from RGB space to another color space such as HSV or L*a*b space for a good distribution of color levels and thereafter a range of more specific pairs of thresholds.

On the other hand, the results found for the image shown in Table 3-f shows that the proposed method is not able to detect the Arab texts oriented or curved. It seems it is required to set up a new descriptor for multi-oriented Arabic texts lines. Finally the isolated Arabic characters with no ligatures are not detected as letters ﺭ ﺍ, ﺡ us is shown in Table 3-c. They may be reintroduced at a later stage.

4 Conclusion and Future Works

We presented a new method for detection and localization of Arabic text in natural scene images based on color. The basic idea of this approach is the consistency of the text color that distinguishes it from the foreground and from the other existing objects in the same image. For this, we propose to use a range of pairs of thresholds to construct a set of binary images rather than dividing the color space in dark and bright. Then, by analyzing the color stability of the connected components, the filtering on the connected components is done regardless to language text candidate regions. They form the entrance to a second filtering according to a criterion related to the Arabic alphabet and get out Arabic regions.

In the future, we aim at enhancing the candidate filtering part in order to be effective for all types of texts and images with complex background. For this, an improvement in the binary maps generation step is suggested either by using a three-dimensional k-means or transition from RGB space to another color space such as HSV or L*a*b space for a good distribution of color levels and thereafter a range of more precise pairs of thresholds. On the other hand, it is needed to set up a new descriptor for multi-oriented Arabic texts lines.

References

1. Shijian, L., Chen, T., Tian, S., Lim, J.H., Tan, C.L.: Scene text extraction based on edges and support vector regression. Int. J. Doc. Anal. Recogn. (IJDAR) **18**(2), 125–135 (2015)
2. Sun, Q., Lu, Y.: Text detection from natural scene images using scale space model. In: Zhang, W., Yang, X., Xu, Z., An, P., Liu, Q., Lu, Y. (eds.) IFTC 2012. CCIS, vol. 331, pp. 156–161. Springer, Heidelberg (2012)
3. Fraz, M., Sarfraz, S.: Exploiting color information for better scene text detection and recognition. Int. J. Doc. Anal. Recogn. **18**(2), 153–167 (2015)
4. Heckbert, P.S.: Color image quantization for frame buffer display. In: SIGGRAPH, pp. 297–307 (1982)

5. Park, J.-H., Yoon, H., Lee, G.-S.: Automatic segmentation of natural scene images based on chromatic and achromatic components. In: Gagalowicz, A., Philips, W. (eds.) MIRAGE 2007. LNCS, vol. 4418, pp. 482–493. Springer, Heidelberg (2007)
6. MacQueen, J.B.: Some methods for classification and analysis of multivariate observations. In: BSMSP, pp. 281–297 (1967)
7. Matas, J., Chum, O., Urban, M., Pajdla, T.: Robust wide baseline stereo from maximally stable extremal regions. In: BMVC, pp. 1–10 (2002)
8. Epshtein, B., Ofek, E., Wexler, Y.: Detecting text in natural scenes with stroke width transform. In: CVPR, pp. 2963–2970 (2010)
9. Chen, H., Tsai, S., Schroth, G., Chen.: Robust text detection in natural images with edge-enhanced maximally stable extremal region. In: ICIP, pp. 2609–2612 (2011)
10. Felhi, M., Bonnier N., Tabone, S.: A skeleton based descriptor for detecting text in real scene images. In: ICPR, pp. 282–285 (2012)
11. Xiaoming, H., Shen, T., Wang, R., Gao, C.: Text detection and recognition in natural scene images. In: ICEDIF, pp. 44–49 (2015)
12. Jain, A.K., Bhattacharjee, S.K.: Address block location on envelopes using gabor filters. Pattern Recogn. **25**, 1459–1477 (1992)
13. Mao, W., Chung, F., Lam, K., Siu, W.: Hybrid chinese/english text detection in images and video frames. In: ICPR, vol. 3, pp. 1015–1018 (2002)
14. Chucai, Y., Yingli, T.: Text extraction from scene images by character appearance and structure modeling. Comput. Vis. Image Underst. **117**, 182–194 (2012)
15. Anouel, H.: Detection and location text in natural scene images: application to the detection of moroccan number plates. Doctoral thesis. Mohammed V-Agdal University (2012)
16. Kim, S.K., Kim, D.W., Kim, H.J.: A recognition of vehicle license plate using a genetic algorithm based segmentation. In: ICIP, vol. 1, pp. 661–664 (1996)
17. Gllavata, J., Ewerth, R., Freisleben, B.: Text detection in images based on unsupervised classification of high-frequency wavelet coefficients. In: ICPR, vol. 1, pp. 425–428 (2004)
18. Li, H., Doermann, D., Kia, O.: Automatic text detection and tracking in digital video. IEEE Trans. Image Process. **9**, 147–156 (2000)
19. Yin, X.C., Yin, X., Huang, K., Hao, H.W.: Robust text detection in natural scene images. IEEE Trans. Pattern Anal. Mach. Intell. **36**(5), 970–983 (2014)
20. Zhong, Y., Karu, K., Jain, A.: Locating text in complex color images. In: ICDAR, vol. 1, pp. 146–149 (1995)
21. Ohya, J., Shio, A., Akamatsu, S.: Recognizing characters in scene images. IEEE Trans. Pattern Anal. Mach. Intell. **16**, 214–220 (1994)

Measuring Spectral Reflectance and 3D Shape Using Multi-primary Image Projector

Keita Hirai[✉], Ryosuke Nakahata, and Takahiko Horiuchi

Graduate School of Advanced Integration Science, Chiba University,
1-33, Yayoi-cho, Inage-ku, Chiba 263-8522, Japan
{hirai,horiuchi}@faculty.chiba-u.jp

Abstract. This paper presents a method to measure spectral reflectance and 3D shape of an object. For realizing these measurements, we applied a multi-primary image projector as a computational illumination system. This multi-primary image projector employs a light source which is programmable and can reproduce any spectral power distributions. In other words, the projector can reproduce 2D pattern projections with arbitrary spectra. In our actual measurements, we developed an imaging system by synchronizing the multi-primary image projector and a highspeed monochrome camera. First, the surface spectral reflectance of an object in a darkroom was obtained based on a finite-dimensional linear model of spectral reflectances. In the spectral reflectance measurements, nine basis images were projected and captured by the synchronized imaging system. Then spectral reflectance at each camera image coordinate was estimated from the captured nine images. Next, structured lights were projected for reconstructing 3D shape. We applied eight binary image projections and a conventional 3D shape reconstruction algorithm to our study. In summary, seventeen images were projected and captured for measuring spectral reflectance and 3D shape. The projection and capturing speed of the seventeen images is 0.085 s on the system specification. In the validation experiments, we could obtain spectral reflectance of X-rite ColorChecker with the average color difference ΔE_{ab}^* of approximately 4. We also confirmed that precise 3D shapes could be reconstructed by our method.

Keywords: Spectral reflectance · 3D shape · Fast measurement · Computational illumination system · Multi-primary image projector

1 Introduction

Measurements of object reflectance properties are important works in the research fields of computer vision, computer graphics, and color image analysis. Notably, color and geometric information are significant factors to determine object reflectance characteristics. For measuring these properties, various techniques have been proposed. In particular, computational illumination techniques and active lighting systems have been developed as useful tools to measure the reflectance properties.

© Springer International Publishing Switzerland 2016
A. Mansouri et al. (Eds.): ICISP 2016, LNCS 9680, pp. 137–147, 2016.
DOI: 10.1007/978-3-319-33618-3_15

Structured light projections have been applied to geometric calibrations and 3D shape measurements [1–3]. In these cases, a projector is generally used as a computational pattern illumination system. However, these researches mainly focus on the measurement of only geometric information. Almost related researches for measuring geometric information have not addressed accurate color measurements.

On the other hand, the techniques for measuring object color information have been also developed. Since measurements of surface spectral reflectance provide accurate color reproduction, various approaches based on active lighting systems have been recently proposed for measuring spectral reflectance [4–8]. In these previous systems, LEDs or spectral light sources are mainly used as active lighting systems. Then it is difficult for these lighting systems to implement 3D shape acquisitions based on the structured light projections.

In the research area of computer vision, a lot of methods based on inverse rendering techniques have been actively developed for recovering surface reflectance properties of both 3D shape and RGB color information [9–11]. In addition, several studies for digital archiving have measured 3D shape and spectral information simultaneously, because spectral information is significant for precise color recording in cultural heritage [12–17]. In these conventional methods, multi-band or multi-spectral cameras were used for acquiring spectral information. However, there are no projector-based computational illumination systems (active lighting systems) and techniques for rapidly measuring 3D shape and spectral reflectance.

In this research, therefore, we propose an imaging system to measure these reflectance properties at high speed. For achieving the goal, we apply a multi-primary image projector [18,19] to our measurement. The projector was developed to reproduce 2D image patterns with arbitrary spectra. This projector is a useful tool to project both structured light and spectrally-modulated illumination. Then we synchronized the projector with a highspeed monochrome camera for projecting and capturing computationally-illuminated images. In our measurements, first, surface spectral reflectance of an object in a dark-room is obtained based on the lighting technique with five spectral basis functions [5]. Then, binary stripe patterns [1] are projected for reconstructing 3D shape. Finally, we will discuss the measurement accuracies and time of spectral reflectance and 3D shape through our experiments. In addition, we apply the measured data to object relighting.

2   Multi-primary Image Projector

In this section, we briefly introduce the multi-primary image projector [18,19]. Figure 1 shows the configuration and projection principle of the projector. The image projection principle is practically the same as that used by digital light processing (DLP) projectors. The projected multi-primary images are produced by multiplexing time-sequential 2D pattern projections with various primary illuminant spectra. The time-sequential 2D image patterns correspond to the spatial weight distributions of each primary illuminant. Observers (cameras)

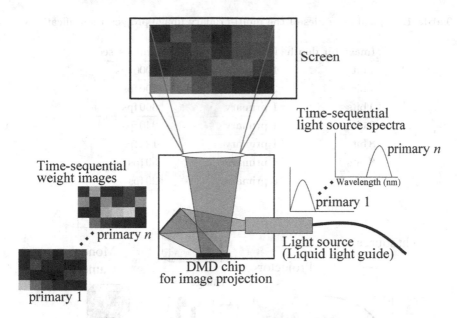

Fig. 1. Configuration and projection principle of the multi-primary image projector

perceive projected patterns that are expressed by spatially weighted SPDs of mixed multi-primary illuminants.

As shown in Fig. 1, the multi-primary image projector is mainly configured with a light source component and an image projection component. The light source component of the projector consists of Optronic Laboratories OL490, which is programmable using a computer. It is composed of a xenon lamp source, grating, a DMD chip, and a liquid light guide. The wavelength resolution is in the range of 380–780 nm. In this study, the sampling pitch for calculating the spectra is set at an interval of 10 nm. This sampling pitch is sufficient for practical spectral reflectance calculations. The image projection component of our prototype is based on a Texas Instruments DLP Lightcrafter. The original LED-based RGB primary colors were replaced with the above spectral light source. The present system uses a DMD chip with a resolution of 608×684 pixels for the image projection.

In summary, the grating and the DMD in the light source of the projector produces spectra, whereas the DMD in an image projection reproduces a monochromatic image with each light source spectrum. The light source and the image projection components are both controlled by a computer to project image sequences synchronously. A trigger signal is sent from the image projection component to the light source component. Table 1 shows the specifications of our multi-primary image projector. The increase of the number of time-sequential primaries means the decrease of light energy of each primary color. In other words, if it is necessary to reproduce high-intensity projection and reduce imaging noises, the projection speed of each primary should be lower.

Table 1. Typical examples of the multi-primary image projector specifications

Image bit depth	Number of primaries	Frames/sec
1 bit	1 primary	4000 fps
1 bit	20 primaries	200 fps
4 bits	1 primary	360 fps
6 bits	1 primary	240 fps
8 bits	1 primary	120 fps
8 bits	4 primaries	30 fps
8 bits	6 primaries	20 fps

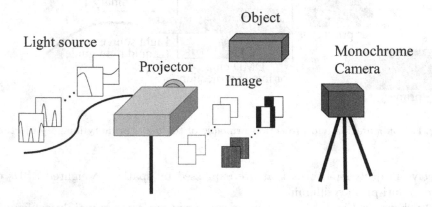

Fig. 2. Overview of our measurement system

3   Measurement System and Algorithms

3.1   Measurement System

Figure 2 shows the overview of our measurement system using the multi-primary image projector and a highspeed monochrome camera. The projector and camera are completely synchronized by a trigger signal. Thus there are no flicker effects between projections and captures in our measurements. As shown in Fig. 3, the projector reproduces nine basis images for estimating spectral reflectance (see Sect. 3.2) and eight binary stripe patterns for reconstructing 3D shape (see Sect. 3.3). Then, we project seventeen images in total for the measurement.

The highspeed monochrome camera is EPIX SV642M (resolution: 640×476 pixels, quantization bit depth: 10 bits, frame rate: 200 fps). In an ideal case, we project binary images (maximum projection speed is 4000 fps as shown in Table 1) and capture them (maximum capturing speed is 200 fps). Then, the projection and capturing speed of the seventeen images is 0.085 s (17 images divided by 200 fps) on the system specification. However, in our actual measurements, for increasing illumination intensities and reducing imaging noises,

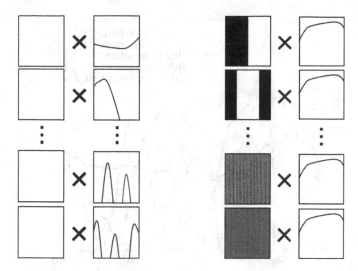

Fig. 3. Projected images: (left) nine basis images for spectral reflectance estimation (nine spectral basis light sources with a white image), and (right) eight stripe images for 3D shape reconstruction (eight stripe pattern images with a white light source).

the practical projection and capturing speed is later than the theoretical one (see also experimental discussions in Sect. 4).

3.2 Estimating Spectral Reflecntance

We use a set of orthonormal basis functions $\psi_m(\lambda)$ to represent surface spectral reflectance [5]. Surface spectral reflectance $S(\lambda)$ can be expressed as

$$S(\lambda) = \sum_{m=1}^{M} w_m \psi_m(\lambda) \quad (m = 1, 2, \ldots, M), \tag{1}$$

where M is the number of the orthonormal basis functions, w_m are the weights of the functions and λ indicates the wavelength. In this study, we selected five spectral basis functions, i.e., $M = 5$. The basis functions were computed by the principal component analysis (PCA) of a spectral reflectance database with 507 samples. Now, if we irradiate an object surface with spectrum $E_m(\lambda)$ of the orthonormal basis functions divided by the camera sensitivity $R(\lambda)$, the camera output O_m can be modeled as

$$O_m = \int E_m(\lambda) R(\lambda) S(\lambda) d\lambda$$

$$= \int (\psi_m(\lambda)/R(\lambda)) R(\lambda) \sum_{m=1}^{M} w_m \psi_m(\lambda) d\lambda \tag{2}$$

$$= w_m.$$

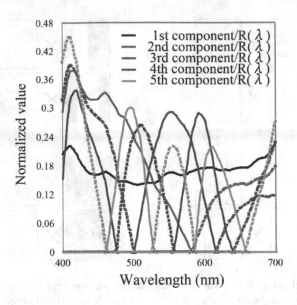

Fig. 4. Projected waveforms of orthonormal basis functions. The waveforms divided by the camera sensitivity are decomposed into positive and negative orthogonal basis (Color figure online).

As shown in Eq. (2), we can directly obtain the weights w_m from the camera outputs which are obtained by the projections based on the orthonormal basis functions. In actual case, we were unable to irradiate an object surface with the spectral basis functions based on PCA, because the orthonormal basis functions include negative values. In this study, we decompose the orthonormal basis functions into positive and negative functions. Then the absolute values of the decomposed negative functions are used as the projected illumination. Finally we estimate surface spectral reflectance using following values:

$$\psi_m(\lambda) = \psi_m^+(\lambda) - \psi_m^-(\lambda), \quad w_m = O_m^+ - O_m^-. \tag{3}$$

Figure 4 shows the projected spectra designed for estimating spectral reflectance. The figure shows the waveforms of nine orthonormal basis functions with the negative values inverted and which are divided by the camera spectral sensitivity $R(\lambda)$. The solid lines are the waveforms that are calculated by dividing the positive original orthonormal bases by the camera spectral sensitivity, and a dashed lines are the waveforms that are obtained by dividing the reversed negative components by the camera sensitivity. The second to fifth principle components include negative values and require illumination of two sources each. Then, nine waveforms are projected for spectral reflectance estimation.

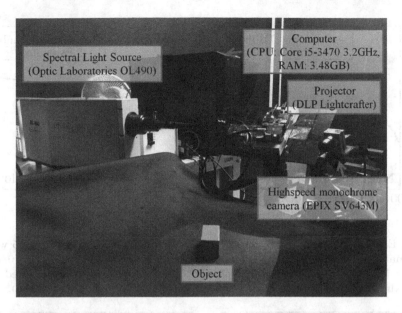

Fig. 5. Experimental setup for measuring spectral reflectance and 3D shape

3.3 Reconstructing 3D Shape

We apply the binary pattern image projection technique [1] to our 3D shape reconstruction. In general, N image patterns can express 2^N stripes. As shown in Fig. 3(b), we project eight pattern images ($N = 8$). Once binary image patterns are projected onto an object, there are 256 (2^8) unique areas coded with unique stripes. The 3D coordinates (X, Y, Z) can be computed for all 256 points along each horizontal line. Finally, 3D shape of an object can be reconstructed based on a triangulation principle and preliminary geometric calibrations.

4 Experimental Results and Discussions

Figure 5 shows our experimental setup for measuring spectral reflectance and 3D shape of an object. The actual experiments were conducted in a dark room. As the preliminary geometric calibration for precise 3D shape reconstruction, we used 75 reference points of a cube.

For validating the spectral reflectance estimation, we used an X-Rite Mini ColorChecker. Figure 6 shows examples which color differences ΔE_{ab}^* are the minimum and maximum in the ColorChecker. The average root mean square error (RMSE), goodness-of-fit coefficient (GFC) [20] and color difference ΔE_{ab}^* of 24 colors are 0.033, 0.9930 and 4.37, respectively. Compared with a conventional work [8], our system can estimate spectral reflectance with sufficient accuracy.

For verifying the accuracy of the 3D shape reconstruction, we used several single-color objects. Figure 7 shows an example of a measured object

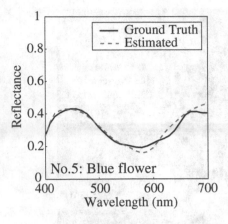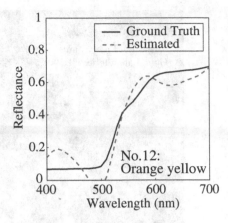

Fig. 6. Estimated spectral reflectances: (left) reflectance of ColorChecker No.5 which is estimated with the minimum color difference ($RMSE = 0.024$, $GFC = 0.9978$, $\Delta E_{ab}^* = 1.25$), and (right) reflectance of ColorChecker No.12 which is estimated with the maximum color difference ($RMSE = 0.074$, $GFC = 0.9872$, $\Delta E_{ab}^* = 10.96$).

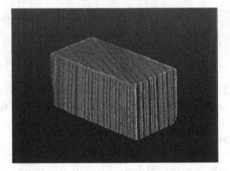

Fig. 7. Measured object (yellow cuboid made of wood) and its 3D mesh representation (Color figure online)

(yellow cuboid made of wood). As shown in the mesh data of Fig. 7, the 3D shape seems to be well reconstructed. We also confirmed that our 3D shape reconstruction had good accuracy compared with a commercial RGB-D camera (Kinect v2).

In the measurement of the spectral reflectance and 3D shape of the yellow object, the projection and capturing speed of seventeen images was 0.425 s. In our current system, if we need to measure more accurate data, making the measurement speed slower is required for achieving higher-intensity projections and less imaging noises. Similarly, we can make the measurement speed faster when we don't require such measurement accuracies. For achieving more rapid and accurate measurements, it is necessary to use a high-intensity light source and a high-sensitivity camera.

Fig. 8. Relighted objects: (left) relighting by illuminant A located at left-side position, and (right) relighting by illuminant D65 located at right-side position.

Finally, we applied the measured data to the object relighting (Fig. 8). The image rendering based on spectral calculations was implemented on PBRT (physically based rendering system). Through a brief experiment, we confirmed that the appearance of the rendered image is similar to the one of actual objects under the illuminations.

5   Conclusions

In this study, we have developed an imaging system for measuring spectral reflectance and 3D shape of scene objects. In our measurement system, we used the multi-primary image projector for computational spatial-spectral pattern projections. The average color difference ΔE_{ab}^* between the measured reflectances and the ground truths of X-Rite Mini ColorChecker was 4.37. We also reconstructed proper 3D shapes of colored objects. Finally, we demonstrated the object relighting using the measured spectral reflectances and 3D shapes.

In the experiments in this paper, we used single-color diffuse objects. For further discussion, we will conduct more experiments using objects with non-diffuse reflectance (specular, transmittance, etc.) and scenes with multiple textured objects. In addition, as discussed in Sect. 4, one problem with our system is the low projection and capturing speed in practical measurements. This is due to the avoidance of noisy image capturing caused by the low illumination intensities. This could be improved in the future by using a high-power light source and a noiseless camera. The improved system will provide rapid and accurate measurements. Finally, as a further future work, we would like to develop a technique for a real-time relighting system.

Acknowledgments. This work was partially supported by JSPS Grant-in-Aid for Scientific Research (C) (Grant Number 25330184).

References

1. Geng, J., Waterman, M.S.: Structured-light 3D surface imaging: a tutorial. Adv. Opt. Photonics **3**(2), 128–160 (2011)
2. Salvi, J., Pages, J., Batlle, J.: Pattern codification strategies in structured light systems. Pattern Recogn. **34**(4), 827–849 (2004)
3. Bimber, O., Raskar, R.: Spatial Augmented Reality: Merging Real and Virtual Worlds. A.K. Peters/CRC Press, Natick (2005)
4. Park, J.I., Lee, M.H., Grossberg, M.D., Nayar, S.K.: Multispectral imaging using multiplexed illumination. In: IEEE 11th International Conference on Computer Vision (ICCV), pp. 1–8 (2007)
5. Tominaga, S., Horiuchi, T.: Spectral imaging by synchronizing capture and illumination. J. Opt. Soc. Am. A **29**(9), 1764–1775 (2012)
6. Hirai, K., Tanimoto, T., Yamamoto, K., Horiuchi, T., Tominaga, S.: An LED-based spectral imaging system for surface reflectance and normal estimation. In: The 9th International Conference on Signal-Image Technology & Internet-Based Systems (SITIS), pp. 441–447 (2013)
7. Han, S., Sato, I., Okabe, T., Sato, Y.: Fast spectral reflectance recovery using DLP projector. Int. J. Comput. Vis. **110**(2), 172–184 (2014)
8. Nakahata, R., Hirai, K., Horiuchi, T., Tominaga, S.: Development of a dynamic relighting system for moving planar objects with unknown reflectance. In: Trémeau, A., Schettini, R., Tominaga, S. (eds.) CCIW 2015. LNCS, vol. 9016, pp. 81–90. Springer, Heidelberg (2015)
9. Sato, Y., Wheeler, M.D., Ikeuchi, K.: Object shape and reflectance modeling from observation. In: SIGGRAPH, pp. 379–387 (1997)
10. Oxholm, G., Nishino, K.: Shape and reflectance from natural illumination. In: Fitzgibbon, A., Lazebnik, S., Perona, P., Sato, Y., Schmid, C. (eds.) ECCV 2012, Part I. LNCS, vol. 7572, pp. 528–541. Springer, Heidelberg (2012)
11. Patow, G., Pueyo, X.: A survey of inverse rendering problems. Comput. Graph. Forum **22**(4), 663–687 (2003)
12. Tonsho, K., Akao, Y., Tsumura, N., Miyake, Y.: Development of goniophotometric imaging system for recording reflectance spectra of 3D objects. In: Proceedings of SPIE, vol. 4663, pp. 370–378 (2001)
13. Manabe, Y., Parkkinen, J., Jaaskelainen, T., Chihara, K.: Three dimensional measurement using color structured patterns and imaging spectrograph. In: 16th International Conference on Pattern Recognition (ICPR), pp. 649–652 (2002)
14. Tominaga, S., Tanaka, N.: Spectral image acquisition, analysis, and rendering for art paintings. J. Electron. Imaging **17**(4), 043022:1–043022:13 (2008)
15. Mansouri, A., Lathuiliere, A., Marzani, F.S., Voisin, Y., Gouton, P.: Toward a 3D multispectral scanner: an application to multimedia. IEEE MultiMedia **14**(1), 40–47 (2007)
16. Chane, C.S., Schutze, R., Boochs, F., Marzani, F.S.: Registration of 3D and multispectral data for the study of cultural heritage surfaces. Sensors **13**(1), 1004–1020 (2013)
17. Sitnik, R., Krzesłowski, J., Maczkowski, G.: Archiving shape and appearance of cultural heritage objects using structured light projection and multispectral imaging. Opt. Eng. **51**(2), 021115:1–021115:8 (2012)
18. Hirai, K., Irie, D., Horiuchi, T.: Multi-primary image projector using programmable spectral light source. J. Soc. Inf. Display (2016). doi:10.1002/jsid.422

19. Hirai, K., Irie, D., Horiuchi, T.: Photometric and geometric measurements based on multi-primary image projector. In: Colour and Visual Computing Symposium (CVCS), pp. 1–5 (2015)
20. Romero, J., García-Beltrán, A., Hernández-Andrés, J.: Linear basis for representation of natural and artificial illuminants. J. Opt. Soc. Am. A **14**(5), 1007–1014 (1997)

Computer Vision Color Constancy from Maximal Projections Mean Assumption

Elkhamssa Lakehal[1]([✉]) and Djemel Ziou[2]

[1] LAMIE Laboratory, LAMIE, faculté des mathématiques et de l'informatique,
Université Batna 2, 05110 Fesdis Batna, Algeria
lakehal_elkhamssa@yahoo.fr
[2] DMI, Université de Sherbrooke, Québec, Canada

Abstract. In this paper, we propose a fast solution for the problem of illuminant color estimation. We present a physics-based algorithm that uses the mean projections maximization assumption. We investigated this hypothesis on a large images dataset and used it afterwords to estimate the illuminant color. The proposed algorithm reduces the illuminant estimation problem to an uncentred PCA problem. The evaluation of the algorithm on two well-known image datasets results in lower angular errors.

Keywords: Color constancy · Scene illuminant estimation · Dichromatic model · Principal component analysis

1 Introduction

The appearance of objects is the result of light, surface, and camera sensor interactions. Hence, the human visual system is able to preserve the appearance of objects by adjusting the gain in the different cones. This ability is called the human vision color constancy. In the case of an imaging device, the sensed image depends on surface reflectances, light color and camera spectral sensitivity. When light color changes, the sensed image colors change even if the surface reflectances and the camera spectral sensitivity remain the same. Chromatic adaptation [21] or computer vision color constancy allows to adjust image colors according to an estimate of the light color. This estimate is the camera sensed light originating from one or several sources that illuminate a scene. It is generally the output of a color constancy algorithm [14,16] used to correct image colors and enhance image contents [30]. For these algorithms, surface reflectances and scene illuminant are unknown. To estimate the scene illuminant, color constancy algorithms use some assumptions and prior knowledge. Dichromatic model [25], lambertian model [22], Grey world assumption [3] or other independent assumptions [2,8] can be used to estimate the scene illuminant since it is considered as an under-constrained problem. Based on assumptions and prior knowledge used, existing algorithms can be divided into two major categories: dichromatic model based

© Springer International Publishing Switzerland 2016
A. Mansouri et al. (Eds.): ICISP 2016, LNCS 9680, pp. 148–156, 2016.
DOI: 10.1007/978-3-319-33618-3_16

methods [5, 26] and lambertian model based methods. Depending on the strategy used, the lambertian algorithms can be subdivided into two categories: static methods [3, 10, 19, 29] and learning methods [11].

This work is based on the dichromatic model to formulate an additional hypothesis based on the fact that the scene illuminant is within bright colors. This hypothesis is close to the hypothesis used in [8]. From this assumption we found that the scene illuminant is the eigenvector of the inner product matrix of image chromaticities. The paper is organized as follows: Sect. 2 presented the new hypothesis and its use for illuminant color estimation. The evaluation of the proposed algorithm on large datasets is presented in Sect. 3.

2   Problem Formulation

2.1   Maximal Square Projections' Mean Assumption

Objects in nature are composed of different surface types. Dielectric objects are widely present in natural scenes. For dielectric surfaces the reflectance is a linear composition of two parts: the specular reflectance and the diffuse one. When imaged under a given light source, the resulting image is also a linear combination of specular and diffuse components. The diffuse part encodes the color of the surface as it is a function of the surface reflectance properties. However, the specular part is independent of surface reflectance properties and hence is considered as the image of the scene light called the illuminant. Based on these observations, pixels of dielectric surface image can be represented in a 2D subspace known as dichromatic space [25], spanned by the specular vector and the diffuse vector.

Considering real scenes, where more than one surface may exist, and several 2D sub-spaces corresponding to the existing surfaces can be defined. Now, if the scene is illuminated by a single light source, just one specular component (i.e. illuminant) is present while several diffuse components, each of which represents a surface, exist (see Fig. 1). It follows that the estimation of the illuminant is equivalent to subspaces intersection estimation [20, 24, 27]. However, this requires the prior knowledge of the existing surfaces in the scene and hence an image segmentation. Another way to proceed is to consider just one surface plane and impose some constraints on sub-spaces [9, 28]. The prior segmentation can be avoided by investigating the relationship that may exist between the specular vector and sub-spaces vectors. Let us assume that there exist several chromaticities close to specular axis more than any other diffuse axis. These chromaticities belong to one or more surfaces, but their identification is not a trivial task. In fact, there are several works that try to identify them like in [5]. We argue that it is not required to identify exactly all the chromaticities close to the specular axis, but a vague subset of them is enough to estimate the illuminant. The subset cardinality must not be large to reduce the computational complexity, but sufficient for carrying statistical estimation, with acceptable bias. The specification of the subset will be explained in Sect. 2.3.

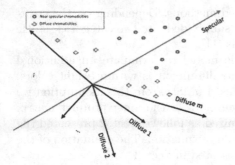

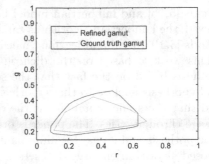

Fig. 1. Representation of dichromatic sub-spaces points and their distances to the specular component for dielectric surfaces.

Fig. 2. The refined gamut calculated from three datasets ([1,4,12]) (Color figure online).

As it is shown in Fig. 1, all the chromaticities have the $(0,0)$ origin. Moreover, being interested in the illuminant color, the chromaticity vectors are normalized such that their magnitude is one. In this case, the proximity between the chromaticity vector c and any other vector x_i, where $i \in [1, n]$ can be measured using the dot product between them. Since the chromaticity components are all positive, it follows that the angles between them and c is less or equal to 90 degrees. In this configuration, the dot product and the Euclidean distance between c and a given chromaticity are equivalent. Note that, other proximity measures can be used. In other words, given a set of normalized near specular chromaticities $\mathcal{L} = \{x_i\}$ and an estimator c of the real illuminant, we search for the vector c that is the most close, in terms of dot product, to all elements of $\mathcal{L}$. However, one could use the dot product square as objective function. The resulting function $m_{I,\mathcal{L}}$ can be interpreted in terms of dispersion of the chromaticities on the axis c. For the n chromaticities which will be chosen, the objective function is the sum of the squares of dot products. More formally,

$$m_{I,\mathcal{L} } = argmax_c \sum_{i=1}^{n} (\vec{x_i} . \vec{c})^2 \text{ subject to the constraint } c^t c = 1 \qquad (1)$$

It can be rewritten in matrix form as follows:

$$m_{I,\mathcal{L}} = argmax_c \, c^t \Sigma c \text{ subject to the constraint } c^t c = 1 \qquad (2)$$

With $\Sigma = X^t X$ is the inner product matrix of selected chromaticities $\mathcal{L}$. One can think that the illuminant estimation problem is equivalent to PCA problem. However, the chromaticities are not centred and therefore, the problem in 2 is not a classical PCA problem. It is, as stated by [17], another PCA variant called uncentred PCA.

2.2   Assumption Validation

In order to validate our assumption, we carried out the following experimentation. We started using the SFU Lab dataset [1] which contains 321 images with corresponding true illuminants. We selected the set $\mathcal{L}$ of chromaticities closest to the true illuminant l. Several chromatic spaces could be used to calculate chromaticities. We made the same observation with [6], the rg-chromaticity space is the most familiar space for calculating image chromaticities. Then, for each image I all the selected chromaticities $\mathcal{L}$ including the illuminant l were projected on each other and the vector c which maximises the square projections' mean was recorded. To compare recorded vectors and real illuminants, we use the dot product. We validated our assumption by using 1 % of chromaticities closest to real illuminants. This percentage contains a sufficient amount of points for doing statistical analysis. Numerically, we used 2981 chromaticities closest to the real illuminant l. Real illuminants and chromaticities yielding the maximal square projections' mean were depicted in Fig. 3. We noted that the majority of these chromaticities were close to real illuminants of the dataset. Indeed, We found that in 98.75 % of the dataset images, the maximal square projections' mean was obtained by projecting the chromaticities on chromaticities having less then 3 degrees from the real illuminants. The binned histogram of angular errors between these chromaticities and true illuminants, in Fig. 4, had an obvious maximum image count near the origin, which means several of chromaticities producing the maximal square projections' mean were true illuminants. This experimentation showed that the maximal mean square projections' assumption is realistic.

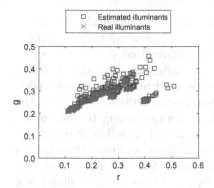

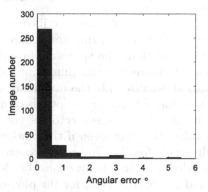

Fig. 3. The set of true illuminants and estimated illuminants (i.e. vectors yielding the maximal projections mean).

Fig. 4. The binned histogram of angular errors between true illuminants and chromaticities maximising the mean projection.

2.3   Chromaticities Selection

The accuracy of the estimated illuminant depends on the chromaticities $\mathcal{L}$ involved in the estimation of the inner product matrix Σ. The cardinality of $\mathcal{L}$ must be small in order to reduce the computational time but large enough to produce lower estimation errors. The closest chromaticities to the true illuminant l are always the bright pixels of the image [18]. So a representative sample set from all chromaticities can be selected according to an adequate threshold. This leads us to ask the following question: is there a useful way to avoid the use of an arbitrary or inadequate threshold? In this section, we propose to take the bright pixels in a gamut of suited chromaticities that we called the refined gamut. Hence, we take first a percentage $T\%$ of bright pixels and we kept from this set, chromaticities that are inside the refined gamut. If the number of resulting chromaticities is not enough to do statistical analysis, we take a greater percentage and search for chromaticities inside the refined gamut. To construct the refined gamut, we run our algorithm using different percentages $(1\%, 3\%, 5\%, 7\%, 10\%)$ on three well-known datasets ([1,4,12]) and gather chromaticities allowing the best illuminant estimator. The construction of the refined gamut is done separately in the training step. The refined gamut and the gamut of real illuminants of the three datasets are plotted in Fig. 2. One can observe that, the gamut of real illuminants is inside the refined gamut. This means that the selected chromaticities involved in the illuminant estimation are always inside the gamut of real illuminants i.e. the selected chromaticities are physically feasible.

2.4   Maximal Square Projections' Mean Algorithm

Based on experimentation described in Sect. 2.2, for a given image the illuminant c is the vector maximizing the square projections' mean of its projected data. Let us recall that, the space of chromaticities is normalized (i.e., $r + g + b = 1$) and therefore the illuminant intensity cannot be estimated. This is not a limitation because only the illuminant direction is used to correct image colors. The solution of this convex optimization problem is straightforward. Indeed, the illuminant c is the eigenvector of the matrix Σ corresponding to the largest eigenvalue. However, even if the mathematical solution is possible, it might not be physically feasible. In order to overcome this problem, additional constraints are needed: The illuminant c must be close to physically feasible illuminants. One can add a new constraint for the physical feasibility of the estimated illuminant like the fact that it belongs to the real illuminants' gamut. This constraint is unnecessary because it is already fulfilled in the selection phase described in Sect. 2.3. Moreover, none of the components of the illuminant vector c can be negative. We propose then to impose the constraint $c - \epsilon > 0$. Taking into account all constraints, we propose to minimize their linear combination. The illuminant estimation problem with constraints can be written as:

$$m_{I,\mathcal{L}} = argmin_c \ -c^t \Sigma c + \lambda_1(\epsilon - c) + \lambda_2(c^t c - 1) \qquad (3)$$

Another important issue concerns the chromaticities which can be centred or not, the Σ matrix can then take positive or negative values. When the chromaticities are centred this matrix is simply the covariance matrix. In the case of uncentred chromaticities, the matrix Σ is the inner product of chromaticities. In this case the dimensionality reduction method is called the mean vector component analysis [17] which preserves the Euclidean length and the direction of the mean vector. For our case (i.e. illuminant estimation) the mean vector direction m is a good implicit constraint on the estimated illuminant c. That means, the mean m of bright chromaticities is generally a color close to the physically feasible illuminants' colors. Moreover, Σ is a strictly positive matrix which is irreducible and then the Perron-Frobenuis theorem [23] can be applied on it. According to this theorem, there exists a largest eigenvalue λ to which corresponds an eigenvector v which is composed only of positive elements. Therefore, using the diagonalization method of Perron-Frobenuis the problem can be rewritten without the explicit vector positivity constraint as in 4. Consequently, we propose the use of Perron-Frobenuis theorem to calculate the eigenvector of inner product matrix Σ as an illuminant estimator.

$$m_{I,\mathcal{L}} = argmax_c \ c^t \Sigma c + \lambda(c^t c - 1) \tag{4}$$

3   Experimental Results

The performance evaluation of the proposed algorithm is carried out in two experimentations. In the first experimentation, we used the SFU lab dataset, a collection of 321 laboratory images of size 637×468 consisting of 31 objects imaging under 11 lights. We used also the SFU Grey Ball collection [4] which consists of 11346 images (874×583) dataset taken through a video registration of indoor and outdoor scenes. The data collection includes a wide variety of scenes and illumination conditions. For both collections the ground truth is available.

For the sake of comparison, we reported the accuracy of some well-known algorithms that are: Grey world (GW) [3], White patch (Max-RGB) [19], Shades of grey (SHGR) [10], the Grey edge (GRED) [29]. From the learning category the Natural image statistics (NIS) [15] algorithm is selected. The Zeta image (Zeta) [5] represents the dichromatic based category. For the implementation of algorithms GW, Max-RGB, SHGR, GRED, we used the software platform [29], while for Zeta and NIS we compared with scores reported in [5,15]. For comparison purposes algorithm which gives the best scores is considered as the best algorithm. In which follows, we refer to the proposed algorithm by maximum projection algorithm (**MPA**).

The performance measures are the mean and the median of angular errors. They are widely used in the state-of-the-art methods, we used them to allow fair comparison. The angular error (Eq. 5) is the dot product of the normalized estimated illuminant vector c and the normalized ground truth vector e. Because it is illumination intensity free, Hordley [16] claimed that this measure can be used to evaluate algorithms that estimate only the illuminant chromaticity.

Let us recall that MPA operates in 2D chromatic space whereas other tested algorithms operate in RGB space. Finlayson et al. in [7] argued that the performance of an algorithm designed for RGB color space like the Grey world deteriorates when it was tested in the 2D chromaticity space.

$$Ang\_Error = \arccos(\frac{c^t e}{\|c\| \|e\|}) \tag{5}$$

The second experimentation is devoted to evaluate the MPA computational accuracy compared to GW, Max-RGB, SHGR, GRED algorithms. The datasets used are the SFU Lab dataset [1], and the SFU Grey Ball dataset [4].

3.1   Algorithm Performance

Scores of selected algorithms including the MPA algorithm on three datasets SFU Lab, Color Checker, and SFU Grey Ball are reported in Table 1. The obtained scores confirm that MPA algorithm outperforms the other algorithms in terms of mean and median angular errors on the three datasets. For the SFU Lab dataset, MPA algorithm reduces the mean and median errors given by best algorithm Zeta by 43 % and 57 % respectively. Scores obtained with the SFU Grey ball dataset show that MPA algorithm enhances by roughly 21 % and 12 %, respectively, the mean and median errors achieved by the best algorithm NIS. These improvements might be considered as important since an enhancement over 5–6% is considered as perceptually significant [13].

Table 1. Mean and median angular errors estimated on two datasets (SFU Lab [1], and Gray Ball [4]) with computational times in seconds.

Method	Data sets					
	SFU lab			Grey ball		
	Mean	Median	Time	Mean	Median	Time
GW [3]	9.8°	7.0°	22.4	7.9°	7.0°	481.6
Max-RGB [19]	9.1°	6.5°	**21.3**	6.8°	5.3°	475.1
SHGR [10]	6.4°	3.7°	30.8	6.1°	5.3°	548.1
GRED [29]	5.6°	3.2°	45.4	5.9°	4.7°	567.6
Zeta [5]	4.3°	1.9°	-	6.8°	4.7°	-
NIS [15]	-	-	-	5.2°	3.9°	-
MPA	**2.3°**	**0.8°**	28.4	**4.1°**	**3.4°**	**453.5**

We investigate also the computational accuracy of MPA algorithm as function of the content and the size of images compared to four algorithms. We run the different algorithms on Alienware machine with Intel Core i7-3820 Processor and 16 GB of RAM memory. One can note that, MPA algorithm achieves least computational time compared to the tested algorithms on two over three datasets. The Max-RGB, the fast algorithm among the first four tested algorithms treats 23 images per second, while, MPA estimates illuminants of 25 images per second from the SFU Grey Ball dataset. However, MPA takes more time for SFU Lab dataset (i.e. over 11 images per second) compared to GW (over 14 images per second) and Max-RGB (over 15 images per second). This is due to iterations made by MPA algorithm to reach an acceptable set cardinality of selected chromaticities.

4   Conclusion

In this paper, we presented the maximum projection algorithm for illuminant color estimation. We observed that the projection of selected chromaticities on illuminant vector allows to derive an efficient and fast algorithm for the illuminant estimation. This algorithm is no other than uncentred PCA problem since we search for the sub-space which maximises the dispersion of chromaticities projected on it. Instead of using all chromaticities of an image, only a subset of them is used which makes the algorithm faster. The method is tested on three images collections and the angular errors obtained are lower compared to previous works. In further work, we will investigate other performance measures and refine the chormaticities selection criterion.

References

1. Barnard, K., Martin, L., Funt, B., Coath, A.: A data set for color research. Color Res. Appl. **27**(3), 147–151 (2002)
2. Brainard, D.H., Freeman, W.T.: Bayesian color constancy. JOSA A **14**(7), 1393–1411 (1997)
3. Buchsbaum, G.: A spatial processor model for object colour perception. J. Franklin Inst. **310**(1), 1–26 (1980)
4. Ciurea, F., Funt, B.: A large image database for color constancy research. In: CIC, vol. 2003, pp. 160–164. Society for Imaging Science and Technology (2003)
5. Drew, M.S., Joze, H.R.V., Finlayson, G.D.: The Zeta-image, illuminant estimation and specularity manipulation. Comput. Vis. Image Underst. **127**, 1–13 (2014)
6. Finlayson, G.D., Drew, M.S., Lu, C.: Intrinsic images by entropy minimization. In: Pajdla, T., Matas, J.G. (eds.) ECCV 2004. LNCS, vol. 3023, pp. 582–595. Springer, Heidelberg (2004)
7. Finlayson, G.D., Hordley, S.D., Hubel, P.M.: Color by correlation: a simple unifying framework for color constancy. IEEE Trans. PAMI **23**(11), 1209–1221 (2001)
8. Finlayson, G.D., Hordley, S.D., Tastl, I.: Gamut constrained illuminant estimation. IJCV **67**(1), 93–109 (2006)
9. Finlayson, G.D., Schaefer, G.: Solving for colour constancy using a constrained dichromatic reflection model. IJCV **42**(3), 127–144 (2001)
10. Finlayson, G.D., Trezzi, E.: Shades of gray and colour constancy. In: CIC, vol. 2004, pp. 37–41 (2004)
11. Forsyth, D.A.: A novel algorithm for color constancy. IJCV **5**(1), 5–35 (1990)

12. Gehler, P.V., Rother, C., Blake, A., Minka, T., Sharp, T.: Bayesian color constancy revisited. In: IEEE Conference on CVPR 2008, pp. 1–8. IEEE (2008)
13. Gijsenij, A., Gevers, T., Lucassen, M.P.: Perceptual analysis of distance measures for color constancy algorithms. JOSA A **26**(10), 2243–2256 (2009)
14. Gijsenij, A., Gevers, T., Van De Weijer, J.: Computational color constancy: survey and experiments. IEEE Trans. Image Process. **20**(9), 2475–2489 (2011)
15. Gijsenij, A., Gevers, T.: Color constancy using natural image statistics and scene semantics. IEEE Trans. PAMI **33**(4), 687–698 (2011)
16. Hordley, S.D.: Scene illuminant estimation: past, present, and future. Color Res. Appl. **31**(4), 303–314 (2006)
17. Jenssen, R.: Mean vector component analysis for visualization and clustering of nonnegative data. IEEE Trans. NNLS **24**(10), 1553–1564 (2013)
18. Joze, H.R.V., Drew, M.S., Finlayson, G.D., Rey, P.A.T.: The role of bright pixels in illumination estimation. In: CIC, vol. 2012, pp. 41–46
19. Land, E.H.: The Retinex Theory of Color Vision. Scientific America, New York (1977)
20. Lee, H.C.: Method for computing the scene-illuminant chromaticity from specular highlights. JOSA A **3**(10), 1694–1699 (1986)
21. MacAdam, D.L.: Chromatic adaptation. JOSA **46**(7), 500–513 (1956)
22. Phong, B.T.: Illumination for computer generated pictures. Commun. ACM **18**(6), 311–317 (1975)
23. Pillai, U.S., Suel, T., Cha, S.: The Perron-Frobenius theorem: some of its applications. IEEE Signal Process. Mag. **22**(2), 62–75 (2005)
24. Schaefer, G.: Robust dichromatic colour constancy. In: Campilho, A.C., Kamel, M.S. (eds.) ICIAR 2004. LNCS, vol. 3212, pp. 257–264. Springer, Heidelberg (2004)
25. Shafer, S.A.: Using color to separate reflection components. Color Res. Appl. **10**(4), 210–218 (1985)
26. Shi, L., Funt, B.: Dichromatic illumination estimation via hough transforms in 3D. In: CGIV, vol. 2008, pp. 259–262
27. Tominaga, S., Wandell, B.A.: Standard surface-reflectance model and illuminant estimation. JOSA A **6**(4), 576–584 (1989)
28. Toro, J.: Dichromatic illumination estimation without pre-segmentation. Pattern Recognit. Lett. **29**(7), 871–877 (2008)
29. Van De Weijer, J., Gevers, T., Gijsenij, A.: Edge-based color constancy. IEEE Trans. Image Process. **16**(9), 2207–2214 (2007)
30. Kerouh, F., Ziou, D., Lahmar, K.N.: Content based computational chromatic adaptation. In: Proceedings of the 11th Joint Conference on Computer Vision, Imaging and Computer Graphics Theory and Applications, vol. 2, pp. 39–47 (2016)

Demosaicking Method for Multispectral Images Based on Spatial Gradient and Inter-channel Correlation

Shu Ogawa[1(✉)], Kazuma Shinoda[1], Madoka Hasegawa[1],
Shigeo Kato[1], Masahiro Ishikawa[2], Hideki Komagata[2],
and Naoki Kobayashi[2]

[1] Graduate School of Engineering, Utsunomiya University,
7-1-2 Yoto, Utsunomiya, Tochigi 321-8585, Japan
14ogawa@mclaren.is.utsunomiya-u.ac.jp
[2] Faculty of Health and Medical Care, Saitama Medical University,
1397-1 Yamane, Hidaka, Saitama 350-1241, Japan

Abstract. Multispectral images have been studied in various fields such as remote sensing and sugar content prediction in fruits. One of the systems that captures multispectral images uses a multispectral filter array based on a color filter array. In this system, demosaicking processing is required because the captured multispectral images are mosaicked. However, demosaicking is more difficult for multispectral images than for RGB images owing to the low density between the observed pixels in multispectral images. Therefore, we propose a demosaicking method for multispectral images based on spatial gradient and inter-channel correlation. Experimental results demonstrate that our proposed method outperforms the existing methods and is effective.

Keywords: Demosaicking · Multispectral filter array · Interpolation · Inter-channel correlation · Spatial gradient

1 Introduction

Multispectral images (MSIs) consist of a higher number of color components than RGB images. Therefore, MSIs have been studied in fields that require accurate color representation such as remote sensing and the diagnosis by pathological images [1].

Various systems have been proposed for the capture of MSIs. These systems can be classified into the following three categories: (i) multi-camera-one-shot systems, (ii) single-camera-multi-shot systems, and (iii) single-camera-one-shot systems [2]. In this paper, we focus on the single-camera-one-shot systems that obtain an MSI by using a single image sensor with a multispectral filter array (MSFA). An MSFA is based on the color filter array (CFA) used for capturing RGB images. Therefore, mosaicked MSIs that have a single band at each pixel location can be captured by using an MSFA. The MSI can be obtained faster with this system than with the single-camera-multi-shot system. Further, the cost of capturing the MSI is lower than in the case of multi-camera-one-shot systems that use multiple cameras. Demosaicking processing is required in order to

© Springer International Publishing Switzerland 2016
A. Mansouri et al. (Eds.): ICISP 2016, LNCS 9680, pp. 157–166, 2016.
DOI: 10.1007/978-3-319-33618-3_17

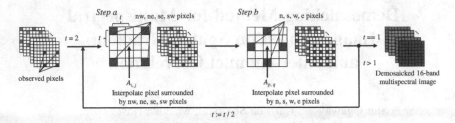

Fig. 1. Interpolation flow of Step 1 in MLDI.

restore the missing pixels. However, demosaicking is more difficult for MSIs than for RGB images because the density between observed pixels for the MSIs captured by an MSFA is lower than that for the RGB images. Earlier studies [3–5] can be applied to any MSFA, however, these methods are based on either inter-channel correlation [3, 4] or spatial gradient [5]. Although the methods based on both have been proposed [6, 7], it is difficult to apply them to any MSFA because they are demosaicking methods proposed for a particular MSFA.

In this paper, we propose multispectral local directional interpolation (MLDI) for some MSFAs. This method is based on local directional interpolation (LDI) that considers spatial gradient and inter-channel correlation, which is proposed by Zhang et al. [8] for CFAs. Experiments performed on test images by using our proposed method and existing methods demonstrate the effectiveness of the proposed method.

The rest of the paper is organized as follows: In Sect. 2, we describe the proposed demosaicking method. We present and discuss the experimental results in Sect. 3, and state the conclusion in Sect. 4.

2   Multispectral Local Directional Interpolation (MLDI)

2.1   Overview of Proposed Demosaicking Method

In this section, we explain the demosaicking algorithm of MLDI that consists of three steps: (1) First, the missing pixels are interpolated by extending LDI; (2) Next, the restored MSI obtained in Step 1 is updated by using the eight neighboring pixels; (3) Then, the artifacts of the restored MSI obtained in Step 2 are removed by using a median filter.

In Step 1, the missing pixels of the mosaicked MSI are interpolated by extending LDI. In this step, we assume that a $2^x \times 2^x$ ($x = 1, 2, \ldots$)-band MSFA is arranged in $2^x \times 2^x$ pixels to interpolate the canter pixel surrounded by the four observed or previously interpolated pixels. Figure 1 shows an overview of Step 1. First, the center pixel surrounded by the peripheral pixels named *north-west* (*nw*), *north-east* (*ne*), *south-east* (*se*), and *south-west* (*sw*) pixels is interpolated. Then, the center pixel surrounded by the peripheral pixels named *north* (*n*), *south* (*s*), *west* (*w*), and *east* (*e*) pixels is interpolated. This process is repeated until all the missing pixels are

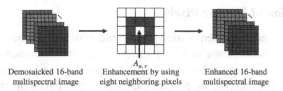

Demosaicked 16-band   Enhancement by using   Enhanced 16-band
multispectral image   eight neighboring pixels   multispectral image

Fig. 2. Updating the restored image of Step 1 by using eight neighboring pixels (Step 2 in MLDI).

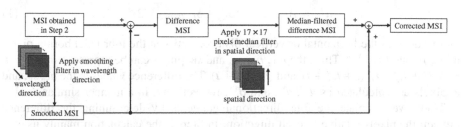

Fig. 3. Removing artifacts in the image obtained in Step 2 (Step 3 in MLDI).

interpolated because the density between observed pixels of the mosaicked MSI is lower than that of the mosaicked RGB image. The interpolation in Step 1 is based on the interpolation of red and blue components in LDI, which use previously interpolated pixels in green component. However, MSFA do not necessarily contain a band that the density between observed pixels is high such as the green component. Therefore, in Step 1, we use a band observed in the interpolation target pixel instead of green component in order to use the observed values at the same pixels as the pixels in green component used in LDI. However, this band may not be observed in pixels used for the interpolation because all pixels in green component have been already interpolated. Therefore, this band is interpolated previously when it is used.

Then, in Step 2, we improve the quality of the restored image obtained in Step 1 by using the eight neighboring pixels. Figure 2 shows an overview of Step 2. In Step 1, the bands and pixels used for each interpolation are different because the interpolation target band, the band observed in the interpolation target pixel and previously interpolated pixels are mainly used for other interpolation. Therefore, in Step 2, we use more bands and pixels than that in Step 1 by using the eight neighboring pixels that have been already interpolated in Step 1.

Finally, in Step 3, we apply a median filter to correct impulse noise as shown in Fig. 3, which is based on the chromatic regularity step of Buades et al. [9]. The chromatic regularity step of [9] decomposes RGB into YUV components, applies a 3×3 median filter to UV components, then recomposes the filtered UV into RGB components. Instead of UV components, we use the difference between the input and smoothed MSI, and remove the noise by using a median filter.

In Sects. 2.2, 2.3, and 2.4, we provide a detailed description of Step 1, Step 2, and Step 3, respectively.

2.2   Interpolation of Missing Pixels

Let the band targeted for interpolation be A, the position of the pixel targeted for interpolation be (i, j) as shown in Fig. 1 (*Step a*), and the reference band be S. Here, the reference band denotes the band in which the pixel value was observed at (i, j) in the mosaicked MSI. In Step 1, we predict the difference between the pixel values of the target and reference bands at (i, j), and calculate the target pixel value by using the difference value at (i, j). First, the difference value between the target and the reference bands at the *nw* pixel is calculated as follows:

$$d^{nw} = A_{i-t, j-t} - (S_{i,j} + S_{i-2t, j-2t})/2, \tag{1}$$

where t denotes the horizontal or vertical distance between the four neighboring pixels and (i, j), and $t = 2^{x-1}$. Thus, the *nw*, *ne*, *se*, and *sw* pixels can be represented as $(i - t, j - t)$, $(i + t, j - t)$, $(i + t, j + t)$, and $(i - t, j + t)$. The difference values at the *ne*, *se*, and *sw* pixels are calculated as d^{ne}, d^{se}, and d^{sw}, respectively, in a manner similar to (1).

Then, we calculate the four directional gradients by determining the difference between the pixels relative to each direction. In Step 1, the calculation mainly use the interpolation target band and the band in which the pixel value was observed at (i, j) in the mosaicked MSI instead of the green component. The directional gradient weight at *nw* is calculated as follows:

$$w^{nw} = 1/(|A_{i-t, j-t} - A_{i+t, j+t}|| + |S_{i-2t, j-2t} - S_{i,j}| + |\tilde{S}_{i-t, j-t} - S_{i,j}| + \varepsilon), \tag{2}$$

where $\tilde{S}_{i,j}$ denotes the value of the band S at (i, j) calculated by bilinear interpolation, and ε is a small positive number that prevents the gradients from attaining a value of zero. Further, the gradient weights in the *ne*, *se*, and *sw* directions are calculated as w^{ne}, w^{se}, and w^{sw}, in a manner similar to (2). Then, a difference value at (i, j) is predicted by calculating the weighted average of the four difference values at the *nw*, *ne*, *se*, and *sw* pixels using these gradient weights as follows:

$$\bar{d} = \frac{w^{nw}d^{nw} + w^{ne}d^{ne} + w^{se}d^{se} + w^{sw}d^{sw}}{w^{nw} + w^{ne} + w^{se} + w^{sw}}. \tag{3}$$

Finally, the pixel value at (i, j) is obtained as follows:

$$\bar{A}_{i,j} = S_{i,j} + \bar{d}. \tag{4}$$

Next, let the position of the pixel targeted for interpolation be (p, q), as shown in Fig. 1 (*Step b*). First, the difference value between the target and the reference bands at the *n* pixel is calculated as follows:

$$d^n = A_{p, q-t} - (S_{p, q} + S_{p, q-2t})/2. \tag{5}$$

Further, the difference values at the *s*, *w*, and *e* pixels are calculated as d^s, d^w, and d^e, in a manner similar to (5).

Then, we calculate the four directional gradients. The directional gradient weight at n is calculated as follows:

$$w^n = 1/(|S_{p,q-2t} - S_{p,q}| + \sum_{k=1}^{t} (|M_{p,q-(t+(k-1))} - M_{p,q+(t-(k-1))}|)$$
$$+ \sum_{k=1}^{t} (W_k|M_{p-k,q-2t} - M_{p-k,q}|) + \sum_{k=1}^{t} (W_k|M_{p+k,q-2t} - M_{p+k,q}|) + \varepsilon) \,,$$

$$(6)$$

where $M_{p,q}$ denotes the pixel value at (p, q) of the mosaicked MSI, and W_k is calculated as follows:

$$W_k = \frac{\exp(-k^2/(2\sigma^2))}{2 \sum_{l=1}^{t} \exp(-l^2/(2\sigma^2))},$$

$$(7)$$

where σ is a parameter. Further, the gradient weights in the s, w, and e directions are calculated as w^s, w^w, and w^e, in a manner similar to (6). Then, the difference value at (p, q) is predicted by calculating the weighted average of the four difference values at the n, s, w, and e pixels using these gradient weights.

Finally, the pixel value at (p, q) is obtained in a manner similar to (4). Then, t is assigned a value of $t/2$, and the process in Step 1 is repeated while t is greater than one.

2.3 Enhancement by Using Eight Neighboring Pixels

In Step 2, each pixel is updated by using the same process as that in Step 1 and by using the eight neighboring pixels. Let the band targeted for update be A, the position of the pixel targeted for update be (u, v) as shown in Fig. 2, and the reference band be S. First, the difference value between the target and reference bands at the nw pixel is calculated as follows:

$$d^{nw} = A_{u-1,v-1} - S_{u-1,v-1}. \tag{8}$$

Further, the difference values at the other neighboring pixels are calculated as d^{ne}, d^{se}, d^{sw}, d^n, d^s, d^w, and d^e, in a manner similar to (8). In addition, the directional gradient weights are calculated using a method similar to that in Step 1 with $t = 1$, and $M_{u,v}$ modified to $A_{u,v}$. Then, a difference value at (u, v) is predicted by calculating the weighted average of the eight difference values and these gradient weights.

Finally, the pixel value at (u, v) is obtained in a manner similar to (4).

2.4 Removal of Artifacts by Applying Median Filter

In Step 3, the artifacts of the updated MSI obtained in Step 2 are removed by using a median filter. As shown in Fig. 3, first, a 1-D smoothing filter is applied to the updated MSI in the wavelength direction. The 1-D smoothing filter is defined as follows:

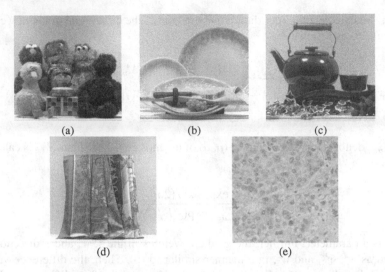

Fig. 4. Test images: (a) *Toys*, (b) *Dishes*, (c) *Kettle*, (d) *Scarf*, (e) *Pathological Image* (*PI*). The size of these images is 512 × 512 pixels.

$$f = [1/3 \quad 1/3 \quad 1/3]. \tag{9}$$

$$y = f * x, \tag{10}$$

where x is an N-band vector of the updated MSI, y is an N-band vector of the smoothed MSI, $*$ is the convolution, and N is the number of bands of the MSI. This process is a pixel-by-pixel convolution. The one band of the smoothed MSI corresponds to the power of three bands, and we treat this value as an alternative of Y. This calculate an average among targeted band and two adjacent bands in the wavelength direction. This processing is applied to each band of MSI. For example, in the case of 16-band MSI whose bands are numbered in ascending order of their wavelengths, the average among band 1, band 2, and band 3 is calculated when the target band is band 2.

The rest of the process is almost the same as [9]. The difference between the updated MSI and smoothed MSI is calculated. Then, a 2-D median filter is applied to the calculated difference in the spatial direction. Finally, we obtain the corrected MSI by adding the smoothed MSI to the median-filtered difference.

3   Experimental Results

We show the validation of the proposed method through an experiment. In this experiment, we compare our proposed method with bilinear interpolation, the method proposed by Brauers et al. [4], the method proposed by Miao et al. [5], and Step 1 in MLDI by applying these methods to the 16-band MSIs shown in Fig. 4. In Fig. 4, the 16-band images are converted to sRGB images. The size of these images is 512 × 512 pixels. The spectral sensitivities of the camera used for capturing *Toys*, *Dishes*, *Kettle*,

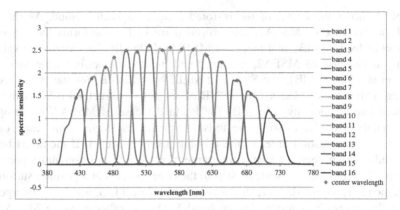

Fig. 5. The spectral sensitivities of the camera used by capturing *Toys*, *Dishes*, *Kettle*, and *Scarf*. The center wavelengths of each band are 424, 448, 469, 482, 500, 517, 535, 554, 566, 584, 602, 622, 644, 666, 687, and 720 nm. (Color figure online)

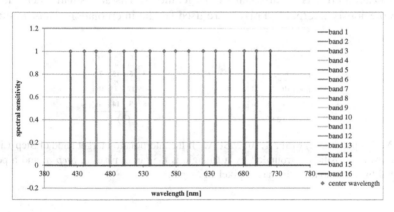

Fig. 6. The spectral sensitivities of the camera used by capturing *PI*. The center wavelengths of each band are 420, 441, 459, 480, 501, 519, 540, 561, 579, 600, 621, 639, 660, 681, 699, and 720 nm. (Color figure online)

and *Scarf* is shown in Fig. 5, and that used for capturing *PI* is shown in Fig. 6. The pathological tissue is of an H&Estained liver (US Biomax, Hepatocellular Carcinoma Tissue Array C054). The imaging system uses an optical microscope (Olympus, BX53), liquid crystal tunable filters (CRi, Varispec VIS), and monochrome CCD (Point Grey, Grasshopper 3). In MLDI, we assumed $\sigma = 0.5$ and $\varepsilon = 1$; the window size of the 2-D median filter is set to 17×17, and the length of the 1-D smoothing filter is set to 3. We assumed that the 16-band MSFA is arranged in 4×4 ($x = 2$) pixels, as shown in Fig. 7. The bands are numbered in ascending order of their wavelengths. We obtain the mosaicked MSI by sampling the pixel values from the original MSI that captured by single-camera-multi-shot systems. Next, we obtain the restored images of the mosaicked MSI by applying each demosaicking method, and then, evaluate these methods based on peak signal-to-noise ratio (PSNR) and visual observation.

Table 1 shows the PSNR of the restored images for each method. As shown in Table 1, in the case of MSFA1, our proposed method outperforms the method of Brauers et al. by 1.75 [dB], and Step 1 in MLDI by 0.96 [dB] for the average value. In addition, in the case of MSFA2, our proposed method outperforms the method of Brauers et al. by 2.93 [dB], and Step 1 in MLDI by 1.22 [dB] for the average value. However, in the case of MSFA1, the PSNR of our proposed method is lower than that of bilinear interpolation by 0.56 [dB] for PI. In the case of MSFA2, our proposed method outperforms the existing methods for all the test MSIs. This result can be related to the interpolation order of the missing pixels in Step 1. If the target band is band 1 and t is two, then, in *Step a*, the target pixel is at a position surrounded by a triangle as shown in Fig. 7. Next, in *Step b*, the target pixel is at a position surrounded by a diamond. Thus, in MSFA1, the positions of bands 11, 3, and 9 are interpolated sequentially during the interpolation of band 1. On the other hand, in MSFA2, the positions of bands 2, 3, and 4 are interpolated sequentially during the interpolation of band 1. In Step 1, when the wavelength of the target and the reference bands are close, the correlation between those bands is strong, then, interpolation accuracy is high. If the interpolation error is small when t is large, the error is also small when t is small because previously interpolated pixels are used for the interpolation. Thus, in the case

(a)   (b)

Fig. 7. MSFA pattern: (a) MSFA1, (b) MSFA2. If the interpolation target band of Step 1 is band 1 and t is two, a position surrounded by a triangle is the target pixel in *Step a*, and a position surrounded by a diamond is the target pixel in *Step b*.

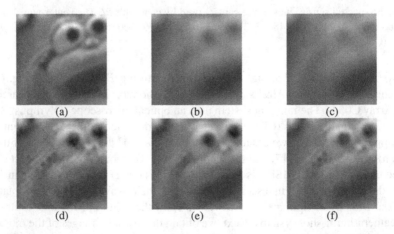

(a)   (b)   (c)

(d)   (e)   (f)

Fig. 8. Comparison between demosaicked images of *Toys* in the case of MSFA2: (a) Original, (b) Bilinear, (c) Miao et al. [5], (d) Brauers et al. [4], (e) MLDI (Step 1), (f) MLDI.

Table 1. Comparison of each method in terms of PSNR: (a) MSFA1, (b) MSFA2.

Method	Toys	Dishes	Kettle	Scarf	PI	Average
(a)						
Bilinear	29.46	27.32	26.70	28.10	**32.83**	28.88
Miao	29.61	27.64	26.87	28.20	32.60	28.98
Brauers	31.40	29.74	29.05	29.00	31.72	30.18
MLDI (Step 1)	32.19	30.88	29.81	29.78	32.26	30.99
MLDI (Step 1-3)	**33.18**	**32.35**	**31.20**	**30.63**	32.27	**31.93**
(b)						
Bilinear	29.44	27.31	26.66	28.09	32.82	28.86
Miao	29.60	27.64	26.83	28.20	32.60	28.97
Brauers	31.55	29.83	29.08	29.27	31.95	30.34
MLDI (Step 1)	32.91	31.22	30.04	31.32	34.75	32.05
MLDI (Step 1-3)	**34.43**	**32.95**	**31.74**	**32.36**	**34.86**	**33.27**

of MSFA2, interpolation accuracy is high because the wavelength of the target and the reference bands are close when t is large. Therefore, for MLDI, MSFA2 is more suitable than MSFA1.

In addition, Fig. 8 shows the sRGB versions of the images obtained by applying each method to the image *Toys* in the case of MSFA2. As shown in Fig. 8, the restored image obtained by applying MLDI has fewer artifacts than the one obtained by applying the other existing methods. This result can be attributed to the consideration of inter-channel correlation and spatial gradient in MLDI.

The proposed method has a room for improvement by changing the number of neighboring pixels of Step 2, and this is one of our future work. We use eight neighboring pixels in this step, but observed pixels are not included in the window when a pixel of band 1 is interpolated at the triangle position of Fig. 7. It has the potential to be improved by adjusting the windows size depending on the dense of the observed pixels.

In future work, it is necessary for our proposed method to consider the distance between the interpolation target and the reference bands in the wavelength direction for the interpolation in order to improve the quality of the restored image because the quality of the restored image obtained by our proposed method is poorer than the original image.

4 Conclusion

In this paper, we proposed MLDI that is based on LDI and considers inter-channel correlation and spatial gradient. We evaluated the performance of our proposed method by comparing it with existing methods. Experimental results show that our proposed method outperforms the existing methods. In future work, we plan to enhance MLDI and compare it with existing methods for various MSFAs.

Acknowledgement. This work was supported by JSPS KAKENHI Grant Number 15K20899. We would like to thank Masahiro Yamaguchi at the Tokyo Institute of Technology for providing the test images used in our experiments.

References

1. Tashiro, M., Murakami, Y., Yamaguchi, M., Obi, T., Ohyama, N., Abe, T., Yagi, Y.: Efficient implementation of dye amount adjustment in pathological images using multispectral pathological imaging. Med. Imaging Technol. **26**(4), 240–246 (2008)
2. Monno, Y., Tanaka, M., Okutomi, M.: Multispectral demosaicking using adaptive kernel upsampling. In: Proceedings of IEEE International Conference on Image Processing (ICIP), pp. 3218–3221 (2011)
3. Kopf, J., Cohen, M.F., Lischinski, D., Uyttendaele, M.: Joint bilateral upsampling. ACM Trans. Graphics **26**(3), 96-1–96-5 (2007)
4. Brauers, J., Aach, T.: A color filter array based multispectral camera. In: Proceedings of Workshop Farbbildverarbeitung (2006)
5. Miao, L., Qi, H., Ramanath, R., Snyder, W.E.: Binary tree-based generic demosaicking algorithm for multispectral filter arrays. IEEE Trans. Image Process. **15**(11), 3550–3558 (2006)
6. Monno, Y., Tanaka, M., Okutomi, M.: Multispectral demosaicking using guided filter. In: Proceedings of SPIE, vol. 8299, pp. 82990O-1–82990O-7 (2012)
7. He, K., Sun, J., Tang, X.: Guided image filtering. In: Daniilidis, K., Maragos, P., Paragios, N. (eds.) ECCV 2010, Part I. LNCS, vol. 6311, pp. 1–14. Springer, Heidelberg (2010)
8. Zhang, L., Wu, X., Buades, A., Li, X.: Color demosaicking by local directional interpolation and nonlocal adaptive thresholding. J. Electron. Imaging **20**(2), 023016-1–023016-16 (2011)
9. Buades, A., Coll, B., Morel, J.-M., Sbert, C.: Self-similarity driven color demosaicking. IEEE Trans. Image Process. **18**(6), 1192–1202 (2009)

Image Filtering, Segmentation
and Super-Resolution

Single Image Super-Resolution Using Sparse Representation on a K-NN Dictionary

Liu Ning[(⊠)] and Liang Shuang

School of Mathematical, Peking University, Science Building in Peking University,
No 5. Yiheyuan Road, Beijing, People's Republic of China
liuning19880928@gmail.com, liangshuang12@pku.edu.cn

Abstract. This paper presents a new method of generating a high-resolution image from a low-resolution image. We use a sparse representation based model for low-resolution image patches. We use large patches instead of small ones of existing methods. The size of the dictionary must be large to guarantee its completeness. For each patch in the low-resolution image, we search for similar patches in the dictionary to obtain a sub-dictionary. To define the similarity and to speed up the searching process, we present a Restricted Boltzmann Machine (RBM) based binary encoding method to get binary codes for the low-resolution patches, and use Hamming distance to describe the similarity. With the KNN dictionary of each low-resolution patch, we use a sparse representation method to get its high-resolution version. Experimental results illustrate that our method outperforms other methods.

Keywords: Super-resolution · Sparse representation · Restricted Boltzmann machine · Binary encoding

1 Introduction

Single image super-resolution (SR) refers to the task of generating a high-resolution (HR) image from a low-resolution (LR) image. It is useful in many applications, such as medical imaging, video surveillance and remote sensing imaging. Since many HR images can produce the same LR images, and SR is the reverse process, so SR is inherently ill-posed. Various SR methods have been proposed to stabilize the inversion of this ill-posed problem.

SR methods can be roughly classified into three categories: interpolation based, reconstruction based and learning based methods. Interpolation based methods (e.g., [1,2]) are simple and fast, while they tend to smooth edges and cause blurring problems. Reconstruction based methods (e.g. [4]) apply various smoothness priors, and the enforced priors are typically designed to reduce edge artifacts. The performance of reconstruction based SR methods degrades rapidly when the number of available input images is small or the desired magnification factor is large. Learning based methods are the most popular ones. These methods either exploit internal similarities of the same image [5,13], or reconstruct

© Springer International Publishing Switzerland 2016
A. Mansouri et al. (Eds.): ICISP 2016, LNCS 9680, pp. 169–178, 2016.
DOI: 10.1007/978-3-319-33618-3_18

the high frequency details from a training set of LR and HR patch pairs [6,7]. However, these methods use a unique dictionary for all the patches, and the patch size is relatively small, which may limit the SR result.

In this paper, we propose a novel SR algorithm which is based on sparse representation. Unlike existing sparse representation methods, ours employ an RBM based binary encoding method for nearest neighbor searching and uses KNN as the dictionary of each patch to conduct sparse representation.

The contributions of this paper are summarized as follows: (1) An RBM based binary encoding method is used to retrieve the KNN of each patch. (2) Using KNN as dictionary for each patch minimizes the reconstruction error in sparse representation, which leads to better SR result. (3) Large patches are employed instead of small ones as the atoms of dictionaries. Since a large patch contains more meaningful information than a small one, more high frequency details are retained in SR results.

2   Methods

In this section, we present our sparse representation based super-resolution method. In Sect. 2.1, we will introduce dictionary preparation related work. RBM based binary encoding method is introduced in Sect. 2.2. We use this method to encode each LR patch in D_l and the input LR image. We use the KNN of each LR patch retrieved by the binary codes to conduct sparse representation reconstruction, which is introduced in Sect. 2.3. The flowchart of our method is shown in Fig. 1.

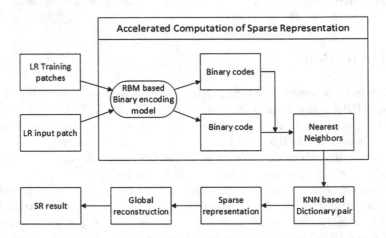

Fig. 1. The flowchart of our super-resolution algorithm.

2.1 Dictionary Preparation

Sparse representation based methods are widely used in learning-based super-resolution field [16,17]. An over-complete dictionary pair is important for these methods. Many SR methods focus on learning an efficiency dictionary [3,15]. To prepare the dictionary pair, we download HR images from Internet as our training set. For each HR training image, we generate the corresponding LR image by blurring and down-sampling. For LR images, we conduct bicubic interpolation to ensure that their sizes are the same as their HR images. We are interested in the patches with ample texture. For this purpose, we use Canny operator to get edges in the LR images, and extract the LR patches that center at edges. HR patches are extracted at the same position in the corresponding HR images.

We use large patches instead of small ones to combine the dictionary pair D_l and D_h, and set the patch size as 19×19. To ensure the completeness of the dictionary with large patches, we set its size as 10^8. Since the dictionaries are huge, (for instance, the LR dictionary D_h, with the feature dimension $d = 19 \times 19 = 361$, and patch number $N = 10^8$,) the total integer number is over than 10^{10}, which needs about tens of Gigabytes. Obviously, computer memory can not load them all at once, so we divide them into 100 blocks respectively and handle them in block order.

2.2 RBM Based Binary Encoding Model

RBM based binary encoding model was proposed in [10]. Compact binary codes are learned via a stack of RBMs, each of which is trained by using the hidden activities of the previous RBM as its training data. This type of network is capable of capturing higher order correlations between different layers of the network. Each time a new RBM is added to this stack, the model has a better variational lower bound on the log probability of the data.

An RBM is a fully connected bipartite graph with one visible input (feature) layer $\mathbf{v} \in \mathbb{R}^{I \times 1}$ and one hidden (coding) layer $\mathbf{h} \in \mathbb{R}^{J \times 1}$, in which I and J represent the number of units of feature layer and coding layer respectively. Each unit has an input bias: represented as c_i for the feature layer and b_j for the coding layer. The layers are connected via undirected weights $\mathbf{W} \in \mathbb{R}^{I \times J}$. The activation probabilities of units are computed by sampling from the opposite layer with a sigmoid activation function, formulated as follows:

$$P(h_j|\mathbf{v}) = \text{sigmoid}(b_j + \sum_{i \in I} \omega_{ij} v_i), \tag{1}$$

$$P(v_i|\mathbf{h}) = \text{sigmoid}(c_i + \sum_{j \in J} \omega_{ij} h_j), \tag{2}$$

where v_i and h_j represent the state of units in the visible and hidden layers respectively.

The energy function of the RBM [10] is formulated as:

$$E(\mathbf{v}, \mathbf{h}) = -\log P(\mathbf{v}, \mathbf{h})$$
$$= -\sum_{i \in I} \sum_{j \in J} v_i \omega_{ij} h_j - \sum_{i \in I} c_i v_i - \sum_{j \in J} b_j h_j \tag{3}$$

The parameters $\mathbf{W} \in \mathbb{R}^{I \times J}$, $\mathbf{b} \in \mathbb{R}^{J \times 1}$ and $\mathbf{c} \in \mathbb{R}^{I \times 1}$ are updated with the objective of minimizing the energy function. The optimization method is called contrastive divergence (CD). A detailed introduction of the optimization process is given in [11]. With this optimization method, the update rules of parameters are formulated as:

$$\Delta w_{ij} = \epsilon(<v_i h_j>_{data} - <v_i h_j>_{recon}), \tag{4}$$
$$\Delta b_j = \epsilon(<h_j>_{data} - <h_j>_{recon}), \tag{5}$$
$$\Delta c_i = \epsilon(<v_i>_{data} - <v_i>_{recon}), \tag{6}$$

where ϵ is the learning rate, $< \cdot >_{data}$ represents the sample result, and $< \cdot >_{recon}$ represents the distribution of the model.

We implement this model with four layers: an input layer, two hidden layers and an output layer. The unit numbers used in each layer are $1444 - 1444 - 722 - 64$. The input unit number is determined by the high-frequency feature number of an LR patch, which is with the patch size as 19 and 4 directional high-frequency features. The output unit number 64 is the length of binary codes. The unsupervised training phase is executed layer by layer from input to output. We use the trained parameters to generate binary codes for patches in D_l and LR image. To reduce noise, we use the probabilities rather than the stochastic binary states in the generate process. The binary codes are the binarization results of output values of output units.

Figure 2 shows an example of similar patches retrieved in the LR dictionary D_l. From this figure, we get that the proposed binary encoding method preserves the local characteristics of patches.

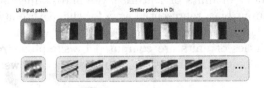

Fig. 2. Example of similar patches retrieved in the LR dictionary D_l.

2.3   Sparse Representation Based Super Resolution

In this section, we present our sparse representation based super-resolution method. Unlike existing sparse representation methods, ours uses KNN as dictionary for each LR patch. And it is realized by the RBM based binary encoding method presented in the previous section. We first conduct binary encoding to D_l and the LR patch x_i, and search the nearest neighbors of x_i in D_l using the hamming distance of their binary codes. The nearest neighbors compose the sub-dictionary $D_l(i)$. Since the atoms in the dictionaries are similar to their corresponding patches, the dictionaries are efficient enough, so that we do not need any dictionary learning method.

For each LR patch x_i in the original LR image, we get its LR dictionary $D_l(i)$ by KNN and the corresponding HR dictionary $D_h(i)$. The patch x_i can be represented as a sparse linear combination in dictionary $D_l(i)$, and the problem of finding the sparsest representation of x_i can be formulated as

$$\min \|\alpha\|_0 \quad \text{s.t.} \quad \|FD_l(i)\alpha - Fx_i\|_2^2 \leq \epsilon, \tag{7}$$

where F is a high-frequency (HF) feature extraction operator, which is composed of the following high-pass operators:

$$f_1 = \begin{pmatrix} +1 & +2 & +1 \\ 0 & 0 & 0 \\ -1 & -2 & -1 \end{pmatrix}, \quad f_2 = \begin{pmatrix} +1 & 0 & -1 \\ +2 & 0 & -2 \\ +1 & 0 & -1 \end{pmatrix},$$

$$f_3 = \begin{pmatrix} 0 & +1 & +2 \\ -1 & 0 & +1 \\ -2 & -1 & 0 \end{pmatrix}, \quad f_4 = \begin{pmatrix} +2 & +1 & 0 \\ +1 & 0 & -1 \\ 0 & -1 & -2 \end{pmatrix}.$$

We concatenate the four different directional HF features as one vector as the HF feature extraction operator F.

Since the optimization problem (7) is NP-hard, we approximate the ℓ_0 norm with the ℓ_1 norm, which can be formulated as

$$\min \|\alpha\|_1 \quad \text{s.t.} \quad \|FD_l(i)\alpha - Fx_i\|_2^2 \leq \epsilon \tag{8}$$

Theoretical study results [8] prove that as long as the coefficient α is sufficiently sparse, the solutions of optimization problems (7) and (8) are equivalent. Lagrange multipliers offer an equivalent formulation to (8), which is formulated as

$$\alpha^* = \operatorname*{argmin}_{\alpha} \lambda\|\alpha\|_1 + \frac{1}{2}\|FD_l(i)\alpha - Fx_i\|_2^2, \tag{9}$$

where the parameter λ balances the fidelity of the approximation to x_i and sparsity of the solution. We recommend to set $\lambda \in [0.1, 0.3]$. In statistical literature, this problem is called LASSO [9].

Another important issue is to guarantee the compatibility of adjacent patches. We solve this problem by a one-pass algorithm similar to the method in [14]. The basic idea is that the reconstruction result $D_h(i)\alpha$ should be close to the previously computed adjacent HR patches in the overlapping areas. With this constraint, the optimization problem can be formulated as

$$\min \|\alpha\|_1 \quad \text{s.t.} \begin{aligned} \|FD_l(i)\alpha - Fx_i\|_2^2 &\leq \epsilon_1, \\ \|PD_h(i)\alpha - \omega\|_2^2 &\leq \epsilon_2, \end{aligned} \tag{10}$$

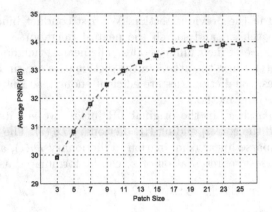

Fig. 3. Average PSNR results of ten benchmark images with different patch sizes.

where the matrix P extracts the overlap region between the previously reconstructed HR result and the current patch, and ω contains the previously reconstructed HR image on the overlap. The optimization problem (10) can be rewritten as

$$\alpha^* = \underset{\alpha}{\operatorname{argmin}} \lambda \|\alpha\|_1 + \frac{1}{2} \|\hat{D}\alpha - \hat{x}\|_2^2, \tag{11}$$

where $\hat{D} = \begin{bmatrix} FD_l(i) \\ PD_h(i) \end{bmatrix}$ and $\hat{x} = \begin{bmatrix} Fx_i \\ \omega \end{bmatrix}$. After computing the optimal solution α^* of (11), the HR patch can be reconstructed as $x_i^* = D_h(i)\alpha^*$.

After patch-based reconstruction, a global reconstruction constraint is enforced to get final super-resolution result. The global constraint can be formulated as:

$$Y^* = \underset{Y}{\operatorname{argmin}} \|Y - Y_{sr}\| \quad \text{s.t.} \quad X = DBY, \tag{12}$$

where Y_{sr} is the SR result of patch-based sparse representation method, X represents the LR version of Y, B represents the blurring filter, and D represents the down-sampling operator.

Formula (12) is solved using back-projection method by an iterative strategy, which is formulated as

$$Y_{t+1} = Y_t + ((X - DBY_t) \uparrow s) * p, \tag{13}$$

where Y_t is the estimated high-resolution image after the t-th iteration, $\uparrow s$ represents up-sampling by the factor of s, and p is the "back-projection" filter. The details of this global reconstruction constraint is explained in [6].

3 Experiments

We apply our algorithm to benchmark images including Pepper, Lena, Foreman etc., and compare the results with those of the bicubic, NE [12], Freeman and

Fig. 4. SR results of image Lena. From top to bottom, left to right: ground truth, bicubic interpolation, NE based [12], Freeman and Liu [7], Yang et al. [6], Peleg and Elad [18], SRCNN [19] and proposed method. The magnification factors is 2.

Fig. 5. SR results of image Foreman. From top to bottom, left to right: ground truth, bicubic interpolation, NE based [12], Freeman and Liu [7], Yang et al. [6], Peleg and Elad [18], SRCNN [19] and proposed method. The magnification factors is 4.

Liu [7], Yang et al. [6], Peleg and Elad [18] and SRCNN [19] methods. We test with different magnification factors respectively, and use PSNR to measure and compare these methods.

3.1 Parameter Settings

There are three important parameters in this algorithm: patch size, dictionary size and sub-dictionary size (the KNN number of a patch). To investigate the impact of different patch sizes, we fix all other parameters of this algorithm and record the average PSNR indicators of ten benchmark images. Experimental results in Fig. 3 show that larger patches result in better SR results. While the calculation time increases rapidly with an increase of patch size. To balance the

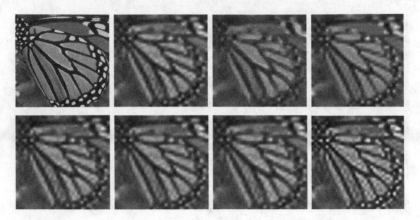

Fig. 6. SR results of image Butterfly. From top to bottom, left to right: ground truth, bicubic interpolation, NE based [12], Freeman and Liu [7], Yang et al. [6], Peleg and Elad [18], SRCNN [19] and proposed method. The magnification factors is 8.

efficiency and performance, we choose the patch size as 19 in our experiments (Fig. 4).

Theoretically, larger dictionary size and sub-dictionary size result in better SR results, while larger dictionary means more retrieve time and storage space.

Table 1. Experimental results of PSNR index on benchmark images

	MF	Lena	Girl	Baboon	Butterfly	Flowers	Foreman	Zebra	Pepper	Starfish	Average
Bicubic	2	31.35	36.86	24.36	26.51	29.03	31.39	29.25	32.04	28.75	29.95
	4	27.66	34.23	22.06	21.79	24.93	26.78	23.63	28.44	24.48	26.01
	8	24.72	32.18	21.01	17.68	21.96	23.10	19.57	25.24	21.49	22.99
NE [12]	2	31.17	36.90	24.28	26.30	29.14	31.52	29.09	32.15	28.69	29.92
	4	27.55	34.17	22.17	21.61	24.82	26.91	23.98	28.49	24.59	26.03
	8	24.61	32.01	21.21	17.83	21.82	23.18	19.79	25.19	21.61	23.03
Freeman and Liu [7]	2	31.48	36.87	24.28	26.49	29.18	31.54	29.17	32.72	28.72	30.05
	4	27.61	34.61	22.29	21.91	25.02	27.01	23.71	28.61	24.61	26.15
	8	24.92	32.42	21.51	18.17	22.01	23.72	19.92	25.64	21.94	23.36
SC [6]	2	32.80	36.58	24.42	27.33	29.61	31.91	29.50	32.34	29.21	30.41
	4	27.66	34.18	22.06	22.02	25.01	26.66	23.99	28.45	24.53	26.06
	8	24.72	32.16	21.01	17.98	22.18	23.09	19.84	25.26	21.56	23.07
Peleg and Elad [18]	2	32.19	36.25	23.83	26.83	29.71	31.26	29.61	32.73	29.31	30.19
	4	27.86	34.19	21.12	21.87	24.82	26.15	24.01	28.38	24.72	25.90
	8	24.71	32.01	19.89	17.10	22.19	22.98	19.71	25.01	21.46	22.79
SRCNN [19]	2	32.79	36.54	24.29	26.50	28.48	31.28	28.13	32.01	29.02	29.89
	4	27.12	33.61	22.70	22.20	24.23	27.16	22.62	27.78	23.67	25.68
	8	24.91	32.71	21.81	18.01	22.81	23.27	20.19	25.53	21.71	23.44
Our method	2	**33.28**	**37.13**	**25.31**	**27.49**	**30.17**	**32.58**	**30.19**	**33.17**	**30.62**	**31.10**
	4	**28.11**	**34.89**	**22.98**	**22.38**	**25.19**	**27.28**	**24.20**	**28.78**	**25.01**	**26.54**
	8	**25.17**	**32.81**	**22.01**	**18.22**	**23.17**	**24.11**	**20.28**	**26.16**	**21.90**	**23.76**

Limited by the capability of our computer, we set dictionary size as 10^8, and sub-dictionary size as 2000.

3.2 Experimental Results and Comparison

We compare our algorithm with other algorithms under different magnification factors (MF). Figure 6 shows the SR results with different magnification factors. From the first row to the third row, the magnification factors are 2, 4 and 8 respectively. Table 1 shows the PSNR results tested on several benchmark images. From this figure and table, we get that our algorithm outperforms others. And the advantage is obvious when the magnification factor is large (Fig. 5).

4 Conclusion

Experimental results demonstrate the effectiveness of our SR method, especially when the magnification factor is large. We adopt a RBM based binary encoding model for super-resolution, and use the KNN of a patch to combine its sub-dictionary. Because the KNN dictionary can minimize the reconstruction error, and the large patch size contains more information, the super-resolution result is better than the state-of-art of super-resolution methods.

Further improvement can be realized through a property hashing method, which can accelerate the KNN searching process. On the other hand, a fast dictionary learning method may be added to make the dictionary more compact, which may further improve the super-resolution result.

References

1. Keys, R.: Cubic convolution interpolation for digital image processing. IEEE Trans. Acoust. Speech Signal Process. **29**(6), 1153–1160 (1981)
2. Li, X., Orchard, M.T.: New edge-directed interpolation. IEEE Trans. Image Process. **10**(10), 1521–1527 (2001)
3. Juefei-Xu, F., Savvides, M.: Single face image super-resolution via solo dictionary learning. In: IEEE International Conference on Image Processing, pp. 2239–2243 (2015)
4. Morse, B., Schwartzwald, D.: Image magnification using level-set reconstruction. In: IEEE Conference on Computer Vision and Pattern Recognition, pp. 333–340 (2001)
5. Freedman, G., Fattal, R.: Image and video upscaling from local self-examples. TOG **30**(2), 12 (2011)
6. Yang, J., Wright, J., Huang, T., Ma, Y.: Image super-resolution via sparse representation. IEEE Trans. Image Process. **19**(11), 2861–2873 (2010)
7. Freeman, W.T., Liu, C.: Markov random fields for super-resolution and texture synthesis (Chap. 10). In: Blake, A., Kohli, P., Rother, C. (eds.) Advances in Markov Random Fields for Vision and Image Processing. MIT Press, Cambridge (2011)
8. Donoho, D.L.: For most large underdetermined systems of linear equations, the minimal ℓ1-norm solution is also the sparsest solution. Comm. Pure Appl. Math. **59**(6) (2006)

9. Tibshirani, R.: Regression shrinkge and selection via the lasso. J. Roy. Stat. Soc. B **58**(1), 267–288 (1996)
10. Hinton, G., Salakhutdinov, R.: Reducing the dimensionality of data with neural networks. Science **313**(5786), 504–507 (2006)
11. Hinton, G.: Training products of experts by minimizing contrastive divergence. Neural Comput. **14**(8), 1771–1800 (2002)
12. Chang, H., Yeung, D.-Y., Xiong, Y.: Super-resolution through neighbor embedding. In: IEEE Conference on Computer Vision and Pattern Recognition, vol. 1 (2004)
13. Huang, J.B., Singh, A., Ahuja, N.: Single image super-resolution from transformed self-exemplars. In: IEEE Conference on Computer Vision and Pattern Recognition, pp. 5197–5206 (2015)
14. Freeman, W.T., Jones, T.R., Pasztor, E.C.: Example based super-resolution. IEEE Comput. Graphics Appl. **22**(2), 56–65 (2002)
15. Xie, J., Chou, C.C., Feris, R., et al.: Single depth image super resolution and denoising via coupled dictionary learning with local constraints and shock filtering. In: IEEE International Conference on Multimedia and Expo, pp. 1–6 (2014)
16. Rao, A.B., Rao, J.V.: Super resolution of quality images through sparse representation. In: Satapathy, S.C., Avadahani, P.S., Udgata, S.K., Lakshminarayana, S. (eds.) ICT and Critical Infrastructure: Proceedings of the 48th Annual Convention of CSI - Volume II. AISC, vol. 249, pp. 49–56. Springer, Heidelberg (2014)
17. Wang, Y.-H., Fu, P.: Sparse representation based medical MR image super-resolution. Int. J. Adv. Comput. Technol. **4**(19) (2012)
18. Peleg, T., Elad, M.: A statistical prediction model based on sparse representations for single image super-resolution. IEEE Trans. Image Process. **23**(6), 2569–2582 (2014)
19. Dong, C., Loy, C.C., He, K., et al.: Image super-resolution using deep convolutional networks (2015)

Super-Resolved Enhancement of a Single Image and Its Application in Cardiac MRI

Guang Yang[1,2]($\boxtimes$), Xujiong Ye[3], Greg Slabaugh[4], Jennifer Keegan[1,2], Raad Mohiaddin[1,2], and David Firmin[1,2]

[1] Cardiovascular MR Unit, Royal Brompton Hospital, London SW3 6NP, UK
g.yang@imperial.ac.uk
[2] National Heart & Lung Institute, Imperial College London,
London SW7 2AZ, UK
[3] School of Computer Science, University of Lincoln,
Lincoln LN6 7TS, UK
[4] Department of Computer Science, City University London,
London EC1V 0HB, UK

Abstract. Super-resolved image enhancement is of great importance in medical imaging. Conventional methods often require multiple low resolution (LR) images from different views of the same object or learning from large amount of training datasets to achieve success. However, in real clinical environments, these prerequisites are rarely fulfilled. In this paper, we present a self-learning based method to perform super-resolution (SR) from a single LR input. The mappings between the given LR image and its downsampled versions are modeled using support vector regression on features extracted from sparse coded dictionaries, coupled with dual-tree complex wavelet transform based denoising. We demonstrate the efficacy of our method in application of cardiac MRI enhancement. Both quantitative and qualitative results show that our SR method is able to preserve fine textural details that can be corrupted by noise, and therefore can maintain crucial diagnostic information.

1 Introduction

High resolution (HR) images are in demand for cardiac magnetic resonance imaging (CMRI). However, HR CMRI images are often costly to acquire. In particular, the quality and resolution of CMRI images can be limited dramatically by low signal to noise ratio, cardiac and respiratory motion, and restricted scanning time due to patient symptoms etc. In consequence, noise corrupted and low resolution (LR) images are produced that may reduce the visibility of vital pathological details and potentially compromise the clinical outcomes.

Instead of optimizing hardware settings (e.g., improved cardiac gating and respiratory navigation) and reducing scanning time (e.g., accelerated by parallel imaging and compressed sensing), image super-resolution (SR) provides an alternative solution to boost the perceptual quality of CMRI images in terms of the

G. Yang—This work has been funded by NIHR.

© Springer International Publishing Switzerland 2016
A. Mansouri et al. (Eds.): ICISP 2016, LNCS 9680, pp. 179–190, 2016.
DOI: 10.1007/978-3-319-33618-3_19

spatial resolution enhancement. Essentially, the goal of SR methods is to recover a HR image from a single or multiple LR images [1]. Comprehensive reviews on various SR methods can be found elsewhere [2,3], and here we briefly review the most relevant publications. Existing SR algorithms can be broadly categorized into three classes including interpolation based, reconstruction based, and learning or example based methods [4]. Widely used interpolation based SR methods, which assume that images are spatially smooth, typically result in overly smoothed edges with ringing and jagged artifacts [4,5]. Reconstruction based algorithms, which solve an inverse problem by recovering the HR image by fusing multiple LR images, are time-consuming and limited to an upsampling factor of two [4–6]. For learning or example based methods, the mapping function between LR and HR images (or their patches) is learned from a representative set of training image pairs. Once the mapping function is learned, it is applied to a single testing image to achieve SR. Despite numerous learning or example based methods (e.g., [7–10]) claiming success for single-image SR, these methods hinge on the availability of training data of LR and HR image pairs; therefore, we define them as *pseudo-single-image* SR.

Compared to pseudo-single-image SR methods, Glasner et al. [1] proposed a self-similarity based single-image SR method using a training dataset that is directly established from the LR input, by exploiting patch redundancy among in-scale and cross-scale images in an image pyramid to enforce constraints for recovering the unknown HR image [4]. In this method, no extrinsic large training dataset is required as a priori, but the abundance of self-similar patches is crucial for successful SR recovery. Instead of searching for similar image patches, Yang and Wang [11] used support vector regression (SVR) to learn SR models from patches at different image scales. They also applied a sparse representation to extract effective image features for SVR to make their SR algorithm more computationally feasible for real applications, following the application of sparse representation originally proposed for solving the SR problem by Yang et al. [12]. More recently, Singh and Ahuja [13] added sub-band energy constraints for the self-similarity based SR method, and Huang et al. [14] enriched the dataset of self-similar patches by looking at their transformed exemplars. Although these studies have demonstrated promising results, the SR methods were applied on natural images, which are relatively clean. Therefore, the performance of these methods for noisy inputs, e.g., CMRI images, hasn't been demonstrated.

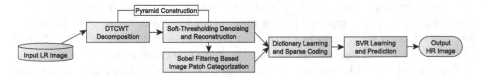

Fig. 1. Flowchart of our approach including both learning and prediction.

In this paper, we propose an SVR based SR method that learns a sparse representation as robust and effective features across various down-sampled and denoised versions (using dual-tree complex wavelet transform, i.e., DTCWT) of a single input LR image. Once the SVR has been trained, we can apply the best model to predict the final SR image from a single LR image (Fig. 1). Compared to the previous learning based methods [7–9], our method does not require construction of paired LR and HR training datasets. Compared to Glasner et al. [1] (Fig. 2(a)) and more recent work by Singh and Ahuja [13], our method does not assume self-similarity of image patches. In contrast to the SR methods [11,15], in which SVR was originally applied, we use DTCWT to suppress the noise, and we hypothesize that our method is more applicable for medical imaging applications [16], in particular for the CMRI images.

2   Method

The overall workflow of our method is summarized in Fig. 1, and details of each step are described below.

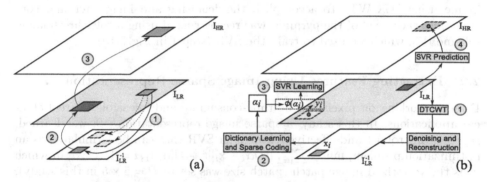

Fig. 2. Schematic diagram of (a) conventional self-similarity based SR method and (b) our self-learning based SR approach. Panel (a): In step 1, the input LR image I_{LR} (yellow) is downsampled by a factor of two recursively into several lower levels, and here only one downsampled level (I_{LR}^{-1}) is shown for illustration purposes. Then k nearest neighbors of the example patch (brown patch P_{LR} in I_{LR}) are located in the downsampled level. For simplicity, we show the case where the most similar patch (red patch in I_{LR}^{-1}) is used (i.e., $k = 1$). In step 2, the corresponding patch at the same location (red patch in I_{LR}) is used as the HR predictor (notice the larger size). In step 3, this patch is copied and pasted in the HR image (I_{HR}). In the case of $k > 1$, multiple predictors are averaged and then pasted; Panel (b): Four major steps of our method and details are described in Sects. 2.1–2.3 Instead of downsampling using bicubic interpolation, DTCWT based denoising and reconstruction was applied to construct the image pyramid. (Color figure online)

2.1 Denoising and Pyramid Construction Using DTCWT

Most previous self-similarity or self-learning methods (e.g., [1,11,13]) used bicubic interpolation to construct the image pyramid, but this can be susceptible to noise. Intuitively, discrete wavelet transform (DWT) based denoising has an intrinsic multiscale structure of decomposition and reconstruction, and therefore can be suitable for the pyramid construction task while effectively suppressing the noise. In addition, the dual-tree complex wavelet transform (DTCWT) overcomes two shortcomings of the widely used conventional DWT: lack of shift-invariance and lack of directional selectivity [17]. Regarding memory usage, the DTCWT is an over-complete transform with a redundancy factor of four for 2D image processing while DWT is non-redundant. An alternative method to obtain the orientation selective sub-bands is using steerable pyramid decomposition [13], which is over-complete by a factor of $4k/3$ (where k denotes the number of orientation sub-bands) [18]. Regarding computational complexity, the DTCWT is linear $\mathcal{O}(N)$ where N is the number of input pixels. In contrast, the steerable pyramid decomposition has a complexity of $\mathcal{O}(N \log N)$. By considering both memory and computational complexity, instead of using steerable pyramid decomposition to overcome limitations of DWT, we decomposed the original image using DTCWT. To accomplish the denoising and image pyramid construction, each level of the pyramid was reconstructed using a soft-thresholding scheme [17], which we used to train the SVR (step 1 in Fig. 2(b)).

2.2 Extracting Features Using Image Sparse Representation

Directly working on pixels can be time-consuming and infeasible for real clinical applications. In this study, a sparse image representation [19] was learned, representing robust and effective features for SVR that can be formulated as an optimization problem, $\min \frac{1}{n} \sum_{i=1}^{n} ||D\alpha_i - x_i||_2^2 + \lambda ||\alpha_i||_1, i = 1, \ldots, n$, in which x_i is the vectorized image patch (patch size was set to $P = 5 \times 5$ in this study), and is denoted as $x = \text{vectorize}(P_{LR}) - \text{mean}(P_{LR}) \in \mathbb{R}^{P \times 1}$, and the subtraction of the mean value of each LR patch ($\text{mean}(P_{LR})$) indicates the learning of local pixel value variations instead of learning absolute pixel values. Here n is the number of training patches and D is the over-complete dictionary to be learned, α_i is the corresponding sparse coefficient vector, and λ is the Lagrange multiplier term that regularizes the model sparsity (l_1-norm term) and the l_2-norm based residual. According to previous research [11], better SR performance can be achieved by patch categorization, i.e., clustering patches into low and high spatial frequency ones and learning their dictionaries separately. We applied a Sobel filter in this study, such that any patch including an edge derived from the Sobel filter is considered to have high spatial frequency. In doing this, two dictionaries (D_l and D_h) for low and high spatial frequency patches have been learned separately. Accordingly, we used the corresponding sparse coefficient vectors α_l and α_h as the features for the SVR models (step 2 in Fig. 2(b)).

2.3   Support Vector Regression

Finally, support vector regression (in this study we used ν-SVR) [20], which can fit the data in a high dimensional feature space without assuming the data distribution, was applied to model the relationship between the input sparse coefficient vector α and the associated SR pixel value. In the training procedure, the SVR solves the following optimization problem,

$$\min \frac{1}{2}\|\omega\|^2 + \rho\left(\nu\epsilon + \frac{1}{n}\sum_{i=1}^{n}(\xi_i + \xi_i^*)\right)$$
$$\text{subject to } y_i - \langle\omega, \Phi(\alpha_i)\rangle - b \leq \epsilon + \xi_i$$
$$\langle\omega, \Phi(\alpha_i)\rangle + b - y_i \leq \epsilon + \xi_i^*$$
$$\xi_i, \xi_i^* \geq 0, \ \epsilon \geq 0, \ i, \ldots, n$$

in which y_i denotes the associated target variable, i.e., pixel value at the center of the patch considered in the HR image (mean(P_{LR})) is also subtracted from each corresponding y_i). $\Phi(\alpha_i)$ is the sparse image patch features in the transformed space; thus, $\Phi(\alpha_i)$ and y_i form the feature and target variable pairs for training. And ω is the norm vector of the nonlinear mapping function to be learned. In addition, ρ is the tradeoff between the generalization and the upper and lower bounds of training errors ξ_i and ξ_i^* subject to a margin of ϵ, and ν controls the amount of support vectors in the resulting model. $K(\alpha_i, \alpha_j) \equiv \Phi(\alpha_i)^T\Phi(\alpha_j)$ is called the kernel function. In this study, we used a nonlinear Gaussian Radial Basis Function (RBF) kernel $K(\alpha_i, \alpha_j) = \exp(-\gamma\|\alpha_i - \alpha_j\|^2)$ with scaling-factor, $\gamma > 0$, to map feature vectors into a nonlinear transformed feature space. SVR parameters (ρ and γ) were estimated using grid search with cross-validation. Furthermore, SVR model selection was achieved according to a minimum-error-rate classification rule based on Bayesian decision theory [11], and the trained best SVR model was applied to predict the final SR output for a test LR input (steps 3 and 4 in Fig. 2(b)).

2.4   Experimental Settings and Performance Measure

First, ex-vivo swine heart MR imaging data were acquired on a Siemens Skyra 3T MRI system (Erlangen, Germany). The subject was scanned using a 4-element receive coil setup and a 3D fast low-angle shot sequence (3D FLASH, TR/TE = 50 ms/5.36 ms, flip angle = 35°, voxel resolution = 0.6 mm³, and reconstructed into 0.3 mm³ isotropically). Second, in-vivo patient data were acquired on a Siemens Avanto 1.5T MRI system. Ten subjects were scanned using a navigator-gated inversion-prepared 3D segmented gradient echo sequence with late gadolinium enhancement (TR/TE = 5.2 ms/2.3 ms, flip angle = 20°, voxel resolution = $1.5 \times 1.5 \times 4$ mm³, and reconstructed into $0.7 \times 0.7 \times 2$ mm³) [21].

For the ex-vivo data, we extracted the central slice from the axial and saggital views respectively in order to test the efficacy of our method on both in-plane and out-of-plane slices. The original resolution is 400×400 pixels for both slices, and used as HR ground truth for SR results evaluation. Inputs were synthesized by downsampling (by a factor of 2 and 4 denoted as x2 and x4 resulted in 200×200

and 100×100 inputs respectively), and degrading (by various additive noises [($\sigma = 10, 15, 20$, and 25) and run 10 times for each noise level]). Evaluations have been done qualitatively by visual inspection and quantitatively using peak signal to noise ratio (PSNR) and mean squared error (MSE) against the HR ground truth. The performance of our method was compared with bicubic interpolation with standard low-pass Gaussian filter based denoising and the self-learning based SR approach (SLSR) proposed in [11]. For the in-vivo data, we randomly chose 40 ROIs (each of 200×200 pixels) from 10 patient cases. For these 40 noise corrupted LR slices, we have no HR ground truth available. In addition to visual inspection of x2 SR, we compared the line profiles extracted from the results of three SR methods, namely, bicubic (with standard low-pass Gaussian filter based denoising), SLSR, and ours, and estimated the remaining noise in the SR results using the method described in [22].

3   Results

Figure 3(a) shows the synthesized LR input by a downsampling factor of two. The added noise ($\sigma = 15$) is shown in Fig. 3(b). Figure 3(c) is the zoomed-in ROI of the HR ground truth. Compared to the results of using bicubic interpolation and SLSR method (Fig. 3(d) and (e)), our SR result (Fig. 3(f)) is much more homogeneous in the myocardium region. In addition, green arrows pointed at three example fine structures that are much clearer in our SR result. Figure 3(g)–(i) are the results recovered from the synthesized LR input by an x4 downsampling with additive noise ($\sigma = 15$). Pink arrows pointed at textures that have been preserved using our SR method (Fig. 3(i)) while missing in the bicubic interpolation and SLSR method (Fig. 3(g) and (h)). Tables 1 and 2 show the PSNR and MSE with various additive noises, and the standard deviations were calculated by running the random noise simulation 10 times at each noise level ($\sigma = 10, 15, 20$, and 25). In addition, our SR results (both PSNR and MSE in Fig. 4) showed significant improvement compared to the results of bicubic interpolation and SLSR (statistical significances were given by two-sample Wilcoxon rank-sum test between the results of each two SR methods with significance level of $p < 0.05$). There is no significant difference between bicubic interpolation and SLSR when the noise level is high (e.g., when $\sigma = 25$).

Figure 5(a)–(c) shows the x2 SR results for one ROI of an in-vivo late gadolinium enhancement scan. Our SR result (Fig. 5(c)) shows noise suppression in the blood pool region of the left atrium, and therefore less confounding artifacts with similar intensities as the real late gadolinium enhancement of the myocardial wall. In addition, line profiles (Fig. 5(d) and (e)) across the SR results show that bicubic interpolation and SLSR method tend to be much noisier. Furthermore, the noise level estimations have been performed according to [22], and our method obtained a lower level of remaining noise (Table 3 shows that $\sigma = 32.04 \pm 4.17$ compared to $\sigma = 35.76 \pm 3.67$ obtained by bicubic interpolation and $\sigma = 40.17 \pm 4.89$ obtained by SLSR method, and noise level of the original LR input is $\sigma = 53.52 \pm 5.48$).

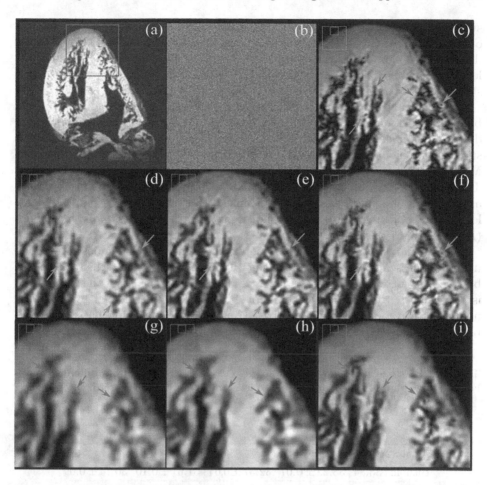

Fig. 3. (a) Synthesized input LR image (sagittal view of a swine heart MRI slice) that is downsampled (x2) and noise corrupted (red box showing the ROI; contrast has been altered for better visualization of the background noise); (b) Random noise ($\sigma = 15$) added to the original HR image; (c) ROI of the original HR image without blurring or noise (ground truth); Panels (d)–(f): x2 SR results; (d) ROI of the bicubic interpolation result; (e) ROI of the SLSR result; (f) ROI of our result; Green arrows pointed three example fine structures that have been super-resolved using our method, but much more blurred using bicubic interpolation and SLSR method; Panels (g)–(i): x4 SR results; (g) ROI of the bicubic interpolation result; (h) ROI of the SLSR result; (i) ROI of our result; Pink arrows point to three example textures that have been preserved using our method, but which are more vague in the results of using bicubic interpolation or the SLSR method. (Color figure online)

4   Discussion and Conclusion

The objective of this study was to develop an image post-processing method to super-resolve LR cardiac MR images from single input while effectively suppressing the noise. Results of this work provide compelling evidence that our single image SR method, which is coupled with multiscale DTCWT based denoising, is capable of reconstructing superior HR results with significantly lower remaining noise compared with conventional bicubic interpolation and a state-of-the-art self-learning based SR approach, i.e., SLSR.

Kernel based single image SR methods (example kernels including linear, bicubic, and Lanczos kernel) are the most widely used in clinical applications due to their efficiency. Results of our experiments on ex-vivo cardiac MR images showed that bicubic kernel based interpolation obtained lower PSNR and higher MSE than SLSR or our methods when the noise level $\sigma \leq 20$ (Tables 1 and 2). This can be attributed to the fact that bicubic interpolation makes strong assumptions on spatial smoothness of images that can result in blurred edges, loss of fine textures, and averaged noisy pixels with their less noisy neighbors (Fig. 3(d) and (g)).

Self-similarity based methods and later proposed self-learning based methods utilize a multiscale decomposition of the LR image to understand the relationship between its current scale and its lower resolution versions. Then the HR output is reconstructed either using prediction from candidates selected by k-nearest neighbors method (self-similarity based) or SVR (self-learning based). To the best of our knowledge, previously published self-similarity or self-learning based

Table 1. PSNR of x2 and x4 SR on ex-vivo cardiac MRI data from different views. For $\sigma > 0$ we run 10 times for each noise level to obtain the mean $\pm$ std.

	PSNR				
	N0	N10	N15	N20	N25
Axial x2					
Bicubic	33.84	33.22 ± 0.07	32.37 ± 0.04	31.61 ± 0.10	30.74 ± 0.09
SLSR	36.01	35.28 ± 0.11	33.96 ± 0.14	32.54 ± 0.13	31.35 ± 0.18
Ours	39.81	37.54 ± 0.13	35.00 ± 0.13	33.14 ± 0.10	31.70 ± 0.16
Sagittal x2					
Bicubic	31.96	31.30 ± 0.02	30.60 ± 0.06	29.77 ± 0.03	28.96 ± 0.07
SLSR	33.47	32.54 ± 0.04	31.40 ± 0.09	30.21 ± 0.13	28.96 ± 0.26
Ours	36.63	34.88 ± 0.09	32.46 ± 0.10	30.69 ± 0.10	29.31 ± 0.11
Axial x4					
Bicubic	26.80	26.66 ± 0.01	26.47 ± 0.02	26.23 ± 0.03	25.96 ± 0.04
SLSR	27.86	27.76 ± 0.05	27.51 ± 0.05	27.19 ± 0.05	26.82 ± 0.08
Ours	30.36	30.31 ± 0.02	29.91 ± 0.05	29.02 ± 0.07	27.71 ± 0.09
Sagittal x4					
Bicubic	25.53	25.37 ± 0.01	25.19 ± 0.01	24.93 ± 0.02	24.66 ± 0.02
SLSR	26.40	26.34 ± 0.04	26.07 ± 0.04	25.74 ± 0.02	25.62 ± 0.04
Ours	28.39	28.36 ± 0.04	28.08 ± 0.04	27.30 ± 0.05	26.21 ± 0.21

Table 2. MSE of x2 and x4 SR on ex-vivo cardiac MRI data from different views. For $\sigma > 0$ we run 10 times for each noise level to obtain the mean $\pm$ std.

| | MSE | | | | |
	N0	N10	N15	N20	N25
Axial x2					
Bicubic	26.91	31.76 $\pm$ 0.13	37.88 $\pm$ 0.11	46.21 $\pm$ 0.50	56.88 $\pm$ 0.43
SLSR	17.34	20.79 $\pm$ 0.21	28.12 $\pm$ 0.37	39.22 $\pm$ 0.43	54.55 $\pm$ 1.04
Ours	6.85	12.11 $\pm$ 0.16	21.41 $\pm$ 0.30	33.23 $\pm$ 0.56	46.60 $\pm$ 0.70
Sagittal x2					
Bicubic	32.79	38.23 $\pm$ 0.16	45.00 $\pm$ 0.36	54.40 $\pm$ 0.30	65.99 $\pm$ 0.40
SLSR	23.18	28.68 $\pm$ 0.26	37.55 $\pm$ 0.28	50.09 $\pm$ 0.63	68.00 $\pm$ 0.78
Ours	11.19	16.86 $\pm$ 0.19	29.51 $\pm$ 0.41	44.22 $\pm$ 0.71	61.38 $\pm$ 0.70
Axial x4					
Bicubic	135.78	140.46 $\pm$ 0.42	146.53 $\pm$ 0.51	154.86 $\pm$ 0.99	164.91 $\pm$ 1.38
SLSR	106.35	109.02 $\pm$ 1.25	115.27 $\pm$ 1.25	124.12 $\pm$ 1.41	135.40 $\pm$ 2.43
Ours	59.91	60.60 $\pm$ 0.33	66.32 $\pm$ 0.76	81.56 $\pm$ 1.31	110.33 $\pm$ 1.98
Sagittal x4					
Bicubic	144.20	149.61 $\pm$ 0.28	155.90 $\pm$ 0.51	165.51 $\pm$ 0.77	176.35 $\pm$ 0.62
SLSR	118.01	119.72 $\pm$ 0.98	127.25 $\pm$ 1.10	137.29 $\pm$ 1.68	152.61 $\pm$ 1.85
Ours	74.59	75.17 $\pm$ 0.68	80.27 $\pm$ 0.71	95.97 $\pm$ 1.10	126.70 $\pm$ 1.32

methods (e.g., [1,11,13]) are demonstrated on natural images, which are assumed with less or no noise contamination. Results of the SLSR method tested on ex-vivo data with various additive noises showed that for the noise level $\sigma \leq 20$ SLSR outperformed bicubic interpolation with significant differences (Fig. 3(e) and (h) and Tables 1 and 2). This may be attributed to the fact that SVR learns local pixel value variations nonlinearly, while negative lobes on the bicubic kernel tend to create ringing artifacts. When $\sigma = 25$ SLSR performed similar to bicubic interpolation (no significant difference) demonstrating that SLSR results can be affected by noise significantly. Tellingly, with noise suppression in each level of the multiscale pyramid our method showed significant improvement of both PSNR and MSE even for the dense noise contamination with high magnification factor (Tables 1 and 2). Both line profiles and remaining noise estimation further confirmed the merits of our SR method (Fig. 5(d) and (e) and Table 3).

Table 3. Noise estimation of in-vivo late gadolinium enhancement data for randomly selected 40 ROIs to obtain the mean $\pm$ std.

	Original LR Image	Bicubic	SLSR	Ours
Noise Level	53.52 $\pm$ 5.48	35.76 $\pm$ 3.67	40.17 $\pm$ 4.89	32.04 $\pm$ 4.17

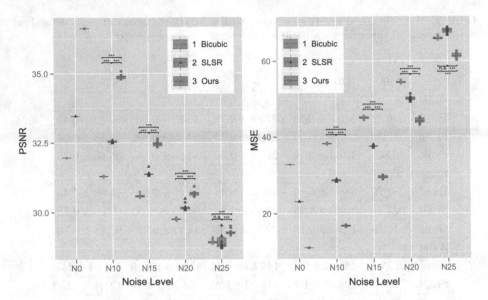

Fig. 4. Left: Boxplot of the PSNR (Sagittal x2 SR); Right: Boxplot of the MSE (Sagittal x2 SR). Statistical significant between each two groups are showing above the boxplot (*** stands for $p < 0.05$ and n.s. means no significant difference between two groups).

Although previous research demonstrated the success of using paired LR and HR training datasets to super-resolve a given new LR image [9], in this study we emphasize the practical infeasibility of this class of methods for CMRI images where acquiring HR training data can require prohibitively long scan times. For clinical CMRI studies, total scanning time per patient is already long (typically 60 min) and this can not easily be extended for HR data acquisition without having a significant input on patient throughput. A method, which doesn't require the use of HR training data, is therefore highly desirable. Moreover, there are potential hazards include painful peripheral nerve stimulation for prolonged scanning time. We are aware that our proof of concept study may have two limitations. First, there are several parameters that can be tuned in our framework, e.g., the thresholds for the calculated gradient magnitude in Sobel filtering and DTCWT denoising. Currently they are based on trial and error; however, we envisage that future assessment of the robustness of the SR framework will include parameter perturbation. Second, we explicitly assumed an additive Gaussian noise for simplicity, but more complex noise modeling and suppression could be easily plugged-in to the current framework. In summary, our SR framework, which couples SVR and DTCWT, can achieve promising HR CMRI results while effectively suppressing the noise.

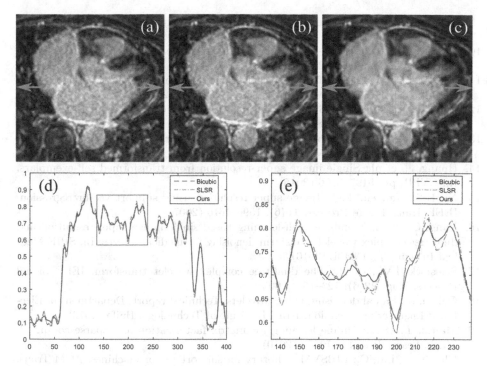

Fig. 5. Panels (a)–(c): x2 SR results of an in-vivo late gadolinium enhancement scan using bicubic interpolation, SLSR method and our approach respectively; (d) Horizontal line profiles through the green arrows of the SR results; (e) Zoomed-in line profiles of the pink region in (d). (Color figure online)

References

1. Glasner, D., et al.: Super-resolution from a single image. In: ICCV, pp. 349–356 (2009)
2. Van Reeth, E., et al.: Super-resolution in magnetic resonance imaging: a review. Concepts Magn. Reson. Part A **40**(6), 306–325 (2012)
3. Nasrollahi, K., Moeslund, T.B.: Super-resolution: a comprehensive survey. Mach. Vis. Appl. **25**(6), 1423–1468 (2014)
4. Yang, C.-Y., Huang, J.-B., Yang, M.-H.: Exploiting self-similarities for single frame super-resolution. In: Kimmel, R., Klette, R., Sugimoto, A. (eds.) ACCV 2010, Part III. LNCS, vol. 6494, pp. 497–510. Springer, Heidelberg (2011)
5. Kangi, L., et al.: Self-learning-based low-quality single image super-resolution. In: MMSP, pp. 1–6 (2013)
6. Lin, Z.C., Shum, H.Y.: Fundamental limits of reconstruction-based super-resolution algorithms under local translation. IEEE Trans. Pattern Anal. Mach. Intell. **26**(1), 83–97 (2004)
7. Chang, H., et al.: Super-resolution through neighbor embedding. In: CVPR, pp. 1–8 (2014)
8. Yang, J., et al.: Coupled dictionary training for image super-resolution. IEEE Trans. Image Process. **21**(8), 3467–3478 (2012)

9. Trinh, D.H., et al.: Novel example-based method for super-resolution and denoising of medical images. IEEE Trans. Image Process. **23**(4), 1882–1895 (2014)
10. Hidane, M., et al.: Super-resolution from a low-and partial high-resolution image pair. In: ICIP, pp. 2145–2149 (2014)
11. Yang, M.C., Wang, Y.C.F.: A self-learning approach to single image super-resolution. IEEE Trans. Multimedia **15**(3), 498–508 (2013)
12. Yang, J., et al.: Image Super-resolution via sparse representation. IEEE Trans. Image Process. **19**(11), 2861–2873 (2010)
13. Singh, A., Ahuja, N.: Sub-band energy constraints for self-similarity based super-resolution. In: ICPR, pp. 4447–4452 (2014)
14. Huang, J., et al.: Single image super-resolution from transformed self-exemplars. In: CVPR, pp. 5197–5206 (2015)
15. Ni, K.S., Nguyen, T.Q.: Image super-resolution using support vector regression. IEEE Trans. Image Process. **16**(6), 1596–1610 (2007)
16. Yang, G., et al.: Combined self-learning based single-image super-resolution and dual-tree complex wavelet transform denoising for medical images. In: SPIE Medical Imaging, p. 97840L (2016)
17. Selesnick, I.W., et al.: The dual-tree complex wavelet transform. IEEE Signal Process. Mag. **22**(6), 123–151 (2005)
18. Cohen, R.: Signal denoising using wavelets. Technical report, Department of Electrical Engineering Technion, Israel Institute of Technology, Haifa (2012)
19. Mairal, J., et al.: Online learning for matrix factorization and sparse coding. J. Mach. Learn. Res. **11**, 19–60 (2010)
20. Chang, C., Lin, C.: LIBSVM: a library for support vector machines. ACM Trans. Intell. Syst. Technol. **2**(5), 1–39 (2011)
21. Keegan, J., et al.: Improved respiratory efficiency of 3D late gadolinium enhancement imaging using the continuously adaptive windowing strategy (CLAWS). Magn. Reson. Med. **71**(3), 1064–1074 (2014)
22. Liu, X., et al.: Single-image noise level estimation for blind denoising. IEEE Trans. Image Process. **22**(12), 5226–5237 (2013)

Signal Processing

Speaker Classification via Supervised Hierarchical Clustering Using ICA Mixture Model

Muhammad Azam[1](✉) and Nizar Bouguila[2]

[1] Department of Electrical and Computer Engineering,
Concordia University, Montreal, QC, Canada
mu_azam@encs.concordia.ca
[2] Concordia Institute for Information Systems Engineering,
Concordia University, Montreal, QC, Canada
nizar.bouguila@concordia.ca

Abstract. In this paper, speaker classification using supervised hierarchical clustering is provided. Bounded generalized Gaussian mixture model with ICA is adapted for statistical learning in the clustering framework. In the presented framework ICA mixture model is learned through training data and the posterior probability is used to split the training data into clusters. The class label of the training data is further selected to mark each cluster into a specific class. The cluster-class information from the training process is taken as reference for the classification of test data into different speaker classes. This framework is employed for the gender and 10 speakers classification and TIMIT and TSP speech corpora are selected to validate and test the classification framework. This classification framework also validate the statistical learning of our recently proposed ICA mixture model. In order to examine the performance of the ICA mixture model, the classification results are compared with same framework using Gaussian mixture model. It is observed that: (i) presented clustering framework performs well for the speaker classification, (ii) ICA mixture model outperforms Gaussian mixture model in the statistical learning based on the classification accuracy for gender and multi-class scenarios.

Keywords: Bounded Generalized Gaussian Mixture Model (BGGMM) · Independent Component Analysis (ICA) · Speaker classification · Supervised hierarchical clustering · ICA mixture model

1 Introduction

Speaker classification is a fundamental component of speaker recognition systems which performs two alternative tasks: speaker identification and verification. The goal of speaker identification is to label an unknown speech file with a speaker identity. The task of speaker verification is to validate and confirm the claim of a speaker about its identity [1,2]. Speaker classification has been used in

© Springer International Publishing Switzerland 2016
A. Mansouri et al. (Eds.): ICISP 2016, LNCS 9680, pp. 193–202, 2016.
DOI: 10.1007/978-3-319-33618-3_20

human-machine dialog systems, forensics, medical and many other applications. One interesting application of speaker classification is in the speech recognition and keyword spotting as preprocessing to reach the speaker of interest which is further useful in many security applications. Mixture models have been widely adopted to address the speaker classification task [3]. Recently Mixture model have been employed to address the object recognition and classification tasks through clustering in [4,5]. A two level hierarchical clustering framework based on inverted Dirichlet mixture model is presented in [6] which is selected for object clustering and recognition. In this work, the same hierarchical clustering framework is adapted using bounded generalized Gaussian mixture model (BGGMM) with ICA and employed for speaker classification. In this paper, gender and 10 speakers classification is performed through the hierarchical clustering framework using ICA mixture model. Bounded generalized Gaussian mixture model with ICA presented in [7] is applied for the statistical learning of the clustering framework. Speaker classification based on supervised hierarchical clustering also serves the purpose to validate the effectiveness of ICA mixture model in speaker recognition and statistical learning. The gender speaker classification is performed on TIMIT and TSP speech databases and 10 speakers classification is conducted on TSP speech database. Both classification frameworks are also implemented using Gaussian mixture model in order to compare the performance of ICA mixture model in statistical learning. It is observed that classification framework based on hierarchical clustering performs well for both classification scenarios and ICA mixture model outperforms the GMM in model learning based on the classification rate. It is also observed that conventional problem of female speaker recognition is improved by employing multi-cluster model instead of classical model during the learning.

2   Supervised Hierarchical Clustering via ICA Mixture Model

In this section, supervised hierarchical clustering framework based on ICA mixture model is presented, which is applied to the speaker classification. The ICA mixture model is trained using training data and the posterior probability is employed to compute the specific cluster membership for each observation of the training data. The class label of the training data is selected to decode the clusters into particular class. The posterior probability is computed for the testing data and cluster-class information from the training is employed to find the particular class for each observation of the testing data. Since the class label of the training data is used to decode the clusters in the particular class and ICA mixture model is adapted for the statistical learning, therefore this framework is called the supervised hierarchical clustering framework based on ICA mixture model. Let us consider the training data represented as $\mathcal{X} = (\boldsymbol{X}_1, \ldots, \boldsymbol{X}_N)$ where each observation is D-dimensional random variable $\boldsymbol{X}_i = (X_1, \ldots, X_D)$. The random variable $\boldsymbol{X}$ follows a K components mixture distribution if its probability distribution is written in the following form:

$$p(\boldsymbol{X}_i|\Theta) = \sum_{j=1}^{K} p(\boldsymbol{X}_i|\theta_j)p_j \tag{1}$$

provided $p_j \geq 0$ and $\sum_{j=1}^{K} p_j = 1$. In Eq. (1), $\Theta = \{p_1, \ldots, p_K, \theta_1, \ldots, \theta_K\}$ where θ_j is the set of parameters of the jth component and p_j represents the mixing proportion for the jth component of the mixture model. For the training data $\mathcal{X}$ having N independent and identically distributed vectors, the mixture model with K components can be expressed as follows:

$$p(\mathcal{X}|\Theta) = \prod_{i=1}^{N}\sum_{j=1}^{K} p(\boldsymbol{X}_i|\theta_j)p_j \tag{2}$$

For each random variable $\boldsymbol{X}_i$, let Z_i be a K dimensional vector representing the missing group indicator which suggests to which component $\boldsymbol{X}_i$ belongs, such that Z_{ij} will be equal to 1 if $\boldsymbol{X}_i$ belongs to class j and 0 otherwise. The complete data likelihood is then:

$$p(\mathcal{X}, Z|\Theta) = \prod_{i=1}^{N}\sum_{j=1}^{K} \left(p(\boldsymbol{X}_i|\theta_j)p_j\right)^{Z_{ij}} \tag{3}$$

The complete data log-likelihood can be written as:

$$L(\Theta, Z, \mathcal{X}) = \sum_{i=1}^{N}\sum_{j=1}^{K} Z_{ij} \log\left(p(\boldsymbol{X}_i|\theta_j)p_j\right) \tag{4}$$

By replacing each Z_{ij} by its expectation, defined as posterior probability that the ith observation belongs to jth component of the mixture model as follows:

$$Z_{ij} = p(j|\boldsymbol{X}_i) = \frac{p(\boldsymbol{X}_i|\theta_j)p_j}{\sum_{j=1}^{K} p(\boldsymbol{X}_i|\theta_j)p_j} \tag{5}$$

The membership of $\boldsymbol{X}_i$ computed from the posterior probability can be selected to mark the clusters into a particular class. This information will further help for decoding the clusters into particular class for testing data using the membership function of the posterior probability for the observations of test data. If testing data is represented as $\mathcal{Y} = (\boldsymbol{Y}_1, \ldots, \boldsymbol{Y}_L)$, the posterior probability for $\boldsymbol{Y}_l$ can be computed using the trained mixture model and is represented as follows:

$$p(j|\boldsymbol{Y}_l) = \frac{p(\boldsymbol{Y}_l|\theta_j)p_j}{\sum_{j=1}^{K} p(\boldsymbol{Y}_l|\theta_j)p_j} \tag{6}$$

The supervised hierarchical framework for gender speaker classification is shown in Fig. 1. The speech data contains the MFCC features for male and female speakers and the class label is also provided. The ICA mixture model is trained in unsupervised fashion and the posterior probability for each observation of the

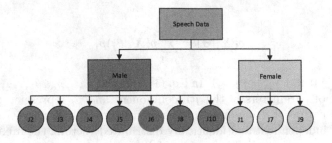

Fig. 1. Gender speaker classification using clustering

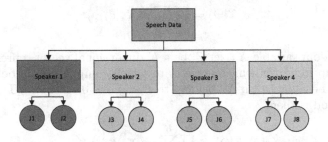

Fig. 2. Multi-speakers classification using clustering

training data is computed. The posterior probability marks each observation to a specific cluster and the class information of the training data can be selected to mark each cluster to a specific class to whom it belongs. For instance, if X_i belongs to the male class and it lies in the cluster 2, then cluster 2 is marked as male cluster. All the clusters can be marked as male or female from the training information and class label. In Fig. 1, it is assumed that the ICA mixture model is learned with 10 mixture densities and we have the class label for each observation. From posterior probability it is inferred that female observations from the speech data belongs to cluster J1, J7 and J9, so these clusters can be further labeled as female class and rest of the clusters were inferred as male class in the same way. It is worth mentioning that training of the ICA mixture model is unsupervised because the speech data is adopted without any class label during the training. However, the clustering framework is supervised because class label is employed after the training to mark the clusters into specific class. In the 10 speakers classification, the same binary classification framework is extended for 10 classes (see Fig. 2) and clusters obtained from the posterior probability are decoded into particular classes based on class label of the training data. In the classification using clustering, one important aspect is to accurately mark the number of classes representing data. In the classical approach, data is modeled by a fixed number of components of the mixture model which is equal to the number of classes. There are two problems associated with classical approach: (i) one single density component for each class does not necessarily fit the class data (ii) there is an overlap between the classes when using a single distribution to

---

Algorithm 1. Model Learning with BGGMM using ICA

1: **Input**:Dataset $\mathcal{X} = \{X_1, \ldots, X_N\}$, t_{min}.
2: **Output**: Θ.
3: **{Initialization}**: K-Means Algorithm. Set $\lambda = 2$.
4: **while** relative change in log-likelihood $\geq t_{min}$ **do**
5:     {[**E Step**]}:
6:         **for all** $1 \leq j \leq K$ **do**
7:             Compute $p(X_i|\theta_j)$ for $i = 1, \ldots, N$.
8:             Compute $p(j|X_i)$ for $i = 1, \ldots, N$.
9:         **end for**
10:    {[**M step**]}:
11:        **for all** $1 \leq j \leq K$ **do**
12:            **start** ICA Algorithm
13:                Update the basis functions A_j.
14:                Update the bias vector b_j.
15:                Update the shape parameter λ_j.
16:            **end** ICA
17:            Update the mixing parameter p_j.
18:            Update the mean μ_j.
19:            Update standard deviation σ_j.
20:        **end for**
21: **end while**

---

model each class [6]. In speaker recognition, while modeling several speakers in one class or even a single speaker in one class may have the above problems. This is because the several speakers in a single class always have some distinct features and even same speaker will have dissimilar behavior while pronouncing the same words or utterances on different times. Due to the problems associated with classical model, we have adopted multi-cluster model which improve the learning of classification framework. There is another problem with the learning of female speakers and it is reported that speaker recognition performance of female speakers is almost worse as compare to the male speakers [8,9]. It is observed that in the multi-cluster modeling, the performance of female speakers is improved during learning for their particular class. Bounded generalized Gaussian mixture model with ICA proposed in [7] is employed as statistical model for learning which uses the maximization of log-likelihood and ICA model for the estimation of its parameters. In an ICA mixture model, it is assumed that observed data comes from a mixture model and it can be categorized into mutually exclusive classes which means that each class of the data is modeled as an ICA [10–12]. The mixture model represented in Eq. (2) is composed of bounded generalized Gaussian distributions (BGGDs) which has mean μ, standard deviation σ and shape parameter λ as its parameters. The idea of bounded support mixture models and bounded generalized Gaussian mixture model was proposed in [13] and [14] respectively. For the ICA mixture model, each D-dimensional data vector $X_i = (X_{i1}, \ldots, X_{iD})$ can be represented as: $X_i = A_j s_{j,i} + b_j$ where A_j is $L \times D$ basis functions, $s_{j,i}$ is D-dimensional source vector and b_j is an L-dimensional bias vector for a particular mixture j [10–12,15]. For the simplicity, number of linear combinations (L) is considered to be equal to the number of sources (D) for each observation of the dataset. In an ICA mixture model, we need to estimate the basis functions A_j and bias vector b_j along with the parameters of the mixture model. The parameters mean, standard deviation and prior probability are estimated using the maximization of the log-likelihood. The shape parameters, basis functions and bias vector are estimated using the standard ICA model and gradient ascent. The parameter estimation for BGGMM with ICA is provided in [7] and complete learning procedure is given in Algorithm 1.

3   Experiments and Results

3.1   Design of Experiments

In this section, experimental framework for male/female and 10 speakers classification based on supervised hierarchical clustering is presented, which uses ICA mixture model for the statistical learning as described in section II. In the pre-processing stage, voice activity detection (VAD) is employed to distinguish between speech and non-speech parts of the speech sequences. By introducing the VAD in the pre-processing it is assured that the training of ICA mixture model is not inferred with the non-speech segments of the data set. The next stage is feature extraction and Mel Frequency Cepstral Coefficients (MFCCs) are selected as features. MFCCs have demonstrated their effectiveness in speech recognition and speaker classification and we have computed 13 dimensional features same as standard hidden Markov model toolkit (HTK). The ICA mixture model is trained using training part of the speech databases and the posterior probability is employed to determine the membership of an observation to a particular cluster. The class label for the training data is adopted to decode the clusters into particular class. The posterior probability is computed for the testing data and clustering information from the training is selected to find the particular class for each observation of the testing data. This classification framework is called the supervised hierarchical clustering based on ICA mixture model and presented in a detail in section II. This framework is also implemented using Gaussian mixture model in order to compare and examine the validity of the statistical learning of ICA mixture model in speaker classification.

3.2   Experimental Framework and Results

The speaker classification based on supervised hierarchical clustering is evaluated on TIMIT and TSP speech databases [16,17]. The TIMIT speech corpus consists of 6300 speech utterances which contains 4620 speech utterances for training and 1680 speech utterances for testing. The TSP speech database consists of 1378 speech utterances spoken by 23 speakers (11 male, 12 female). For gender speaker classification, 6 speakers are selected for testing from the TSP and rest of the data is dedicated for training. For 10 speakers classification, 10 speakers (5 male, 5 female) having 60 speech utterances for each speaker are selected from the TSP with 40 speech utterances for training and 20 utterances for testing. The TIMIT speech corpus is employed for gender speaker classification whereas TSP database is selected for both classification scenarios. In the clustering framework for both scenarios, each speech utterance is segmented into frames of 25 ms with a window shifting of 10 ms, where each frame is represented by 13 MFCCs. The VAD is applied before feature extraction in order to have only speech frames in the training and testing data. The k-means is employed to initialize the parameters of ICA mixture model, with shape parameter set to 2 for each component of the mixture model. For the gender speaker classification, ICA mixture model is trained using the training sets of both speech databases separately. From the posterior probability, speech utterances are divided into clusters by the membership of particular component of the mixture model. The class label for each utterances is provided for the training data which further leads to label the clusters into particular class. Once the clusters are labeled into the particular classes, the cluster-class information can be selected to decode the testing data into male/female speakers. The classification framework is evaluated using classification accuracy computed from the confusion matrices. For the TIMIT speech corpus, the classification accuracy is computed for different number of component of mixture model between 2–100 and plotted in Fig. (3a). In the classification accuracy curve for both classes, it is observed that by increasing the number of components of the mixture model, the classification rate is increased. However after 30 components of the mixture model, the increase in classification accuracy is slow. The classification framework having ICA mixture model is compared with the same framework having GMM on the basis of classification rate. The overall classification rate for ICA mixture model in the setting of 100 mixture components is 88.92 % whereas in same setting for GMM, the classification rate is 81.87 %. It is also noted that for smaller number of mixture components, the recognition of female speakers is very poor which is improved for higher number of mixture components. It is also observed that multi-cluster model has improved the model learning for both classes as compared to the classic model. In the classic model, the female speakers have poor performance while fitting the data in one class. In comparison with GMM, ICA mixture model has performed well which validates the effectiveness of ICA mixture model for speaker classification and statistical learning. For the TSP speech database, the speech utterances from 17 speakers (8 male, 9 female) are adopted to train the ICA mixture model whereas 6 speakers (half male, half female) are employed for the testing with each speaker having 60 speech utterances. The classification accuracy for different number of components of ICA mixture model and GMM in gender speaker classification framework is computed and plotted in Fig. (3b). The highest value for overall classification accuracy is observed at 40 mixture components (86.94 %) for ICA mixture model and at 50 mixture components (81.11 %) for GMM. For the 10 class speaker classification TSP speech database is employed for tuning the speaker classification framework. In this scenario, 10 speakers are chosen and 40 speech utterances for each speaker are selected for training and 20 speech utterances for each speaker are adopted for testing. The classification results are computed for different number of mixture components and the resulting confusion matrices for classic and multi-cluster models are shown in Table (1a), (1b) and (1c). In order to have a comparison of ICA mixture model with GMM for 10 speakers classification, the same framework is

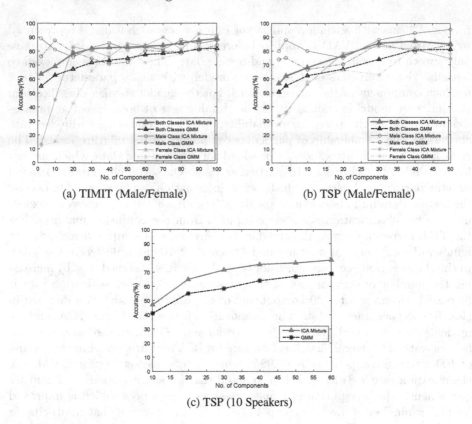

(a) TIMIT (Male/Female)

(b) TSP (Male/Female)

(c) TSP (10 Speakers)

Fig. 3. Classification accuracy for male/female and 10 speakers using ICA mixture and GMM (Colour figure online)

implemented with GMM and overall classification rate is plotted for both models in Fig. (3c). The highest classification rate is observed at 60 mixture components for both scenarios of 10 speakers classification (78.50 % for ICA mixture & 69 % for GMM) which demonstrates the effectiveness of ICA mixture model in this setting.

Table 1. 10 speakers classification confusion matrix using TSP database.

(a) ICA Mixture, M=10

	MH	MI	MJ	MK	ML	FH	FI	FJ	FK	FL
MH	12	1	2	1	3	0	1	0	0	0
MI	2	9	1	4	1	1	0	1	0	1
MJ	1	3	11	1	2	0	1	0	0	1
MK	2	1	5	9	1	1	0	1	0	0
ML	1	1	2	1	10	1	1	1	2	0
FH	1	0	1	1	0	8	1	2	4	2
FI	0	1	0	2	1	5	7	1	1	2
FJ	0	0	1	1	0	0	1	12	2	3
FK	1	1	0	1	0	2	1	3	9	2
FL	1	1	0	1	0	1	2	5	2	7

(b) ICA Mixture, M=40

	MH	MI	MJ	MK	ML	FH	FI	FJ	FK	FL
MH	15	1	1	1	1	0	0	1	0	0
MI	0	13	2	2	1	1	0	0	0	1
MJ	1	1	17	1	0	0	0	0	0	0
MK	1	1	1	16	1	0	0	0	0	0
ML	0	1	0	1	18	0	0	0	0	0
FH	1	0	0	1	0	13	1	2	1	1
FI	0	1	0	0	0	1	15	1	1	1
FJ	0	0	1	0	0	1	1	14	1	2
FK	1	0	0	0	0	1	1	2	14	1
FL	0	0	0	0	1	0	1	1	1	16

(c) ICA Mixture, M=60

	MH	MI	MJ	MK	ML	FH	FI	FJ	FK	FL
MH	17	1	0	1	1	0	0	0	0	0
MI	1	16	1	0	1	1	0	0	0	0
MJ	0	1	18	0	0	1	0	0	0	0
MK	2	0	1	14	1	1	0	1	0	0
ML	0	1	2	1	13	1	1	0	0	1
FH	0	0	0	0	0	15	1	1	2	1
FI	0	0	0	0	0	1	17	1	0	1
FJ	0	1	0	0	0	1	0	16	1	1
FK	1	0	1	0	0	1	3	1	13	0
FL	0	0	0	0	0	1	1	0	0	18

4   Conclusion

In this paper supervised hierarchical clustering framework is presented which is adopted for speaker classification. The first stage of the clustering is performed by the ICA mixture model and in the second stage, clusters received from the posterior probability are further classified using the class label of the training data. The cluster-class label information from training process is used for the classification of testing data. The classification framework is validated on TIMIT and TSP speech corpora. This framework also validates the statistical learning of ICA mixture model proposed in [7]. In order to examine the performance of the ICA mixture model, the classification framework is also implemented with GMM and the classification accuracy in different modes is compared. The proposed framework having ICA mixture model is employed for gender and 10 speakers classification. It is concluded that supervised hierarchical clustering framework has performed considerably well for the speaker classification and ICA mixture model surpass the GMM in the classification rate and model learning. It is also concluded that multi-cluster model has improved the problem of female speakers to fit the class data as compared to classic model.

Acknowledgment. The completion of this research was made possible thanks to the Natural Sciences and Engineering Research Council of Canada (NSERC).

References

1. Hansen, J., Hasan, T.: Speaker recognition by machines and humans: a tutorial review. Sig. Process. Mag. IEEE **32**, 74–99 (2015)
2. Markowitz, J.: The many roles of speaker classification in speaker verification and identification. In: Mller, C. (ed.) Speaker Classification I. LNCS, vol. 4343, pp. 218–225. Springer, Berlin (2007)
3. Reynolds, D.A., Quatieri, T.F., Dunn, R.B.: Speaker verification using adapted gaussian mixture models. Digital Sig. Process. **10**(1), 19–41 (2000)
4. Bourouis, S., Mashrgy, M.A., Bouguila, N.: Bayesian learning of finite generalized inverted Dirichlet mixtures: application to object classification and forgery detection. Expert Syst. Appl. **41**, 2329–2336 (2014)
5. Bdiri, T., Bouguila, N., Ziou, D.: Visual scenes categorization using a flexible hierarchical mixture model supporting users ontology. In: 2013 IEEE 25th International Conference on Tools with Artificial Intelligence, pp. 262–267, Herndon, VA, USA, 4–6 Nov 2013
6. Bdiri, T., Bouguila, N., Ziou, D.: Object clustering and recognition using multi-finite mixtures for semantic classes and hierarchy modeling. Expert Syst. Appl. **41**, 1218–1235 (2014)
7. Azam, M., Bouguila, N.: Unsupervised keyword spotting using bounded generalized Gaussian mixture model with ICA. In: 2015 IEEE Global Conference on Signal and Information Processing (General Symposium), Orlando, USA (2015)
8. Nguyen, P., Le, T., Tran, D., Huang, X., Sharma, D.: Fuzzy support vector machines for age and gender classification. In: INTERSPEECH, pp. 2806–2809 (2010)

9. Vergin, R., Farhat, A., O'Shaughnessy, D.: Robust gender-dependent acoustic-phonetic modelling in continuous speech recognition based on a new automatic male/female classification. In: Fourth International Conference on Spoken Language, ICSLP 1996, Proceedings, vol. 2, pp. 1081–1084 (1996)
10. Salazar, A.: ICA and ICAMM methods. In: On Statistical Pattern Recognition in Independent Component Analysis Mixture Modelling. Springer Theses, vol. 4, pp. 29–55. Springer, Berlin (2013)
11. Lee, T.-W., Lewicki, M.S.: The generalized Gaussian mixture model using ICA. In: International Workshop on Independent Component Analysis, ICA 2000, pp. 239–244 (2000)
12. Lee, T.-W., Lewicki, M.S., Sejnowski, T.J.: ICA mixture models for unsupervised classification with non-Gaussian sources and automatic context switching in blind signal separation. In: IEEE Transactions on Pattern Recognition and Machine Learning (2000)
13. Lindblom, J., Samuelsson, J.: Bounded support Gaussian mixture modeling of speech spectra. IEEE Trans. Speech Audio Process. **11**, 88–99 (2003)
14. Nguyen, T.M., Wu, Q.J., Zhang, H.: Bounded generalized Gaussian mixture model. Pattern Recogn. **47**, 3132–3142 (2014)
15. Lee, T.-W., Lewicki, M.S.: Unsupervised image classification, segmentation, and enhancement using ICA mixture models. IEEE Trans. Image Process. **11**(3), 270–279 (2002)
16. Garofolo, J.S., Lamel, L.F., Fisher, W.M., Fiscus, J.G., Pallett, D.S., Dahlgren, N.L.: DARPA TIMIT acoustic phonetic continuous speech corpus CDROM (1993). http://www.ldc.upenn.edu/Catalog/LDC93S1.html
17. Kabal, P.: TSP Speech Database. Technical report, Department of Electrical and Computer Engineering, McGill University, Montreal, Quebec, Canada (2002)

Speaker Discrimination Using Several Classifiers and a Relativistic Speaker Characterization

Siham Ouamour, Zohra Hamadache, and Halim Sayoud[✉]

USTHB University, Algiers, Algeria
{siham.ouamour,halim.sayoud}@uni.de,
zohra.hamadache@yahoo.fr

Abstract. Automatic Speaker Discrimination consists in checking whether two speech signals belong to the same speaker or not. It is often difficult to decide what could be the best classifier to use in some specific circumstances. That is why, we implemented nine different classifiers, namely: Linear Discriminant Analysis, Adaboost, Support Vector Machines, Multi-Layer Perceptron, Linear Regression, Generalized Linear Model, Self Organizing Map, Second Order Statistical Measures and Gaussian Mixture Models. Moreover, a special feature reduction was proposed, which we called Relativistic Speaker Characteristic (*RSC*). On the other hand we further intensified the feature reduction by adding a second step of feature transformation using a Principal Component Analysis (*PCA*). Experiments of speaker discrimination are conducted on Hub4 Broadcast-News. Results show that the best classifier is the SVM and that the proposed feature reduction association (*RSC-PCA*) is extremely efficient in automatic speaker discrimination.

Keywords: Speaker discrimination · Speaker verification · Relativistic speaker characteristic · PCA reduction · Classification models

1 Introduction

Speaker discrimination consists in checking whether two different pronunciations (speech signals) are uttered by the same speaker or by two different speakers [1]. This research domain has several applications such as automatic speaker verification [2], speech segmentation [3] or speaker based clustering [4]. All these tasks can be performed either by generative classifiers or by discriminative classifiers.

However, existing approaches are not robust enough in noisy environment or in telephonic speech. Any new model must therefore improve the reliability of existing discriminative systems, without altering their architectures.

To address the above issue, we implemented 9 different classifiers and applied the PCA with these different classifiers. Furthermore, a new relativistic characteristic is proposed: we called it "Relativistic Speaker Characteristic" [5]. Basically, the introduction of the relative notion in speaker modelization allows getting a flexible relative speaker template, more suitable for the task of speaker discrimination in difficult environments. Moreover, to further intensify the feature reduction, a PCA reduction is

© Springer International Publishing Switzerland 2016
A. Mansouri et al. (Eds.): ICISP 2016, LNCS 9680, pp. 203–212, 2016.
DOI: 10.1007/978-3-319-33618-3_21

applied to reduce again the RSC feature. For that purpose, several speaker discrimination experiments are conducted on a subset of Broadcast-News dataset.

The overall structure of this paper is organized as follows: In Sect. 2, we describe some related works and explain the motivation of this investigation. Section 3 defines the nine used classifiers. Section 4 describes the RSC notion employed for the task of speaker discrimination and feature reduction. Experiments of speaker discrimination are presented in Sect. 5 and finally a general conclusion is presented at the end of this manuscript.

2 State of the Art in Feature Reduction Based Speaker Recognition

Speaker discrimination is the ability to check whether two utterances come from the same speaker or from different speakers, but in a broader sense, speaker recognition is the task of recognizing the true speaker of a given speech signal. Hence, in this section, we will shortly quote some recent works of speaker recognition using feature reduction (*such as PCA reduction*).

In 2008, Li *et al.* [6] proposed a novel hierarchical speaker verification method based on PCA and Kernel Fisher Discriminant (*KFD*) classifier. Later on, Zhao *et al.* [7] presented a new method which takes full advantage of both vector quantization and PCA. Also in 2009, Jayakurnar *et al.* [8] presented an effective and robust method for speaker identification based on discrete stationary wavelet transform (*DSWT*) and principal component analysis techniques. Ingeniously, Zhou *et al.* [9] proposed a method to reduce feature dimension based on Canonical Correlation Analysis (*CCA*) and PCA. In the same period, Mehra *et al.* (Mehra, 2010) presented a detailed comparative analysis for speaker identification by using lip features, PCA, and neural network classifiers: it was a multimodal feature combination. Then, Xiao-chun *et al.* [10] proposed a text-independent (*TI*) speaker identification method that suppresses the phonetic information by a subspace method: a Probabilistic Principle Component Analysis (*PPCA*) is utilized to construct these subspaces. Recently, Jing *et al.* (Jing, 2014) introduced a new method of extracting mixed characteristic parameters using PCA. This speaker recognition technique is based on the performance of the PCA on the Linear Prediction Cepstral Coefficients (*LPCC*) and Mel Frequency Cepstral Coefficients (*MFCC*). All of these works (*or at least most of them*) used the principal component analysis to reduce the feature space dimensionality without altering the recognition performances.

In this investigation, we not only propose a completely different feature reduction technique, but we also combine it with PCA reduction to further enhance both the memory size and recognition precision. Moreover, we evaluate the RSC-PCA efficiency in real environment (*Broadcast News*) and with 9 different classifiers.

3 Description of the Classifiers and Classification Process

The choice of the optimal classifier is crucial before any application of pattern recognition that is why we have decided to implement 9 classifiers and evaluate them in the same experimental conditions.

The different classification methods are described in the following sub-sections. However, since we are limited by the pages number of the article, we will only give the general definition of the different classifiers; the details could be found in the cited references.

3.1 LDA: Linear Discriminant Analysis

Linear discriminant analysis (*LDA*) is a method used in statistics, pattern recognition and machine learning to find a linear combination of features which characterizes or separates two or more classes of objects or events.

Consider a set of observations $\vec{x}$ (also called features, attributes, variables or measurements) for each sample of an object or event with known class y. This set of samples is called the training set. The classification problem is then to find a good predictor for the class y of any sample of the same distribution (not necessarily from the training set) given only an observation $\vec{x}$.

LDA approaches the problem by assuming that the conditional probability density functions $p(\vec{x}|y = 0)$ and $p(\vec{x}|y = 1)$ are both normally distributed with mean and covariance parameters $(\vec{\mu}_0, \Sigma_0)$ and $(\vec{\mu}_1, \Sigma_1)$, respectively. Under this assumption, the Bayes optimal solution is to predict points as being from the second class if the log of the likelihood ratios is below a threshold T [11].

3.2 AdaBoost: Adaptive Boosting

AdaBoost, short for "Adaptive Boosting", is a machine learning meta-algorithm. It can be used in conjunction with many other types of learning algorithms to improve their performance. The output of the other learning algorithms ('*weak learners*') is combined into a weighted sum that represents the final output of the boosted classifier. AdaBoost is adaptive in the sense that subsequent weak learners are tweaked in favor of those instances misclassified by previous classifiers.

AdaBoost refers to a particular method of training a boosted classifier. A boost classifier is a classifier in the form

$$F_T(x) = \sum_{t=1}^{T} f_t(x) \tag{1}$$

where each f_t is a weak learner that takes an object x as input and returns a real valued result indicating the class of the object. The sign of the weak learner output identifies the predicted object class and the absolute value gives the confidence in that classification. Similarly, the T-layer classifier will be positive if the sample is believed to be in the positive class and negative otherwise [12].

3.3   SVM: Support Vector Machines

In machine learning, support vector machines (*SVMs*) are supervised learning models with associated learning algorithms that analyze data and recognize patterns. They are used for classification and regression analysis.

The basic SVM takes a set of input data and predicts, for each given input, which of two possible classes forms the output, making it a non-probabilistic binary linear classifier.

Given a set of training examples, each marked as belonging to one of two categories, a SVM training algorithm builds a model that assigns new examples into one category or the other. A SVM model is a representation of the examples as points in space, mapped so that the examples of the separate categories are divided by a clear gap that is as wide as possible. New examples are then mapped into that same space and predicted to belong to a category based on which side of the gap they fall on [13].

3.4   MLP: Multi Layer Perceptron

MLP is a feed-forward neural network classifier that uses the errors of the output to train the neural network: it is the "training step" [14].

MLP is organized in layers, one input layer of distribution points, one or more hidden layers of artificial neurons (*nodes*) and one output layer of artificial neurons (*nodes*).

Each node, in a layer, is connected to all other nodes in the next layer and each connection has a weight (*which can be zero*). MLPs are considered as universal approximators and are widely used in supervised machine learning classification. The MLP can use different back-propagation schemes to ensure the training of the classifier.

3.5   LR: Linear Regression

Linear regression is the oldest and most widely used predictive model. The method of minimizing the sum of the squared errors to fit a straight line to a set of data points was published by Legendre in 1805 and by Gauss in 1809. Linear regression models are often fitted using the least squares approach, but they may also be fitted in other ways, such as by minimizing the "lack of fit" in some other norms (*as with least absolute deviations regression*), or by minimizing a penalized version of the least squares loss function as in ridge regression [15, 16].

In linear regression, data are modeled using linear predictor functions, and unknown model parameters are estimated from the data. Such models are called linear models.

Usually, the predictor variable is denoted by the variable X and the criterion variable is denoted by the variable y. Most commonly, linear regression refers to a model in which the conditional mean of y given the value of X is an affine function of X. Less commonly, linear regression could refer to a model in which the median of the conditional distribution of y given X is expressed as a linear function of X.

3.6   GLM: Generalized Linear Model

In statistics, the generalized linear model (*GLM*) is a flexible generalization of ordinary linear regression that allows for response variables that have error distribution models other than a normal distribution. The GLM generalizes linear regression by allowing the linear model to be related to the response variable via a link function and by allowing the magnitude of the variance of each measurement to be a function of its predicted value [17].

3.7   SOM: Self Organizing Map

A self-organizing map (*SOM*) is a type of artificial neural network that is trained using unsupervised learning to produce a low-dimensional, discretized representation of the input space of the training samples, called a map. Self-organizing maps are different from other artificial neural networks in the sense that they use a neighborhood function to preserve the topological properties of the input space.

This makes SOMs useful for visualizing low-dimensional views of high-dimensional data. The model was first described as an artificial neural network by Kohonen, and is sometimes called a Kohonen map. A Self-organizing Map is a data visualization technique developed by Kohonen in the early 1980's [18, 19].

Like most artificial neural networks, SOMs operate in two modes: training and mapping. The training builds the map using input examples, while the mapping automatically classifies the input vector.

3.8   SOSM: Second Order Statistical Measure

The proposed method uses mono-gaussian models based on the second order statistics, and provides some similarity measures able to make a comparison between two speakers (*speech segments*) according to a specific threshold. We recall bellow the most important properties of this approach [20].

Let $\{x_t\}_{1 \leq t \leq M}$ be a sequence of M vectors resulting from the P-dimensional acoustic analysis of a speech signal uttered by speaker x. These vectors are summarized by the mean vector $\bar{x}$ and the covariance matrix X.

Similarly, for a speech signal uttered by speaker y, a sequence of N vectors $\{y_t\}_{1 \leq t \leq N}$ can be extracted. These vectors are summarized by the mean vector $\bar{y}$ and the covariance matrix Y.

The Gaussian likelihood based measure μ_G is defined by:

$$\mu_G(x,y) = \frac{1}{P}\left[-\log(\frac{\det(Y)}{\det(X)}) + tr(YX^{-1}) + (\bar{y} - \bar{x})^T X^{-1}(\bar{y} - \bar{x})\right] - 1 \qquad (2)$$

we have:

$$\underset{x}{Argmax}\, \overline{G}x(y_1^N) = \underset{x}{Argmin}\, \mu_G(x,y) \qquad (3)$$

where "det" represents the determinant and "tr" represents the trace of the matrix.

The μ_g mesasure is widely used in speech analysis for the task of speaker recognition.

3.9   GMM: Gaussian Mixture Model

A Gaussian Mixture Model (GMM) is a parametric probability density function represented as a weighted sum of Gaussian component densities. GMMs are commonly used as a parametric model of the probability distribution of continuous measurements or features in a biometric system, such as vocal spectral features in a speaker recognition system. GMM parameters are estimated from training data using the iterative Expectation-*Maximization* algorithm or *Maximum A Posteriori* estimation from a well-trained prior model.

A Gaussian mixture model is a weighted sum of M component Gaussian densities as given by the equation,

$$p(\mathrm{X}|\lambda) = \sum_{i=1}^{M} w_i \, g(\mathrm{X}|\mu_i, \Sigma_i), \tag{4}$$

where x is a D-dimensional continuous-valued data vector, wi, i = 1,..., M, are the mixture weights, and g(x|μi,_i), i = 1,..., M, are the component Gaussian densities. Each component density is a D-variate Gaussian function of the form,

$$g(X|\mu_i, \Sigma_i) = \frac{1}{(2\pi)^{D/2}|\Sigma_i|^{1/2}} \exp\left\{ -\frac{1}{2}(X - \mu_i)' \, \Sigma_i^{-1}(X - \mu_i) \right\}, \tag{5}$$

with mean vector μi and covariance matrix Σ_i. The mixture weights satisfy the constraint that Pм i = 1 wi = 1.

The complete Gaussian mixture model is parameterized by the mean vectors, covariance matrices and mixture weights from all component densities. Herein, we wish to estimate the parameters of the GMM, which in some sense best matches the distribution of the training feature vectors. There are several techniques available for estimating the parameters of a GMM [21]. By far the most popular and well-established method is the *maximum likelihood* estimation.

In general GMMs are considered as the state-of-the-art classifier in speaker recognition.

3.10   PCA Features Reduction

PCA provides an interesting way to reduce a complex data set to a lower dimension to reveal the sometimes hidden, simplified dynamics that often underlie it [22]. PCA is mathematically defined as an orthogonal linear transformation that transforms the data to a new coordinate system such that the greatest variance by some projection of the data comes to lie on the first coordinate (i.e. the first principal component), the second greatest variance on the second coordinate, and so on.

In our investigation, PCA has been intensively used to further reduce the dimensionality of the features of the relative characteristic RSC. This fact has three advantages: reducing the processing time, avoiding the need of high training data and making the features more pertinent with regards to the discrimination task.

4 Relativity in Speaker Discrimination: Notion of RSC

We propose a new relative characteristic called RSC derived from the Mel Frequency Spectral Coefficients MFSC and which is used for the task of speaker discrimination.

This relativity approach is proposed in order to reduce the features dimension, optimize the learning classifiers training, without modifying the classifier architecture and without changing the input features either (Fig. 1).

The previous formula 1 gives us a similarity measure between a speech signal uttered by a speaker y and the reference model of the speaker x.

We derive from this formula the following one:

$$\psi^*(x,y) = \frac{1}{P}[-\log(\det(\Re)) + tr(\Re))] - 1 \tag{6}$$

We have called the $\Re$ ratio: **Relative Speaker Characteristic** (RSC)

$$\Re = RSC(x,y) = \frac{Y}{X} = Y*X^{-1} \tag{7}$$

Hence, $\psi^*(x,y)$ appears to be a function of the RSC.

5 Experiments of Speaker Discrimination on Hub4 Broadcast News

Several speech segments are extracted from "Hub4 Broadcast-News 96" dataset, containing some recordings from "CNN early edition". They are composed of clean speech, music, telephonic calls, noises, etc. The sampling frequency is 16 kHz and the speech signals are extracted and arranged into segments of about 4 s or 3 s. The corpus contains 14 different speakers (*most of them journalists, speaking about the news*) organized into 259 speaker combinations for the training and 195 speaker combinations for the testing.

The training dataset is composed of speech segments of 4 s each, whereas the testing set consists of speech segments of 3 s each. The choice of 3 s is due to the fact that previous works showed that the minimal speech duration for good speaker recognition is 3 s.

The general experimental protocol is described as follows:

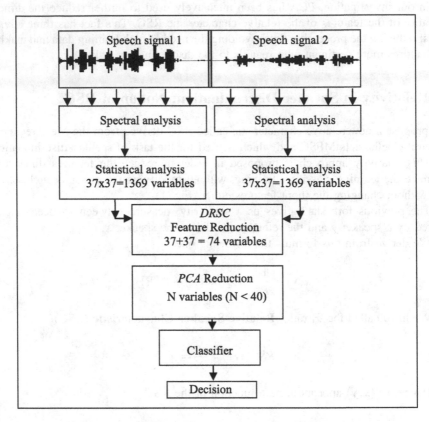

Fig. 1. The general experimental classification protocol

And the different results obtained during these experiments are summarized in the following table (*Table 1*).

Table 1. Scores of good speaker discrimination in %

Method	without PCA Reduction	after PCA Reduction
1. SOM map	76,92	80,51
2. SOSM-muGc	82,56	82,56 (*without PCA*)
3. Adaboost	68,21	84,62
4. MLP	77,95	85,64
5. GMM	*failure*	87,18
6. LDA	75,38	89,23
7. Lin Regress	75,38	89,74
8. GLM Regress	75,90	90,26
9. SVM	83,08	91,28

The first observation, we can make, is that the PCA reduction allowed the improvement of the accuracy for almost all the classifiers and the reduction of the features size (*and then the computation time too*).

The second observation is related to the comparative evaluation of the 9 classifiers: we can see that the 4 classifiers namely: LDA, Linear regression, GLM regression and SVM are the most accurate classifiers with a score about 90 % of good discrimination. The SVM is the best one by providing a score of 91.28 % of good classification. The 3 classifiers namely: Adaboost, MLP and GMM are relatively less accurate with a score of about 85 %. Although those 3 classifiers are known to be quite robust, however, the lack of training data made them not very efficient. Finally, for the 2 remaining classifiers, namely: SOM and SOSM, the performances noticed during the discrimination experiments, show that those classifiers are not suitable for the task of speaker discrimination, since the score of good classification is about only 80 %. However, one must note that the SOSM approach remains quite interesting since it does not require any training step (distance measure). Moreover, in the present experiments, no PCA reduction was applied for the SOSM (*technically not possible*). That is, if we observe the scores without PCA, we do notice that the SVM and SOSM provide the best performances (about 83 %).

6 Conclusion

In this paper, we dealt with the problem of speaker discrimination on Broadcast News speech segments. For that purpose, we implemented 9 different classifiers and proposed a new reduced pertinent characteristic called RSC, which has been successfully employed in association with the PCA (Principal Component Analysis).

The association RSC-PCA was applied to reduce the size of the features and speed up the training/testing process. This investigation has shown that this association did not only reduce the features dimensionality but it also further improved the classification accuracy.

The experiments of speaker discrimination were conducted on a subset of HUB-4 Broadcast News. Results have shown, on one hand, an important enhancement of the discrimination accuracy by using the new RSC characteristic; on the other hand, this investigation has allowed us to compare the performances of the different classifiers on the same experimental conditions.

The best speaker discrimination score is over 91 %, reached by the SVM, and which appears to be the best classifier used in our experiments.

As perspectives, we intend to implement some fusion architectures between the different classifiers in order to further enhance the discrimination performances.

References

1. Rose, P.: Forensic speaker discrimination with Australian English vowel acoustics. In: ICPhS, XVI (2007)
2. Matrouf, D., Bonastre, J.F.: Accurate log-likelihood ratio estimation by using test statistical model for speaker verification. In: The Speaker and Language Recognition Workshop, Odyssey (2006)

3. Meignier, S., et al.: Step- by- step and integrated approaches in broadcast news speaker diarization. Comput. Speech Lang. **20**, 303–330 (2006)
4. Meignier, S.: Indexation en locuteurs de documents sonores: segmentation d'un document et Appariement d'une collection. Ph.D. thesis, LIA Avignon, France (2002)
5. Ouamour, S., Guerti, M., Sayoud, H.: A new relativistic vision in speaker discrimination. Can. Acoust. J. **36**(4), 24–34 (2008). ISSN 0711-6659
6. Li, M., Xing, Y., Luo, R.: Hierarchical speaker verification based on PCA and kernel fisher discriminant. In : 4th International Conference on Natural Computation, pp. 152–156 (2008)
7. Zhao, Z.D., Zhang, J., Tian, J.F., Lou, Y.Y.: An effective identification method for speaker recognition based on PCA and double VQ. In: Proceedings of the Eighth International Conference on Machine Learning and Cybernetics, Baoding, pp. 1686–1689 (2009)
8. Jayakurnar, A., Vimal Krishnan, V.R., BabuAnto, P.: Text dependent speaker recognition using discrete stationary wavelet transform and PCA. In: International Conference on the Current Trends in Information Technology CTIT, pp. 1–4 (2009)
9. Zhou, Y., Zhang, X., Wang, J., Gong, Y.: Research on speaker feature dimension reduction based on CCA and PCA. In: International Conference on Wireless Communications and Signal Processing (WCSP), pp. 1–4 (2010)
10. Xiao-chun, L., Jun-xun, Y., A.: Text-independent speaker recognition system based on probabilistic principle component analysis. In: 3rd International Conference on System Science, Engineering Design and Manufacturing Informatization, pp. 255–260 (2012)
11. Contributors of Wikipedia: Linear discriminant analysis. https://en.wikipedia.org/wiki/Linear_discriminant_analysis. Accessed Nov 2015
12. Contributors of Wikipedia: Adaboost. https://en.wikipedia.org/wiki/AdaBoost. Accessed Nov 2015
13. Contributors of Wikipedia: Support vector machine. https://en.wikipedia.org/wiki/Support_vector_machine. Accessed Nov 2015
14. Sayoud, H.: Automatic speaker recognition – connexionnist approach. Ph.D. thesis, USTHB University, Algiers (2003)
15. Contributors of Wikipedia: linear discriminant analysis. https://en.wikipedia. Last Accessed Nov 2015, Wikipedia, "Linear regression". http://en.wikipedia.org/wiki/Linear_regression. From Wikipedia, Last Accessed 28 Mar 2013
16. Huang, X., Pan, W.: Linear regression and two-class classification with gene expression data. Bioinformatics **19**(16), 2072–2078 (2003)
17. Contributors of Wikipedia, 2015. Generalized linear model. Last Accessed Nov 2015. https://en.wikipedia.org/wiki/Generalized_linear_model
18. Kohonen, T.: The self-organizing map. Proc. IEEE **78**(9), 1464–1480 (1990). doi:10.1109/5.58325. Invited Paper
19. Tambouratzis, G., Hairetakis, G., Markantonatou, S., Carayannis, G.: Applying the SOM Model to Text Classification According to Register and Stylistic Content. Int. J. Neural Syst. **13**(1), 1–11 (2003)
20. Bimbot, F., Magrin-Chagnolleau, I., Mathan, L.: Second-Order Statistical Measures for text-independent Broadcaster Identification. Speech Commun. **17**(1–2), 177–192 (1995)
21. Reynolds, D.A.: Speaker identification and verification using Gaussian mixture speaker models. Speech Commun. **17**(1–2), 91–108 (1995)
22. Shlens, J.: A tutorial on principal component analysis - Derivation, Discussion and Singular Value Decomposition. Version 1, (2003). www.cs.princeton.edu/picasso/mats/PCA-Tutorial-Intuition_jp.pdf

Speaker Discrimination Based on a Fusion Between Neural and Statistical Classifiers

Siham Ouamour[✉] and Halim Sayoud

USTHB University, Algiers, Algeria
{siham.ouamour,halim.sayoud}@uni.de

Abstract. Speaker discrimination consists in checking whether two (or more) speech segments belong to the same speaker or not. In this framework, we propose a new approach developed for the task of speaker discrimination, this approach results from the fusion between a neural network classifier (NN) and a statistical classifier, this fusion is obtained once by combining the scores of the simple classifiers weighted by some confidence coefficients and another time, by using the scores of the statistical classifier as an additional input of the Multi-Layer Perceptron (MLP), in order to optimize the NN training (Hybrid model).

In one hand, we notice that the fusion has improved the results obtained by each approach alone and in the other hand we notice that the fusion using the sum of weighted scores, obtained by each classifier alone, seems to be better than the hybrid method. The experiments, done on a subset of Hub4 Broadcast News database, have shown the efficiency of that fusion in speaker discrimination, where the Equal Error Rate (EER) is about 7 %, with short segments of 4 s only.

Keywords: Speaker discrimination · Fusion · Speech processing

1 Introduction

Speaker discrimination (*by voice*) represents an important field in biometry, since the voice remains the unique method used at distance (via telephone). This particularity, has given to speaker discrimination a great importance, especially in secure applications which require very high accuracy. Speaker discrimination consists in checking whether two different pronunciations (*speech segments*) are uttered by the same speaker or by two different speakers. One means used to compare the utterances is to extract the vocal characteristics from each segment, in order to detect the degree of similarity between them.

Speaker discrimination has applications in several domains, like speaker verification, biometry, multimedia segmentation and speaker based clustering.

Different approaches were developed for this purpose, among those two approaches are investigated in this paper: a neural network and a 2nd order statistical measure, but we also propose two other approaches based on the association between the two previous classifiers.

© Springer International Publishing Switzerland 2016
A. Mansouri et al. (Eds.): ICISP 2016, LNCS 9680, pp. 213–221, 2016.
DOI: 10.1007/978-3-319-33618-3_22

These different approaches are evaluated on a sub-set of Broadcast News (1996) [1] and our results show that this fusion is really interesting.

2 Some Techniques Related to Speaker Discrimination and Parameterization

Several techniques were developed for the task of speaker discrimination, like GMM (Gaussian Mixture Models) [2], NN (Neural Networks) [3], statistical measures [4], HMM (Hidden Markov Models) [5] …etc. In our research work, we have approached the discrimination problem with four methods; MLP (Multi-Layer Perceptron), statistical measures, Hybrid method and the fusion based on the sum of weighted scores. These different methods are described below.

For the parameterization, we used 37 MFSC coefficients (Mel Frequency Spectral Coefficients) obtained from the calculation of the energies in the mel spectral scale [6, 7]. This dimension has been chosen after a thorough investigation done on the optimal spectral resolution [8, 9].

2.1 Statistical Method

One of the referential methods used for the task of speaker discrimination is the statistical measure of similarity (μ_{Gc}) which is based on the covariance matrix. The statistical measure is used in order to determine the similarity degree (with regards to speaker's features) between the different speech segments.

We recall bellow the most important properties of the approach [10, 11].

Let $\{x_t\}_{1 \leq t \leq M}$ be a sequence of M vectors resulting from the P-dimensional acoustic analysis of a speech signal uttered by speaker x. These vectors are summarized by the mean vector $\bar{x}$ and the covariance matrix X:

$$\bar{x} = \frac{1}{M} \sum_{t=1}^{M} x_t \tag{1}$$

and

$$X = \frac{1}{M} \sum_{t=1}^{M} (x_t - \bar{x})(x_t - \bar{x})^T \tag{2}$$

Similarly, for a speech signal uttered by speaker y, a sequence of N vectors can be $\{y_t\}_{1 \leq t \leq M}$ extracted.

By assuming that all acoustic vectors extracted from the speech signal uttered by speaker x are distributed like a Gaussian function, the likelihood of a single vector y_t uttered by speaker y is:

$$G(y_t/\mathbf{x}) = \frac{1}{(2\pi)^{P/2}(\det X)^{1/2}} e^{(1/2)(y_t - \bar{x})^T X^{-1}(y_t - \bar{x})} \tag{3}$$

If we assume that all vectors y_t are independent observations, the average log-likelihood of $\{y_t\}_{1 \leq t \leq M}$ can be written as

$$\bar{Lx}(y_1^N) = \frac{1}{N}\log G(y_1 \cdots y_N | X) = \frac{1}{N}\sum_{t=1}^{N} \log G(y_t | \mathbf{x}) \tag{4}$$

We also define the minus-log-likelihood $\mu(\mathbf{x}, y_t)$ which is equivalent to similarity measure between vector y_t (uttered by y) and the model of speaker x, so that

$$\underset{x}{Arg\,\max}\ G(y_t/\mathbf{x}) = \underset{x}{Arg\,\min}\ \mu(\mathbf{x}, y_t) \tag{5}$$

We have then:

$$\mu(\mathbf{x}, y_t) = -\log G(y_t/\mathbf{x}) \tag{6}$$

The similarity measure between test utterance $\{y_t\}_{1 \leq t \leq M}$ of speaker y and the model of speaker x is then

$$\mu(\mathbf{x}, \mathbf{y}) = \mu(\mathbf{x}, y_1^N) = \frac{1}{N}\sum_{t=1}^{N} \mu(\mathbf{x}, y_t)$$
$$= -\bar{Lx}(y_1^N) \tag{7}$$

After simplifications, we obtain

$$\mu(\mathbf{x}, \mathbf{y}) =$$
$$\frac{1}{P}\left[-\log\left(\frac{\det(Y)}{\det(X)}\right) + tr(YX^{-1}) + (\bar{y} - \bar{x})^T X^{-1}(\bar{y} - \bar{x}) \right] - 1 \tag{8}$$

This measure is equivalent to the standard Gaussian likelihood measure (asymmetric μ_G) defined in [8].

A variant of this measure called μ_{Gc} is deduced from the previous one by assuming that $\bar{y} = \bar{x}$ (inter-speaker variability of the mean is negligible).

Thus, the new formula becomes:

$$\mu_{GC}(\mathbf{x}, \mathbf{y}) = \frac{1}{P}\left[-\log\left(\frac{\det(Y)}{\det(X)}\right) + tr(YX^{-1}) \right] - 1 \tag{9}$$

2.2   Neural Approach for Speaker Discrimination

Knowing the high discriminative capacities of the NNs (neural networks) [12], we opted for the use of a MLP (Multi-Layer Perceptron) with one or two hidden layers and with only one output. Experiments are done on audio signals, of three or four seconds each and extracted from Hub-4 Broadcast News.

The goal of this neural network [13] is to discriminate the different speakers by their speech signals. For this purpose, an input vector extracted from the MFSC coefficients is used.

The NN must have at its input a number of receptive cells equal to the dimension of the example vector [7]. Thus, in case of using a vector with N MFSC coefficients [6, 7], the number of input receptive cells is equal to $2.N$ (corresponding to two different utterances).

The training is performed by the back-propagation algorithm and the NN output will give then an indication on the correlation between the two utterances:

- *If $NN_{OUTPUT} = 0$ then it is the same speaker,*
- *If $NN_{OUTPUT} = 1$ then the speakers are different,*

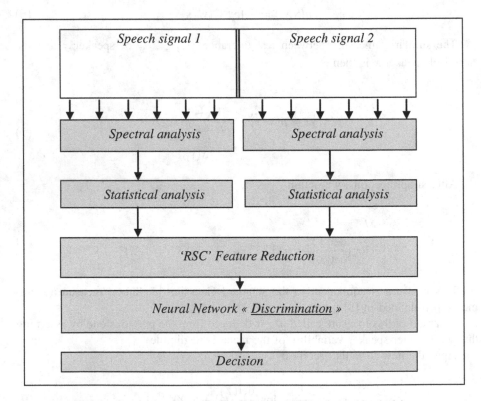

Fig. 1. Comparison between 2 utterances and discrimination decision

If the two segments (utterances) have different characteristics (characterization of the speaker), then we can affirm that these segments belong to the same speaker, otherwise, these segments belong to two different speakers.

Concerning the acoustical-spectral analysis of the signal, a segmentation by windows of 35 ms (ensuring the stationarity) is used in each segment where a spectral analysis is made, in giving one series of MFSC vectors for each segment [6, 7].

This vectors set goes through a statistical process which allows extracting the covariance diagonal elements in each segment. Thereafter, a feature reduction is applied by using a RSC or Relative Speaker Characterization (see section C). These elements are directly injected to the input of the NN which will decide whether the two segments belong to the same speaker or not: see Fig. 1.

2.3   Hybrid Method

Since it has been proved that NNs have an excellent discriminative property, we thought to mix the statistical measure with the neural inputs in order to improve the NN performance: this is the hybrid method.

Thus, a new input is added to the NN, into which we inject the discrimination result given by the statistical measure for each couple of segments, with the corresponding segments and then the training of the NN with this new input is performed as shown in Fig. 2 below.

The hybrid method is summarized as follows: First, the features are extracted from the two segments, then; the statistical measure μ_{Gc} is computed and injected to the NN together with the reduced features, called RSC (*Relative Speaker Characteristic*) [14]. The training is then enhanced by the information brought by the statistical approach.

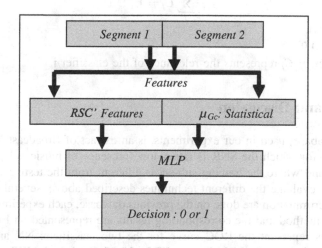

Fig. 2. The hybrid method.

2.4   Fusion

In order to enhance the discrimination performance, we usually use several classifiers which are combined in order to get a better precision: this combination is called Fusion. The fusion in the broad sense can be performed at different hierarchical levels or processing stages. A very commonly encountered taxonomy of data fusion is given by the following three-stage hierarchy [15, 16]:

(a) *Feature level* where the feature sets of different modalities are combined. Fusion at this level provides the highest flexibility but classification problems may arise due to the large dimension of the combined (concatenated) feature vectors.
(b) *Score (matching) level* is the most common level where the fusion takes place. The scores of the classifiers are usually normalized and then they are combined in a consistent manner.
(c) *Decision level* where the outputs of the classifiers establish the decision via techniques such as majority voting. Fusion at the decision level is considered to be rigid for information integration.

In our case, we chose the fusion at the score level.

If the simple scores are denoted by S_j, then the fusion score Sf is given by:

$$Sf = \sum_{j=1}^{N} C_j S_j \tag{10}$$

where C_j represents the weighing coefficient (confidence) for the classifier "j" and N denotes the classifiers number.

With

$$\sum_j C_j = 1 \tag{11}$$

and $C_j \in [0.1, 0.9]$

The coefficient C_j represents the relevance of the classifier j.

3   Results and Discussion

The audio database, used in our experiments, is an extract of Broadcast News "CNN early edition", for which the SNR is rather low (presence of music, telephonic calls, noises...etc.) and where the training sub-set is different from the testing one.

In order to evaluate the different techniques described above, several experiments of speaker discrimination are done on the previous database, each experiment concerns one particular method and the corresponding results are represented on Figs. 3 and 4.

The figures represent the ROC curve for the two classifiers: NN and statistical measure. We notice that the NN gives an EER of 9.25 % while the EER given by the statistical measure is 11.75 %. The NN looks better than the statistical method in the middle area, whereas at the borders of the ROC curve, the statistical measure looks better.

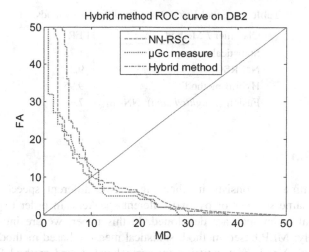

Fig. 3. Speaker discrimination –Hybrid Method-

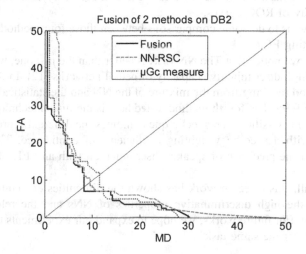

Fig. 4. Speaker discrimination –Fusion NN/μ_{Gc}-

In the other hand, this EER is about 9.95 % when we use the hybrid method (Fig. 3), which means an improvement of 1.8 % with respect to the statistical measure score and a degradation of 0.7 % with respect to the NN.

Results of fusion between the two classifiers: NN and μ_{Gc} are shown in Fig. 4, where we can notice that the fusion gives an EER better than the EER given by each method alone. The fusion EER is only 7.88 % (Table 1) which shows that the fusion is useful. The overall results are summarized in Table 1.

Table 1. Equal Error Rates for different methods.

Classifier / Method	EER %
Statistical measure	11.75
NN-RSC	9.25
Hybrid method	9.95
Fusion (*weighted sum*): NN- μ_{Gc}	7.88

4 Conclusion

Speaker discrimination consists in checking if two different speech segments are uttered by the same speaker or by two different speakers. In order to deal with this problem, several techniques are developed. In this paper, we are interested in four methods, namely: MLP based method, statistical measure based method (μ_{Gc}), hybrid method (MLP-μ_{Gc}) and even a fusion (at score level) based method for the task of discrimination. All those methods are evaluated on a sub-set extracted from Hub4 Broadcast News database and the different scores obtained by each method are represented in a way of ROC curves.

Results allow us to do some comparisons between those four methods according to their corresponding EER.

In one hand, we notice that The NN EER is better than the μ_{Gc} one, which confirms once again the high discriminative capacity of neural networks [12]. In the other hand, the hybrid method resulting from the mixture of the NN and the statistical method has a medium EER of 9.95. The fourth method tested here is the fusion technique carried out with the two basic classifiers. This technique combines the different scores obtained by each method, with a specific weighting coefficients of confidence. This fusion has highly improved the precision of speaker discrimination with an EER of 7.88 % (best score obtained).

In the overall, this research work has shown the difficulties encountred in speaker discrimination, the high discriminative properties of NNs and the relevance of the fusion technique. For future works, we hope to expand our experiments to other fusion techniques used for the same task.

References

1. Woodland, P.C., Gales, M.J.F., Pye, D., Young, S.J.: The Development of the 1996 HTK broadcast news transcription system. In: Workshop DARPA Speech Recognition, pp. 97–99 (1997)
2. Motlicek, P., Dey, S., Madikeri, S., Burget, L.: Employment of subspace gaussian mixture models in speaker recognition. In: 2015 IEEE International Conference on Acoustics, Speech and Signal Processing (ICASSP), South Brisbane, pp. 4445–4449, 19–24 April 2015
3. Richardson, F., Reynolds, D., Dehak, N.: Deep neural network approaches to speaker and language recognition. IEEE Sig. Process. Lett. **22**(10), 1671–1675 (2015)

4. Ouamour, S., Sayoud, H.: Speaker detection on telephone calls using fusion between SVMs and statistical measures. In: International Conference on Cyber-Enabled Distributed Computing and Knowledge Discovery, Beijing, China, 10–12 October 2013
5. Alam, M.M., Uddin, M.S., Uddin, M.N.: Text dependent speaker identification using hidden Markov model and mel frequency cepstrum coefficient. Int. J. Comput. Appl. **104**(14), 33–37 (2014)
6. Lee, H.S., Tsoi, A.C.: Application of multi-layer perceptron in estimating speech / noise characteristics for speech recognition in noisy environment. Speech Commun. **17**(1–2), 59–76 (1995)
7. Sayoud, H., Ouamour, S., Boudraa, M.: 'ASTRA' an automatic speaker tracking system based on SOSM measures and an interlaced indexation. acta. Acustica **89**(4), 702–710 (2003)
8. Sayoud, H., Ouamour, S.: Reconnaissance automatique du locuteur en milieu bruité. In: JEP 2000 Conference, Aussois Juin, pp. 345–348 (2000)
9. Ouamour, S., Sayoud, H.: Looking for the best spectral resolution in automatic speaker recognition. In: 3rd IEEE-GCC Conference, Manama Bahrain, 19–22 March (2006)
10. Bimbot, F., Magrin-Chagnolleau, I., Mathan, L.: Second-order statistical measures for text-independent broadcaster identification. Speech Commun. **17**(1–2), 177–192 (1995)
11. Bonastre, F., Besacier, L.: Traitement Indépendant de Sous-bandes Fréquentielles par des méthodes Statistiques du Second Ordre pour la Reconnaissance du Locuteur. Actes du 4ème Congrès Français d'Acou., Marseille pp. 357–360, 14–18 Apr 1997
12. Bennani, Y.: Approches connexionnistes pour la reconnaissance du locuteur: modélisation et identification. Ph. D. thesis, Université Paris XI (1992)
13. Sayoud, H.: Automatic speaker recognition using neural approaches. Ph. D. thesis, USTHB University, Algiers (2003)
14. Ouamour, S., Guerti, M., Sayoud, H.: A new relativistic vision in speaker discrimination. Can. Acoust. J. **36**(4), 24–34 (2008). Publisher: Canadian Acoustics Association, Canada
15. Dasarathy, B.V.: Decision Fusion. IEEE Computer Society Press, Los Alamitos (1994)
16. Kitler, J.: Multiple classifier systems in decision-level fusion of multimodal biometric experts. 1st BioSecure residential workshop, Paris, France 1–26 August (2005)

Multiple-Instance Multiple-Label Learning for the Classification of Frog Calls with Acoustic Event Detection

Jie Xie[✉], Michael Towsey, Liang Zhang, Kiyomi Yasumiba,
Lin Schwarzkopf, Jinglan Zhang, and Paul Roe

Electrical Engineering and Computer Science School,
Queensland University of Technology, Brisbane, Australia
xiej8734@gmail.com
https://www.ecosounds.org/

Abstract. Frog call classification has received increasing attention due to its importance for ecosystem. Traditionally, the classification of frog calls is solved by means of the single-instance single-label classification classifier. However, since different frog species tend to call simultaneously, classifying frog calls becomes a multiple-instance multiple-label learning problem. In this paper, we propose a novel method for the classification of frog species using multiple-instance multiple-label (MIML) classifiers. To be specific, continuous recordings are first segmented into audio clips (10 s). For each audio clip, acoustic event detection is used to segment frog syllables. Then, three feature sets are extracted from each syllable: mask descriptor, profile statistics, and the combination of mask descriptor and profile statistics. Next, a bag generator is applied to those extracted features. Finally, three MIML classifiers, MIML-SVM, MIML-RBF, and MIML-kNN, are employed for tagging each audio clip with different frog species. Experimental results show that our proposed method can achieve high accuracy (81.8 % true positive/negatives) for frog call classification.

Keywords: Frog call classification · Acoustic event detection · Multiple-instance multiple-label learning

1 Introduction

Recently, human activity and climate change put a negative effect on frog biodiversity, which makes frog monitoring become ever more important. Compared with the traditional monitoring method such as field observation, acoustic sensors have greatly extended acoustic monitoring into larger spatio-temporal scales [1]. Correspondingly, large volumes of acoustic data are generated, which makes it essential to develop automatic methods.

Several papers have already described automated methods for the classification of frog calls. Han et al. combined spectral centroid, Shannon entropy, Renyi

© Springer International Publishing Switzerland 2016
A. Mansouri et al. (Eds.): ICISP 2016, LNCS 9680, pp. 222–230, 2016.
DOI: 10.1007/978-3-319-33618-3_23

entropy for frog call recognition with a k-nearest neighbour classifier [2]. Gingras et al. proposed a method based on mean value for dominant frequency, coefficient of variation of root-mean square energy, and spectral flux for anuran classification [3]. Bedoya et al. used Mel-frequency cepstral coefficients (MFCCs) for the recognition of anuran species with a fuzzy classifier [4]. Xie et al. proposed a method based on track duration, dominant frequency, oscillation rate, frequency modulation and energy modulation to do frog call [5]. All those previous methods achieve a high accuracy rate in recognition and classification, but recordings used in those papers are assumed that there is only a single frog species present in each recording.

Unfortunately, all the recordings used in this study are low signal to noise ratio and contain many overlapping animal vocal activities including frogs, birds, crickets and so on. To solve this problem, the multiple-instance multiple-label classifier for supervised classification is formulated [6]. In the previous study, Briggs et al. has already introduced the MIML classifiers for acoustic classification of multiple simultaneous bird species [7]. In their method, a supervise learning classifier was employed for segmenting acoustic events, which required lots of annotations.

In this study, we introduced the MIML algorithm for frog call classification. Rather than using a supervised learning method for syllable segmentation, acoustic event detection is first employed to separate frog syllables. Then, three feature sets, mask descriptor, profile statistics, and the combination of mask descriptor and profile statistics, are calculated from each syllable. After applying a bag generator to those extracted feature sets, three classifiers, MIML-SVM [6], MIML-RBF [8], and MIML-kNN [9], are lastly used for the recognition of multiple simultaneous frog species. Experimental results show that our proposed method can achieve high classification accuracy.

2 Materials and Methods

2.1 Materials

Digital recordings in this study were obtained with a battery-powered, weather-proof Song Meter (SM2) box. Recordings were two-channel, sampled at 22.05 kHz and saved in WAC4 format. Here, a representative sample of 342 10-s recordings was selected to train and evaluate our proposed algorithm for predicting which frog species are present in a recording. All those examples were collected between 02/2014 to 03/2014, because it is the frog breeding season with high calling activity. All the species that are present in each 10-s recording were manually labelled by an ecologist who studies frog calls. There are totally eight frog species in the recordings: Canetoad (CAD) ($F_0 = 560\,\text{Hz}$), Cyclorana novaehollandiae (CNE) ($F_0 = 610\,\text{Hz}$), Limnodynastes terraereginae (LTE) ($F_0 = 610\,\text{Hz}$), Litoria fallax (LFX) ($F_0 = 4000\,\text{Hz}$), Litoria nasuta (LNA) ($F_0 = 2800\,\text{Hz}$), Litoria rothii (LRI) ($F_0 = 1800\,\text{Hz}$), Litoria rubella (LRA) ($F_0 = 2300\,\text{Hz}$), and Uperolela mimula (UMA) ($F_0 = 2400\,\text{Hz}$). Here, F_0 is the mean dominant frequency for each frog species. Each recording contains between 1 and 5 species. Following the prior work [7], we assume that recordings without any frog calls can be detected by acosutic event detection.

2.2 Signal Processing

All the recordings were re-sampled at 16 kHz and mixed to mono. A spectrogram was then generated by applying short-time Fourier transform to each recording. Specifically, each recording was divided into frames of 512 samples with 50 % frame overlap. A fast Fourier transform was then performed on each frame with a Hamming window, which yielded amplitude values for 256 frequency bins, each spanning 31.25 Hz. The final decibel values (S) were generated using $S_{tf} = 20*log_{10}(A_{tf})$, where A is the amplitude value, $t = 0, ..., T-1$ and $f = 0, ..., F-1$ represent frequency and time index, T and F are 256 frequency bins and 625 frames, respectively.

2.3 Acoustic Event Detection for Syllable Segmentation

Acoustic event detection (AED) aims to detect specified acoustic event in an audio stream. In this study, we use AED to segment frog syllables. Since all the recordings are collected from the field, there are much overlapping vocal activities. Traditional methods for audio segmentation are based on time domain information [10,11], which cannot address those recordings. Here, we modified the AED method developed by Towsey et al. [12] to segment recordings with overlapping activities. The detail of our AED method is described as follows:

Step 1: Wiener filter

To de-noise and smooth the spectrogram, a 2-D Wiener filter is applied to the spectrogram image over a 5 × 5 time-frequency grid, where the filter size is selected after considering the trade-off between removing the background graininess and blurring the acoustic events.

$$\hat{S_{tf}} = \mu + \frac{(\sigma^2 - \nu^2)}{\sigma^2}(S_{tf} - \nu) \tag{1}$$

where μ and σ^2 are local mean and variance, respectively. ν^2 is the noise variance estimated by averaging all local variances.

Step 2: Spectral subtraction

After Wiener filter, the graininess has been removed. However, some noises such as wind, insect, motor engine that cover the whole recording cannot be removed. Here, a modified spectral subtraction is used for dealing with those noise [13].

Step 3: Adaptive thresholding

After noise reduction, the next step is to convert the noise reduced spectrogram $\hat{S'_{tf}}$ into the binary spectrogram S^b_{tf} for events detection. Different from the hard threshold in Towseys work, an adaptive thresholding method named *Otsu thresholding* is used to convert the smoothed spectrogram into binary spectrogram. Otsus method assumes that the spectrogram is composed of two classes: acoustic events and background noise. An optimal threshold value is used for

Algorithm 1. Modified Spectral Subtraction

Data: $\hat{S}_{tf}$, spectrogram after Wiener filtering.

Result: $\hat{S'}_{tf} = \hat{S}_{tf}$, noise reduced spectrogram.

begin

    Construct an array of the modal noise values for all frequency bins;

    for $f \in F$ **do**

        1. calculate the histogram of the intensity value over each frequency bin

        2. smooth the histogram array with a moving average window of size 7

        3. regard the modal noise intensity at the position of maximal bin in the left-side of the histogram

    Smooth the array with a moving average filter with window of size 5;

    for $f \in F$ **do**

        1. subtract the modal noise intensity

        2. truncated negative decibel values to zero

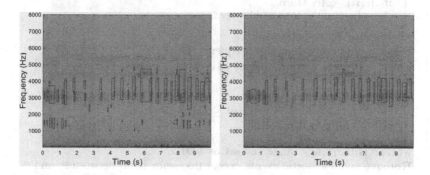

Fig. 1. Acoustic event detection results before (Left) and after (Right) event filtering based on dominant frequency. Here, blue rectangle means the time and frequency boundary of each detected event.

the decision. After thresholding, each group of contiguous positive pixels will be regarded as a candidate event (Fig. 1).

Step 4: Events filtering using dominant frequency and event area

After aforementioned process, not all detected events are correspond to frog vocalizations. To further remove those events that are from the listed frog species in Sect. 2.1, dominant frequency (F_0) and area within the event boundary (Ar) are used for filtering.

Step 5: Region growing

Region growing algorithm is utilized to obtain the contour of the particular acoustic event [14]. To get the accuracy boundary of each acoustic event and improve the discrimination of extracted features, a 2-D region growing algorithm is applied for obtaining the accuracy event shape within each segmented event. First, a maximal intensity value within each segmented event is selected as the seed point. Then, if the difference between the neighbourhood pixels and the seed(s) is smaller than the threshold, the neighbourhood pixels will be located and assigned to the output image. Next, the new added pixels are used as seeds for further processing until all the pixels that satisfy the criteria are added to the output image. The final results after region growing are shown in Fig. 2. Here, the threshold value is empirically set as 5 dB.

Algorithm 2. Event filtering based on dominant frequency and event area

---

Data: S_{tf}^b, spectrogram; $t_s(n)$, $t_e(n)$, $f_l(n)$, $f_h(n)$, location of each acoustic
        event n; $F_0(i)$, dominant frequency of frog species i.
Result: $\tilde{S}_{tf}$, spectrogram after events filtering.
begin
    Calculate the area of each acoustic event n.
    $Area(n) = (t_e(n) - t_s(n)) * (f_h(n) - f_l(n))$
    for $n \in N_{e1}$ **do**
        if $Ar(n) \geq Ar_l$ **then**
             split event n into small events
    where Ar_l is set as 3000 pixels.
    Filter events using dominant frequency $f_d(n) = \sum_{t=t_s(n)}^{t_e(n)} F(t)/t_e(n) - t_s(n)$
    where $F(t)$ is the peak frequency of each frame within the event area
    for $n \in N_{e2}$ **do**
        for $i \in I$ **do**
            if $f_d(n) \geq F_0(i) + \theta$; $f_d(n) \leq F_0(i) - \theta$ **then**
                 $f_d(n) = 0$;
    where θ is frequency range and set as 300 Hz.
    Remove small acoustic events except frequency band between θ_l and θ_h
    for $n \in N_{e2}$ **do**
        if $Ar(n) \leq Ar_s$ **then**
             remove event n
    where Ar_s is set at 300 pixels, θ_l and θ_h are set as 300 Hz and 800 Hz,
    respectively. Because the area of LTE is smaller than Ar_s.

2.4   Feature Extraction

Based on acoustic event detection results, two feature sets are first calculated to describe each event (syllable): mask descriptor and profile statistic [7]. Here, we exclude histogram of orientation from our feature sets, because the previous study has already demonstrated its poor classification performance [7]. For mask descriptor, it is used to describe the syllable shape including minimum frequency, maximum frequency, bandwidth, duration, area, perimeter, non-compactness, rectangularity. For profile statistics, there are time-Gini, frequency-Gini, frequency-mean, frequency-variance, frequency-skewness, frequency-kurtosis, frequency-max, time-max, mask-mean, and mask standard deviation. The third feature set consists of all features.

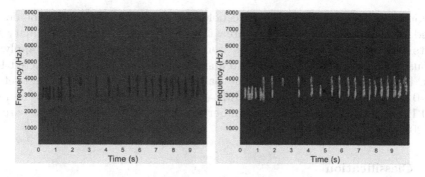

Fig. 2. Acoustic event detection results after region growing. Left: binary segmentation results; Right: segmented frog syllables.

Table 1. Accuracy measure for MIML classifiers with different feature sets. Here, ↓ indicates the smaller the better, while ↑ indicates the bigger the better.

Feature	Algorithm	Hamming loss ↓	Rank loss ↓	One-error ↓	Coverage ↓	Micro-AUC ↑
MD	MIML-SVM	0.253	0.186	0.308	3.147	0.745
MD	MIML-kNN	0.205	0.153	0.298	2.647	0.771
MD	MIML-RBF	**0.182**	**0.132**	**0.223**	**2.352**	**0.828**
PS	MIML-SVM	0.239	0.208	0.323	3.544	0.728
PS	MIML-kNN	0.211	0.153	0.298	2.647	0.777
PS	MIML-RBF	0.186	0.161	0.338	3.161	0.746
AF (MD+PS)	MIML-SVM	0.261	0.199	0.279	3.588	0.761
AF (MD+PS)	MIML-kNN	0.205	0.160	0.264	2.735	0.787
AF (MD+PS)	MIML-RBF	0.191	0.142	0.220	2.632	0.821

3 Multiple-Instance Multiple-Label Classifiers

After feature extraction, three MIML algorithms are evaluated for the classification of multiple simultaneous frog calls: MIML-SVM, MIML-RBF, and MIML-kNN. With some form of event-level distance measure, the MIML problem has been reduced to a single-instance multiple-label problem by associating each event with a event-level feature [7]. Here, the maximal and average Hausdorff distances between two syllables are used by MIML-SVM and MIML-RBF, separately. For MIML-kNN, the nearest neighbour is used to assign syllable-level features.

4 Experiment Results

4.1 Parameter Tuning

There are three modules whose parameters need to be discussed: signal processing, acoustic event detection, and classification. For signal processing, the window size and overlap are 512 samples and 50 %, respectively. During the process of acoustic event detection, four thresholds for event filtering need to be determined, which are small and large area threshold, and frequency boundary for events filtering. All those thresholds were determined empirically by applying various combinations of thresholds to a small number of randomly selected 10 s clips. For MIML-SVM classifiers, the parameters used are (C, γ, r) and set as (0.1, 0.6, 0.2) experimentally. For MIML-RBF, the parameters are (r, μ) and set as (0.1,0.6). For MIML-kNN, the number of references (k) and citers (k') are 10 and 20, respectively.

4.2   Classification

In this study, all the algorithms were programmed in Matlab 2014b. Each MIML algorithm is evaluated with five-fold cross-validation on the collection of 342 species-labelled recordings. Five measures including Hamming loss, rank loss, one-error, coverage, and micro-AUC are used to characterize the accuracy of each algorithm [15,16]. The definition of each measure can be found in [7], the positive/negatives is defined as $1-$Hamming loss and it is 0.818 for MIML-RBF with MD. Mask descriptor (MD) and profile statistical (PS), and all features (AF) are put into the three classifiers, respectively. The performance of each MIML classifier is shown in Table 1. Here, the best classification accuracy is achieved by MIML-RBF using MD. For each classifier, the classification accuracy of MD is higher than PS and AF, which shows that the event shape have higher discrimination power than the event content. To give a concrete view of predictions, the results of 5 randomly selected recordings using MIML-RBF are shown in Table 2. Recordings of No. 1 and No. 3 are accurately predicted.

Table 2. Example predictions with MIML-RBF.

No.	Ground truth	Predicted labels
1	UMA	UMA
2	LNA, LRI, UMA	LNA, LRA, UMA
3	LNA, UMA	LNA, UMA
4	LNA, LFX, LRA	LNA, LFX, LRI, LRA
5	LNA, LFX, LRA	LNA, LRA

5   Conclusion

In this study, we propose a novel method for the classification of multiple simultaneous frog species in environmental recordings. To the best of our knowledge, this is the first study that applies the MIML algorithm to frog calls. Since frogs tend to call simultaneously, the MIML algorithm is more suitable for dealing with those recordings than single-instance single-label classification. After applying acoustic event detection algorithm to each 10 s recording, each frog syllable is segmented. Then, three feature sets are calculated based on those segmented syllables. Finally, three MIML classifiers are used for the classification of frog calls with the best accuracy (81.8 % true positive/negatives). Future work will focus on the study of novel features and MIML classifiers for further improving the classification performance.

References

1. Wimmer, J., Towsey, M., Planitz, B., Williamson, I., Roe, P.: Analysing environmental acoustic data through collaboration and automation. Future Gener. Comput. Syst. **29**(2), 560–568 (2013)
2. Han, N.C., Muniandy, S.V., Dayou, J.: Acoustic classification of Australian Anurans based on hybrid spectral-entropy approach. Appl. Acoust. **72**(9), 639–645 (2011)
3. Gingras, B., Fitch, W.T.: A three-parameter model for classifying Anurans into four genera based on advertisement calls. J. Acoust. Soc. Am. **133**(1), 547–559 (2013)
4. Bedoya, C., Isaza, C., Daza, J.M., López, J.D.: Automatic recognition of Anuran species based on syllable identification. Ecol. Inf. **24**, 200–209 (2014)
5. Xie, J., Towsey, M., Truskinger, A., Eichinski, P., Zhang, J., Roe, P.: Acoustic classification of Australian Anurans using syllable features. In: 2015 IEEE Tenth International Conference on Intelligent Sensors, Sensor Networks and Information Processing (IEEE ISSNIP 2015), Singapore, April 2015
6. Zhou, Z.-H.Z.M.-L.: Multi-instance multi-label learning with application to scene classification. In: Advances in Neural Information Processing Systems, pp. 1609–1616 (2007)
7. Briggs, F., Lakshminarayanan, B., Neal, L., Fern, X.Z., Raich, R., Hadley, S.J., Hadley, A.S., Betts, M.G.: Acoustic classification of multiple simultaneous bird species: a multi-instance multi-label approach. J. Acoust. Soc. Am. **131**(6), 4640–4650 (2012)
8. Zhang, M.-L., Wang, Z.-J.: MIMLRBF: RBF neural networks for multi-instance multi-label learning. Neurocomputing **72**(16), 3951–3956 (2009)
9. Zhang, M.-L.: A k-nearest neighbor based multi-instance multi-label learning algorithm. In: 22nd IEEE International Conference on Tools with Artificial Intelligence (ICTAI), vol. 2, pp. 207–212. IEEE (2010)
10. Somervuo, P., et al.: Classification of the harmonic structure in bird vocalization. In: IEEE International Conference on Acoustics, Speech, and Signal Processing (ICASSP 2004), vol. 5, pp. V–701. IEEE (2004)
11. Huang, C.-J., Yang, Y.-J., Yang, D.-X., Chen, Y.-J.: Frog classification using machine learning techniques. Expert Syst. Appl. **36**(2), 3737–3743 (2009)
12. Towsey, M., Planitz, B., Nantes, A., Wimmer, J., Roe, P.: A toolbox for animal call recognition. Bioacoustics **21**(2), 107–125 (2012)
13. Xie, J., Towsey, M., Zhang, J., Roe, P.: Image processing and classification procedure for the analysis of Australian frog vocalisations. In: Proceedings of the 2nd International Workshop on Environmental Multimedia Retrieval, ser. EMR 2015, New York, NY, USA, pp. 15–20. ACM (2015)
14. Mallawaarachchi, A., Ong, S., Chitre, M., Taylor, E.: Spectrogram denoising and automated extraction of the fundamental frequency variation of dolphin whistles. J. Acoust. Soc. Am. **124**(2), 1159–1170 (2008)

15. Zhou, Z.-H., Zhang, M.-L., Huang, S.-J., Li, Y.-F.: MIML: a framework for learning with ambiguous objects. CORR abs/0808.3231 (2008)
16. Dimou, A., Tsoumakas, G., Mezaris, V., Kompatsiaris, I., Vlahavas, I.: An empirical study of multi-label learning methods for video annotation. In: Seventh International Workshop on Content-Based Multimedia Indexing, CBMI 2009, pp. 19–24. IEEE (2009)

Feature Extraction Based on Bandpass Filtering for Frog Call Classification

Jie Xie[✉], Michael Towsey, Liang Zhang, Jinglan Zhang, and Paul Roe

Electrical Engineering and Computer Science School,
Queensland University of Technology, Brisbane, Australia
{j3.xie,168.zhang}@qut.edu.au,
{m.towsey,jinglan.zhang,p.roe}@hdr.qut.edu.au
https://www.ecosounds.org/

Abstract. In this paper, we propose an adaptive frequency scale filter bank to perform frog call classification. After preprocessing, the acoustic signal is segmented into individual syllables from which spectral peak track is extracted. Then, syllable features including track duration, dominant frequency, and oscillation rate are calculated. Next, a k-means clustering technique is applied to the dominant frequency of syllables for all frog species, whose centroids are used to construct a frequency scale. Furthermore, one novel feature named bandpass filter bank cepstral coefficients is extracted by applying a bandpass filter bank to the spectral of each syllable, where the filter bank is designed based on the generated frequency scale. Finally, a k-nearest neighbour classifier is adopted to classify frog calls based on extracted features. The experiment results show that our proposed feature can achieve an average classification accuracy of 94.3 % which outperforms Mel-frequency cepstral coefficients features (81.4 %) and syllable features (88.1 %).

Keywords: Frog call classification · Spectral peak track · k-means clustering · Filter bank · k-nearest neighbour

1 Introduction

Recently, frog biodiversity has been threatened due to human activity and climate change [1]. Therefore, frog monitoring is becoming ever more important. Compared with traditional monitoring methods such as field observation, acoustic sensors can extend the monitoring into larger spatiotemporal scales [2]. Correspondingly, the use of acoustic sensor generates large volumes of acoustic data, which makes it essential to develop automatic acoustic data processing techniques.

Several papers have already described automated methods for detection and classification of animal calls. Since an elementary unit for frog call classification is one syllable [3], the first step of one frog call classification system is often syllable segmentation. In prior work, different features have already been explored for syllable segmentation, including energy [4,5], zero-crossing rate (ZCR) [4,5],

© Springer International Publishing Switzerland 2016
A. Mansouri et al. (Eds.): ICISP 2016, LNCS 9680, pp. 231–239, 2016.
DOI: 10.1007/978-3-319-33618-3_24

amplitude [3], spectrogram [6,7]. Compared with energy, ZCR, and amplitude, syllable segmentation based on spectrogram is more robust to the background noise [8]. With segmented syllables, feature extraction is the next crucial step for the performance of classification system. Lee et al. used Mel-frequency cepstrum coefficients (MFCCs) for classifying frog and cricket calls with linear discriminant analysis [9]. Chen et al. developed a method for frog call classification based on syllable duration and a multi-stage average spectrum [4]. Bedoya et al. used MFCCs as the feature for the recognition of anuran species with a fuzzy clustering technique [10]. Jie et al. explored image features for frog call classification with a k-nearest neighbour classifier [11]. All the previous work achieves a high accuracy rate in recognition and classification of frog calls. However, most features used are transplanted from speech processing directly, which might be not suitable for studying frog calls.

In this paper, one novel feature based on an adaptive frequency scale bandpass filter bank is proposed for frog call classification. Following our prior work [7], spectrogram is first investigated for segmentation. Then, spectral peak track is extracted from each segmented syllable for feature calculation: track duration, dominant frequency and oscillation rate. Next, a frequency scale is constructed by applying a k-means clustering technique to the dominant frequency of segmented syllables. Furthermore, a bandpass filter bank is designed based on the frequency scale, and applied to the spectral of each frog call syllable for extracting bandpass filter bank cepstral coefficients (BFCCs). Finally, a k-nearest neighbour (k-NN) classifier is used for frog call classification with extracted features. The experimental results show that our proposed feature can achieve the highest classification accuracy for classifying frog calls, which outperforms MFCCs and syllable features (SFs).

2   Materials and Methods

Our frog call classification system consists of four steps including pre-processing, syllable segmentation, feature extraction and classification. Detailed description of each step is shown in the following parts.

2.1   Data Description and Pre-processing

In this study, eighteen frog species which are widely spread in Queensland, Australian are selected for the experiment. All the recordings are obtained from David Stewart's CD [12]. Each recording includes one frog species, with duration ranged from 8 to 55 s. For pre-processing, human voice are first excluded from the recordings. Then, all the recordings are re-sampled at 16 kHz and mixed to mono.

2.2   Syllable Segmentation

After pre-processing, each recording consists of continuous frog calls, which is made up of multiple syllables. Here, one syllable is an elementary unit of frog vocalizations for species detection [3]. For syllable segmentation, the iterative amplitude-frequency information is explored based on Härmä's method [6]. The amplitude-frequency information is generated by applying STFT to the frog calls, where the window function is Kaiser window with the size and overlap being 512 samples and 25 %. A Gaussian filter (7×7) is optionally used before applying Härmä's method for segmentation. The filter size used is set taking into account a trade-off between connecting gaps within one syllable and separating adjacent syllables.

2.3 Spectral Peak Track Extraction

For frogs, related species often share more similar advertisement calls than distant species [13]. Applying STFT to those advertisement calls, each frog species is found to occupy one particular frequency band. Therefore, we explore the spectral peak track (SPT) to represent the dominant frequency trace of frog calls. The reasons for using SPT is (1) Isolate the desired signal from background noise; (2) Extract corresponding features based on SPT. The SPT extraction method used is briefly summarized here, with further details provided in [7]. In this SPT extraction algorithm, seven parameters need to be pre-defined (Table 1). The process for selecting those parameters is explained in Sect. 3.

Table 1. Parameters used for spectral peak extraction

Parameter	Description
I (dB)	Minimum intensity threshold for peak selection
T_c (s)	Maximum time domain interval for peak connection
T_s (s)	Minimum time interval for stopping growing tracks
f_c (Hz)	Maximum frequency domain interval for peak connection
d_{min} (s)	Minimum track duration
d_{max} (s)	Maximum track duration
β (0 1)	Minimum density value

Before applying SPT extraction algorithm, each syllable is transformed to the spectrogram by dividing it into frames of 128 samples with 85 % overlap. For the generated spectrogram, selecting the maximum intensity (real peak) from each frame with a minimum required value I is the first step. Then, the time and frequency domain intervals between two successive peaks are calculated for satisfying T_c and f_c. If so, one initial track will be generated, then linear regression is applied to the generated track for calculating the position of next predicted peak. Next, the time and frequency domain intervals between predicted peak and the real peak are recalculated for satisfying T_c and f_c. If so, the real peak will be added to the initial track. This iterative process continues until T_s is no longer satisfied. After one track stops growing, comparing the duration and density of the track with d_{min}, d_{max}, and β is the next step. If all conditions are satisfied, then the track will be saved to the track list. The SPT results for *Neobatrachus sudelli* are shown in Fig. 1. During the process of track extraction, time domain gaps of the track are generated where the intensity threshold I is not reached. These gaps can be filled by predicting the correct frequency bin using linear regression, as illustrated in Fig. 1.

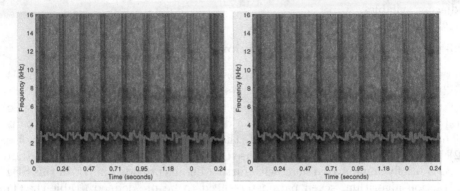

Fig. 1. Spectral peak track extraction results for *Neobatrachus sudelli* (left: selected peaks whose frequency are zero mean that the peaks do not satisfy the intensity threshold I and are set to zero, right: spectral peak track with predicted peaks using linear regression).

Based on each spectral peak track, syllable features are calculated including track duration, dominant frequency and oscillation rate [7]. Here, track duration is the length of track; dominant frequency is calculate by averaging the frequency of the peak within the track; oscillation rate represents the pulse rate within one track.

2.4   Bandpass Filtering for Feature Extraction

After calculating the dominant frequency for all frog species, some frog species are found to have similar dominant frequency but different spectral distribution. In this study, we explore the bandpass filtering technique for capturing the spectral information. First, frequency scale is generated by applying k-means clustering algorithm to the dominant frequency of all frog syllables. Here, k is selected as 18, which is the same with the number of frog species to be classified; the distance function is city block function. After applying the k-means clustering, 18 centroids ($C_i, (i = 1, ..., 18)$) are saved for design the bandpass filter.

Bandpass Filter Design for Feature Extraction. In this study, a cascade of a 20th-order equalizer and a band-pass filter (Butter-worth filter) is used to design a filter bank for feature extraction.

Algorithm 1. Design of a bandpass filter bank

Data: $C_i(i = 1 : N)$, where C_i is the centroid of the clustering results; N is the number of frog species to be classified.

Result: Bandpass filter bank

begin

    Step 1: Sort the centroid C and calculate the difference between the consecutive vectors of C, save the results as $d_j(j = 1 : N - 1)$

    Step 2: Design a filter bank with N bandpass filters based on the centroids. Here, $k = 1 : N$ is the index of bandpass filter; LF and HF represent the low and high cutoff frequency.

    if $k = 1$ then

       | $HF(k) = C_k + \frac{d_k}{2}$;

       | $LF(k) = C_k - \frac{d_k}{2}$;

    else if $k = N$ then

       | $HF(k) = C_k + \frac{d_{k-1}}{2}$;

       | $LF(k) = C_k - \frac{d_{k-1}}{2}$;

    else

       | $\varepsilon = min(\frac{d_{k-1}}{2}, \frac{d_k}{2})$

       | $HF(k) = C_k + \varepsilon$;

       | $LF(k) = C_k - \varepsilon$;

With the generated bandpass filter bank, we apply it to the spectrum of each frog syllable $x(n)$. Detailed steps for calculating bandpass filter bank cepstral coefficients (BFCCs) are described as follows:

Step 1: Apply bandpass filter bank to $X(k)$

Filter $X(k)$ with the generated filter bank, and save the filtered results of each bandpass filter as $B(i, j), j = 1, ..., J$. Where $X(k)$ is the result after applying fast Fourier transform to the windowed signal $x(n)$, i is the number of coefficients for each bandpass filter, j is the index of the filter.

Step 2: Calculate the energy of filtered result for each frequency band

$$E_{i,j} = \sum_{i=1}^{M_i}[B(i,j)]^2 \tag{1}$$

where M_i means the number of coefficients after bandpass filtering.

Step 3: Perform discrete cosine transform on the logarithm energy and obtain the feature BFCCs for each windowed signal

$$BFCCs(d) = \sum_{i=1}^{I} logE_{i,j}cos(\frac{d(i - 0.5)}{I}\pi) \tag{2}$$

where $d = 1, 2, ..., D$, and D is the dimension of BFCCs and set as 12. i is the index of energy for each bandpass filter.

Step 4: Average BFCCs over the temporal direction

$$BFCCs = \frac{\sum_{f=1}^{F} BFCCs(d, f)}{F} \tag{3}$$

where f is the index of windowed signal, F is the number of windowed signal after windowing.

3   Experiments and Discussion

3.1   Parameter Tuning

In this study, parameters of two parts need to be discussed: spectral peak track extraction and feature calculation. For spectral peak track, seven parameters were determined empirically by applying various combinations of thresholds to a small randomly selected syllables. Here, minimum and maximum duration are 60 ms and 1000 ms. The density value is 0.8, which describes the integrity of one syllable. The minimum intensity value is 3 dB. The maximum time interval for connecting peaks is 1.5 ms, and the maximum frequency interval is 500 Hz. For feature extraction, MFCCs are used as the baseline [9], where the window size and overlap are 512 samples and 50 %.

3.2   Classification

The k-NN classifier has been successfully employed for classifying bioacoustic signal [3,7,14]. In this experiment, the k-NN classifier is used to learn a model on the training examples with 10-fold cross-validation for frog classification. Since the k-NN classifier is sensitive to the local structure of the data as well the initial cluster centroids, we run the k-NN classifier for 10 times based on different initial points. The feature performance is evaluated by the classification accuracy, which is defined as

$$Accuracy(\%) = \frac{N_c}{N_t} * 100\% \tag{4}$$

where N_c is the number of syllables that are correctly classified, and N_t is the total number of syllables for one frog species. Three features are put into the classifier: syllable features (SFs), MFCCs, and BFCCs. The averaged classification accuracy is shown in Table 2.

   In this experiment, the averaged classification accuracy for MFCCs and SFs is 81.4 % and 88.1 % respectively. Our proposed feature achieves the highest classification accuracy (94.3 %). For MFCCs, the classification accuracy of *Neobatrachus sudelli* and *Philoria kundagungan* is 100 %, because their spectrum is different from other frog species. Compared with MFCCs and SFs, the classification accuracy of all frog species using BFCCs are higher than 90 % except *Mixophyes fleayi*. Since the spectrum of *Mixophyes fleayi* and *Limnodynastes terraereginae* are similar, the classification accuracy of them are relatively low.

However, the duration and oscillation rate between *Mixophyes fleayi* and *Limno-dynastes terraereginae* are different, which leads to a higher classification accuracy for SFs. For MFCCs, the spectrum is extracted based on the Mel-scale filter bank, which is designed based on the human auditory rather than the character of frog calls. With derived dominant frequency which has shown its ability for discriminating frog species [7,13], the designed bandpass filter bank is more suitable for the frequency scale of frog species to be classified. Compared with SFs, the use of bandpass filter bank captures not only the information of dominant frequency but also the distribution of the frog calls through all frequency bands.

Table 2. Classification accuracy (mean and standard deviation) for 18 frog species with three different features.

Scientific name	No. of syllables	Classification accuracy		
		MFCCs	SFs	BFCCs
Assa darlingtoni	36	23.3 ± 26.0	85.0 ±16.6	100.0 ± 0.0
Crinia parinsignifera	32	93.3 ± 13.3	76.7 ± 26.0	100.0 ± 0.0
Crinia signifera	22	60.0 ± 32.7	50.0 ± 22.4	100.0 ± 0.0
Limnodynastes tasmaniensis	16	50.0 ± 40.0	35.0 ± 22.9	90.0 ± 30.0
Limnodynastes terraereginae	54	86.7 ± 12.5	96.0 ± 8.0	95.0 ± 7.6
Litoria chloris	35	76.7 ± 15.3	77.5 ± 17.5	90.0 ± 15.3
Litoria latopalmata	172	98.2 ± 2.7	97.6 ± 3.9	100.0 ± 0.0
Litoria nasuta	74	85.0 ± 9.4	87.1 ± 13.5	98.8 ± 3.8
Litoria revelata	130	93.8 ± 5.8	99.2 ± 2.3	100.0 ± 0.0
Litoria rubella	37	93.3 ± 13.3	90.0 ± 16.6	96.7 ± 10.0
Litoria tyleri	71	90.0 ± 10.9	98.6 ± 4.3	98.8 ± 3.8
Litoria verreauxii verreauxii	28	80.0 ± 33.2	100.0 ± 0.0	100.0 ± 0.0
Mixophyes fasciolatus	33	95.0 ± 10.0	90.0 ± 15.3	92.5 ± 16.0
Mixophyes fleayi	16	70.0 ± 45.8	100.0 ± 0.0	40.0 ± 29.0
Neobatrachus sudelli	22	100.0 ± 0.0	90.0 ± 20.0	100.0 ± 0.0
Philoria kundagungan	22	100.0 ± 0.0	100.0 ± 0.0	100.0 ± 0.0
Uperoleia fusca	39	95.0 ± 10.0	87.5 ± 12.5	97.5 ± 7.5
Uperoleia laevigata	25	75.0 ± 33.5	100.0 ± 0.0	100.0 ± 0.0
Averaged accuracy	864	81.4 ± 18.0	88.1 ± 13.7	**94.3 ± 7.9**

For testing the robustness of the syllable features, a Gaussian white noise signal, with signal to noise ratio (SNR) of 40 dB, 30 dB, 20 dB, and 10 dB was added to the original audio data. The results from running the classifier on audio data with artificially added background noise are shown in Fig. 2, which show the ability of our feature extraction method for dealing with background noise.

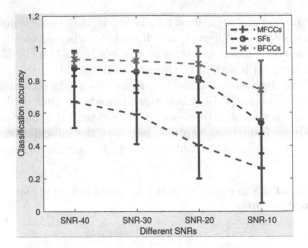

Fig. 2. Classification accuracy with MFCCs, SFs, and BFCCs under different levels of noise contamination.

4 Conclusion

This study presents a novel feature extraction method for frog call classification. After segmenting the audio data into syllables, the SPT algorithm is applied to each syllable. Then, syllable features are calculated including track duration, dominant frequency and oscillation rate. Based on the dominant frequency, a frequency scale is constructed with a k-means clustering algorithm for generating the bandpass filter bank. Finally, a feature set is extracted with generated filter bank for classifying frog calls using a k-NN classifier. The experimental results are promising with an average classification accuracy of 94.3 % for BFCCs. Future work will include additional experiments that test a wider variety of frog calls from different geographical and environment conditions.

References

1. Stuart, S.N., Chanson, J.S., Cox, N.A., Young, B.E., Rodrigues, A.S., Fischman, D.L., Waller, R.W.: Status and trends of amphibian declines and extinctions worldwide. Science **306**(5702), 1783–1786 (2004)
2. Wimmer, J., Towsey, M., Planitz, B., Williamson, I., Roe, P.: Analysing environmental acoustic data through collaboration and automation. Future Gener. Comput. Syst. **29**(2), 560–568 (2013)
3. Huang, C.-J., Yang, Y.-J., Yang, D.-X., Chen, Y.-J.: Frog classification using machine learning techniques. Expert Syst. Appl. **36**(2), 3737–3743 (2009)
4. Chen, W.-P., Chen, S.-S., Lin, C.-C., Chen, Y.-Z., Lin, W.-C.: Automatic recognition of frog calls using a multi-stage average spectrum. Comput. Math. Appl. **64**(5), 1270–1281 (2012)
5. Jaafar, H., Ramli, D.A.: Automatic syllables segmentation for frog identification system. In: 2013 IEEE 9th International Colloquium on Signal Processing and Its Applications (CSPA), pp. 224–228. IEEE (2013)

6. Harma, A.: Automatic identification of bird species based on sinusoidal modeling of syllables. In: Proceedings of the 2003 IEEE International Conference on Acoustics, Speech, and Signal Processing (ICASSP 2003), vol. 5, pp. V–545. IEEE (2003)
7. Xie, J., Towsey, M., Truskinger, A., Eichinski, P., Zhang, J., Roe, P.: Acoustic classification of Australian anurans using syllable features. In: 2015 IEEE Tenth International Conference on Intelligent Sensors, Sensor Networks and Information Processing (IEEE ISSNIP 2015), Singapore, April 2015
8. Colonna, J.G., Cristo, M., Salvatierra, M., Nakamura, E.F.: An incremental technique for real-time bioacoustic signal segmentation. Expert Syst. Appl. **4221**, 7367–7374 (2015)
9. Lee, C.-H., Chou, C.-H., Han, C.-C., Huang, R.-Z.: Automatic recognition of animal vocalizations using averaged MFCC and linear discriminant analysis. Pattern Recogn. Lett. **27**(2), 93–101 (2006)
10. Bedoya, C., Isaza, C., Daza, J.M., López, J.D.: Automatic recognition of anuran species based on syllable identification. Ecol. Inform. **24**, 200–209 (2014)
11. Xie, J., Towsey, M., Zhang, J., Dong, X., Roe, P.: Application of image processing techniques for frog call classification. In: 2015 IEEE International Conference on Image Processing (ICIP), pp. 4190–4194, September 2015
12. Stewart, D.: "Australian frog calls: subtropical east," Audio CD (1999). http://www.naturesound.com.au/cd_frogsSE.htm
13. Gingras, B., Fitch, W.T.: A three-parameter model for classifying anurans into four genera based on advertisement calls. J. Acoust. Soc. Am. **133**(1), 547–559 (2013)
14. Han, N.C., Muniandy, S.V., Dayou, J.: Acoustic classification of Australian anurans based on hybrid spectral-entropy approach. Appl. Acoust. **72**(9), 639–645 (2011)

Biomedical Imaging

Classification of Eukaryotic Organisms Through Cepstral Analysis of Mitochondrial DNA

Emmanuel Adetiba$^{(\boxtimes)}$ and Oludayo O. Olugbara

ICT and Society Research Group, Durban University of Technology,
Durban 4001, South Africa
{emmanuelal,oludayoo}@dut.ac.za

Abstract. Accurate classification of organisms into taxonomical hierarchies based on genomic sequences is currently an open challenge, because majority of the traditional techniques have been found wanting. In this study, we employed mitochondrial DNA (mtDNA) genomic sequences and Digital Signal Processing (DSP) for accurate classification of Eukaryotic organisms. The mtDNA sequences of the selected organisms were first encoded using three popular genomic numerical representation methods in the literature, which are Atomic Number (AN), Molecular Mass (MM) and Electron-Ion Interaction Pseudopotential (EIIP). The numerically encoded sequences were further processed with a DSP based cepstral analysis to obtain three sets of Genomic Cepstral Coefficients (GCC), which serve as the genomic descriptors in this study. The three genomic descriptors are named AN-GCC, MM-GCC and EIIP-GCC. The experimental results using the genomic descriptors, backpropagation and radial basis function neural networks gave better classification accuracies than a comparable descriptor in the literature. The results further show that the accuracy of the proposed genomic descriptors in this study are not dependent on the numerical encoding methods.

Keywords: Atomic number · Cepstral · EIIP · Genomic · Molecular mass · mtDNA

1 Introduction

Taxonomy is a hierarchical system that is employed to group organisms up to the species level. It is the principal method used to estimate organism's diversity and makes the study of living organisms highly convenient [1]. DNA based classification of organisms into groups within taxonomical hierarchies has applications in areas such as evolutionary characterization, bio-diversity research, forensic studies, food and meat authentication, detection of relationship within and between organisms as well as species identification [2]. Some of the traditional methods for nuclear DNA based classification of organisms include sequence alignment and analysis of compositional bias. According to [3], sequences that may not seem to have resemblance using sequence alignment may be found to be similar using compositional bias. This is because biases within the nuclear DNA genomes of the same organism are smaller than

© Springer International Publishing Switzerland 2016
A. Mansouri et al. (Eds.): ICISP 2016, LNCS 9680, pp. 243–252, 2016.
DOI: 10.1007/978-3-319-33618-3_25

that between different organisms. The availability of more genomic data in recent times has however presented evidences of huge variation in sequences within the same category of organisms, which has impacted negatively on the efficacy of these two traditional methods. Thus, a number of other DNA based methods have been developed to replace traditional methods. One of the most reliable, sensitive and specific of these modern methods is mitochondrial DNA (mtDNA) sequencing. The mtDNA sequencing generate mitochondria genomic sequences from the cells of eukaryotic species. The mtDNA sequences represent a minute fraction of the total DNA sequences in the eukaryotic cells. mtDNA sequences have a lot of attributes that make them suitable for taxonomic classification of eukaryotic species. One of these attributes is the ease with which the sequences can be isolated from organisms even with degraded or low amount of samples. Another vital attribute is the substantial variation in the mtDNA sequences of organisms belonging to different species [4].

Given the abovementioned attractive attributes, some studies in the literature have utilized bioinformatics and Genomic Signal Processing (GSP) techniques to process mtDNA so as to solve species classification or identification problems. Vijayan et al. [5] extracted Frequency Chaos Game Representation (FCGR) features from the chaos game representation images of mtDNA sequences of eight eukaryotic organisms to train Artificial Neural Networks (ANN) classifier. The authors reported a classification accuracy of 92.3 % with Probabilistic Neural Network (PNN) using 64 element feature vector. When the feature vector was reduced to 16 elements by exploiting the fractal nature of the mtDNA, the authors reported that the network complexity was radically reduced with no appreciable reduction in classification accuracy since an average accuracy of 90.1 % was obtained. Rastogi et al. [6] carried out a study on species identification of various animal samples using mtDNA and nuclear sequences obtained from their tissues. The bioinformatics tools utilized for the study are BLAST, Molecular Evolutionary Genetic Analysis (MEGA) v3.1 and ClustalW program. The result of this study showed that the mtDNA sequences are more efficient for species identification and authentication than nuclear sequences. According to the authors, the superiority of mtDNA sequences emanates from their relatively rapid evolution at the sequence level due to the mitochondrial inability to repair damages in the DNA. Kitpipit et al. [7] undertook a study on Tiger species identification using mtDNA from two individuals of four of the five subspecies of Tiger. The authors successfully sequenced and processed a total of 7891 bp which represent 46.4 % of the total tiger mtDNA using FINCH TV 1.4.0 and ClustalX bioinformatics tools. Based on the result in this study, there was no sequence variation within the 7891 bp that can be used to reliably differentiate the Tiger subspecies. This study further validates the low variability in intra-species mtDNA which make it highly potent for interspecies differentiation.

Genomic sequences other than mtDNA have also been employed for taxonomic classification in the literature. A study was carried out in [8] to classify the genomic sequences of four pathogenic viruses which include ebolavirus, enterovirus D68, dengue and hepatitis c viruses. The authors used Genomic Cepstral Coefficients (GCC) and Gaussian Radial Basis Function (RBF) to achieve classification rate of 97.3 %.

The compact and highly discriminatory GCC utilized in [8] and the strong inter-species variability of mtDNA as illustrated in [5] provided the motivation for the study at hand. Firstly, we acquired the genome of eight eukaryotic organisms from the

National Center for Biotechnology Information (NCBI) organelle database and numerically encoded them using three Physico-Chemical Property Based Mapping (PCPBM) schemes, which are Atomic Number (AN), Molecular Mass (MM) and Electron Ion Interaction Potential (EIIP) [9, 10]. Secondly, we computed Genomic Cepstral Coefficients (GCC) from the encoded genomes to obtain three different set of descriptors from the eukaryotic organisms. These descriptors are named in this study as AN-GCC, MM-GCC and EIIP-GCC. Thirdly, experiments were performed using each of the three descriptors as well as Back Propagation Neural Network (BPNN) and Radial Basis Function Neural Network (RBFNN) as utilized in [5]. The classification results obtained from the experiments were compared with the FCGR descriptor reported in [5]. Furthermore, we compared the results obtained using the three descriptors in this study so as to determine the most discriminatory of them.

The rest of this paper is organized as follows. Section 2 contains the materials and methods, Sect. 3 contains the results and discussion, while the paper is concluded in Sect. 4.

2 Materials and Methods

2.1 Dataset

We extracted mitochondrial DNA (mtDNA) genomes of Eukaryotic organisms, which belong to eight different taxonomical categories as the dataset for this study [5]. These data are from NCBI organelle database (www.ncbi.nlm.nih.gov/genome/browse/?report=5) and were extracted on the 31st of October, 2015. On this database, a search by organism query was carried out using the names of the Eukaryotic organisms (Table 1) to obtain the mtDNA genome accession numbers of the organisms in each category. The statistics of the dataset in the current study are shown in Table 1. As shown in the Table, the cumulative size of the dataset is 1,249, with Protostomia and Vertebrata each having the highest number of organisms (198) while Porifera has the lowest number of organisms (60). The size ranges of the genome for each of the Eukaryotic organism is also shown in Table 1. Notably, an organism in Plant category has the smallest genome size of 288 and another organism in the same category has the highest genome size of 1,555,935. As earlier established, the huge variation in genome lengths within the same class of organisms as shown in the Table is bound to impact negatively on the outcome of traditional organism classification methods such as sequence alignment and compositional bias analysis.

2.2 Numerical Representation of the mtDNA Genomes

Genome sequences are biologically represented with the collection of the four nucleotides, which are adenine, thymine, cytosine and guanine. The sequences are symbolized using character strings that consist of the letters A for Adenine, T for Thymine, C for Cytosine and G for Guanine. The use of Digital Signal Processing (DSP) in the literature to solve some critical problems in genomics has been possible through numerical representation of genome sequences and this has given birth to a

Table 1. Eukaryotic organisms extracted for this study

S/N	Eukaryotic organisms	Number of organisms	Range of genome size
1	Acoelomata (Flatworms)	83	13,387 – 27,133
2	Cnidaria	124	2,811 – 22,015
3	Fungi	196	1,136 – 235,849
4	Plant	271	288 – 1,555,935
5	Porifera	60	5,596 – 28,958
6	Protostomia	198	8,118 – 48,161
7	Pseudocoelomata(Nematodes)	119	12,626 – 26, 194
8	Vertebrata	198	3,427 – 22,184

branch of bioinformatics named Genomic Signal Processing (GSP) [11]. The methods for numerical representation of sequences in the GSP literature are classified into two, which are Fixed Mapping (FM) and Physico Chemical Property Based Mapping (PCPBM). FM methods use binary, real or complex number to transform genome sequences into a series of arbitrary numerical sequences while the PCPBM methods numerically transform genome sequences such that the biological principals and structures in the sequences can be detected [10]. The PCPMB methods is highly relevant for the study at hand because our goal is to use the inherent biology structures in the mtDNA sequences to classify unknown organism into the appropriate Eukaryotic category. Other attributes that are paramount for the numerical representation of the mtDNA sequences in this study are (i) single and non-redundant representation (ii) fixed magnitude representation for each nucleotide (iii) non-derivation from other numerical representation methods and (iv) accessibility to DSP analysis. All these attributes are essential for low computational overhead, memory conservation and detection of the inherent periodicity in genome sequences [10]. The three PCPBM methods in the literature, which fully satisfy the foregoing criteria are Atomic Number (AN), Molecular Mass (MM) and Electron-Ion Interaction Pseudopotential (EIIP) [9–11]. Hence, these methods were nominated for numerical representation of the mtDNA dataset in this study. Table 2 shows the nucleotides and their corresponding AN, MM and EIIP values. In this study, all the sequences of the organisms shown in Table 1 were numerically transformed based on the values of each nucleotide in the respective methods shown in Table 2.

Table 2. Numerical representation of the four nucleotides using AN, MM and EIIP

Nucleotide	Atomic Number (AN)	Molecular Mass (MM)	Electron-Ion Interaction Potential (EIIP)
A	70	134	0.1260
G	78	150	0.0806
C	58	110	0.1340
T	66	125	0.1335

2.3 Signal Cepstral Analysis

The application of the principle used in Fourier Transform (FT) for the detection of periodicity components in a Fourier spectrum is referred to as cepstrum analysis [12]. Given a numerically represented mtDNA sequence, which is a discrete signal denoted as $\hat{x}(n)$, with a spectrum denoted as $X(w)$, the cepstrum can be computed as the inverse FT of the logarithmic spectrum as follows:

$$\hat{x}(n) = \frac{1}{2\pi} \int_{-\pi}^{\pi} \log(X(w))e^{jwt}dw \tag{1}$$

Since $X(w)$ is a complex and even function, $\hat{x}(n)$ is usually referred to as a complex cepstrum even if the input signal is real. However, a real cepstrum can be computed by considering the spectrum magnitude $|X(w)|$ as:

$$c_x(n) = \frac{1}{2\pi} \int_{-\pi}^{\pi} \log(|X(w)|)e^{jwt}dw \tag{2}$$

As reported in [8], the real cepstrum in Eq. (2) consistently outperformed the complex cepstrum for all the experiments carried out in the previous study. Furthermore, it is a usual practice to restrict the number of cepstral coefficients that preserves the spectral envelope while removing the fine spectrum information. Retaining the first fifteen coefficients to represent the signal envelope gave better performance than the lower coefficients experimented in the aforementioned previous study [8]. Hence, for the study at hand, the first fifteen coefficients of the real cepstrum of the numerically encoded genome sequences form the GCC descriptors for each of the organisms. Based on the three different PCPBM methods earlier selected, three sets of descriptors, which are AN-GCC, MM-GCC and EIIP-GCC, were computed for the Eukaryotic organisms in this study. The algorithms for these descriptors were implemented in MATLAB R2014a programming environment. Each of the descriptors contains 15 element vector per organism and culminates in a $15 \times 1{,}249$ data matrix for the selected Eukaryotic organisms. One of the major benefits of utilizing the 15 element GCCs is that the complexity of the succeeding supervised classifier is drastically reduced.

2.4 Supervised Classification

In supervised classification, the training dataset is represented as $\{(x_j, c_j)\}$, with $j \in \{1, \ldots, N\}$ where each x_j contains n features and the class labels $c_j \in \{1, \ldots, l\}$ where l is the number of classes in the data. The supervised classification task involves the development of a model based on the set of N instances (i.e. the training data). The developed model is thereafter used to assign class labels to unknown instances using the values of the n features. Adapting the supervised classification paradigm to this study, symbols $N = 1{,}249$, $n = 15$ and $l = 8$. One of the most popularly used supervised classification methods in the bioinformatics and species classification literature is

Artificial Neural Network (ANN) [2, 10]. Since it is not known a priori which ANN topologies is more suitable for our dataset in this study, we experimented with the Backpropagation Neural Network (BPNN) and Radial Basis Function Neural Network (RBFNN) as was done in a closely related study reported in [5].

BPNN is reputed to be very good at learning various patterns [13]. In this study, the BPNN was tested for one, two and three number of layers and different number of neurons in each of the layers respectively [5]. The input layer contains 15 neurons, which is equal to the number of features in the training dataset and the output layer contains 8 neurons since there are 8 classes of Eukaryotic organisms in the dataset. The linear activation functions were selected for both the input and the output layers [10], the tansigmoid function was selected for the hidden layers while Levenberg-Marquardt training algorithm with a learning rate of 0.1 and Mean Square Error (MSE) goal of 0, was used for all the configurations [5].

RBFNN is suitable when there is a large training dataset and its design is very fast. RBFNN comprises of the input layer, which contains 15 neurons in this study, only one hidden layer, whose number of neurons are determined and created during training and the output layer, which is configured with 8 neurons. The two additional parameters that are supplied to RBFNN are the MSE goal and the spread factor.

The performances of the BPNN and RBFNN supervised classifiers were captured using accuracy and training time [5]. The implementations of the two classifiers in the Neural Network Toolbox of MATLAB R2014a were used in this study.

2.5 Experiments

The experiments in this study were performed on a computer system that contains an Intel Core i5-3210 M CPU, which operates at 2.50 GHz speed, 6.00 GB RAM, and runs 64-bit Windows 8 operating system. 70 % of the experimental dataset was used for training, 15 % for testing and the remaining 15 % for validation. The first experiment involved training each of the configurations of the BPNN five times using the AN-GCC, MM-GCC and EIIP-GCC descriptors one after the other. We needed to carry out five different trainings and obtained the average accuracy and training time for each BPNN configuration because the network normally begins with random weights. These initial random weights often culminate in the same network configuration, with the same training dataset, generating different accuracies when trained at different times. In the second experiment, we configured the RBFNN with an MSE goal of 0.0 and a spread factor of 1 and trained the network using AN-GCC, MM-GCC and EIIP-GCC respectively to obtain the accuracies and training times. All the results we obtained in the foregoing experiments are hereafter reported and discussed.

3   Results and Discussion

The results of the first experiment are shown in Table 1. As shown in the Table, the highest average accuracy after the BPNN was trained with AN-GCC is 88.04 % when the BPNN was configured with two hidden layers of 25 neurons in the first hidden layer and 15 neurons in the second hidden layer. The highest average accuracy was 88.70 % when the BPNN was trained using MM-GCC and configured with three hidden layers having 30, 20 and 10 neurons in the first, second and third hidden layers respectively. When the BPNN was trained with EIIP-GCC, the highest average accuracy was 88.66 % with two hidden layers of 50 and 30 neurons respectively. Although, the MM-GCC gave marginally higher average accuracy (88.70 %) compared to AN-GCC (88.04 %) and EIIP-GCC (88.66 %) trained classifiers, this little improvement is not significantly better, given the complexity of the BPNN configuration (three hidden layers) that generated this level of accuracy.

It is noteworthy that across all the configurations of the BPNN, the performances of the three descriptors are very similar. Hence, it is difficult to claim that any of them is the best. The similarity in the performance accuracies of the three descriptors is also illustrated in Fig. 1. As shown in the figure, there is a strong overlap in the average classification accuracies obtained using the three descriptors. Figure 1 also shows the plot of the average classification accuracies obtained using the FCGR descriptor proposed in [5] to train the same BPNN configurations. It is clearly shown in the figure that all the three descriptors in this study gave better average classification accuracies than the FCGR descriptor. As expected, the training times for BPNN configurations with 20 to 60 neurons in one hidden layer require less than 2 min while the configurations with two or three hidden layers took approximately 3 min for all the three descriptors (Table 3). Even though the BPNN with the FCGR descriptor took shorter time for training as shown in Fig. 2, the better performance obtained using our proposed descriptors is a justification for the relatively longer training time.

Table 3. Results of the first experiment

Number of hidden layer	Number of neurons in the hidden layer	Average accuracy (%)			Training time (min:sec)		
		AN-GCC	MM-GCC	EIIP-GCC	AN-GCC	MM-GCC	EIIP-GCC
1	20	83.49	81.73	85.73	0:32	0:55	0:72
1	40	81.52	86.98	84.23	1:04	0:88	0:81
1	60	83.49	86.44	88.22	1:66	1:98	1:82
1	80	78.50	87.05	81.06	2:72	3:01	2:42
2	[20 10]	84.32	86.61	85.41	2:81	3:02	2:14
2	[25 15]	**88.04**	86.76	87.81	3:00	2:39	2:74
2	[30 15]	85.24	85.88	85.25	2:56	2:84	2:54
2	[50 25]	86.87	82.83	86.84	3:01	3:00	3:01
2	[50 30]	83.92	84.13	**88.66**	3:02	3:02	3:01
3	[20 15 10]	86.36	86.10	80.34	3:00	2:83	3:00
3	[25 20 15]	87.05	84.88	85.14	3:00	3:00	3:00
3	[30 15 5]	81.32	84.40	85.08	3:00	3:00	3:00
3	[30 20 10]	83.97	**88.70**	82.13	3:01	3:00	3:00
3	[30 25 20]	83.99	87.45	83.64	3:00	3:00	3:01

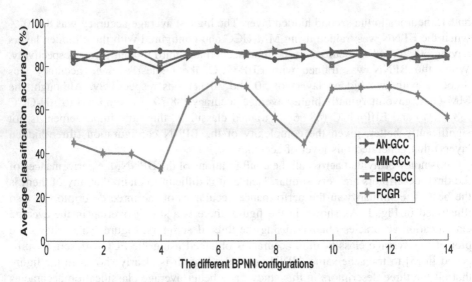

Fig. 1. Plots of the average classification accuracies for the first experiment

We carried out the second experiment so as to determine if RBFNN can give better classification accuracies than the result we obtained in the first experiment [10]. The RBFNN configurations earlier described, was trained with AN-GCC, MM-GCC and EIIP-GCC descriptors. Higher classification accuracy of 98.8 % and training time of approximately 3 min were obtained for each of the three descriptors respectively. This accuracy is better than the results in the first experiment and the results that was obtained using the FCGR descriptor and RBFNN in [5].

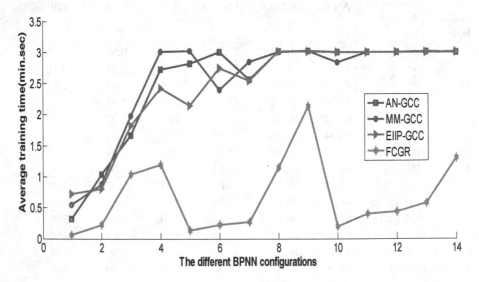

Fig. 2. Plots of the training time for the first experiment

The foregoing experimental results clearly show that the AN-GCC, MM-GCC and EIIP-GCC genomic descriptors have better efficacy than the comparable descriptor in the literature [5]. The results obtained from the two classifiers (BPNN and RBFNN) further implies that the three genomic descriptors in this study are not dependent on any of the three PCPBM method. It can therefore be unequivocally stated that, using any of the three descriptors in this study with RBFNN for classification of Eukaryotic organisms in real time will produce acceptable performance.

4 Conclusion

In this paper, we have been able to successfully obtain three highly discriminatory genomic descriptors for Eukaryotic organism classification based on mtDNA, cepstral analysis and RBFNN classifier. The descriptors were also shown to be independent of the numerical encoding methods utilized, since each of them produced 98.8 % accuracy with RBFNN. These descriptors have high prospect of being applicable for taxonomical classification of organisms in fields as diverse as bio-diversity study, food authentication, forensics, clinical diagnosis and host of others. In the future, we hope to utilize other genomic numerical encoding methods so as to determine their efficacy for the development of discriminatory genomic descriptors. We also hope to utilize other signal processing techniques such as power cepstral, linear predictive coding and higher order spectrum for enhanced genomic based taxonomical classification of organisms.

Acknowledgements. Emmanuel Adetiba is on postdoctoral fellowship at the ICT and Society (ICTAS) Research Group, funded by the Durban University of Technology, South Africa. He is on postdoctoral research leave from the Department of Electrical & Information Engineering, College of Engineering, Covenant University, Ota, Ogun State, Nigeria.

References

1. Komarek, J., Kastovsky, J., Mares, J., Johansen, J.R.: Taxonomic classification of cyanoprokaryotes (cyanobacterial genera) 2014, using a polyphasic approach. Preslia **86**(4), 295–335 (2014)
2. Nair, V.V., Nair, A.S.: Combined classifier for unknown genome classification using chaos game representation features. In: Proceedings of the International Symposium on Biocomputing, p. 35. ACM (2010)
3. Zanoguera, F., De Francesco, M.: Protein classification into domains of life using Markov chain models. In: IEEE Computational Systems Bioinformatics Conference, CSB 2004, pp. 517–519 (2004)
4. Yang, L., Tan, Z., Wang, D., Xue, L., Guan, M.X., Huang, T., Li, R.: Species identification through mitochondrial rRNA genetic analysis. Sci Rep. **4**(4089), 1–11 (2014)
5. Vijayan, K., Nair, V.V., Gopinath, D.P.: Classification of Organisms using Frequency-Chaos Game Representation of Genomic Sequences and ANN. In 10th National Conference on Technological Trends (NCTT 2009), pp. 6–7 (2009)

6. Rastogi, G., Dharne, M.S., Walujkar, S., Kumar, A., Patole, M.S., Shouche, Y.S.: Species identification and authentication of tissues of animal origin using mitochondrial and nuclear markers. Meat Sci. **76**, 666–674 (2007)

7. Kitpipit, T., Linacre, A., Tobe, S.S.: Tiger species identification based on molecular approach. Forensic Sci. Int Genet. Suppl. Ser. **2**, 310–312 (2009)

8. Adetiba, E., Olugbara, O.O., Taiwo, T.B.: Identification of pathogenic viruses using genomic cepstral coefficients with radial basis function neural network. In: Pillay, N., Engelbrecht, A.P., Abraham, A., du Plessis, M.C., Snášel, V., Muda, A.K. (eds.) Advances in Nature and Biologically Inspired Computing. AISC, vol. 419, pp. 281–291. Springer, Heidelberg (2016)

9. Kwan, J.Y.Y., Kwan, B.Y.M., Kwan, H.K.: Spectral analysis of numerical exon and intron sequences. In: 2010 IEEE International Conference on Bioinformatics and Biomedicine Workshops (BIBMW), pp. 876–877 (2010)

10. Adetiba, E., Olugbara, O.O.: Lung Cancer Prediction Using Neural Network Ensemble with Histogram of Oriented Gradient Genomic Features. The Scientific World Journal, pp. 1–17 (2015)

11. Abo-Zahhad, M., Ahmed, S.M., Abd-Elrahman, S.A.: Genomic analysis and classification of exon and intron sequences using DNA numerical mapping techniques. Int. J. Inf. Technol. Comput. Sci. (IJITCS) **4**(8), 22 (2012)

12. Liang, B., Iwnicki, S.D., Zhao, Y.: Application of power spectrum, cepstrum, higher order spectrum and neural network analyses for induction motor fault diagnosis. Mech. Syst. Sign. Proces. **39**, 342–360 (2013)

13. Yu, S.N., Chou, K.T.: Combining independent component analysis and backpropagation neural network for ECG beat classification. In: 28th Annual International Conference EMBS 2006, pp. 3090–3093 (2006)

A Novel Geometrical Approach for a Rapid Estimation of the HARDI Signal in Diffusion MRI

Ines Ben Alaya[1]([✉]), Majdi Jribi[2], Faouzi Ghorbel[2], and Tarek Kraiem[1]

[1] Laboratory of Biophysics and Medical Technology,
Higher Institute of Medical Technology of Tunis,
Tunis Elmanar University, 1006 Tunis, Tunisia
{benalayaines,kraiemtarek}@yahoo.fr
[2] CRISTAL Laboratory, GRIFT Research Group,
National School of Computer Sciences,
La Manouba University, 2010 La Manouba, Tunisia
{majdi.jribi,faouzi.ghorbel}@ensi.rnu.tn

Abstract. In this paper, we address the problem of the diffusion signal reconstruction from a limited number of samples. The HARDI (High Angular Resolution Diffusion Imaging) technique was proposed as an alternative to resolve the problems of crossing fibers in the case of Diffusion Tensor Imaging (DTI). However, it requires a long scanning time for the acquisition of the Diffusion Weighted (DW) images. This fact makes hard the clinical applications. We propose here a novel geometrical approach to accurately estimate the HARDI signal from a few number of *DW* images. The missing diffusion data are obtained according to their neighborhood from a reduced set of diffusion directions on the sphere of the q-space. The experimentations are performed on both synthetic data and many digital phantoms simulating crossing fibers on the brain tissues. The obtained results show the accuracy of the reconstruction of the Fiber Orientation Distribution (FOD) function from the estimated diffusion signal.

Keywords: Diffusion signal · MRI · HARDI · Spherical deconvolution · FOD · Reconstruction · Delaunay · Simulated data · Digital phantoms · Crossing fibers

1 Introduction

Diffusion Magnetic Resonance Imaging (dMRI) is the only non-invasive tool to obtain information about the neural architecture within the white matter of the brain in vivo. Several medical applications can be considered such as the 3D fibers reconstruction, the characterization of neuro-degenerative diseases and the surgical planning. The diffusion MRI consists in the study of the water molecules movement. In the case of brain tissues, this diffusion is anisotropic.

© Springer International Publishing Switzerland 2016
A. Mansouri et al. (Eds.): ICISP 2016, LNCS 9680, pp. 253–261, 2016.
DOI: 10.1007/978-3-319-33618-3_26

Therefore, we need to perform models that characterize the diffusion and reproduce the preferred directions.

High Angular Resolution Diffusion Imaging (HARDI) [2] has become one of the most widely used methods to characterize the underlying fiber configurations in the presence of complex fiber crossings from diffusion-weighted MRI data. This technique is based on sampling the signal on a single or many spheres of the q-space. Among the HARDI techniques, there are the QBI (Q-Ball Imaging) method [7] and the spherical deconvolution one [3]. The first approach consists in the definition of a spherical function, the Orientation Distribution Function (ODF), that characterizes the probability of diffusion along a given angular direction. The second technique estimates the Fiber Orientation Distribution function (FOD) in each imaging voxel. It models the diffusion MRI signal as the convolution of the diffusion signal with a single fiber response.

However, although able to identify complex fiber configurations, HARDI techniques require a very large number of DW images to reach a satisfactory angular resolution and to give an adequate characterization of all the features of the diffusion signal. A long measurement time is, therefore, needed. It is problematic for clinical studies involving children and people afflicted with certain diseases.

For this reason, a large variety of methods have been recently proposed in the literature to shorten the acquisition time of the HARDI techniques. Donoho [10] was among the first to address this challenging field. He proposed a novel method qualified by Compressive Sensing (CS) to accurately reconstruct a signal from under sampled measurements acquired below the Shannon-Nyquist rate by using different representations. This method was applied in a large range of domains including image and video compression as well as geophysics and medical imaging. The CS technique was already applied in High Angular Resolution Diffusion Imaging (HARDI) to reduce the acquisition time.

Michailovich et al. [11] used this technique to represent the HARDI signals in the basis of spherical ridgelets by using a relatively small number of representation coefficients. Tristn-Vega et al. [12] proposed to represent the probabilistic Orientation Distribution Function (ODF) in the frame of Spherical Wavelets (SW). Duarte-Carvajalino et al. [4] directly estimated the constant solid angle orientation distribution function (CSA-ODF) from under-sampled multi-shell high angular resolution diffusion imaging (HARDI) datasets. Daducci et al. [5] used the CS method to estimate the FOD function with the spherical deconvolution method from limited samples.

In this work, we propose a novel method to reduce the acquisition time of the HARDI technique. It is based on a geometrical approach to construct the diffusion signal from a reduced number of gradient directions. These missing gradient directions will be obtained according to their neighborhood from a reduced set of data on the sphere of the q-space. The experimentations will be performed on simulated data and on digital phantoms.

Thus, this paper will be structured as follows: We present in the second section a brief recall of the principle of the HARDI acquisition technique. In the third section, we detail all the steps of the proposed approach. We test its accuracy to perform a good estimation of the FOD function using the Constrained Spherical Deconvolution (CSD) method on both simulated and digital phantoms in the fourth section.

2   Brief Recall of the HARDI Acquisition

Diffusion MRI provides a serie of images which is obtained by a direction variation of the encoding gradient. The application of a single pulsed gradient produces one Diffusion Weighted (DW) image that corresponds to one position in the q-space [9]. In HARDI imaging, the N discrete gradient directions are uniformly distributed on a single or many spheres of the q-space as illustrated in Fig. 1 (the case of one sphere). Each red dot on the surface of the unit sphere corresponds to a specific direction of the diffusion gradient. Along each of these gradient directions $g_i(x_i, y_i, z_i), 1 < i < N$, a DW signal S$(g_i)$ is measured.

Hence, the diffusion signal $S = \{S(g_1), S(g_2), ...S(g_N)\}$ is obtained by the collection of the magnitudes in all diffusion-weighted images of the brain.

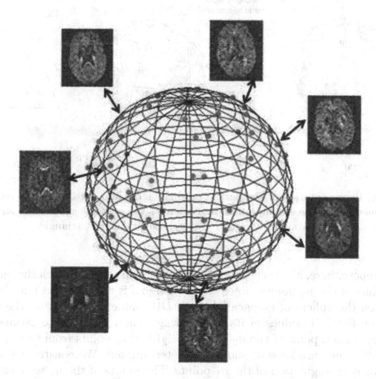

Fig. 1. Explanation of the diffusion-weighted images acquisition procedure in the HARDI technique. (Color figure online)

3   Proposed Approach

This work investigates the possibilities of the reconstruction of the diffusion signal with a reduced number of gradient directions. Therefore, the acquisition procedure time is reduced and thus make the HARDI technique clinically feasible. We propose here a novel approach to characterize the complete water diffusion process in the white matter, with a small number of measurements.

Let N denote the full set of uniformly distributed directions on the sphere with their 3D coordinates. The value of N is chosen to be able to ensure a good construction of the DW signal. We consider $(n_1 < N)$ a subset of the full set of directions with their DW signal values. It is qualified here by the partial original signal. We intend to estimate the $(n_2 = N - n_1)$ DW signal values. They correspond to the rest of points from the full set of directions. Figure 2-A illustrates the n_1, n_2, and the N points on the sphere. The blue dots denote the partial original diffusion data and red ones correspond to those the DW signal values are to be estimated.

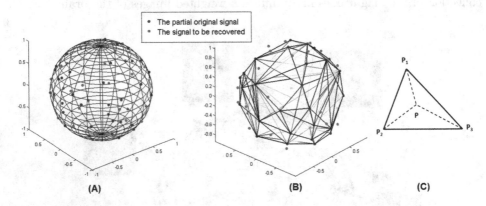

Fig. 2. (A) Representation of the partial original signal and the data to be recovered on the sphere. (B) The Delaunay triangulation of the original signal (the n_1 set of points). (C) An illustration of a point P (of n_2) and its nearest triangle.

We propose, here, a novel geometrical approach in order to reach the real DW signal values of the n_2 points. Since the DW signal is a continuous one that was sampled on the sphere of q-space [8], each DW value of a point on the sphere depends on the DW values of its neighboring points. In order to estimate the DW value of each point of the n_2 set, its neighboring points from the n_1 points (their DW values are known) should be determinated. We construct therefore the Delaunay triangulation of the n_1 points. The points of the n_1 set composing the nearest triangle to a point of n_2 are considered as its neighboring ones. This nearest triangle corresponds to the one that has the minimum Euclidean distance between the considered point of n_2 and all the triangles obtained after the Delaunay triangulation. Figure 2-B illustrates the Delaunay triangulation of the set of points n_1. Let P be a point of the set n_2 and $T_{P_1 P_2 P_3}$ its nearest triangle composed by the points P_1, P_2 and P_3 as showed in Fig. 2-C. The DW values of P (that we denote here by $DW(P)$) depends on the DW values respectively of P_1, P_2 and P_3. We propose that $DW(P)$ will be estimated as a linear combination of $DW(P_1)$, $DW(P_2)$ and $DW(P_3)$ as follows:

$$DW(P) = \alpha_1 DW(P_1) + \alpha_2 DW(P_2) + \alpha_3 DW(P_3) \tag{1}$$

with $\alpha_1 + \alpha_2 + \alpha_3 = 1$.

α_1, α_2 and α_3 are computed in the following sense:

We denote by $T_{PP_1 P_2}$, $T_{PP_1 P_3}$ and $T_{PP_2 P_3}$ the three triangles composed respectively by the points $(P, P_1$ and $P_2)$, $(P, P_1$ and $P_3)$ and $(P, P_2$ and $P_3)$ as shown in Fig. 2-C.

We qualify by $A_{T_{P_i P_j P_k}}$ the area of a triangle composed by the point P_i, P_j and P_k. The values $\{\alpha_i, 1 \leq i \leq 3\}$ characterize respectively the participation of the point $\{P_i, 1 \leq i \leq 3\}$ in the estimation of $DW(P)$. The more P is close to P_i the more α_i should be large. The two triangles containing the point p_i will be used for the estimation of the value of α_i. In the case of the point p too close to p_i, the areas of these two triangles are small. We formulate the value of α_i as follows to ensure a better participation of the point p_i in the estimation of α_i.

Then:

$$\alpha_i = 1 - A_{p_i} \tag{2}$$

Where

$$A_{p_i} = \frac{A_{T_{PP_i P_j}} + A_{T_{PP_i P_k}}}{A_{T_{PP_i P_j}} + A_{T_{PP_i P_k}} + A_{T_{PP_j P_k}}} \tag{3}$$

A_{p_i} corresponds to the normalized portion of the area of the two triangles containing the point P_i.

α_i is equal to $(1 - A_{p_i})$ to ensure that the value of α_i is large when P is too close to P_i. Therefore,

$$\alpha_1 = 1 - \frac{A_{T_{PP_1 P_2}} + A_{T_{PP_1 P_3}}}{A_{T_{PP_1 P_2}} + A_{T_{PP_1 P_3}} + A_{T_{PP_2 P_3}}} \tag{4}$$

$$\alpha_2 = 1 - \frac{A_{T_{PP_2 P_1}} + A_{T_{PP_3 P_2}}}{A_{T_{PP_1 P_2}} + A_{T_{PP_1 P_3}} + A_{T_{PP_2 P_3}}} \tag{5}$$

$$\alpha_3 = 1 - \frac{A_{T_{PP_3 P_1}} + A_{T_{PP_2 P_3}}}{A_{T_{PP_1 P_2}} + A_{T_{PP_1 P_3}} + A_{T_{PP_2 P_3}}} \tag{6}$$

4   Experimental Results

In order to evaluate the accuracy of the proposed method to estimate the HARDI signal, we will use the Constrained Spherical Deconvolution (CSD) [6] method. This technique aims to estimate the Fiber Orientation Distribution (FOD) within each voxel directly from the diffusion-weighted (DW) data, using the concept of Spherical Deconvolution (SD) [3]. Tournier et al. [1] prove that a minimum of 45 DW directions is sufficient to fully characterize the DW signal with a maximum harmonic degree of 8 (Lmax = 8) and for a b-value equal to $3000\,\text{s/mm}^2$ (The b-value is a parameter that reflects the intensity and the duration of the gradient pulses used to generate the diffusion-weighted images).

We used a full set of directions $N = 65$ uniformly distributed on the sphere to avoid issues with imperfections in the uniformity of the DW gradient directions [1] and we varied the subsets n_1 from 26 to 40 in order to evaluate the impact of the number of samples. After recovering the missing data with the proposed method, we obtain a new diffusion signal composed by the n_1 directions and the recovered data. Then, we calculated the fiber orientation distribution (FOD) using CSD (Lmax = 8). We reconstruct the FOD function from HARDI data with the novel estimated signal. The obtained FOD with the full original set directions (the N original values of DW signal) is used as a ground truth. In order to test the performance of the proposed method, we generate a two-tensor model simulating two fibers crossing in different angles: 50, 70, and 90. We also evaluate our method on the data acquired from many digital phantoms of fibers crossing.

Results on Simulated Data. We simulate fiber crossing by generating Noise free DW data from the sum of two exponentials characterized by two identical fibers described by a diffusion tensor equal to $[0.3\ 0.3\ 1.7] \times 10^{-3}\,\text{mm}^2/\text{s}$ using 65 directions and a b-value equal to $3000\,\text{s/mm}^2$

$$S(g_i) = \exp(-bg_i^t D_1 g_i) + \exp(-bg_i^t D_2 g_i) \tag{7}$$

Where D_1 is a diagonal matrix with diagonal entries $[0.3\ 0.3\ 1.7] \times 10^{-3}\,\text{mm}^2/\text{s}$ and D_2 corresponds to D_1 rotated respectively by the angles 90, 70 and 50. For the first part of the experimentation, we calculate the FOD function. For the second one, we extract the local maxima of the FOD to calculate the crossing angle. By increasing the number of the n_1 points set from 26 to 40, we show that as few as 34 diffusion directions are sufficient to obtain an accurate FOD estimation. Therefore, we can reduce the number of gradient acquisition by approximately a half and thus the scan time is reduced by 50 %. Table 1 illustrates the obtained crossing angles according to the values of n_1. Figure 3 illustrates the obtained result for $n_1 = 34$ directions for the angles 90, 70 and 50. From the observation of the obtained results, we can note that the reconstruction of the diffusion signal from under-sampled data using the proposed method yields accurate results compared with the full HARDI acquisition (ground truth).

Results on Digital Phantoms. We used the software Phantomαs[1] to generate the diffusion weighted images that consist of two fiber bundles crossing at

---

[1] http://www.emmanuelcaruyer.com/phantomas.php.

Table 1. Angular values estimation according to the n_1 points set on simulated data.

	Angle value = 90	Angle value = 70	Angle value = 50
Ground truth: 65	89.9360	73.7964	53.0413
26	89.9175	72.2064	46.2389
28	94.6525	74.7271	47.6331
30	92.1995	71.5084	48.4864
32	86.8856	73.9298	47.9856
34	89.6054	71.4659	48.4340
36	89.8957	71.9182	51.2044
38	89.9124	72.4520	55.4363
40	89.9022	71.4684	55.3474

various angles 50, 70 and 90. The data were acquired using 65 gradient directions with b = $3000 \, \text{s/mm}^2$. Here, we select the region (voxel) corresponding to the intersection zone between the fibers. The first column of Fig. 4 illustrates the generated images and the selected voxels. In order to study the impact of the initial set of n_1 points for the estimation of the FOD function, we variate the values of n_1 from 26 to 40. Table 2 illustrates the obtained results. Figure 4 illustrates the obtained results using the digital phantoms for $n_1 = 34$. These results confirm the accuracy of the proposed method. In fact, the crossing angles values are too close to the ground truth. We show, therefore, with both synthetic diffusion signal and digital phantomas that using only 34 directions is enough to reconstruct the FOD function.

Table 2. Angular values estimation according to the n_1 point set of digital phantoms.

	Angle 90	Angle 70	Angle 50
Ground truth: 65	90.1719	74.5425	53.4923
26	93.0370	72.0239	54.5815
28	90.1467	76.1030	57.6006
30	90.2952	74.7498	64.1872
32	91.9319	71.6433	60.1589
34	89.9877	73.9948	55.6366
36	89.9869	76.0433	60.2174
38	89.9897	76.1030	60.2356
40	89.9379	76.7925	60.2579

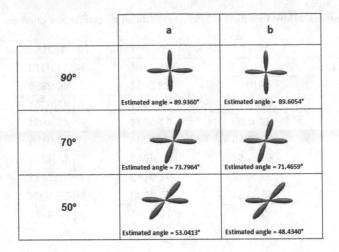

Fig. 3. FOD reconstruction on simulated data from: (a) the full set directions (b) the novel estimated signal for $n_1 = 34$.

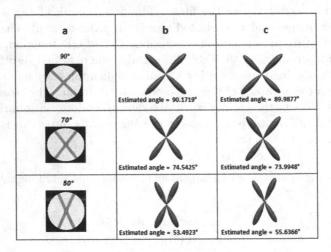

Fig. 4. FOD reconstruction on digital phantoms from: (b) the full set directions (c) the novel estimated signal for $n_1 = 34$.

5   Conclusion

In this paper, we have proposed a new solution to accelerate the acquisition time of the HARDI technique. In fact, it requires a big number of gradient directions. We proposed in this work a novel geometrical approach to accurately reconstruct the HARDI signal from reduced number of samples. It is based on recovering non-acquired data obtained according to their neighborhood from a reduced set of data on the sphere of the q-space. The experiments were conducted on both synthetic data and digital phantoms simulating crossing fibers. We computed the FOD function to evaluate the accuracy of the proposed method to estimate the diffusion weighted signal. We have shown that as few as 34 directions are sufficient to obtain accurate FOD estimation.

In future works, we intend to test the accuracy of the proposed method in real data. It will be also interesting to study the robustness of the method under many types of noise.

References

1. Tournier, J.D., Calamante, F., Connelly, A.: Determination of the appropriate b value and number of gradient directions for highangular- resolution diffusion-weighted imaging. NMR in Biomed. **26**, 1775–1786 (2013)
2. Tuch, D., Belliveau, J., Reese, T., Wedeen, V.: High angular resolution imaging of the human brain. In: Proceedings of the International Society for the Magnetic Resonance in Medicine, p. 321 (1999)
3. Tournier, J.D., Calamante, F., Gadian, D.G., Connelly, A.: Direct estimation of the fiber orientation density function from diffusion- weighted mri data using spherical. Neuro-Image **23**, 1176–1185 (2004)
4. Duarte-Carvajalino, J.M., Lenglet, C., Xu, J., Yacoub, E., Ugurbil, K., Moeller, S., Carin, L., Sapiro, G.: Estimation of the CSA-ODF using bayesian compressed sensing of multi-shell HARDI. Magn. Reson. Med. **72**, 1471–1485 (2014)
5. Daducci, A., Van De Ville, D., Thiran, J.P., Wiaux, Y.: Sparse regularization for fiber ODF reconstruction: from the suboptimality of l2 and l1 priors to l0. Med. Image Anal. **18**, 820–833 (2014)
6. Tournier, J.D., Calamante, F., Connelly, A.: Robust determination of the fibre orientation distribution in diffusion mri: nonnegativity constrained super-resolved spherical deconvolution. Neuro-Image **35**, 1459–1472 (2007)
7. Tuch, D.: Q-Ball imaging. Magn. Reson. Med. **52**, 1358–1372 (2004)
8. Caruyer, E.: Q-space Diffusion MRI: Acquisition and Signal Processing. Ph.D. Thesis (2012)
9. Mori, S.: Introduction to Diffusion Tensor Imaging. Elsevier, Amsterdam (2007)
10. Donoho, D.: Compressed sensing. IEEE Trans. Inf. Theory **52**, 1289–1306 (2006)
11. Michailovich, O., Rathi, Y.: Fast and accurate reconstruction of HARDI data using compressed sensing. In: Jiang, T., Navab, N., Pluim, J.P.W., Viergever, M.A. (eds.) MICCAI 2010, Part I. LNCS, vol. 6361, pp. 607–614. Springer, Heidelberg (2010)
12. Tristán-Vega, A., Westin, C.-F.: Probabilistic ODF estimation from reduced HARDI data with sparse regularization. In: Fichtinger, G., Martel, A., Peters, T. (eds.) MICCAI 2011, Part II. LNCS, vol. 6892, pp. 182–190. Springer, Heidelberg (2011)

Detection of Activities During Newborn Resuscitation Based on Short-Time Energy of Acceleration Signal

Huyen Vu[1($\boxtimes$)], Trygve Eftestøl[1], Kjersti Engan[1], Joar Eilevstjønn[2], Ladislaus Blacy Yarrot[3], Jørgen E. Linde[4,6], and Hege Ersdal[5,6]

[1] Department of Electrical Engineering and Computer Science, University of Stavanger, Stavanger, Norway
vtphuyen1987@yahoo.com
[2] Strategic Research, Laerdal Medical AS, Stavanger, Norway
[3] Research Institute, Haydom Lutheran Hospital, Haydom, Manyara, Tanzania
[4] Department of Pediatrics, Stavanger University Hospital, Stavanger, Norway
[5] Department of Anesthesiology and Intensive Care, Stavanger University Hospital, Stavanger, Norway
[6] Department of Health Sciences, University of Stavanger, Stavanger, Norway

Abstract. *Objectives:* Clinical intervention for non-breathing newborns due to birth asphyxia needs to be conducted within the first minute of life. The responses of the babies are affected by complicated interactions between physiological conditions of the newborns and the combination of various clinical treatments, e.g., drying thoroughly, stimulation, manual bag-mask ventilation, chest compression, etc. Previously, we have proposed methods to detect and parameterize various events regarding bag mask ventilation. However, the outcome of the resuscitation is likely influenced by not only ventilation but also other therapeutics activities. The detection of the existence of activities using information from acceleration signals is illustrated in this paper. *Methods:* Short time energy of the acceleration signal is calculated. A thresholding method is applied on the amplitude of the energy signal to determine activity or rest. *Results:* The average sensitivity and specificity of the detection of activities are 90 % and 80 % respectively. *Conclusions:* The performance of the detection algorithm indicates the possibility to use acceleration signal to detect the presence of various activities during resuscitation procedure.

Keywords: Short time energy · Acceleration signal · Energy signal · Thresholding · Resuscitation activities

1 Introduction

Save the Children organization recently reported that birth asphyxia is one of the main causes of nearly a quarter of the estimated 3 million newborn deaths worldwide every year [1,2]. Skilled and equipped birth attendants are needed to identify asphyxiation during the birth process. In case the babies are not

© Springer International Publishing Switzerland 2016
A. Mansouri et al. (Eds.): ICISP 2016, LNCS 9680, pp. 262–270, 2016.
DOI: 10.1007/978-3-319-33618-3_27

breathing, according to the guidelines of the International Liaison Committee on Resuscitation and the World Health Organization [3, 4], it is necessary to carry out resuscitation steps within the first minute of life - "The Golden Minute" to increase survival chance [5].

Ventilation is an important treatment in helping babies breathe. Physiological events associated with manual bag-mask ventilation have been detected and parameterized from ventilation related signals measured during resuscitation in our previous research work [6]. The framework for data exploration and analysis to investigate the relationship between ventilation parameters and Apgar score as well as heart rate changes has been developed [7–9]. However, other clinical interventions happening at the same time are possibly also significant factors contributing to the effectiveness of newborn resuscitation.

Accelerometers are increasingly used in wearable devices (e.g., smart phones, health status monitors, etc.) in a variety of circumstances. An accelerometer is a device measuring acceleration forces into three orthogonal directions (X, Y and Z axes). Accelerometer-based approach has shown to be a reliable and efficient method in detecting and recognizing human activities during the last decades [10–13]. A method to detect physical activities by using an optimum parameter set including the length of a smoothing filter, the width of the averaging window, and the threshold value applied on the integrated magnitude of the tri-axial acceleration signal was proposed in [13]. Automated recognition of daily human activities using various types of features extracted from acceleration signal has been studied in many research works [10–12].

To improve the treatment recommendations for asphyxiated newborns, studies of the ventilation signals and parameters are necessary, but it is also needed to know if other activities (e.g. thorough drying, stimulation and chest compression) are performed. At the present time, studying videos recorded in the delivery room is necessary to learn which activities the infants are subjected

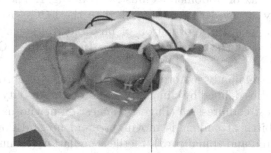

**Accelerometer sensor
attached to ECG-sensor**

Fig. 1. The accelerometer sensor attached to the ECG-sensor placed to the abdomen of a newborn manikin (NeoNatalie, Laerdal Global Health) used for practical training. When the ECG-sensor is placed on a newborn infant after birth it measures ECG- and acceleration signals.

to. However, video recordings may not be available, and video review is time consuming.

In this paper, a method to detect the presence or absence of activity at a specific point of time is proposed. We aim for a system to support clinicians not only in observing videos more easily and quickly but also producing information about activities in situations where videos are not available. The acceleration signal can be measured by a tri-axis accelerometer placed gently on the thorax of the newborn. This paper focuses on answering the question whether an activity is happening at a given time. The hypothesis is that the occurrence of activities could be reflected in the acceleration signal. Specifically, if there are activities happening, the energy of the acceleration signal is high and vice versa. A reliable detection of existence of activities could be used later for further analysis. The objective is to create a computer-aid tool to facilitate investigation of clinical data for the improvement of newborn resuscitation treatment recommendations.

2   Dataset

"Safer Births" is a collaborative project with partners from Haydom Lutheran Hospital in Tanzania and Stavanger University Hospital, University of Stavanger, and Laerdal Global Health in Norway. The data collection is done at Haydom Lutheran Hospital in Tanzania. The goal of the project is to gain new knowledge and develop innovative products to help decrease newborn mortality due to birth asphyxia worldwide.

The Laerdal Newborn Resuscitation Monitor (LNRM) is developed by Laerdal Global Health, Stavanger, Norway and specially designed to be used for research in limited resource settings. LNRM measures the ventilation (airway pressure, flow, CO_2), ECG and acceleration signals. Two stainless steel discs of the ECG-sensor are arranged on each side of a flexible arch to be placed gently over the baby's thorax or abdomen as illustrated in Fig. 1. The acceleration signal is measured by an accelerometer attached to the ECG-sensor. The dataset used in this paper includes information of physiological signals and videos of 30 patients collected at the Haydom Lutheran Hospital from October 2013 to January 2014.

Activities were manually annotated from the videos according to a set of resuscitation activities defined by clinicians. Annotated "Activity" includes seven different types: chest compression (fingers on chest on newborns and compress), stimulation (the birth attendant is moving a hand up and down the back to stimulate the column and spinal cord), tactile stimulation (stimulate on chest or feet), drying thoroughly (using a cloth to wipe the baby), moving baby, moving ECG-sensor, and other (uncategorized movements affecting the energy of the acceleration signal). The 20 manually annotated episodes are referred as the trial set since they are used as the experimental data to find the optimal parameters for the algorithm detecting parts of the acceleration signal corresponding the presence one of these activities.

3   Method

The acceleration signals including 3 axes A_x, A_y, A_z are sampled at 100 Hz. There are two components in the acceleration signal: the high frequency component corresponds to the body movement and the low frequency component is influenced by the gravity. In the pre-processing step, a low pass filter is used to compute the low frequency component as in Eq. (1). In our experiment, the chosen optimal cutoff frequency is 0.1 Hz [14]. The coefficients found for the low pass filter are: $a_1 = 1$, $b_1 = 0.0063$, $a_2 = -0.9937$. The body acceleration is calculated by subtracting the low pass filtered data from the original signal.

$$a_1 \cdot A_{LP}(n) = b_1 \cdot A(n) - a_2 \cdot A_{LP}(n-1) \tag{1}$$

After subtracting the low frequency component in each direction, A_x, A_y, A_z, the magnitude of the acceleration signal is then computed as:

$$A(n) = \sqrt{A_x^2(n) + A_y^2(n) + A_z^2(n)} \tag{2}$$

The amplitude of speech signals varies rapidly over time, and the short time energy (STE) has been used for discriminating voice from unvoiced segments in speech signal in some studies [15,16]. Similarly, the acceleration signal in our dataset fluctuates significantly because of quick movement of the accelerometer sensor during stressful resuscitation process. Thus, the energy associated with acceleration signal is also time varying. The energy of the acceleration signal corresponding to activities is higher than the one without activities. Consequently, short time energy can be used for activity detection. The association of activities and STE of acceleration signal is depicted in Fig. 2

i-th frame of the acceleration signal is represented as:

$$A_i(n) = A(n) \cdot w(i \cdot T - n) \quad i \cdot T - N + 1 \leq n \leq i \cdot T \tag{3}$$

Where i = 1, 2,... $w(n)$ denotes the windowing function with a finite duration of N and T is the frame shift. In this paper, we choose the T = 1, thus the STE is calculated as follows:

$$E(i) = \sum_{n=i-N+1}^{i} [A(n) \cdot w(i-n)]^2 \tag{4}$$

The energy signal is smoothed by an averaging filter to remove high frequency spikes. To detect the occurrence of an activity at a given time, STE of acceleration signal is compared to a threshold value Thr. If the energy value, $E(i)$ is higher than Thr then the sample at i of the acceleration signal is considered to be corresponding with activity otherwise non-activity.

$$Activity(i) = \begin{cases} 1, & \text{if } E(i) \geq Thr \\ 0, & \text{otherwise} \end{cases} \tag{5}$$

The choice of threshold value has an important impact on the sensitivity and specificity of the algorithm. The optimal selection of parameters is determined by using the trial set including 20 manually annotated videos. The energy of the acceleration signal varies for each individual patient because it depends on how stably the accelerometer sensor is positioned on the abdomen of the newborn, whether the newborn is covered with the wrapping blanket, etc. Therefore, Thr needs to be patient dependent but should also contain information of a global minimum energy value as a common starting point for all patients. Thr is determined by the following expression:

$$Thr = G + \delta = r \cdot f + L \cdot f = (r + L) \cdot f \tag{6}$$

Equation 6 has two parts: G is the global minimum energy value. δ is patient dependent. G, δ are then expanded as $G = r \cdot f$ and $\delta = L \cdot f$, where r and f are the parameters that can be learned from the trial set. L represents the local minimum, a value dependent on the characteristics of energy acceleration signal of each patient. L is the average of the values of the baseline points the energy signal as illustrated in Fig. 2.

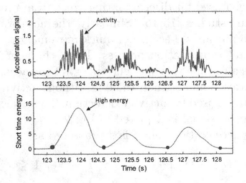

Fig. 2. The acceleration signal (upper plot) and its STE (lower plot). Baseline points are marked in blue color. (Color figure online)

Applying a high threshold on the energy signal might cause small segments in between an activity period to be wrongly detected as non-activity. Thus, in the post-processing step, if one segment detected as non-activity had duration less than 0.5 s, it was then re-labeled as activity. There is also the possibility that small segments of non-activity are detected as activity due to a low threshold. To avoid this situation, the segments that had duration less than 1 s were re-labeled as non-activity because the duration of an activity is not likely to be less than 1 s. Figures 3(a) and (b) show the possible wrongly detected cases because of too high and low applied thresholds respectively.

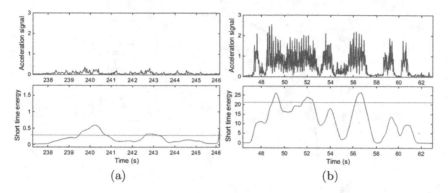

Fig. 3. False positive (a) and false negative (b) due to too low threshold and too high threshold respectively. The blue lines represent the applied thresholds.

4   Results

r and f are chosen in the range $r = 0 : 0.05 : 0.5$ and $f = 0.01 : 0.01 : 1$. The optimal values of r and f are determined from the trial set and applied on the test set to evaluate the activity-detection algorithm. The test set contains 10 videos annotated in a semi-automatic way. Specifically, to facilitate the annotation of those 10 videos, a threshold Thr was preliminarily chosen and the result of the automatic detection was used as the proposed of possible occurrence of activities. To avoid bias, the 10 videos were observed and annotated giving the true manual annotations used as the test set. We experimented with rectangular and Hamming window types and various window length to compute STE. Hamming window with length N = 51 gave the better results on the test set. The average sensitivity and specificity over 20 patients in the trial set are represented in the ROC curve as shown in Fig. 4. The optimal point marked in red color is corresponding with $r_{opt} = 0.25$ and $f_{opt} = 0.19$. The test result is described in Table 1.

Table 1. Performance of algorithm using the optimal value of r and f applying on 10 patients in the test group. The total duration of activities in 10 episodes of the test set was 1299 s.

	Sensitivity	Specificity
Mean	90 %	80 %
Standard deviation	6 %	6 %

5   Discussion

The performance of the detection algorithm depends on the length of the window to compute the STE of the acceleration signal, the length of the average

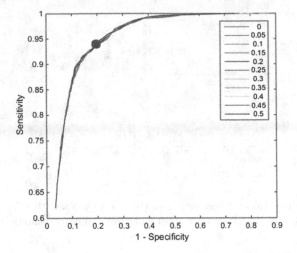

Fig. 4. ROC curve representing the performance of algorithm resulting from 20 patients in the trial set. Optimal point is marked in red color corresponding to $r_{opt} = 0.25$ and $f_{opt} = 0.19$ (Color figure online)

filtering window, and the chosen threshold Thr. The longer the average filter window is, the smoother the energy signal is. However, the more energy lost, the more difficult it is to distinguish between activity and non-activity. To balance sensitivity and specificity, the energy threshold parameter Thr needs to be reasonably chosen. In our approach, the selection of an appropriate threshold value is experimentally chosen as the combination of the global minimum energy value ($G = r \cdot f$) determined from the trial set and the local minimum value $\delta = L \cdot f$ depending on individual patient. Small segments that are wrongly labeled in case of unnecessarily high or low thresholds are re-defined in the post-processing step.

During newborn resuscitation procedures, in addition to ventilation, several different interventions are commonly performed within the first minutes after birth. Bag mask ventilation is a crucial action to save non-breathing babies, but other activities may also influence outcome. In addition to intended treatment, activities like newborn breathing attempts or gasping, movement of the baby, or touching the ECG-sensor by the birth attendants might occur and present as noise in the signal. The noisy data makes detection of true treatment actions more challenging. The detection of the presence and absence true treatment of activities based on the acceleration signal is a further step in developing the automatic system supporting clinicians in reviewing videos.

6   Conclusion

In this paper, we have illustrated an approach to detect activities performed on newborns using the ECG-sensor integrating an accelerometer sensor.

The detection method is based on thresholding the STE of the acceleration signal. The performance of the algorithm allows the possibility to use the detection result as the input for the activity recognition to distinguish among seven different activity classes annotated in our data. Automatic classification of resuscitation activities is the next step in our work. The reliability of our detection needs to be validated by applying more new test data.

References

1. Save the Children: Ending newborn deaths Ensuring every baby survives (2013)
2. Wang, H., et al.: Global, regional, national levels of neonatal, infant, under-5 mortality during 19902013: a systematic analysis for the Global Burden of Disease Study 2013. The Lancet **384**(9947), 957–979 (2014)
3. Perlman, J., Wyllie, J., Kattwinkel, J., et al.: Part 7: neonatal resuscitation: 2015 international consensus on cardiopulmonary resuscitation and emergency cardiovascular care science with treatment recommendations. Circulation **132**, S204–S241 (2015)
4. WHO Library Cataloguing-in-Publication Data: Guidelines on basic newborn resuscitation (2011) ISBN: 978-92-4-150369-3
5. Erdal, H.L., Mduma, E., Svensen, E., Perlman, J.M.: Early initiation of basic resuscitation interventions including face mask ventilation may reduce birth asphyxia related mortality in low-income countries. Resuscitation **83**, 869–873 (2012)
6. Vu, H., Eftestøl, T., Engan, K., Eilevstjnn, J., Linde, J., Ersdal, H.: Automatic detection and parameterization of manual Bag-Mask ventilation on newborns (Accepted for IEEE Journal of Biomedical and Health Informatics)
7. Vu, H., Eftestøl, T., Engan, K., Eilevstjnn, J., Linde, J., Ersdal, H.: Analysis of heart rate changes in newborns to investigate the effectiveness of bag-mask ventilation. In: Proceedings of Computing in Cardiology Conference (2014)
8. Vu, H., Eftestøl, T., Engan, K., Eilevstjønn, J., Linde, J., Ersdal, H.: Exploratory analysis of ventilation signals from resuscitation data of newborns. In: Proceedings of Biosignals (2015)
9. Vu, H., Eftestøl, T., Engan, K., Eilevstjønn, J., Yarrot, L., Linde, J., Ersdal, H.: Exploring the relationship between characteristics of ventilation performance and response of newborns during resuscitation, Communications in Computer and Information Science (To be published). Springer
10. Ravi, N., et al.: Activity recognition from accelerometer data. In: AAAI, vol. 5 (2005)
11. Casale, P., Pujol, O., Radeva, P.: Human activity recognition from accelerometer data using a wearable device. In: Vitrià, J., Sanches, J.M., Hernández, M. (eds.) IbPRIA 2011. LNCS, vol. 6669, pp. 289–296. Springer, Heidelberg (2011)
12. Gupta, P., Dallas, T.: Feature selection and activity recognition system using a single triaxial accelerometer. IEEE Trans. Biomed. Eng. **61**(6), 1780–1786 (2014)
13. Mathie, M.J., Coster, A.C.F., Lovell, N.H., Celler, B.G.: Detection of daily physical activities using a triaxial accelerometer. Med. Biol. Eng. Comput. **41**(3), 296–301 (2003)
14. Bayat, A., Pomplun, M., Tran, D.A.: A study on human activity recognition using accelerometer data from smartphones. Procedia Comput. Sci. **34**, 450–457 (2014)

15. Jalil, M., Butt, F.A., Malik, A.: Short-time energy, magnitude, zero crossing rate and autocorrelation measurement for discriminating voiced and unvoiced segments of speech signals. In: 2013 International Conference onTechnological Advances in Electrical, Electronics and Computer Engineering (TAEECE), pp. 208–212. IEEE, May 2013
16. Bachu, R.G., Kopparthi, S., Adapa, B., Barkana, B.D.: Voiced/unvoiced decision for speech signals based on zero-crossing rate and energy. In: Advanced Techniques in Computing Sciences and Software Engineering, pp. 279–282. Springer, Netherlands (2010)

Geoscience and Remote Sensing

Unsupervised Classification of Synthetic Aperture Radar Imagery Using a Bootstrap Version of the Generalized Mixture Expectation Maximization Algorithm

Ahlem Bougarradh$^{(\boxtimes)}$, Slim Mhiri, and Faouzi Ghorbel

CRISTAL Laboratory, GRIFT Research Group,
National School of Computer Sciences, University of Manouba, Manouba, Tunisia
Ahlem.Bougarradh@gmail.com, {Slim.Mhiri,Faouzi.Ghorbel}@ensi.rnu.tn

Abstract. In this work, we propose a bootstrapped generalized mixture estimation algorithm for synthetic aperture radar image segmentation. The Bootstrap sampling reduces the dependence effect of pixels in real images, and reduces segmentation time. Given an original image, we randomly select small representative set of pixels. Then, a generalized expectation maximization algorithm based on optimal Bootstrap sample is released for mixture identification. The generalized aspect comes from the use of distributions from the Pearson system. We validate the proposed algorithm on the classification of SAR images. The results we obtain show that the bootstrap sampling method yield the same accuracy and robustness of image classification as the basic algorithm while reducing time computing. This fact make possible the integration of such technique in real time applications.

Keywords: Pearson system · Unsupervised Bayesian segmentation · Generalized mixture expectation maximization algorithm · Bootstrap sampling · SAR images

1 Introduction

Synthetic Aperture Radar images (SAR images) of the earth are an important tool for many scientific applications such as high resolution remote sensing for mapping, surface surveillance, search-and-rescue, mine detection, navigation position location, and Automatic Target Recognition. For most of the applications mentioned, besides the importance of segmentation quality in the subsequent analysis for target detection and recognition, the time computing can play a key role. This constraint is difficult to reach because of the large size of SAR images. Amongst several existing works especially designed for SAR data [11,19], one finds the contribution of the unsupervised statistical approach [17,20].

Tree main statistical approaches have been suggested depending on the way that neighborhood influences the classification of a given pixel. The local or blind

© Springer International Publishing Switzerland 2016
A. Mansouri et al. (Eds.): ICISP 2016, LNCS 9680, pp. 273–282, 2016.
DOI: 10.1007/978-3-319-33618-3_28

approaches consider that pixels are spatially independent [18]. Contextual methods [14] take into account a neighborhood of limit extent. Global approaches [17] assume that all pixels in an image influence the classification of the pixel of interest. Different estimation algorithms have been applied to the problem of unsupervised segmentation. The most popular one is the expectation-maximization (EM) algorithm [1,6], with the maximum likelihood (ML) estimation. Many variants of the EM have been presented such as Stochastic EM (SEM) [14], Gibsien EM (GEM) [5], Iterative Conditional Estimation (ICE) [2,4] and Zhang algorithms [21]. Because of the inherent speckle noise, it is now accepted that the statistics of SAR images can be well modeled by the family of probability distributions known as the Pearson system [8,12].

We base our work in the field of statistical approaches; the mixture identification will be performed with the generalized mixture expectation maximization algorithm GMEM where the generalized aspect comes from the use of the Pearson system.

In statistical segmentation, the time increases with the size of training data set. Because of the large size of SAR images, the size of the training data is very large. As a result, the time required to segmentation could be prohibitively large which constrain its use in the real-world applications.

In this context, we propose a fast segmentation algorithm based on the principle of Bootstrap sampling. The Bootstrap [9] has not seen much applications in image analysis and classification. The first attempt to apply the bootstrap to image analysis was by Ghorbel and Banga [10] who introduced a Bootstrap scheme in the context of Bayesian image segmentation under the Gaussian assumption. M'hiri et al. [15,16] extended the technique later and applied them to the segmentation of brain images.

In this paper, we propose to combine the bootstrap technique with the generalized mixture expectation maximization algorithm GMEM for unsupervised SAR image classification. The Bootstrap technique consists on selecting a small representative set a pixels from the original image and mixture identification will be done on bootstrap samples instead of the correlated pixels in the real image. The use of such resampling procedure enables to reduce considerably the computation times while preserving the estimation equality. The reminder of this paper is organized as follow. In Sect. 2, we describe the unsupervised Bayesian segmentation by Bootstrapping GMEM algorithm, Sect. 3 is devoted to experimental results of SAR image classification. Conclusions and future prospects are presented in Sect. 4.

2   Unsupervised Image Segmentation by the BGMEM Algorithm

2.1   Bootsrap Sampling for Image Classification

Efron [9] introduces the Bootstrap term to designate the set of the random resampling procedures of the data observed intended to be approached by simulating the statistics of the underlying distribution. The Bootstrap theory is based on the convergence of the empirical law of the sample towards the underlying unknown law when the sample size is sufficiently large.

Given a random sample $\chi_N = (X_1, X_2, .., X_N)$ of size N from a population with distribution F_X. The bootstrap approximation was to estimate the distribution of a given unknown statistics $R(\chi_N, F_X)$ by the bootstrap distribution noted F_n^* corresponding to the sample $\chi_N^* = X_1^*, X_2^*, .., X_n^*, (n < N)$ where $X_1^*, X_2^*, .., X_N^*$ are randomly selected from χ_N. Since the empirical distribution converges almost surely to the underlying distribution, one can hope that the bootstrap distribution would converge to the true unknown distribution. Details and applications of bootstrap technique can be found in Ref. [3,22].

Ghorbel and Banga [10] introduce a bootstrap sampling scheme for gray levels image analysis. In this case, the whole image distribution is presented only by a small bootstrap sample size but should be representative of the entire image.

Suppose we have a two-dimensional image of $N_r * N_c = N$ pixel resolution with N_r rows and N_c columns. In statistical segmentation, we suppose that the image is a finished population of N observations. It is then noted $Y = (y_1, y_2, ..., y_N)$ that is to say a sample from an unknown distribution. From this original image, we construct the bootstrap sample $Y^* = (y_1^*, ..., y_n^*), (n < N)$ by randomly selecting n pixels $y_i^* = (k_i, l_i)^t$ for $i \in \{1, .., N\}$. k_i and l_i are obtained by making independent uniform random trials under the set $\{1, .., N_r\}$ and the set $\{1, .., N_c\}$ respectively. The $Y^* = (y_1^*, ..., y_n^*)$ is a resample of size n chosen with replacement from Y.

The optimal size of the bootstrap sample is determined by two representative criteria for the use of this technique in image segmentation.

The sample $Y^* = (y_1^*, ..., y_n^*)$ is representative of an image Y when each image gray level (GL) appears at least one time in the samples. It's explicitly shown by the $C1$ and $C2$ equations.

$$C1 : n_0 > 4D \quad with \quad D : \quad the \quad variation \quad of \quad the \quad gray \quad level \qquad (1)$$

$$C2 : n_0 \quad is \quad representative \iff B(n_0) = \sum_{j=1}^{D} \frac{\pi_j e^{-n_0 \pi_j}}{1 - e^{-n_0 \pi_j}} < \epsilon \qquad (2)$$

D is the number of the different gray levels values in the image, $B(n_0)$ is the sampling characteristic function and ϵ is a fixed small value.

The advantage of the $C1$ criterion is to be able to depart from a minimum sample size n_0. The sampling characteristic function $B(n_0)$ defined by the criterion $C2$ takes into account both image pixel distribution and bootstrap sample size . The n_0 is initially computed by the $C1$ criterion then n_0 is progressively increased. The corresponding bootstrap sample is constructed for each size n_0 by random uniform selecting set of pixels from the image and the $C2$ criterion is verified . The bootstrap sample is qualify to be representative when the sampling characteristic function value is lower than the expected precision $\epsilon = 10^{-2}$.

An empirical convergence study based on minimizing the mean integrated square error (MISE) between original density and its estimate based on the bootstrap sample show that the fixed precision $\epsilon = 10^{-2}$ ensure the representativity of the bootstrap sample.

2.2   An Overview of the Pearson System of Distributions

The Pearson system [13] is made up of mainly height families of distributions including Gaussian, Gamma and Beta ones and offers a large variety of shapes (symmetrical or not, with finite or semi-finite support, etc.). Each law can be uniquely defined by its mean μ_1 and its first three centered moments (μ_2, μ_3, μ_4). All of them can be represented in the so-called Pearson diagram (Fig. 1) in which axes β_1 and β_2 are given by $\beta_1 = \frac{(\mu_3)^2}{(\mu_2)^3}$ and $\beta_1 = \frac{(\mu_4)}{(\mu_2)^3}$.

Gaussian distributions are located at $(\beta_1 = 0, \beta_2 = 3)$. Gamma distributions on the straight line $\beta_2 = 1.5\beta_1 + 3$ and inverse gamma distribution on the curve with the equation $\beta_2 = \frac{3}{\beta_1 - 32}(-13\beta_1 - 16 - 2(\beta_1 + 4)^{\frac{3}{2}})$. First kind Beta distributions are located between the lower limit and the gamma line, second kind Beta distributions are located between the gamma and the inverse Gamma distributions, and Type 4 distributions are located between the inverse Gamma distributions and the upper limit. Then it is possible to estimate empirical moments of a distribution from a sample and to assess the family of distributions from coordinates (β_1, β_2) and determine the parameters that precisely characterize the probability density function within its family.

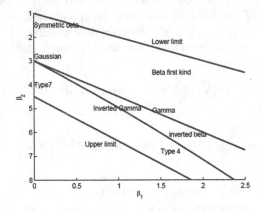

Fig. 1. Eight families of the Pearson system in the (β_1, β_2)-diagram.

2.3   Description of the Bootstrapped Generalized Expectation Maximization Algorithm

Before proceeding with mixture identification by the BGMEM algorithm, a pre-processing step is needed to determine the size of the representative bootstrap sample because the performance of the mixture identification depends on the pre-processing step. The sample size drawn from the image fulfills the criteria proposed by Ghorbel and Banga in Sect. 2.1. Let given an available bootstrap sample $Y^* = (y_1^*, ..., y_n^*)$ from the original image Y.

The mixture identification by BGMEM algorithm is performed using only the representative Bootstrap sample instead of using the entire image. After initializing parameters from the histogram, the two following steps are iterated.

- Expectation Step: For each class, the distribution f_k will be selected from the Pearson system distribution according to the skewness and kurtosis values [7] then the a posterior probability for a pixel y_i^* to belong to class k at the iteration q is given by:

$$\forall k \in \{1, ..., K\} \quad P(x_k | y_i^*, \theta^q) = \frac{\pi_k^{q-1} f_k(y_i^* | \theta_k^{(q-1)})}{\sum\limits_{l=1}^{K} \pi_l^{q-1} f_l(y_i^* | \theta_l^{q-1})} \tag{3}$$

- Maximization Step: the parameters of the mixture are constructed in the following way:

$$\forall k \in \{1, ..., K\} \quad \pi_k^{(q)} = \frac{\sum\limits_{i=1}^{n} P(x_k | y_i^*, \theta^q)}{n} \tag{4}$$

$$\forall k \in \{1, ..., K\} \quad \mu_{1,k}^{(q)} = \frac{\sum\limits_{i=1}^{n} P(x_k | y_i^*, \theta^q) y_i^*}{\sum\limits_{i=1}^{n} P(x_k | y_i^*, \theta^q)} \tag{5}$$

Hight order moments μ_j with $j = 2, 3, 4$ are computed according the equation:

$$\forall k \in \{1, ..., K\} \quad \mu_{j,k}^{(q)} = \frac{\sum\limits_{i=1}^{n} P(x_k | y_i^*, \theta^q)(y_i^* - \mu_{1,k}^{(q)})^j}{\sum\limits_{i=1}^{n} P(x_k | y_i^*, \theta^q)} \tag{6}$$

At the $q^t h$ iteration on the sample the skewness and the kurtosis of the class k are computed as:

$$\beta_{1,k}^{(q)} = \frac{\left(\mu_{3,k}^{(q)}\right)^2}{\left(\mu_{2,k}^{(q)}\right)^3}, \qquad \beta_{2,k}^{(q)} = \frac{\mu_{4,k}^{(q)}}{\left(\mu_{2,k}^{(q)}\right)^2} \tag{7}$$

The algorithm applied to the sample stops when the sample estimated parameters are stagnated.

3   Unsupervised Bayesian Classification of SAR Images

In the unsupervised Bayesian classification, the image is supposed as a realization of mixture distributions and the classification problem consists on mixture identification associated to a Bayesian rule. A large study is done to validate the BGMEM framework on a large data set of both synthetic images and real SAR images. In this section, we will show results only for four SAR images. The original SAR images are $512 * 512$ pixels resolutions presented by 256gray levels classified in four classes. Before proceeding with image classification by the BGMEM algorithm, a pre-processing step is needed to determine the size of the representative bootstrap sample according to the representativity criteria presented in Sect. 2.1. The bootstrap sample size must be large enough to ensure a good estimation and small enough to reduce the computation time. The sample size $n_0 = 3000$ pixels is validate according to the sampling characteristic function equation $(B(3000) < 0.004)$ for the four images.

Table 1. Evaluation of the MSE measure of the mixtures

MSE	GMEM	BGMEM
Image1	1.9010^{-7}	1.8810^{-7}
Image2	1.6810^{-7}	1.3210^{-7}
Image3	1.7410^{-7}	1.6310^{-7}
Image4	7.9210^{-7}	7.5810^{-7}

The Fig. 2a shows the fitting of the estimated densities to the image histogram in the case of classical GMEM algorithm for the four images and the Fig. 2b shows the result in the Bootstapped case. The conditional estimated densities fit the image histogram in the two cases of classical and bootstrapped algorithm.

We present in the Table 1 a comparison of the Mean Square Error MSE between the classical GMEM algorithm and the bootstrapped one. The mean square error shows an improvement of estimation when considering the bootstrapped version of the algorithm. The observations are decorrelated by randomly selecting observations which construct the sample. This fact offer best conditions of application of the GMEM algorithm and so better parameter estimation.

Table 2. Time segmentation in seconds of the SAR images

Time	GMEM	BGMEM
Image1	74669	856
Image2	74449	852
Image3	52997	573
Image4	72118	828

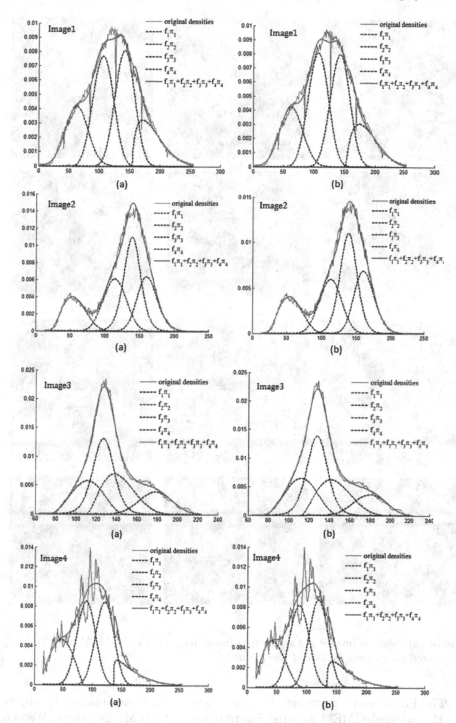

Fig. 2. Plot of estimated distributions by (a) GMEM algorithm (b) BGMEM algorithm

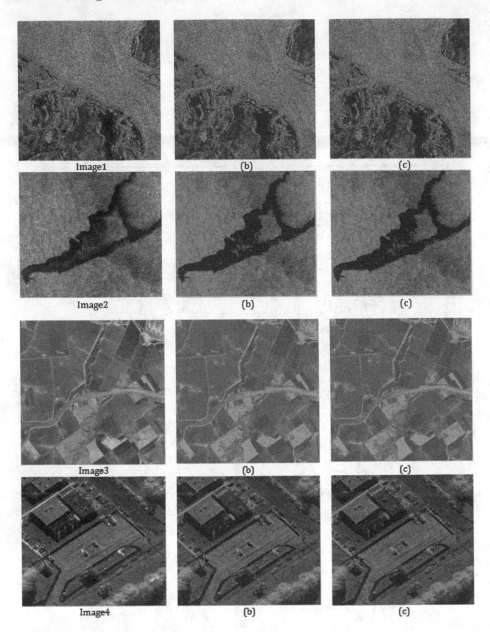

Fig. 3. (a) Original images (b) segmented image from classical GMEM algorithm (c) segmented image from BGMEM algorithm.

The Fig. 3b and c represent the segmentation results we obtained by applying the classical GMEM and the Bootstrapped BGMEM algorithms. We can observe visually a same segmentation quality by the both algorithms which is consequently of good mixture identification. We dont focus our work in the interpretation of the SAR images so the segmentation quality is showed visually but the contribution here was in accelerating the time computing of image classification. The computational time of the Boostrap algorithm and the classical one are given in Table 2. The programs are done with matlab and turned under a core i5 processor time computing may be lower if the algorithms are running on a more powerful processor. On the basis of the bootstrap sample which represents 0.01 of the image size, we have considerable gain in time computing more than a factor of 87 by the boostrapped algorithm with the same accuracy and robustness of image classification.

4   Conclusion

In this paper, we have proposed a Bootstrap model to the unsupervised Bayesian image segmentation. The Bootstrap technique allows an estimation of parameters of the image from a small sized sample instead of the entire image. The principle advantage of the proposed algorithm is the reduction of time computing which make it useful in real-time applications. As future work, we are interest to the study of multivariate Pearson system for the statistical modeling of images acquired by different sensors.

References

1. Ambroise, C., Govaert, G.: Convergence of an EM-type algorithm for spatial clustering. Pattern Recognit. Lett. **19**, 919–927 (1998)
2. Braathen, B., Pieczynski, W., Masson, P.: Global and local methods of unsupervised Bayesian segmentation of images. Mach. Graph. Vis. **2**, 39–52 (1993)
3. Basiri, S., Ollila, E., Koivunen, V.: Robust, scalable, and fast bootstrap method for analyzing large scale data equation. IEEE Trans. Signal Process. **64**(4), 1007–1017 (2015)
4. Caillol, H., Pieczynski, W., Hillion, A.: Estimation of fuzzy Gaussian mixture and unsupervised statistical image segmentation. IEEE Trans. Image Process. **6**, 425–440 (1997)
5. Chalmond, B.: An iterative Gibbsian technique for reconstruction of m-ary images. Pattern Recognit. Lett. **22**, 747–761 (1989)
6. Dempester, A.P., Laird, N.M., Rubin, D.B.: Maximum likelihood from incomplete data via the E.M algorithm. J. R. Stat. Soc., Series B **39**(1), 1–38 (1977)
7. Delignon, Y., Marzouki, A., Pieczynski, W.: Estimation of generalised mixture and its application in image segmentation. IEEE Trans. Image Process. **6**(10), 1364–1375 (1997)
8. Delignon, Y., Garello, R., Hillion, A.: Statistical modelling of ocean SAR images. IEE Proc. Radar, Sonar and Navig. **44**(66), 348–354 (1997)
9. Efron, B.: Bootstrap method : another look at the Jackknife. Ann. Stat. **7**, 1–26 (1979)
10. Ghorbel, F., Banga, C.: Bootstrap sampling applied to image analysis, invited paper, special session. IEEE-ICASSP, Adelaide, S. Aust. **6**, 81–84 (1994)

11. Gong, M.G., Zhou, Z.Q., Ma, J.J.: Change detection in synthetic aperture radar images based on image fusion and fuzzy clustering. IEEE Trans. Image Process. **21**(4), 2141–2151 (2012)
12. Inglada, J.: Change detection on SAR images by using a parametric estimation of the Kullback-Leibler divergence. In: Proceeding IEEE International Conference Geoscience and Remote Sensing (IGARSS), pp. 4104–4106, Toulouse (2003)
13. Johnson, N.L., Kotz, S.: Distribution in Statistics: Continuous Univariate Distributions, vol. 1 and 2. Wiley, New York (1994)
14. Masson, P., Pieczynski, W.: SEM algorithm and unsupervised statistical segmentation of satellite images. IEEE Trans. Geos. Rem. Sen. **31**, 618–633 (1993)
15. Mhiri, S., Cammoun, L., Ghorbel, F.: Speeding up HMRF EM algorithms for fast unsupervised image segmentation by Bootstrap resampling: Application to the brain tissue segmentation. J. Signal Process. **87**, 2544–2559 (2007)
16. M'hiri, S., Mabrouk, S., Ghorbel, F.: Segmentation des IRM cerebrales par une variante bootstrapee du HMRF-EM : etude preliminaire sur fantomes. IRBM **33**(1), 2–10 (2012)
17. Pal, N.R., Pal, S.K.: A review on image segmentation techniques. Pattern Recogn. **26**(9), 1277–1294 (1993)
18. Peng, A., Pieczynski, W.: Adaptive mixture estimation and unsupervised local Bayesian image segmentation. Graph. Models Image Process. **57**, 389–399 (1995)
19. Yang, D., Wang, L., Hei, X., Gong, M.: An efficient automatic Sar segmentation framework in AIS using kernel clustering index and histogram statistics. App. Soft Comput. **16**, 63–79 (2014)
20. Zhang, Y.J.: Evaluation and comparison of different segmentation algorithms. Pattern Recogn. Lett. **18**, 963–974 (1997)
21. Zhang, Y.J., Modestino, J.W., Langan, D.A.: Maximum likelihood parameter estimation for unsupervised stochastic model-based image segmentation. IEEE Trans. Image Process. **3**, 404–420 (1994)
22. Zoubir, A., Iskander, D.: Bootstrap methods and applications : a tutorial for the signal processing practitioner. IEEE Signal Process. Magazine **24**(4), 10–19 (2007)

Palm Trees Detection from High Spatial Resolution Satellite Imagery Using a New Contextual Classification Method with Constraints

Soufiane Idbraim[1]([✉]), Driss Mammass[1], Lahoucine Bouzalim[1], Moulid Oudra[1], Mauricio Labrador-Garca[2], and Manuel Arbelo[3]

[1] IRF-SIC Laboratory, Faculty of Science, Ibn Zohr University, Agadir, Morocco
`s.idbraim@uiz.ac.ma`
[2] GMR Canarias, Tenerife, Canary Islands, Spain
[3] Grupo de Observacin de la Tierra y la Atmsfera (GOTA), La Laguna University, Canary Islands, Spain

Abstract. Palm groves are one of the most characteristic agro-ecosystems of Morocco. Therefore, conservation and monitoring have become a primary objective, not just from an environmental and landscaping point of view but also from the socio-economic. In this context, remote sensing presents an effective tool to map palm groves, to count palm trees and to detect their possible diseases.

The present study attempts to map palm trees from very high resolution WorldView 2 (WV 2) imagery, using a new supervised contextual classification method based on Markov Random Fields and palm trees shadow orientation. A combined layer of pan-sharpened multispectral (MS) bands and eight mean texture measures based Gray Level Co-occurrence Matrices (GLCM) were used as input variables. Total accuracy of 83.4 % palm trees detection was achieved. Using a decision criterion based on palm trees: shape, shadow orientation and the distance, the total accuracy of palm trees detection reached 88.1 %.

Keywords: Palm trees · WORLD VIEW 2 · Contextual classification · ICM

1 Introduction

Palm groves are one of the most characteristic agro-ecosystems of Morocco, not only for their natural and scenic value, but also because over hundreds of years, they have created a favorable environment that man has used to cultivate, taking advantage of the microclimate and protection offered by the palm trees in this arid environment. Therefore, conservation and monitoring have become a primary objective, not just from an environmental and landscaping point of view but also from the socio-economic.

© Springer International Publishing Switzerland 2016
A. Mansouri et al. (Eds.): ICISP 2016, LNCS 9680, pp. 283–292, 2016.
DOI: 10.1007/978-3-319-33618-3_29

In this sense, remote sensing presents an effective tool to map palm groves, to count palm trees, and to detect their possible diseases. To date, no specific document touching the use of remote sensing to map date palms in Morocco has been published. However, some authors have demonstrated the potential of satellite images in other parts of the world not just to identify palm trees, but also to detect the symptoms of diseases. In [1] the authors have mapped the date palm trees in urban and agricultural areas in Kuwait. They have used panchromatic and multispectral sensor of Quickbird with a resolution of 60 cm. Although the results show a level of accuracy 96 %, it should be noted that their study is limited to areas where there are palm trees of 3 m or more in diameter, and most importantly, the distance between them should be greater than 3–8 m. Similar studies were conducted in Malaysia, and in this case the goal was to detect and count the palm oil plantations [2]. The authors used data from an airborne senor with a spatial resolution of 1 m and 20 spectral bands. They scored higher levels of accuracy to 90 %, but always there were no palm trees with an overlap. In [3] although it is not specifically devoted to the classification of palm trees, the authors made a comparative analysis between IKONOS and WorldView-2 imagery to map different species of trees in an urban environment. We note in their results for palm category (all existing species in the studied area), the success rate was only 40 %. They tried to reason with the fact that the diameters of palm trees were small (< 3 m) and the presence of a mixing effect with surfaces below and around the palm trees. We could cite further studies, all with good results but provided that the palm trees are large and separated by a distance from each other.

The process of the classification can be performed in several ways, e.g., supervised or unsupervised, parametric or nonparametric, contextual or non-contextual. In this paper, we focus on the application of a supervised contextual classification method using a Markov Random Fields (MRF). In image processing the fundamental idea of the MRF is to introduce contextual relations on a local neighborhood, with MRF, pixels are not considered any more independently but in their globality. Thus, besides spectral values for each pixel, information from its neighboring pixels is also evaluated. In this regard, we have used the Iterated Conditional Mode (ICM) algorithm [4,5] with a parameter of temperature inspired from the simulated annealing algorithm [6]. Basically, this parametric method models the prior distribution of the image as a locally dependent Markov random field, for which the maximum a posteriori estimate is approximated iteratively.

This paper is organized as follows: in Sect. 2, we present an overview of the processing workflow. In Sect. 3, the developed ICM classification algorithm with constraints is described. Then in Sect. 4, the preliminary results are given and the post-classification decision criterion is used to improve results. Finally, conclusions are given in Sect. 5.

2   The Proposed Workflow

Due to the complexity of the scenes and of the several factors limiting digital palm trees detection, our conceptual workflow incorporates three blocks. The first block is devoted to the pre-processing, the second is related to the classification process and the third block to identify palm trees using shape and shadow direction information. The classified image is compared with the validation samples to determine the level of accuracy of the resulting classification. The workflow outlining steps of our methodology is shown in Fig. 1.

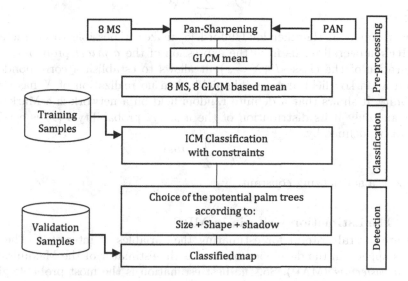

Fig. 1. Processing flow chart of the palm trees mapping.

3   The Classification Developed Method

3.1   The Contextual Image Model

3.1.1   Markov Random Fields in Imagery

We are given an image MxN defined on $\Omega = \{s = (i,j); 1 \leq i \leq M, 1 \leq j \leq N\}$ with value in E, thus, an element x_s of E is a matrix $x = (x_s, s \in \Omega)$ where x_s is for example the gray scale associated to the site s.

To the family $V = \{V(s), s \in \Omega\}$ is associated a class of the distribution probability, called Markov field and characterized by the following property:

$$\begin{cases} P(x_s) \succ 0, \text{ for any configuration } x_s \\ P(x_s|x_r, r \in \Omega - \{s\}) = P(x_s|x_r, r \in V(s) - \{s\}). \end{cases} \tag{1}$$

The probability of a pixel x_s conditional to all the others is equal to the conditional probability of x_s knowing the pixels of its local neighborhood $V(s)$.

The value of the other sites r is supposed known $r \in \Omega - \{s\}$. In the context of land cover classification, this property implies that the same land cover class is more likely to occur in connected regions than isolated pixels.

With a given neighborhood system corresponds a set of cliques. A clique is a set of points of the lattice that are mutually neighboring. The order of a clique is the number of sites which compose it. Two pixels belong to a clique if they are mutually neighboring each other. So, $U(x)$ which can be decomposed on all the cliques of the image, and expressed as a sum of associated potentials to these cliques:

$$U(x) = \sum_{c \subset C} V_c(x). \qquad (2)$$

The theorem of Hammersley-Clifford [5] makes it possible to characterize the MRFs in overall terms from the expression of the *a priori* probability of a configuration of the classes $P(X = x)$. It allows to establish a correspondence between a Markov field and a Gibbs field when no realization of X has a null probability. It shows that a definite random field on a network is a Markovian field if and only if its distribution of the *a priori* probability $P(x)$ is a Gibbs distribution, defined by:

$$P(x) = \frac{1}{Z} e^{-U(x)}, \qquad (3)$$

where Z is a normalizing constant.

3.1.2   The Estimation Criteria in MRF

There are several criteria for estimating the variables of interest x. The one which is applied in the developed method is the estimator of the Maximisation of the *a posteriori* (MAP). So, the best estimation is the most probable given the observed realization y and which amounts to minimize the energy $U(x)$.

In the case of MAP, there exist several methods of researching its solution: deterministic or stochastic. In our work we have opted for a deterministic method, which is the Iterated Conditional Mode method (ICM), because our goal is to process images of large sizes and with this method the convergence is guaranteed with a reasonable time of execution.

3.1.3   Minimization of the Posterior Energy by the ICM

Proposed by Besag [4], by assigning to each site s the class that maximizes the conditional probability to the observation in s and therefore minimizes the function of energy.

Let $Y = \{Y_s = y_s; s \in \Omega\}$ and $X = \{X_s = x_s; s \in \Omega\}$. Each pixel configuration x_s denotes one land cover class. Hence, $x_s \in \{1, ..., L\}$. A simple way to see this method is using Markovian property as follows: developing the *a posteriori* probability compared to a pixel s, we choose as a new value in s the one that maximizes the conditional probability $P(X = x | Y = y)$, which can be written as,

$$X^* = \arg\{\max_X [P(y|x = x_s) P(x_s)]\}, \qquad (4)$$

here, $P(y|x = x_s)$ is the probability that the data point y is observed for the given class of the configuration x in the site s, whereas $P(x_s)$ denotes the a priori probability of the configuration x_s. To calculate the probability $P(y|x = x_s)$, a multivariate Gaussian distribution with mean vector μ_s and covariance matrix Σ_s is assumed for class in x_s:

$$P(y|x = x_s) = \frac{1}{2\pi^{d/2} |\Sigma_s|^{1/2}} \exp[-\frac{1}{2}(y_s - \mu_s)^T \Sigma_s^{-1}(y_s - \mu_s)], \tag{5}$$

where d is the number of spectral bands.
The common covariance matrix is $\Sigma = \frac{1}{L} \sum_{i=1}^{L} \Sigma_i$.
Substituting (4) into (5), yields,

$$X^* = \arg\{\max_X[C \exp(-E(X|Y))]\}, \tag{6}$$

where $C = 1/Z_T(2\pi)^{d/2}$, Z_T is a normalizing constant depends on the temperature T and

$$E(X|Y) = \frac{1}{T}U(x_s) + \frac{1}{2}(y_s - \mu_s)^T \Sigma_s^{-1}(y_s - \mu_s) + \frac{1}{2}\ln(|\Sigma_s|).$$

Since the exponential function is monotonic and C is a constant that is independent of X, (6) can be reduced to

$$X^* = \arg\{\min_X[E(X|Y)]\}. \tag{7}$$

3.2   The Developed ICM Method with Contextual Constraints

The formalism of Markov Random Fields makes it possible to introduce, in a flexible way, the constraints of spatial context through their modeling by some potential functions. In addition to the constraint of the neighbourhood (regularization or smoothing constraint) we have introduced another constraint which is that of the contour (segmentation) [7] in order to minimize more the function of energy E in the classification. The expression of the function of energy, corresponding to the constraints used in the modeling of the a priori probability implemented in our application is as follow:

$$E(X|Y) \propto \frac{1}{T}U(x_s) + f(y_s, \mu_s, \Sigma_s), \tag{8}$$

where

$$U(x_s) = \sum_{all\_constraints} U_{constraint} = U_{smooth}(x_s) + U_{contour}(x_s). \tag{9}$$

For the constraint of regularization, the class the most present in the neighborhood of the pixel is favored. For the constraint of contour, the image of contours used is obtained through a segmentation process cited in [7].

Throughout the algorithm, we will decrease T, nor too quickly to avoid getting blocked around a local minimum, nor too slowly if we want to have a result in a reasonable time.

4   Result and Discussion

4.1   Study Area

The study area is the date palm grove of Mezguita (Fig. 2), in the Draa River Valley, Morocco. It has an extension of 44 km². The mean altitude is near 900 m above sea level. The area is characterized by a prevalence of small property. 85.8 % of farms have a surface lower than 2 ha and only 5.3 % of farms have a surface higher than 5 ha. In this very fragmented zone where date palms coexist with other crops.

4.2   Satellite Data

A 9 km × 4.9 km Worldview-2 (WV2) image of the Mezguita Oasis (Fig. 2), acquired on 13 April 2012 at 11:39 UTM was used. The acquisition was slightly off-nadir at 83.2 satellite elevation. The image was supplied at the nominal spatial resolution of 0.50 m/pixel and 2 m/pixel for the panchromatic and multispectral bands, respectively.

Fig. 2. Worldview-2 image of the Mezguita Oasis

4.3 Image Pre-processing

The acquired WV-2 image was standard ortho ready level and radiometrically corrected. It was converted to top-of-atmosphere spectral radiance using the procedure described in [8]. The resulting image was atmospherically corrected to obtain surface reflectances by mean of FLAASH (Fast Line-of-sight Atmospheric Analysis of Spectral Hypercubes), a first-principles atmospheric correction tool that corrects wavelengths in the visible through near-infrared and shortwave infrared regions [9]. Normally, palms are mixed with the rest of crops and soil uses, and irregularly arranged, which necessitates the highest possible level of detail. This is possible thanks to the panchromatic image with a resolution of 50 cm per pixel, but at the same time we would lose all the 8 spectral information bands of WV-2 satellite. That is why we chose a process of fusion where the multispectral bands were resampled through the Gram-Smith Spectral sharpening with the panchromatic band. Thus, an image is obtained that has not only a higher spatial resolution, but also all the spectral information. In addition to the loss or possible distortion of the spectral information which can occur during this process, there is still another problem arises: the considerable size of the generated image, which forces to use very powerful equipment to reduce the duration of treatment. The fusion method used was developed in [10] This technique solves the two most important problems in the image fusion: on the one hand the color distortion and, on the other hand, the operator dependence. It is about an adjustment by the ordinary least squares (OLS) method between the gray levels of the original multi-spectral images, the panchromatic and the fused bands to improve the color representation (Fig. 3).

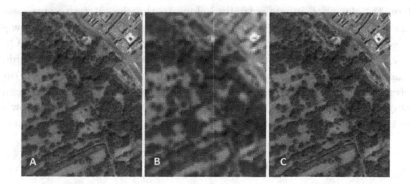

Fig. 3. Fusion process (C) of multi-spectral bands (B) with panchromatic band (A)

4.4 Classification Results

In this section we present the results obtained, first, with the proposed supervised contextual classification represented in the Fig. 4 by comparing it with the most commonly used supervised classification namely maximum likelihood (MLC).

Fig. 4. [4-3-2] bands color composite and Classified result map [palm tree (blue); shadow (cyan)] (Color figure online)

Thereafter, we show the interest of the use of shape and shadow direction information to refine the result of the contextual classification by masking the palm trees.

The confusion matrix in Table 1 shows the results of the validation polygons compared to the classified image. The main diagonal refers to the well-classified areas. In addition, we have calculated the producer's accuracy and at the user's accuracy (Table 2). The first accuracy refers to the probability for a given type of land cover to be well classified, and the second refers to the probability of an object on the classified image actually belong to the class it represents

Generally, it could be said that the non-contextual results did not allow good palm trees class detection (73.2 % total accuracy using ENVI Software). On the contrary, for the ICM method a total palm trees accuracy of 83.4 % was achieved. After having the classified map, the palm trees will be detected based on the shape (circular or elliptical), the orientation angle and the distance between the centers of the adjacent labeled objects of the palm trees class and shadow class to select the potential palm trees. For the choice of the angle of orientation,

Table 1. Confusion matrix of the proposed ICM classification

	Fruit trees	Palm trees	Cultures	No cultures	Total
Fruit trees	347	456	267	0	1070
Palm trees	345	6959	626	0	7930
Cultures	733	452	4935	0	6120
No cultures	0	7	1336	2439	3782
Total classified	1425	7874	7164	2439	18902

Fig. 5. Experimental angle interval of shadow orientation

Table 2. Palm trees producer's accuracy and user's accuracy

	user's accuracy	producer's accuracy
MLC	74,1 %	72,3 %
ICM	82,3 %	84,5 %
ICM+shape+shadow	88,4 %	87,8 %

it was chosen experimentally between $40°$ and $50°$ Fig. 5. The decision may be reformulated as below.

$$Decision = AND(Criterion_{shape}; Criterion_{dist-palm-shadow}; Criterion_{angle}) \tag{10}$$

Tree objects are identified according to their geometric properties (shape rule) as they define compact and elliptical objects and according to the adjacency between palm tree class and shadow class (distance rule). Also, tree objects depend to the directional existence of shadow according to the sun illumination represented by the third rule of angle orientation.

As expected, with the use of the shape and shadow information. This accuracy shows improved to reach 88.1 %.

5   Conclusion

In this paper we have proposed a new supervised classification based on the Model of Markov Region and derived from the ICM (Iterated Conditional Mode). We have added a post-classification decision criterion based on shape, orientation angle and the distance, an improvement was achieved. The application of this method for the detection of palm trees is promising, however, the case of overlapping palm trees still significant issue for further investigation.

Acknowledgments. Satellite imagery and ground truth data of this work are provided in the PALMERA project 2008–2013 included in the POCTEFEX program financed by the FEDER.

References

1. Uddin, S., AL-Dousari, A., AL-Ghadban, A.: Mapping of palm trees in urban and agriculture areas of Kuwait using satellite data. Int. J. Sus. Dev. Plan. 4(2), 1–9 (2009)
2. Helmi, Z., Shafri, M., Nasrulhapiza, H., Iqbal Saripan, M.: Semiautomatic detection and counting of oil palm trees from high spatial resolution airborne imagery. Int. J. Remo. Sens. 38(8), 2095–2115 (2011)
3. Ruiliang, P., Landry, S.: A comparative analysis of high spatial resolution IKONOS and WorldView-2 imagery for mapping urban tree species. Remo. Sens. Env. 124, 516–533 (2012)
4. Besag, J.: Spatial interaction and the statistical analysis of lattice systems. J. Roy. Sta. Soc. 36, 192–236 (1974)
5. Solberg, A.H.S., Taxt, T., Jain, A.K.: A Markov random field model for classification of multisource satellite imagery. IEEE Trans. Geosc. Remo. Sens. 34, 100–113 (1996)
6. Bremaud, P.: Markov Chains Gibbs Field, Monte Carlo Simulation, and Queues. Springer, New York (1999)
7. Idbraim, S., Ducrot, D., Mammass, D., Aboutajdine, D.: An unsupervised classification using a novel ICM method with constraints for land cover mapping from remote sensing imagery. Int. Rev. Comp. Sof. 4, 165–176 (2009)
8. Updike, T., Comp, C.: Radiometric Use of WorldView-2 Imagery. Technical note. Digital Globe Inc., Longmont, Colorado, U.S.A (2010)
9. Matthew, M.W., Adler-Golden, S.M., Berk, A., Richtsmeier, S.C., Levine, R.Y.: Status of atmospheric correction using a MODTRAN4-based algorithm. In: Proceedings of SPIE 4049, Algorithms for Multispectral Hyperspectral and Ultraspectral Imagery VI, pp. 199–207 (2000)
10. Xu, Q., Zhang, Y., Li, B.: Recent advances in pansharpening and key problems in applications. Int. J. Data Im. Fus. 5(3), 175–195 (2014)

Fast Autonomous Crater Detection
by Image Analysis–For Unmanned Landing
on Unknown Terrain

Payel Sadhukhan[✉] and Sarbani Palit

Indian Statistical Institute, 203, B.T. Road, Kolkata 700108, India
payel0410@gmail.com

Abstract. Unmanned landing on unknown terrain such as planetary surfaces requires the in-situ estimation of surface irregularities like craters, ridges and other deformities. Moreover, to facilitate safe landing, the surface estimation has to be done in as little time as possible. In this paper, we present an algorithm to address the above two issues in the context of crater presence on the terrain. Detection of craters is done on images of the probable landing surfaces and the computation time required for the detection is subsequently reduced in the proposed method using image analysis approaches like standard deviation filtering, morphological operations and validation of crater presence by texture extraction. We have achieved a 85–89% true positive (TP) rate on large craters and 79–82 % TP rate on small craters. We have conducted our experiments on real images of Mars and the Moon, collected by space-crafts named 2001 Mars Odyssey and the Lunar Reconnaissance Orbiter, respectively. Empirical evidences indicate that the proposed method achieves a commendable TP rate and a subsequent improvement in the time required for detection as compared to existing methodologies.

Keywords: Crater detection · Mathematical morphology · Contrast change · Texture analysis · Image analysis

1 Introduction

Planetary bodies have remained intriguing to humans since ages unknown. What started with simple observations of the moon, planets and stars, soon evolved into formulating detailed and complex mathematical relationships governing their behaviour and other features. As technology advanced, sophisticated space-crafts and satellites were launched, both manned and unmanned, which, as a part of their mission, provide an enormous volume of planetary images. The availability of legible images of planetary surfaces has further spurred the possibility of crater detection from such images making it a viable tool for space exploration and scientific research.

Geological studies of the planetary surfaces require the detection and subsequent estimation of impact crater ages as well as study of their structures,

© Springer International Publishing Switzerland 2016
A. Mansouri et al. (Eds.): ICISP 2016, LNCS 9680, pp. 293–303, 2016.
DOI: 10.1007/978-3-319-33618-3_30

density and other features. Several such pieces of work involving detection and study of impact craters has been done [3]. Crater catalogue creation is another application which can serve a number of purposes [10]. Some detection work has also focussed towards facilitating autonomous landing on planetary surfaces [3]. Diverse schemes have been used to detect the craters which include arc fitting [6], capturing circularity using Circular Hough Transform [11], ellipse fitting– a more sophisticated but time consuming approach detecting elliptical craters [7], texture and template matching [1,2]. Several machine learning techniques like neural networks [12], SVM [5,12], boosting [8,12], genetic algorithm [4] have also been used. Most of the above mentioned techniques and schemes for crater detection are adequate for off-line studies like geological analysis and crater catalogue implementation. However, these methods require intensive computation and seem fairly unsuitable for real-time tasks like detection for the purpose of autonomous landing.

To address the intensive computation and time requirement issue, it is necessary to conceive of the crater detection task in a simplified fashion. Craters have several features, namely – a circular or elliptical shape, a more or less continuous structure of the rims, a distinct dark-light texture. We can reduce the detection time if we exploit the properties which require a minimal amount of mathematical computations. The proposed approach implements this by attempting detection of the probable crater rims using standard deviation filtering and thresholding, filtering out the crater containing Region-of-Interests (ROIs) by morphological operations and finally detection of craters by contrast change detection in the ROIs. We deliberately avoid the circle or ellipse fitting stage in order to reduce the computation time. Experimental results indicate a commendable detection rate and improvement in time requirement over circle fitting methods.

2   Proposed Method

Figure 1 shows a block diagram of the proposed approach. The approach has three distinct stages. The first one deals with the identification of probable crater rims on the surface image under examination, referred to as the original image, in the block diagram. The ridge map contains actual crater rims as well as undesired surface irregularities. Mathematical morphological operations are used to sift the ROIs (containing craters) from the ridge-map in the second stage. Finally, texture analysis is performed on the ROIs to verify crater presence in them.

2.1   The Steps of the Algorithm

1. **Crater rim identification:** Craters have a unique texture, a lightened half and the darkened other by virtue of their hollow insides. Figure 2 presents a surface image showing multiple such craters. This property gives the rims a different light intensity than its surroundings. This feature is well captured across the crater if we use an extraction technique by which we can gain

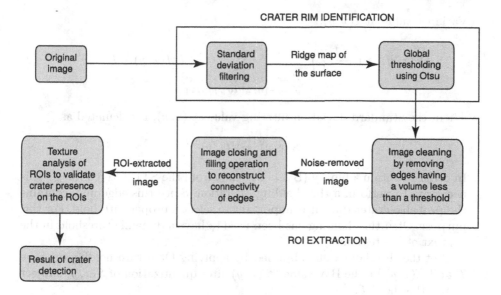

Fig. 1. The proposed crater detection scheme.

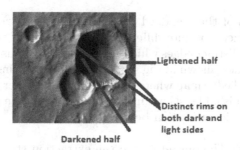

Fig. 2. A surface image showing the presence of distinct crater rims on both darkened and lightened sides of the craters

insight into the localized changes in the gray intensity. This task is accomplished by performing standard deviation (STD) based filtering of the gray scale surface image.

In order to do this, we initially choose the neighbourhood or locality in which the standard deviation will be considered.

Let I be the gray-scale original image, the neighbourhood size be n, and $I(x, y)$ be the $(x, y)^{th}$ pixel for which the STD filtering value will be defined. Without loss of generality, n is assumed to be even.

Mean gray value at $(x, y)^{th}$ pixel,

$$M(x, y) = \left(\frac{1}{n+1}\right)^2 \sum_{\substack{x'=x-\lfloor n/2 \rfloor \; to \; x+\lfloor n/2 \rfloor \\ y'=y-\lfloor n/2 \rfloor \; to \; y+\lfloor n/2 \rfloor}} I(x', y') \qquad (1)$$

Variance value at $I(x, y)$,

$$V(x, y) = \left(\frac{1}{n+1}\right)^2 \sum_{\substack{x'=x-\lfloor n/2 \rfloor \text{ to } x+\lfloor n/2 \rfloor \\ y'=y-\lfloor n/2 \rfloor \text{ to } y+\lfloor n/2 \rfloor}} (M(x, y) - I(x', y'))^2 \quad (2)$$

Then, the Standard deviation filtering value at (x, y), is calculated as

$$S(x, y) = V(x, y)^{0.5}$$

In order to obtain a binary (BW) edge map from the STD filtered image, it is necessary to perform a thresholding operation. Since this edge map contains the probable crater rims, it is important to select a proper threshold. For this purpose, Otsu thresholding has been used to have a dynamic threshold in the context of the test image.

Let the threshold value obtained by applying Otsu thresholding on S be T and $E(x, y)$ be the BW value at (x, y) after quantization of $S(x, y)$ subject to the threshold T.

$$E(x, y) = \begin{cases} 1, & S(x, y) > T \\ 0, & \text{otherwise} \end{cases}$$

The effectiveness of the standard deviation (STD) filtering is illustrated in Fig. 3. The localized absolute difference computation of the image shown in Fig. 3a, gives the distinct edges which represent crater rims both on the darker and the lighter sides, shown in Fig. 3b. Edge detection using the Canny operator gives a meshed edge map where positive rims and other noisy surroundings become indistinguishable, shown in Fig. 3c. I map will be used in subsequent stages with crater identification being the ultimate goal.

2. **ROI extraction:** The output of the rim extraction stage, the E map gives the locations on which ROI extraction will be performed. Edge pixels, *i.e.* the white ones on the E map give the probable locations of crater rims. High frequency noise and other non-relevant surface irregularities also contribute to the edge pixels on the E map apart from the craters. We resort to quantitative (morphological) removal and systematic augmentation of edges to get the continuous crater rims. The crater rims which are enclosed in *Bounding boxes* give the coveted Region-of-Interest, ROI. The various steps involved, are explained below:

(a) *Quantitative removal:* In most cases, crater rims give one or more edges (8-connected set of edge pixels) with higher volume (number of pixels) whereas high frequency noise and non-relevant irregularities give edges with a lesser volume. Following this observation, we ignore edges which have volume (no. of pixels) less than a certain threshold. From observations made on a large set of images, this threshold was empirically set at 1 % of the total no. of white pixels in the edge map E.

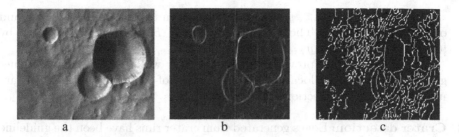

Fig. 3. (a) shows the original image. (b) shows the edge map obtained by standard deviation filtering, crater rims are profoundly seen. (c) shows the Canny edge map, gives indistinguishable crater rims

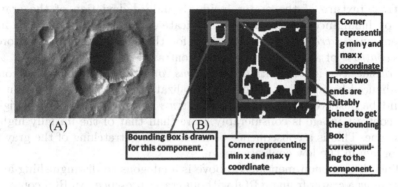

Fig. 4. (A) shows the crater containing original image. (B) shows the *Systematic augmentation* stage output of the same image on which *Bounding Box* is drawn on two connected components. Total seven connected components are seen on (B)

(b) *Systematic augmentation:* As crater rims give disconnected edges, it is important to restore their connectivity before we go for texture analysis in the next segment. For that, we perform closing operation on the remaining edges of E by a single structuring element followed by a hole-filling operation on the modified edges. This gives a somewhat continuous set of probable crater rims.

(c) *Enclosing the probable crater locations in Bounding Boxes:* After establishing structural continuity of the probable crater rims in the previous stage, it is necessary to quantitatively 'mark' those regions for crater detection in the final stage. For this, we draw *Bounding Box* around each of such probable crater rim or connected component. By *bounding box*, we imply a rectangle of least area which totally encloses a connected component or probable crater rim. For each probable crater rim (given as an output of System augmentation stage), we note the maximum and minimum abscissa and ordinate respectively. These four measures coupled together gives the x and y span of the bounding rectangle.

Let x_{max}, x_{min}, y_{max}, y_{min} be the maximum and minimum abscissa and ordinate respectively. The four corners of the *Bounding box* are given by $[(x_{max}, y_{max}), (x_{max}, y_{min}), (x_{min}, y_{max}), (x_{min}, y_{min})]$.

The *Bounding box* provides a visual marker while the coordinate values give the quantitative locations of the Region-of-Interest (ROIs) which are used in the crater detection stage.

3. **Crater detection:** Edges generated from crater rims have been the guideline for extraction of the ROIs in the previous stage. But we cannot deny the presence of non-relevant objects in the ROIs. We distinguish craters (detect craters) from non-crater ones by texture analysis of the ROI locations in I.

The proposed texture analysis is based on capturing the dark-light, high-contrast texture of the crater inside. Standard deviation of the gray values or luminance of an image is indicative of the contrast of an image. Often *rms contrast* is the term used for the same measure [9]. More the *rms contrast* of an image, more is its contrast.

Consider two images with different *rms contrast* values and whose contrast is enhanced by applying histogram equalization to each image separately. It would be observed that the change in *rms contrast* value of the originally low-contrast image is considerably more than that of the initially high contrast one. This is a consequence of the increased stretching of the gray-value histogram in the low contrast image.

The phenomenon mentioned above is analogous to distinguishing an ROI containing a crater from an ROI without crater presence. An ROI containing a crater will possess a high contrast region originally (by virtue of the dark-light texture of the crater), and hence, will show less augmentation in *rms contrast* after contrast enhancement via histogram equalization. On the contrary, a ROI without a crater is generally a low-contrasted one, arising due to surface irregularities and hence shows larger increase in *rms contrast* after histogram equalization. This differential behaviour of the ROIs with a crater present as compared to ROIs devoid of craters, is used to detect the craters.

Let R_1 be a ROI (image segment) to be tested for crater detection and I is the original image.

$S_1 = rms\,contrast$ of R_1.

$S_I = rms\,contrast$ of I.

$RC_1 = R_1$ after contrast enhancement using histogram equalization.

$IC = I$ after contrast enhancement using histogram equalization.

$\acute{S}_1 = rms\,contrast$ of RC_1.

$\acute{S}_I = rms\,contrast$ of IC.

Fitness value, $f = (\acute{S}_1 - S_1) - (\acute{S}_I - S_I)$.

f gives the difference of change in contrast between the ROI concerned and the original image. If the change of contrast in a ROI is less than that of the original image, it indicates the presence of a contrasted texture (dark-light) in the concerned ROI. Contrasted texture is synonymous to crater presence while the reverse indicates the absence. So we quantize the fitness value for crater absence or presence as follows:

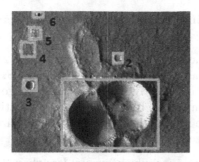

Fig. 5. Crater 1: $f = -23$, detected and present, **Crater 2:** $f = 4.8$, undecided but present (missed), **Crater 3:** $f = -12$, detected and present, **Crater 4:** $f = 18.9$, absent and missing, **Crater 5:** $f = 16$, absent and missing, **Crater 6:** $f = -18$, detected and present

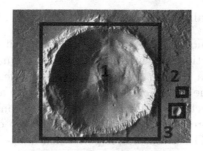

Fig. 6. 1: Large crater, **2 and 3:** Small crater *in the context of the given image.*

$f < 0$,   *Crater is detected in ROI*
$0 < f < 5$,   *Undecided about crater presence*
$f > 5$,   *Crater is absent in ROI*

3   Experimental Validation

Our work is focussed towards autonomous crater detection to facilitate landing on unknown terrain. In order to validate the efficacy of the proposed method, it is necessary to compare the automated detection output with visual probe of the same images by humans.

3.1   Crater Sizes

Crater size is an important parameter which influences the quality of the crater detection task. Missing out a large crater is clearly hazardous for landing but we can expect a 'missed' small one to be detectable in a closer, magnified stage which would be available as the spacecraft approaches the planetary surface. It is important to define a large and small crater clearly. Before proceeding to the evaluation stage, we define two classes of craters – large craters and small craters heuristically.

Large Craters: are the ones which cover more than 2 % of image pixels. [6] has classified a crater as large or small by its size ($Size$ < 8 pixels: Small, $8 < Size \le 60$: Large) irrespective of the surface image size. A more realistic approach of classification should be using crater size relative to the image size — an 8 pixel crater can be regarded small in a 256 pixel size surface image, but a crater with the same size is relatively large in a 32 pixel surface image.

Small Craters: are the ones which occupy less than 2 % of the pixels of the surface image. Such craters which go undetected in the "small" stage may become detectable in the later stages. It happens if the "small" crater gets a good share of the pixels and becomes a "large" one in the magnified view.

3.2 Metrics for Evaluation

In order to facilitate smooth and autonomous landing, it is necessary to have a good recall rate of detection, specially for large craters. Quality of detection is the other important criteria which takes into account the detection of false targets (non-craters) besides the actual craters. In order to have a practical application, time complexity of detection should also be taken into consideration. We use the following three parameters to evaluate the performance of our scheme and the comparing technique. The evaluation is performed image-wise.

- *True detection percentage:* It gives the percentage of 'true' craters detected by the crater detection scheme. It may be noted that 'true' craters refer to those detected manually from a surface image.

$$True\ detection\ percentage\ (TDP) = \frac{TP}{TP + FN} * 100$$

- *False detection rate:* It estimates the percentage of non-craters present in the detected set of craters.

$$False\ detection\ rate\ (FDR) = \frac{FP}{TP + FP} * 100$$

- *Detection time* (DT): The total time taken to detect all the craters present on an image. It is measured in *seconds*.

For crater detection assessment, human detection is considered as the ground truth value. *True positive* (TP) denotes those cases which are classified as craters by the detection scheme as well as the humans. Similarly, *True negative* (TN), are those which are classified as non-craters by both. The ones classified as craters by the autonomous detector but having ground truth (human) value as non-craters denote *False positive* (FP), while the reverse class is denoted by *False negative,* (FN).

3.3   Data Sources

In recent times, spacecraft landings have been made on several planetary surfaces like Mars, Mercury, Venus, Moon and others. These missions have led to the acquisition and transmission of planetary surface images back to earth, as a valuable source of data for exploration and research. We have used images of two diverse heavenly bodies, Mars and the Moon for evaluation of the proposed approach for crater detection. The two major sources of such images for our work have been:

- Martian images captured by the spacecraft Odyssey. One of the chief motivations for acquiring images of the Martian surface was to map the water distribution of the surface.
- Lunar images taken by the Lunar Reconnaissance orbiter (LRO) We convert the RGB images of LRO to gray-scale before proceeding with our algorithm.

3.4   Comparison of Performance

The "Crater Detection" stage, where contrast change detection is performed for crater identification, forms the most transformational juncture and hence the most crucial step of the proposed algorithm. We have made the comparative study of our work with the more general and extensively used, Circular Hough Transform (CHT) based detection method (where we have considered the previous stages to be same as that of our work). Figure 7 illustrates a scenario where an elliptical crater is detected by the proposed schema but CHT fails.

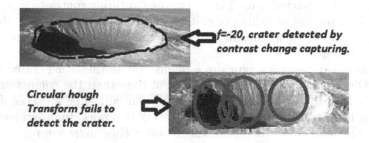

Fig. 7. This figure shows the failure of CHT to detect an elliptical crater

3.5   Results

The results of the comparison of the proposed method with the CHT based method has been given in Table 1. The performance with respect to the evaluating criteria are given for large and small craters separately.

Results have been obtained for 25 images of the Martian surface and 25 of the Lunar surface. A total of 123 craters were found the Martian surface images (including large and small) while 141 were detected on the Lunar surface.

Table 1. Results for crater detection is given. TDP, FDR, DT stands for *True detection percentage*, *False detection rate* and *Detection time* respectively. CHT stands for Circular Hough transform. ↑ indicates higher the value, better the performance on the metric, similarly ↓ indicates the reverse, the lower the better.

		Detection using contrast change			Detection using CHT		
		TDP ↑	FDR ↓	DT ↓ (in s)	TDP ↑	FDR ↓	DT ↓ (in s)
Martian Craters	Large	84.2	22	0.31	79.0	21.3	1.82
	Small	79.9	18.2	0.27	79.6	18.8	1.65
Moon Craters	Large	90.23	20.26	0.32	82.8	16.6	1.46
	Small	81.45	17.46	0.28	82.3	16.4	1.24

The mean criteria values across those images has been presented on Table 1. It is observed from the results that performance of both CHT-based technique and the proposed scheme is better for Lunar images than that of Martian images.

4   Conclusion

This paper presents a fast, autonomous crater detection technique to facilitate landing on unknown surfaces. Validation of its performance has been established through computations made on a large number of actual planetary images captured on various extra-terrestrial missions. Rim continuity detection followed by simplified contrast-change capturing modus operandi enables us to sufficiently reduce the time required. Mathematical morphological operations establish the continuity in the detected rims. The scheme for capturing contrast-change allows us to perform texture matching of craters without having to address the issues of scaling, rotation or alignment which are commonly faced problems during texture matching.

The proposed algorithm provides a unique way of validating crater presence in the ROIs in significantly lesser amount of time than the competing Circular Hough Transform-based technique. A substantially superior *True detection percentage* is the other important achievement of this work. Improvement of performance for small craters and achieving a better *False detection rate* constitute our future direction of work. Extending the algorithm to include other kinds of surface images also form the scope of future research.

References

1. Bandeira, L., Ding, W., Stepinski, T.F.: Detection of sub-kilometer craters in high resolution planetary images using shape and texture features. Adv. Space Res. **49**, 64–74 (2012)
2. Bandeira, L., Saraiva, J., Pina, P.: Impact crater recognition on mars based on a probability volume created by template matching. IEEE Trans. Geosci. Remote Sens. **45**(12), 4008–4015 (2007)

3. Bandeira, L.P.C., Saraiva, J., Pina, P.: Development of a methodology for automated crater detection on planetary images. In: Martí, J., Benedí, J.M., Mendonça, A.M., Serrat, J. (eds.) IbPRIA 2007, Part I. LNCS, vol. 4477, pp. 193–200. Springer, Heidelberg (2007)

4. Bue, B.D., Stepinski, T.F.: Machine detection of martian impact craters from digital topography data. IEEE Trans. Geosci. Remote Sens. **45**(1), 265–274 (2007)

5. Ding, M., Cao, Y., Wu, Q.: Novel approach of crater detection by crater candidate region selection and matrix-pattern-oriented least squares support vector machine. Chin. J. Aeronaut. **26**, 385–393 (2013)

6. Kim, J.R., Muller, J.P., van Gasselt, S., Morley, J.G., Neukum, G.: Automated crater detection, a new tool for Mars cartography and chronology. Photogram. Eng. Remote Sens. **71**(10), 1205–1217 (2005)

7. Leroy, B., Medioni, G., Johnson, E., Matthies, L.: Crater detection for autonomous landing on asteroids. Image Vis. Comput. **19**, 787–792 (2001)

8. Martins, R., Pina, P., Marques, J.S., Silveira, M.: Crater detection by a boosting approach. IEEE Geosci. Remote Sens. Lett. **6**, 127–131 (2009)

9. Moulden, B., Gatley, L.F., et al.: The standard deviation of luminance as a metric for contrast in random-dot images. Perception **19**(1), 79–101 (1990)

10. Salamunićcar, G., Lončarić, S., Pina, P., Bandeira, L., Saraiva, J.: Ma130301gt catalogue of martian impact craters and advanced evaluation of crater detection algorithms using diverse topography and image datasets. Planet. Space Sci. **59**(1), 111–131 (2011)

11. Sawabe, Y., Matsunaga, T., Rokugawa, S.: Automated detection and classification of lunar craters using multiple approaches. Adv. Space Res. **37**(1), 21–27 (2006)

12. Wetzler, P.G., Honda, R., Enke, B., Merline, W.J., Chapman, C.R., Burl, M.C.: Learning to detect small impact craters. In: Seventh IEEE Workshops on Application of Computer Vision, WACV/MOTIONS 2005, vol. 1. IEEE (2005)

Automatic Detection and Classification of Oil Tanks in Optical Satellite Images Based on Convolutional Neural Network

Qingquan Wang[1]([✉]), Jinfang Zhang[1], Xiaohui Hu[1], and Yang Wang[2]

[1] Institute of Software Chinese Academy of Sciences, Beijing, China
{qingquan2014,jinfang,hxh}@iscas.ac.cn
[2] Beijing Information Science & Technology University, Beijing, China
1054334480@qq.com

Abstract. Oil reserves are one of the core interests of a country. The detection of oil tanks is a very important task. So far, most studies only focus on the detection task itself. But the strategic value of different types of oil tanks is obviously different. So we furtherly divide oil tanks into two types: flat crest and cone-shaped crest. In this paper, a four-step method is adopted: (1) prepare dataset; (2) train the classifier; (3) extract candidate regions and (4) classification. The deep network (CNN) Krizhevsky used on cifar-10 dataset is used to train the classifier and ELSD is used to extract candidate regions. In addition, some clustering tricks are used to determine an only candidate region to solve the double-detection problem. The experimental results show that this method can detect and distinguish different types of oil tanks with outstanding performance.

Keywords: Deep learning · Convolutional Neural Network (CNN) · Ellipse and Line Segment Detector (ELSD) · Oil tank detection and classification · Clustering

1 Introduction

Many countries see oil reserves as a national strategy and oil tank detection is one of the most important tasks in the field of remote sensing. It has great significance in security monitoring, disaster prevention and so on. Recently, military actions taken by some western countries against oil depots of the terrorist organization effectively weaken the enemy's strength, furtherly proving its strategic position.

So far, most studies only focus on the detection task itself. In fact, oil tanks roughly includes three types: fixed cone-shaped crest, interior floating crest and exterior floating crest. The first two are cone-shaped crest structure, mainly storing light oil. The last one is flat crest structure and its capacity is mostly more than 10,000 m^3, mainly storing heavy oil. In the recently built oil depots

Q. Wang—Foundation item: Supported by the National Natural Science Foundation of China (NSFC No. U1435220, 41401409).

A. Mansouri et al. (Eds.): ICISP 2016, LNCS 9680, pp. 304–313, 2016.
DOI: 10.1007/978-3-319-33618-3_31

of China, the capacity of most exterior floating crest oil tanks is 100,000 m^3. Obviously, these tanks have more strategic value. So we divide oil tanks into two types (flat crest and cone-shaped crest) and take detecting and distinguishing them as our task.

Most studies are based on the shape feature (circle) of oil tanks. Zhang et al. [1] applied edge detection and Hough transform [2] to the images processed by Brovey transform fusion method. Xu et al. [3] exploited the characteristics of quasi-circular shadow and highlighting arcs of SAR images. Ok and Baseski [4] used the symmetric feature of circle. Zhao et al. [5] improved Hough transform to get a directional and weighted Hough voting method.

Zhang et al. [6] proposed a systematic three-step process: candidate selection, feature extraction, and classification. They used a rapid and efficient algorithm called ELSD [7] (ellipse and line segment detector) for candidate selection and an existing CNN model trained by Krizhevsky [8] in the ILSVRC2012 contest to extract surrounding features. Coupled with the extracted features of HOG, LBP and Gabor, SVM is applied to the feature set. The same process was also used to detect seals [9].

In this paper we demonstrate how to detect and classify oil tanks into flat crest and cone-shaped crest from optical satellite images. The framework includes four steps: (1) prepare dataset; (2) train the classifier; (3) extract candidate regions and (4) classification. In step3, some clustering tricks are used to determine the final position and size of each potential target to solve the double-detection (one target corresponds to multiple candidate regions) problem.

2   Oil Tank Detection and Classification

This framework consists of four steps: (1) prepare dataset; (2) train the classifier with the deep network Krizhevsky [10] used on cifar-10 dataset; (3) extract candidate regions with ELSD [7]; (4) apply the classifier to these candidate regions.

2.1   Prepare Dataset

The type of input data is optical satellite image with RGB mode. From Google Earth, optical images of some oil depots in America, China, Japan and South Korea are collected as raw data. The resolution is between 0.5 and 0.9 m. Some of the collected images are cut into square pieces in the method of sliding window. To simulate different illumination conditions, the HSV color space is exploited to adjust the brightness of images. To simulate different resolutions, images are cut in different scales. Finally, all these pieces are scaled to size of 32×32 to fit the input size of the deep network [10]. To achieve the task of detection and classification, images should be divided into three classes: flat crest tanks, cone-shaped crest tanks and non-tanks.

The final dataset totally contains 60101 labeled images, among which 15131 are flat crest tanks and 12618 are cone-shaped crest tanks. The dataset is split

Table 1. The sizes of training and validation sets. Another 35 original optical satellite images are directly used as testing set. Two of them are shown in Fig. 5.

	Flat	Cone-shaped	Non-tanks
training set	13631	11118	30852
validation set	1500	1500	1500

into training and validation sets. The sizes of these two sets are shown in Table 1. When training the classifier, cross validation is performed on the validation set. The other 35 original optical satellite images collected from Google Earth are directly used as testing set.

2.2   Train the Classifier

The classifier is trained with existing deep network [10] shown in Fig. 1. There are three pooling layers in this network. The first one is max-pooling and the other two are mean-pooling. Max-pooling can efficiently reduce computational complexity while mean-pooling keeps more information of local regions. It tries to find a balance between computational complexity and local details. This network also contains ReLu (Rectified Linear Units) layer and LRN (Local Response Normalization) layer around pooling layer. ReLu is an activation function: $f(x) = max(0, x)$. It directly erases the negative value but keeps the positive value. Therefore, the sparsity is produced, which can effectively accelerate the training process and prevent over-fitting in some extent. The LRN process imitates the lateral inhibition mechanism of nervous system. It highlights the larger response value and as a result enhances the generalization ability of this model.

The classifier is trained with standard SGD (stochastic gradient descent) algorithm. Each layer contains two calculations, forward and backward passes.

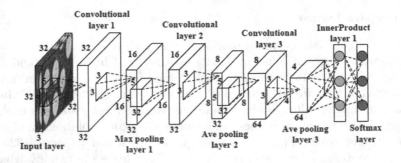

Fig. 1. The deep network structure (CNN) Krizhevsky [10] used on cifar-10 dataset.

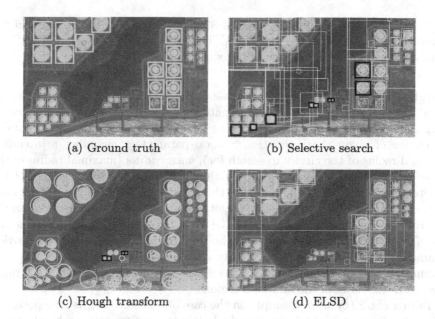

(a) Ground truth   (b) Selective search

(c) Hough transform   (d) ELSD

Fig. 2. Figure (a) shows the ground truth. The size is 1011 × 657. The flat crest tanks are marked with thick boxes and the cone-shaped crest tanks are marked with thin boxes. The other three figures respectively show the results of extracting candidate regions with methods: (b) selective search, (c) Hough transform and (d) ELSD. The tanks in black boxes are missed or not properly surrounded.

The forward pass computes the output given the input for inference. The backward pass computes the gradient given the loss for learning. The weights are initialized with a Gaussian distribution of variance 0.01 and mean 0. The bias is initialized with 0 and the learning rate is set to 0.001. In addition, GPU is used to accelerate the training process. After iterations, parameters finally got can roughly describe the distribution of dataset and be used as classifier for other images.

2.3   Extract Candidate Regions

Existing algorithms for candidate selection in oil tank detection can be roughly classified into two categories: potential targets extraction and circle detection. Among the first one, a widely used method is selective-search [11]. Hough transform [2] and ELSD [7] are typical line segment and elliptical arc detectors which can be used for circle detection.

Selective Search. This method is based on hierarchical grouping algorithm, optimized with three complementary strategies including color spaces, similarity measures and starting regions [11]. Here selective-search is applied to an optical satellite image which contains oil tanks of quite different scales. As shown in

Fig. 2 (b), this method misses 9 out of 39 tanks. Some are not found and the extracted sizes of the others are wrong. The missing rate reaches over 20 %. It greatly reduces the performance of the whole framework.

Hough Transform. The basic principle of Hough transform [2] is that lines in the image space are changed to aggregation points of the parameter space by using the duality of points and lines, so as to validate whether an image contains the curves of given characteristics. Several parameters including min_radius (minimal radius of the circles to search for), max_radius (maximal radius of the circles to search for) and min_dist (minimum distance between centers of the detected circles) need to be provided to this algorithm. To effectively reduce false alarms and meanwhile not miss any target, all target sizes should be between the min_radius and the max_radius. At the same time, the distance between any pair of targets should be greater than the min_dist. Only the request to provide parameters artificially itself will greatly reduce the algorithm's generality and automation ability. What's more, inaccurate parameters will lead to a rapid increase in the number of candidate regions.

Taking Fig. 2 (c) as an example, in the case of 4 missed targets, the potential regions of different tanks have already begun to overlap with each other in a large area. And when ensuring that all targets are not missed by adjusting the parameters, the image space has already been covered by massive false alarms.

ELSD. ELSD [7] is a combined and parameter-free line segment and elliptical arc detector. This detector obeys a 3-step scheme: candidate selection, candidate validation and model selection. The automation and generality ability of object extraction is guaranteed by the characteristic of parameter-free. As shown in Fig. 2 (d), all targets are in some appropriate boxes.

However, due to shadow, texture or other factors, there are many redundant regions. Zhang et al. [6] took a trick to remove most of these regions, in which all discontinuous arcs belonging to a same ring are figured out. Their trick need to compute distances between a center and every aligned pixel of a detected arc, with high computational complexity. We use a rule of concentric circles depending on the center coordinates and radius instead of all aligned pixels.

Step 1: validate whether two discontinuous arcs belong to a same ring.

$$Dist(a, b) = \sqrt{(Cenr_a - Cenr_b)^2 + (Cenc_a - Cenc_b)^2}. \tag{1}$$

$$\frac{Dist(a, b)}{max(r_a, r_b)} \leq \theta, \ \theta \geq 0. \tag{2}$$

$$\frac{|r_a - r_b|}{max(r_a, r_b)} \leq \sigma, \ \sigma \geq 0. \tag{3}$$

where $Cenr$ and $Cenc$, respectively indicate the row and column index of a circle's center, and r is the circle's radius. θ and σ are two constants. The subscripts indicate two different circles. The formula (2) validates whether two circles have a same center and the formula (3) validates whether two circles have a same radius. They are both robust to different resolutions due to the ratio.

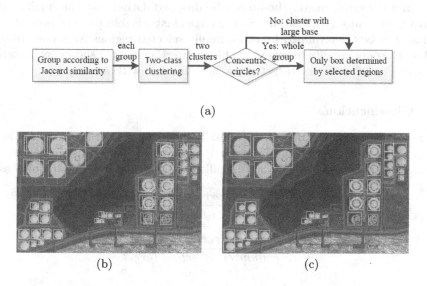

(a)

(b)   (c)

Fig. 3. Figure (a) shows the process to determine an only candidate region for a target. Figure (b) shows the optimization result of Fig. 2 (d) when applying the ratio trick [6]. Figure (c) shows the result when using additional steps to figure (b).

Step 2: compute a aligned ratio that all aligned pixels occupy in total pixels of a ring, same as what proposed in [6].

$$R_{circle} = \frac{k_x(circle)}{l_{circle}}.$$ (4)

where l_{circle} indicates the total pixels of the ring and $k_x(circle)$ is the number of aligned pixels. A threshold is used to select the final validated selections. But after this, there is still phenomenon of double-detection. Figure 3 (b) shows the optimization result of Fig. 2 (d). Additional steps in Fig. 3 (a) are taken.

Step 3: group candidate regions based on Jaccard similarity. Each group corresponds to an only target.

$$J(a, b) = \frac{|area_a \cap area_b|}{|area_a \cup area_b|}.$$ (5)

where $area$ indicates the area of a circle.

Step 4: perform two-class clustering on each group according to the center distance of circles.

If the summaries (average value of the center coordinates and radius for each cluster) of the two clusters meet a constraint of formula (2) but don't satisfy formula (3), the whole group should be selected as representative results. Because the cluster with shorter radius most likely responds to ring contour on flat crest tanks and the small cluster should not be dropped. Otherwise, the small cluster is most likely caused by shadows. So the large cluster is selected as representative results. The box determined by those finally selected regions from one group is used as the only candidate region of this group. Figure 3 (c) shows optimization result of Fig. 3 (b). Every target is properly marked with an only box.

2.4   Classification

After scaled to size of 32 × 32, the classifier can be applied to these candidate regions. The classification performance is evaluated with confusion matrix. We adopt two indicators: precision and recall. For each class, they are defined as:

$$Precision = \frac{number\ of\ correctly\ classified\ targets}{number\ of\ predicted\ targets}. \tag{6}$$

$$Recall = \frac{number\ of\ correctly\ classified\ targets}{number\ of\ actual\ targets}. \tag{7}$$

3   Experiments and Results

In total, 35 optical satellite images are selected as test data from different oil depots on Google Earth. Two of them are shown In Fig. 5. These 35 images totally contain 729 flat crest tanks and 894 cone-shaped crest tanks.

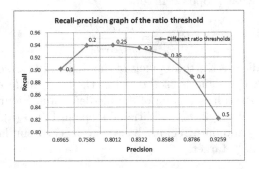

Fig. 4. Recall-precision graph of the ratio threshold in candidate selection. The ratio indicates proportion that aligned pixels occupy in total pixels of a ring.

The optimization method in [6] used to filter out false alarms suggested a threshold of 0.4. Through experiment shown in Fig. 4, 0.3 is selected as our threshold. Eventually 2 flat crest tanks and 97 cone-shaped crest tanks are

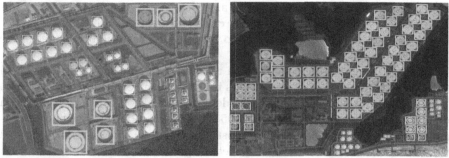

(a) Ground truth. The left one is 1047 × 743 and the right one is 1628 × 1370. The flat crest tanks are marked with thick boxes and the cone-shaped crest tanks are marked with thin boxes.

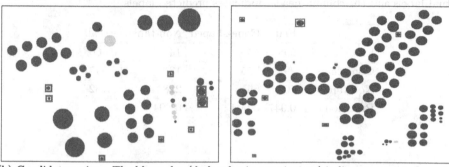

(b) Candidate regions. The blue color (dark color in gray images) indicates extracted candidate regions and the yellow color (light color in gray images) indicates that they are missed. The boxes mark the false alarms.

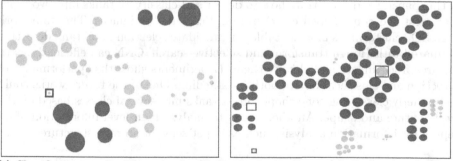

(c) Classification results. The red color (dark color in gray images) indicates that they are predicted to be flat crest and the yellow color (light color in gray images) indicates that they are predicted to be cone-shaped crest. The boxes mark the failure cases.

Fig. 5. Figure (b) shows the final candidate regions extracted from figure (a) and figure (c) shows the classification results of figure (b).

missed. The Fig. 5 (b) shows the final candidate regions extracted from Fig. 5 (a). The reasons for missed detection are mainly the appearance of corrosion and poor imaging conditions. Besides, the scales and shapes of cone-shaped crest tanks can be quite different. Both the smaller cross sectional area and short distance between small tanks make them easier to be missed. These factors challenge the process of classification too.

The Fig. 5 (c) shows the classification results. The confusion matrix (Table 2) shows the performance of flat crest tanks is better than cone-shaped crest tanks. It proves what we analyze before. For detection of all oil tanks, the precision and recall are respectively 0.924 and 0.953. It seems a poor performance in distinguishing the background, because most of the false alarms have been filtered out and produce a very small test dataset of non-tanks.

Table 2. Confusion matrix obtained from this experiment. The row header indicates actual labels and the column header indicates predicted labels.

	Flat	Cone-shaped	Non-tanks	Recall
Flat	698	15	14	0.960
Cone-shaped	29	755	13	0.947
Non-tanks	10	65	228	0.752
Precision	0.947	0.904	0.894	

4   Conclusion

In this paper, we demonstrate how to detect and classify oil tanks into two types (flat crest and cone-shaped crest) from optical satellite images. The framework of ELSD+clustering is more suitable for candidate selection in oil tank detection compared with Hough transform and selective-search. CNN can efficiently learn features from images and classify them. Experiments show that performance of detection and classification are both outstanding. One of the future works could be furtherly classifying cone-shaped crest tanks into several classes based on the crest texture and shape. Another one is to analyze high level information of oil depots for information analysis, such as depot scale or storage structure of oil.

References

1. Zhang, W., Zhang, H., Wang, C., Wu, T.: Automatic oil tank detection algorithm based on remote sensing image fusion. In: IEEE IGARSS, vol. 6, pp. 3956–3958. IEEE (2005)
2. Duda, R.O., Hart, P.E.: Use of the hough transformation to detect lines and curves in pictures. Comm. ACM **15**(1), 11–15 (1972). ACM

3. Xu, H., Chen, W., Sun, B., et al.: Oil tank detection in synthetic aperture radar images based on Quasi-circular shadow and highlighting arcs. J. Appl. Remote Sens. **8**(2), 397–398 (2014). SPIE
4. Ok, A.O., Baseski, E.: Circular oil tank detection from panchromatic satellite images: a new automated approach. IEEE Geosci. Remote Sens. Lett. **12**(6), 1347–1351 (2015). IEEE
5. Zhao, W., Yang, H., Shen, Z., Luo, J.: Oil tanks extraction from high resolution imagery using a directional and weighted hough voting method. J. Indian Soc. Remote **43**(3), 539–549 (2015). Springer India
6. Zhang, L., Shi, Z., Wu, J.: a hierarchical oil tank detector with deep surrounding features for high-resolution optical satellite imagery. IEEE J-STARS **8**(10), 4895–4909 (2015). IEEE
7. Ptrucean, V., Gurdjos, P., von Gioi, R.G.: A parameterless line segment and elliptical arc detector with enhanced ellipse fitting. In: Fitzgibbon, A., Lazebnik, S., Perona, P., Sato, Y., Schmid, C. (eds.) ECCV 2012, Part II. LNCS, vol. 7573, pp. 572–585. Springer, Heidelberg (2012)
8. Krizhevsky, A., Sutskever, I., Hinton, G.E.: ImageNet classification with deep convolutional neural networks. In: NIPS, vol. 25, pp. 1097–1105. NIPS (2012)
9. Salberg, A.-B.: Detection of seals in remote sensing images using features extracted from deep convolutional neural networks. In: IEEE IGARSS, pp. 1893–1896. IEEE (2015)
10. Krizhevsky, A.: Convolutional Deep Belief Networks on CIFAR-10. Univ. of Toronto, Technical report (2010)
11. Uijlings, J., van de Sande, K., Gevers, T., Smeulders, A.: Selective search for object recognition. IJCV **104**(2), 154–171 (2013). Springer, US

Watermarking, Authentication and Coding

Digital Watermarking Scheme Based on Arnold and Anti-Arnold Transforms

M. Abdallah Elayan$^{(\boxtimes)}$ and M. Omair Ahmad

Department of Electrical and Computer Engineering,
Concordia University, Montreal, Canada
{a_alayan,omair}@ece.concordia.ca

Abstract. The goal of an image watermarking scheme is to embed a watermark that is robust against various types of attacks while preserving the perceptual quality of the cover image. In this paper, a discrete cosine transform and singular value decomposition based digital image watermarking scheme that makes use of Arnold transform is proposed. The basic idea behind the proposed Arnold transform based watermarking scheme is to improve the robustness of the watermarked image, while providing complete security to the embedded watermark. The new scheme is shown to retain the perceptibility of the cover image in the watermarked image due to the discrete cosine transform and singular value decomposition based watermark embedding. Extensive experiments are performed to demonstrate the performance of the proposed scheme in providing security to the watermark content, preserving the perceptibility of the cover image and in being robust against various types of attacks on the watermarked image.

Keywords: Digital watermarking · Discrete Cosine Transform (DCT) · Singular Value Decomposition (SVD) · Arnold transform

1 Introduction

With the rapid development of multimedia, it has become easy to obtain the intellectual properties. Consequently, the multimedia owners need more than ever before to protect their data and to prevent the unauthorized use of their data. Digital watermarking has attracted considerable attention and has several applications including copyright protection and fingerprinting of the multimedia for tracing and data authentication [1,2].

According to the embedding domain, watermarking schemes can be categorized into two groups, spatial domain schemes and transform domain schemes. The schemes in the first category have the advantages of low complexity and easy implementation. However, these schemes generally lack the robustness against

---

This work was supported in part by the Natural Sciences and Engineering Research Council (NSERC) of Canada and in part by the Regroupement Strategique en Microelectronique du Quebec (ReSMiQ).

A. Mansouri et al. (Eds.): ICISP 2016, LNCS 9680, pp. 317–327, 2016.
DOI: 10.1007/978-3-319-33618-3_32

lossy image compression. On the other hand, a more robust watermarking can be achieved by the schemes in the second category by embedding the watermark into the transform coefficients of the host multimedia. In an effort to further improve the robustness of these transform domain schemes, in recent years, a number of watermarking schemes have been developed using singular value decomposition in the transform domain [3–7]. A feature of the singular value decomposition pertinent to digital watermarking is that the singular values of an image do not change significantly when common image processing attacks are performed on an image, and thus yields a more robust watermarking.

In [3], the authors have proposed a watermarking scheme based on DCT and SVD, where the watermark image is embedded into the singular value decomposition matrix of the DC values of the transformed cover image. This scheme provides a good robustness against general processing attacks while providing good imperceptibility, but the scheme lacks robustness against other attacks such as, contrast adjustment, rotation and cropping. In 2010, Lai and Tsai [4] proposed a watermarking scheme based on DWT and SVD. The watermark image is divided into two parts and embedded by modifying the singular values of the middle sub-bands of the one-level decomposed cover image. The proposed scheme has a good robustness against some kinds of attacks such as JPEG compression, rescaling and histogram equalization, but not so against other types of attacks such as, noise corruption or rotation. In [6], a DCT-SVD based watermarking scheme has been proposed, where the watermark image is embedded by modifying the singular values of each sub-band of the DCT coefficients by making use of the singular values of the watermark image. The proposed algorithm has a good resistant against general image processing attacks such as, noise corruption, contrast adjustment, and brightening adjustment, but lack the robustness against attacks such as, rotation, histogram equalization and translation. In [7], the authors have proposed a watermarking scheme based on DWT-SVD using Arnold transform. In this scheme, a watermark image is embedded into the low sub-band of the one-level decomposed cover image. The proposed scheme provides a good robustness against rotation, rescaling and contrast adjustment attacks, but not so against other types of attacks such as, gamma correction, histogram equalization and cropping. In general, the main limitation of the watermarking schemes described in [3–7] is that they, in general, are not robust against the different types of attacks.

In this paper, a DCT-SVD based digital image watermarking scheme that makes use of Arnold transform is developed with a view to providing improved robustness against different types of attacks while preserving the perceptual quality of the cover image. The paper is organized as follows. In Sect. 2, image scrambling are briefly reviewed. In Sect. 3, a new DCT-SVD based digital image watermarking scheme that makes use of the Arnold transform is proposed. In Sect. 4, experimental results demonstrating the performance of the proposed algorithm are presented. The performance of the proposed algorithm is also compared with those of other existing algorithms in this section. Finally, Sect. 5 concludes this paper by summarizing and highlighting the salient contributions of this work.

2 Background

2.1 Image Scrambling

Image scrambling process is an important image encryption technique that has been used in digital image watermarking. The objective of digital image scrambling is to transform a meaningful image into unintelligible image that prevents unauthorized users from understanding its true content. Without the knowledge of the image scrambling algorithm and the secret key, an unauthorized user (attacker) would not be able to recover the original watermark, even if it has been extracted from the watermarked data. Thus, scrambling provides an additional security for the digital data. Furthermore, since scrambling of an image, eliminates the spatial correlation of its pixels, the robustness of a watermarking scheme can be further improved.

Arnold Transform. The Arnold transform was introduced by Arnold [8]. For an image C with $N \times N$ pixels, the Arnold transform operation on the position (x, y) pixel is given by

$$\begin{pmatrix} x' \\ y' \end{pmatrix} = \begin{pmatrix} 1 & 1 \\ 1 & 2 \end{pmatrix} \begin{pmatrix} x \\ y \end{pmatrix} \, mod N \tag{1}$$

The Arnold transform, which changes the positions of the pixels, can be repeated many times in order to obtain a scrambled image. However, due to the periodicity of the Arnold transformation, the original image can be restored after a certain number of iterations. Dyson and Falk [9] have studied the properties of the Arnold transform and pointed out that the transform given by (1) has a period $T_N \le N^2/2$, for $N > 2$.

Anti-Arnold Transform. Use of the Arnold transform periodicity on a scrambled image to recover the original image could be achieved at the expense of possibly a large computational complexity depending on how many iterations have already been used to obtain the scrambled image. For this reason the authors in [10] have obtained the anti-Arnold transform. The anti-Arnold transform is given by

$$\begin{pmatrix} x \\ y \end{pmatrix} = \begin{pmatrix} 2 & -1 \\ -1 & 1 \end{pmatrix} \begin{pmatrix} x' \\ y' \end{pmatrix} \, mod N \tag{2}$$

If a scrambled image is obtained by using n iterations of the operation of the Arnold transform, it needs the same number of iterations to recover the original image using the anti-Arnold transform. Therefore, the use of anti-Arnold transform to recover the original image can provide significant savings in computation, if $n \ll T_N$, as depicted in Fig. 1.

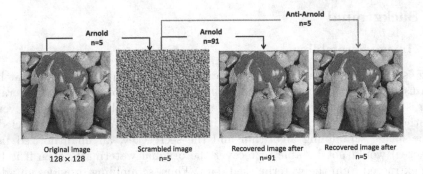

Fig. 1. Arnold and Anti-Arnold transforms.

3   Proposed Watermarking Scheme

3.1   Watermark Embedding Scheme

The discrete cosine transform is first applied to an $M \times M$ cover image, c. Next, the entire array of the DCT coefficients are zig-zag scanned, then the scanned coefficients are mapped in a zig-zag manner into the subbands B_1, B_2, B_3 and B_4 starting from the subband B_1, and ending with the subband B_4, as depicted in Fig. 2. Then, each subband is individually made to undergo an SVD operation. Next, an $N \times N$ $(2N \leq M)$ watermark image is scrambled by applying r iterations of the Arnold transform. The number of iterations r is saved as a secret key, to be used during the extraction process to recover the original watermark image. The singular value matrix of each subband is then modified by adding to this matrix the scrambled watermark image. The resulting subband image $S_k + \alpha W'$ $(k = 1, 2, \ldots, 4)$ is singular value decomposed to obtain the singular value matrix S^*_{wk} of the watermarked subband. The subband watermarked DCT coefficients are obtained by augmenting S^*_{wk} with U_k and V_k as $B^*_k = U_k S^*_{wk} V^T_k$. Finally, the modified DCT coefficients are mapped back to their original positions, followed by an inverse discrete cosine transform operation to obtain the watermarked image. The proposed watermark embedding scheme is presented as Algorithm 1.

Algorithm 1. Watermark embedding algorithm

Step 1 Apply the discrete cosine transform to the cover image, c.

Step 2 Rearrange the 2-D DCT coefficients into four subbands: B_1, B_2, B_3 and B_4, through a zig-zag scanning of the DCT coefficients.

Step 3 Perform SVD operation to each subband: $B_k = U_k S_k V^T_k$ $(k = 1, 2, \ldots, 4)$.

Step 4 Apply r iterations of the Arnold transform on the watermark image W to obtain scrambled watermark image W'.

Step 5 Modify the singular value matrices S_k corresponding to each subband through a watermark embedding as $S_k + \alpha W'$, where α is a scaling factor.

Step 6 Perform the SVD operation on the embedded subband singular value matrices $S_k + \alpha W'$ as $S_k + \alpha W' = U_{wk} S^*_{wk} V^T_{wk}$.

Step 7 Augment the singular value matrix S^*_{wk} with U_k and V_k to obtain the watermarked DCT coefficients as $B^*_k = U_k S^*_{wk} V^T_k$.

Step 8 Map the watermarked DCT coefficients of the subbands back to their original positions.

Step 9 Apply the inverse discrete cosine transform to obtain the watermarked image, c_w.

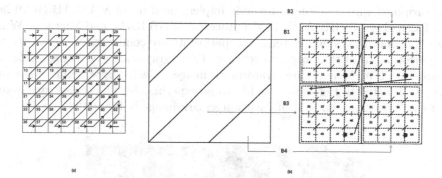

Fig. 2. (a) Zig-zag scanning of the 2-D discrete cosine transform coefficients. (b) Mapping of the scanned DCT coefficients into four subbands.

3.2   Watermark Extraction Scheme

The discrete cosine transform operation is applied to the watermarked image c_w, possibly after attack, followed by a re-arranging of the DCT coefficients into four subbands B_{w1}, B_{w2}, B_{w3} and B_{w4} through a zig-zag scanning of the coefficients. Then, each subband is individually made to undergo an SVD operation. Next, the singular value matrix of each subband S'_{wk} is augmented with U_{wk} and V^T_{wk} to obtain $D'_k = U_{wk} S'_{wk} V^T_{wk}$ $(k = 1, 2, \ldots, 4)$. A scrambled watermark image is extracted from each subband as $W'^*_k = (D'_k - S_k)/\alpha$, followed by an application of r iterations of the anti-Arnold transform to obtain the original watermark image. It should be noted that the number of iterations r of the anti-Arnold transform is used as a secret key during the extraction process. The proposed watermark extraction scheme is summarized as Algorithm 2.

Algorithm 2. Watermark extraction algorithm

Step 1 Apply the discrete cosine transform to the watermarked image, c_w.

Step 2 Rearrange the 2-D DCT coefficients into four subbands: B_{w1}, B_{w2}, B_{w3} and B_{w4}, through a zig-zag scanning of the DCT coefficients.

Step 3 Perform SVD operation to each subband: $B_{wk} = U'_{wk} S'_{wk} V'^T_{wk}$ $(k = 1, 2, \ldots, 4)$.

Step 4 Augment S'_{wk} with U_{wk} and V^T_{wk} to obtain $D'_k = U_{wk}S'_{wk}V^T_{wk}$, where U_{wk} and V_{wk}, are as obtained in Step 6 of Algorithm 1.

Step 5 Extract the scrambled watermark image from each subband as $W'^*_k = (D'_k - S_k)/\alpha$.

Step 6 Apply r iterations of the anti-Arnold transform on the scrambled watermark image W'^*_k to obtain the watermark image W^*_k.

4 Experimental Results and Discussion

The proposed watermarking scheme is implemented using MATLAB (R2012a) on a PC with a 1.6-GHz AMD E-350 processor, 3-GB RAM, and Microsoft Windows 7 operating system. Extensive experiments are conducted to demonstrate the performance of the proposed scheme. Three gray-scale cover images, *Lena*, *Pirate*, and *Couple*, and three watermark images, *Boat*, *Peppers*, and *Cameraman*, as depicted in Fig. 3, are used in these experiments. The size of each cover image is 256 × 256 and that of each watermark image is 128 × 128.

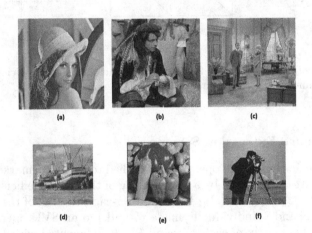

Fig. 3. Cover images: (a) *Lena*, (b) *Pirate*, and (c) *Couple*. Watermark images: (d) *Boat*, (e) *Peppers*, and (f) *Cameraman*.

Figure 4 shows an example of a watermarked image and the extracted watermark image obtained by applying the proposed watermarking scheme. It is seen from this figure that the embedded watermark dose not degrade the perceptual quality of the cover image, and the proposed scheme is able to extract the watermark images successfully from the un-attacked watermarked image.

For objective evaluation of the perceptual quality of watermarked image, the peak signal-to-noise ratio ($PSNR$) is used [11]. The $PSNR$ is given by

$$PSNR = 10\log_{10}\frac{MAX^2}{MSE} \qquad (3)$$

Fig. 4. (a) Cover image, *Lena*. (b) Watermark image, *Boat*. (c) Watermarked image. (d) The watermark image extracted from the watermarked image.

In general, a $PSNR$ value is higher than 30dB is considered to be an indication of good perceptual quality of the watermarked image [11]. Table 1 gives the $PSNR$ values of the various watermarked images obtained by using the proposed scheme. This table clearly indicates that the embedded watermark does not degrade the perceptual quality of the cover image, and thus the proposed embedding scheme guarantees the imperceptibility of the watermark.

Table 1. PSNR values (in dB) of various watermarked images

Cover image	Watermark image		
	Boat	Peppers	Cameraman
Lena	32	32.53	32.79
Couple	31.18	32.13	32.55
Pirate	31.67	32.38	32.83

To investigate the robustness of the proposed watermarking scheme, each watermarked image obtained by using the proposed watermark embedding scheme is subjected to different types of attacks. After each of these attacks, we extract four watermarks using the proposed watermark extraction scheme and then select the one having the largest normalized correlation coefficient between the extracted and the original watermark images. The normalized correlation (NC) between the original $N \times N$ watermark image W and the extracted watermark image W^* is given by

$$NC = \frac{\sum_{i=1}^{N}\sum_{j=1}^{N}(W_{ij})(W_{ij}^*)}{\sqrt{\sum_{i=1}^{N}\sum_{j=1}^{N}(W_{ij}^2)}\sqrt{\sum_{i=1}^{N}\sum_{j=1}^{N}(W_{ij}^{*2})}} \tag{4}$$

Figure 5 shows the watermarked *Lena* images, each subjected to one type of attack, and the watermark images extracted from the attacked images. It is seen from this figure that the proposed effectively resists different types of attacks and is able to extract the watermark images with high perceptual quality.

In order to provide an objective analysis of the robustness of the proposed scheme, the normalized correlation coefficient between the extracted and the

Fig. 5. Watermarked *Lena* image attacked by different types of attacks and the extracted watermark images.

original watermark images is computed. Table 2 gives the values of the correlation coefficient using the cover images, *Lena*, *Couple*, and *Pirate*, and the same watermark image, *Boat*. It is seen from this table that the values of the correlation coefficient are almost invariably larger than 0.9 for the various attacks regardless of the images used in the experiments.

We also implement the SVD based watermarking scheme of [5], the DCT-SVD based watermarking algorithm of [6], and the DWT-SVD based watermarking scheme of [7], in order to compare the performance of the proposed scheme with theirs in terms of the PSNR of the watermarked image measuring the imperceptibility of the watermark and the correlation coefficient measuring the robustness of the watermarking schemes. The performance comparison is given in Table 3. It is seen from this table that the proposed watermarking scheme preserves the perceptual quality of the cover image, and provides an improved robustness against various types of attacks. Thus, the proposed scheme outperforms the other three algorithms used for comparison.

Table 2. Values of the correlation coefficient between the extracted and original watermark images

Attack	Cover image		
	Pirate	Couple	Lena
Rotation 2	0.9643	0.9489	0.9381
JPEG compression (Q = 10)	0.9974	0.9992	0.9993
Histogram Equalization	0.9665	0.9359	0.9371
Gaussian Noise ($\sigma^2 = 0.3$)	0.9870	0.9892	0.9875
Re-scaling (256-128-256)	0.9862	0.9831	0.9955
Contrast adjustment (-20%)	0.9886	0.9956	0.9841
Sharpening (80 %)	0.8137	0.9078	0.8315
Gamma correction ($\gamma = 0.6$)	0.9937	0.9997	0.9998
Cropping (left and right sides by 25 columns)	0.9947	0.9970	0.9998
Blurring (using Gaussian filter)	0.9207	0.9284	0.9530
Median filter (3×3)	0.9805	0.9754	0.9909
Brightening (70 %)	0.9991	0.9994	0.9990
Darkening (70 %)	0.9800	0.9960	0.9979
Contrast adjustment ($+20\%$)	0.9705	0.9939	0.9871

Table 3. Performance, in terms of PSNR and normalized correlation coefficient, of the proposed and three other watermarking schemes against various types of attacks (Cover Image: *Lena*, Watermark Image: *Boat*)

Scheme	Proposed scheme	[5]	[6]	[7]
PSNR	**32**	28.31	24	24.26
	NC			
Rotation 2	**0.9381**	0.8864	0.8157	0.9292
JPEG compression (Q = 10)	0.9993	0.9881	0.9998	0.9981
Histogram Equalization	**0.9371**	0.9316	0.7492	0.5983
Gaussian Noise ($\sigma^2 = 0.3$)	**0.9875**	0.9441	0.9853	0.9767
Re-scaling (256-128-256)	0.9955	0.9785	0.9964	0.9928
Contrast adjustment (-20%)	**0.9841**	0.9626	0.9504	0.9006
Sharpening (80 %)	**0.8315**	0.7449	0.7898	0.8105
Gamma correction ($\gamma = 0.6$)	**0.9998**	0.5960	0.9460	-0.7115
Cropping (left and right sides by 25 columns)	**0.9998**	0.8256	0.9969	0.0155
Blurring (using Gaussian filter)	**0.9530**	0.9501	0.9521	0.9350
Translation (20,20)	**0.9955**	0.9024	0.7101	0.8693
Brightening (70 %)	**0.9990**	0.3524	0.9678	0.9408
Darkening (70 %)	**0.9979**	0.3351	0.9927	-0.9287
Contrast adjustment ($+20\%$)	**0.9871**	0.9742	0.9816	0.9550

Table 4. Execution times of running the proposed and two other watermarking schemes

Watermark embedding/extraction	Execution time in seconds		
	Proposed Scheme	[6]	[7]
Embedding	2.145	2.061	2.848
Extraction	0.339	0.327	0.585

Table 4 gives the execution times of running the proposed watermarking algorithms and that of running the schemes developed in [6,7]. A comparison of the proposed scheme with the scheme of [6] indicates that the use of the Arnold and anti-Arnold transforms for the embedding and extraction of the watermark in the proposed scheme does not add to its computation time. However, the data scrambling using the Arnold transform in the proposed scheme significantly improves its robustness. It is also seen from this table that the proposed scheme provides savings of 24.7 % and 42 % in the execution times of its embedding and extraction parts, respectively, over those of the scheme of [7] that also uses the Arnold transform.

5   Conclusion

In this paper, a DCT-SVD based watermarking scheme, in which the watermark image is embedded using the approach of Arnold transform has been proposed. The DCT coefficients of the cover image are zig-zag scanned and mapped in a zig-zag manner into four subbands. The watermark image is scrambled using the operation of the Arnold transform, and then embedded into the singular value matrices of the four subbands of the array of the re-arranged DCT coefficients.

Extensive experiments have been conducted to evaluate the performance of the proposed scheme. The results of the experiments have demonstrated that the proposed embedding scheme ensures the imperceptibility of the watermark and that the embedded watermark does not degrade the perceptual quality of the cover image. The performance of the proposed scheme has also been compared with three other watermarking schemes. The results of comparison have demonstrated that the proposed watermarking scheme yields a performance superior to that of the other three schemes in preserving the perceptual quality of the cover image, and in providing an improved robustness against various types of attacks.

References

1. Zebbiche, K., Khelifi, F.: Efficient wavelet-based perceptual watermark masking for robust fingerprint image watermarking. IET Image Proc. **8**(1), 23–32 (2014)
2. Li, Z., Ping-ping, Z., Gong-bin, Q., Zhen, J.: Image watermarking with optimum capacity. In: 5th International Conference on Visual Information Engineering, pp. 117–123 (2008)

3. Liu, F., Liu, Y.: A watermarking algorithm for digital image based on DCT and SVD. In: Proceedings of Conference on Image and Signal Processing, vol. 1, pp. 380–383 (2008)
4. Lai, C.C., Tsai, C.C.: Digital image watermarking using discrete wavelet transform and singular value decomposition. IEEE Trans. Instrum. Meas. **59**(11), 3060–3063 (2010)
5. Liu, R., Tan, T.: A SVD-based watermarking scheme for protecting rightful ownership. IEEE Trans. Multi. **4**(1), 121–128 (2002)
6. Gupta, P.K., Shrivastava, S.K.: Improved RST-Attacks resilient image watermarking based on joint SVD-DCT. In: Proceedings of International Conference on Computer and Communication Technology, Allahabad, India, pp. 46–51 (2010)
7. Sushila, K., Maheshkar, V., Agarwal, S., Srivastava, K.: DWT-SVD based robust image watermarking using Arnold map. Int. J. Inf. Technol. **5**(1), 101–105 (2012)
8. Arnold, V., Avez, A.: Ergodic Problems in Classical Mechanics. Benjamin, New York (1968)
9. Dyson, F.J., Falk, H.: Period of a discrete cat mapping. Amer. Math. Mon. **99**, 603–624 (1992)
10. Wu, L., Zhang, J., Deng, W., He, D.: Arnold transformation algorithm and anti-arnold transformation algorithm. In: Proceedings of the Information Science and Engineering International Conference, Nanjing, China, pp. 1164–1167 (2009)
11. Chang, C.C., Lin, C.C., Hu, Y.S.: An SVD oriented watermark embedding scheme with high qualities for the resorted images. Int. J. Innovative Comput. Inf. Control **3**, 609–620 (2007)

A JND Model Using a Texture-Edge Selector Based on Faber-Schauder Wavelet Lifting Scheme

Meina Amar[1,2]([⊠]), Rachid Harba[2], Hassan Douzi[1], Frederic Ros[2],
Mohamed El Hajji[1], Rabia Riad[1,2], and Khadija Gourrame[1]

[1] IRF-SIC Laboratory, Ibn Zohr University, BP 8106,
Cit Dakhla, 80000 Agadir, Morocco
`amar.meina@edu.uiz.ac.ma`
[2] PRISME Laboratory, University of Orlans, 12 Rue de Blois,
45067 Orleans, France

Abstract. Modeling the human visual system has become an important issue in image processing such as compression, evaluation of image quality and digital watermarking. In this paper we present a spatial JND (Just Noticeable-Difference-) model that uses a texture selector based on Faber-Schauder wavelets lifting scheme. This texture selector identify non-uniform and uniform areas. That allows to choose between JNDs models developed by Chou and Qi. The chosen JND will determine the value of the embedding strength in each pixel, related to the identified region. Results show that by this process, we can generally ameliorate the visual quality with the same robustness.

Keywords: Perceptual models · Human Visual System · Digital watermarking · Wavelet · Lifting schemes · JND

1 Introduction

Digital watermarking is an efficient alternative to guarantee safety of multimedia document [1]. The most important in a digital watermark is to solve the trade-off between invisibility, robustness and the capacity for insertion of the watermark [2,3]. To improve the robustness we can increase the embedding strength but this degrade the invisibility of the mark, and vise-versa. If we ameliorate the image quality after watermarking we may lose the robustness of the mark.

To ameliorate at the same time image quality and robustness we can take into account the properties of the Human Visual System (HVS) [4] by developing perceptual models; HVS modeling has become an important issue in the image processing [5,6]. Models based on the HVS determine the maximum quantity that can be added to each pixel without affecting the visual quality of the image. Barni [7] summarized the observations and experiments on the HVS into the following three rules: First degradation are much less visible in highly textured

© Springer International Publishing Switzerland 2016
A. Mansouri et al. (Eds.): ICISP 2016, LNCS 9680, pp. 328–336, 2016.
DOI: 10.1007/978-3-319-33618-3_33

areas than in uniform ones. Second contours are more sensitive to noise addition than textured regions but less sensitive than the uniform regions. Finally degradation are less visible in dark areas than in bright ones.

Digital watermarking is composed of two steps: insertion of the mark in a digital document and detection of the presence of the watermark or its extraction [1,8]. In psychophysical studies, a level of distortion that can be just seen in experimental tests is called JND (just noticeable difference) [1] and is used to determine the invisibility threshold [9]. This allows to adjust the embedding strength, optimally and adaptively with respect to areas of the image. The principle of digital watermarking using JND in spatial domain can be described by the following expression:

$$I_w(x,y) = I_o(x,y) + JND(x,y) * W(x,y) \tag{1}$$

where I_w is the watermarked image, I_o original image, W is a pseudo-random sequence represented the insertion watermark and JND is the parameter strength of the mark that controls the trade-off between visibility and robustness of the watermark.

In the literature, several JND models have been proposed for images [4,10,14]. Here we quote some important models that are designed in different domains, namely the spatial domain and transform domain.

In [10] Chou and Li proposed a spatial domain JND model for compression. This model takes into account the luminance adaptation and texture masking. The JND is defined as the dominant effect between the texture masking and luminance adaptation. In [11] Yang et al. and in [4] Qi et al. ameliorate the texture masking of Chou and Lis JND. One of the first JND model in Discrete Cosine Transform (DCT) domain was developed by Watson et al. [12] for compression. This model estimates the perceptibility changes in each image DCT block. Finally Nguyen et al. [13] proposed JND models in Discreet Wavelet Transform (DWT) domain.

In this paper we propose a JND that combines both JNDs introduced by Qi and Chou and we introduce a texture selector between non-uniform and uniform area. In the case of no textured area we will use luminance masking developed by Chou and Li. Otherwise we use texture masking developed by Qi et al.

The texture selector is based on Faber-Schauder wavelet coefficient. The wavelet coefficient are represented in a mixed scales way. The density of blocs of dominant wavelet coefficient gives an efficient method to select textural region in image [14]. We test the proposed method on several images and we show that the use of texture selector ameliorate the image quality with the same robustness of the watermark compared to method developed by Chou et al. and Qi et al.

This paper is organized as follows. Section 2 presents the JND of Chou and Li and Qi et al. In Sect. 3 we present our watermarking method with JND using Faber-Schauder lifting schemes. In Sect. 4 we present the results obtained for the evaluation of visual quality and robustness on several natural images. Finally in Sect. 5, we end with conclusion and perspectives.

2   Perceptual Models Proposed by Chou and Li and Qi et al.

2.1   Luminance Masking of Chou and Li

A luminance masking has been proposed by Chou and Li [10] wherein the luminance threshold due to the luminance of the background is given by the luminance masking JNDL (x, y). The relationship between noise sensitivity and background luminance is controlled by a subjective test. Thus JNDL (x, y) can be determined by modeling the curve obtained by experiments (Fig. 1-a). Figure 1-b shows an example of luminance masking.

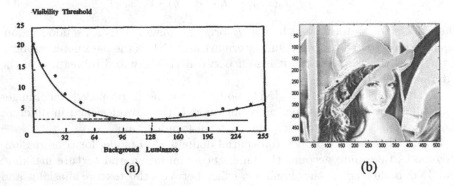

(a)   (b)

Fig. 1. (a) Visibility threshold relatively to background luminance modeled by Chou [10]. (b) Luminance masking JNDL(x,y) (with inversed color) obtained for Lena image. Black parts in the masking correspond to high watermark embedding strength.

Computing the luminance masking is the following for 8-bits gray scale images.

$$JND_L(x,y) = \begin{cases} 17\left(1 - \left(\frac{b_g(x,y)}{127}\right)^{\frac{1}{2}}\right) + 3 & \text{for } b_g \leq 127 \\ \frac{3}{128}(b_g(x,y) - 127) + 3 & \text{for } b_g \geq 127 \end{cases} \quad (2)$$

$$b_g(x,y) = \frac{1}{32}\sum_{i=1}^{5}\sum_{j=1}^{5} I_o(x-3+i, y-3+j).B(x,y), \quad B(i,j) = \begin{bmatrix} 1 & 1 & 1 & 1 & 1 \\ 1 & 2 & 2 & 2 & 1 \\ 1 & 2 & 0 & 2 & 1 \\ 1 & 2 & 2 & 2 & 1 \\ 1 & 1 & 1 & 1 & 1 \end{bmatrix}$$

where $0 \leq x < H, 0 \leq y < W$. H and W denote respectively the height and width of the image I_o. $b_g(x,y)$ is the average luminance of the background calculated using an averaging filter B.

(a)   **(b)**   **(c)**

Fig. 2. (a) Lena image. (b) Texture masking $JND_T(I_o)$ with sliding windows 3×3. (c) Edge masking $JND_L(I_o)$

2.2   Texture and Edge Masking of Qi et al.

For texture masking we use the one proposed by Qi et al. [4]. The texture masking (Fig. 2-b) uses the absolute value of the distance between each pixel and local average value of the pixels within a sliding window LxL, Eq. (4)

$$JND_T(I_o) - |I_o(i,j) - \bar{I}_o(i,j)| \qquad (3)$$

$$\bar{I}_o(i,j) = \frac{1}{(2L+1)^2} \sum_{k=-L}^{L} \sum_{l=-L}^{L} I_o(i+k, j+l)$$

where JND_T is the texture masking, $I_o(i,j)$ is the pixel at the position (i,j), $(2L+1)^2$ represents the number of pixels in the sliding window.

We also consider the edge masking proposed by Qi et al. [4] Fig. 3-c which is a Laplacien filter.

$$JND_E = L(I_o) \qquad (4)$$

3   Proposed Method Based on Lifting Schemes and Using Chou-Qi JND

In order to take advantage of the perceptual models developed by Chou et al. and Qi et al. we propose to introduce an additional performant texture selector which distinguishes between uniform area, textured area and edge area. The fact that the texture selector is based on Faber-Schauder wavelet lifting scheme and the use of an original mixed scale representation of the wavelets coefficients, make the selection between JNDs more efficient. The next scheme represent the proposed perceptual mask (Fig. 3):

3.1   Texture Selector Based on Faber-Schauder Lifting Schemes

The Faber-Schauder wavelet transform (FSWT) and inverse transform (IFSWT) can be giving by the lifting scheme [15]:

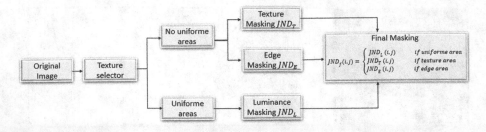

Fig. 3. Final masking, the texture selector uses Faber-Schauder wavelet lifting scheme.

$$FSDWT = \begin{cases} f_{ij}^0 = f_{ij} \text{ for } i,j \in Z \\ \qquad \text{ for } 1 \le k \le N \\ f_{ij} = f_{2i,2j}^{k-1} \\ g_{ij}^k = (g_{ij}^{k1}, g_{ij}^{k2}, g_{ij}^{k3}) \\ g_{ij}^{k1} = f_{2i+1,2j}^{k-1} - \frac{1}{2}(f_{2i,2j}^{k-1} + f_{2i+2,2j}^{k-1}) \\ g_{ij}^{k2} = f_{2i,2j+1}^{k-1} - \frac{1}{2}(f_{2i,2j}^{k-1} + f_{2i+2,2j+2}^{k-1}) \\ g_{ij}^{k3} = f_{2i+1,2j+1}^{k-1} - \frac{1}{4}(f_{2i,2j}^{k-1} + f_{2i,2j+2}^{k-1} + f_{2i+2,2j}^{k-1} + f_{2i+2,2j+2}^{k-1}) \end{cases}$$

$$IFSDWT = \begin{cases} \qquad \text{ for } 0 \le k \le N-1 \, i,j \in Z \\ f_{2i,2j}^k = f_{ij}^k \\ f_{2i+1,2j}^k = g_{ij}^{k+1,1} + \frac{1}{2}(f_{i,j}^{k+11} + f_{i+1,j}^{k+1}) \\ f_{2i,2j+1}^k = g_{ij}^{k+1,2} + \frac{1}{2}(f_{i,j}^{k+1} + f_{i,j+1}^{k+1}) \\ f_{2i+1,2j+1}^k = g_{ij}^{k+1,3} + \frac{1}{4}(f_{i,j}^{k+1} + f_{i+1,j}^{k+1} + f_{i,j+1}^{k+1} + f_{i+1,j+1}^{k+1}) \end{cases}$$

where (f_{ij}^0) represent the image to transform, (f_{ij}^k) and (g_{ij}^k) represents approximation and details wavelet coefficient at scale k.

Usually a pyramidal representation is used to show the result of transformation, but here we privilege a mixed scale representation. In this representation each wavelet coefficient is at the place where its associated wavelet function is localized, so we have one transformed image (instead of pyramidal images) which can be considered as a good description of textural and edge areas in the image [14,15] (Fig. 4). Indeed we can distinguish areas that include edges and textured areas. These high activity regions correspond to a high density of absolute value wavelet coefficients.

The proposed approach is as follows: firstly we transform the image using Faber-Schauder wavelet transform. Then we select significant coefficient with absolute value exceeding a threshold Sc. Finally sliding windows centered on each pixel determine the density of such significant coefficient. The choice of parameter Sc as well as the sliding windows dimension can be adjusted manually or automatically [14]. As explained in [14] for low density we consider that the pixel belong to a uniform region, for medium density the pixel belong to a non-uniform region and maybe considered as an edge-region and for high density the pixel belong to a textured region (Fig. 5).

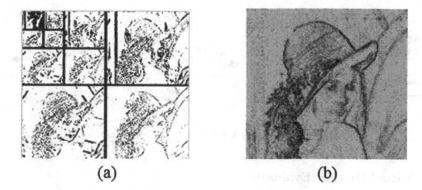

Fig. 4. (a) Pyramidal wavelet scale representation. (b) FSWT mixed-scale representation

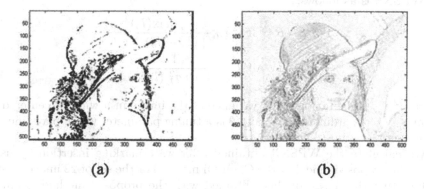

Fig. 5. (a) Texture selector using density of significant wavelet coefficient. (b) Inverted final masking using Chou and Qi models and the FSWT texture selector.

4   Watermarking Proposed Algorithm and Results

We evaluate the performances of the proposed JND model with mixed scale wavelet texture selector and we compare to those developed by Chou and Qi. We use a set of 22 natural images of variable textures and edges, for evaluation.

The watermarking system consists of three steps (Fig. 6): Firstly watermark embedding using perceptual models, second simulated attack are performed to test robustness of watermark and finally detection or extraction of watermark. In our method the watermark is inserted in spatial domain and coded according to a pseudo-random sequence of binary elements as in [16]. The image is divided into 8×8 [1] block and the watermark is embedded into each block. For the extraction of the watermark we calculate the linear correlation between the watermarked image and the coded watermark. Finally we test the visual quality of watermarked image and the robustness of the extraction by calculating respectively the Weighted Peak Signal-to-Noise Ratio (WPSNR) and the Bit-Error-Rate (BER).

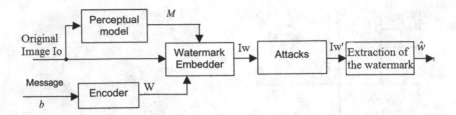

Fig. 6. Scheme of a watermarking system using perceptual models.

4.1   Visual Quality Evaluation

To measure the visual quality of watermarked images, we use the Weighted Peak Signal-to-Noise Ratio (WPSNR) proposed in [17]. For an 8-bit grayscale image, the WPSNR is as follows:

$$WPSNR = 10\log_{10}\frac{\max(I_o)^2}{\parallel (I_w - I_o).NVF \parallel^2} \tag{5}$$

$$\text{with}\quad NVF = \frac{1}{1 + \theta\sigma_{I_o}^2(i,j)}$$

where $\sigma_x^2(i,j)$ denotes the local variance of the image in a window centered on the pixel with coordinates (i,j) and θ is a tuning parameter which plays the role of the contrast adjustment.

We calculate the WPSNR obtained after watermarking insertion by using either the proposed model or the Chou-Qi model. For the set of 22 images tested we find that the image quality obtained with the proposed method is always better than that of Chou-Qi model (Fig. 7).

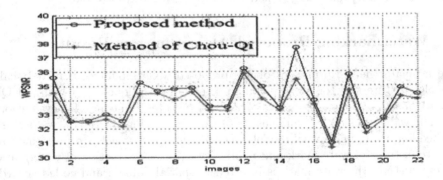

Fig. 7. Curve of WPSNR for 22 images

4.2   Robustness Evaluation

In order to test the robustness of the proposed method, we perform two type of simulated attacks, Pepper noise from 0.1 to 1, Jpeg compression from 80 % to

10 %. Figure 8 is the result for watermark detection. We use the BER to measure the rate of watermark extraction. For impulsive noise the proposed method is better. For Jpeg compression attack robustness of the other method is slightly better.

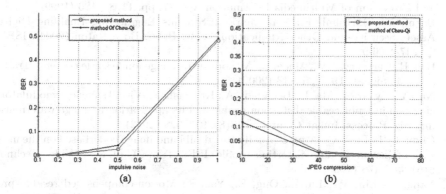

(a)   (b)

Fig. 8. BER curve of attacked watermarked image with different type of attack: (a) density of Impulsive noise. (b) Quality factor of JPEG compression

5   Conclusion and Perspectives

In this paper we propose a new spatial JND model that uses a texture selector based on Faber-Schauder wavelets lifting scheme. The choice of FSWT help us to distinguish very specific areas around the edges and around the textured areas of the image. We tested both the visual quality of our JND and the robustness of the watermark. We show that we can ameliorate the image quality. In order to ameliorate the robustness of the proposed method we project, for future works, to adapt our mixed scale wavelet transform to watermarking in DCT and DWT domain. We also Intend to improve our JND model by integrating other HVS mechanisms like the contrast sensitivity function (CSF). And also we project to do Psychophysical tests in our future work.

References

1. Cox, I.J., Miller, M., Bloom, J., Fridrich, J., Kalker, T.: Digital Watermarking and Steganography. Morgan Kaufmann, San Francisco (2007)
2. Tsai, H.H., Tseng, H.C., Lai, Y.S.: Robust lossless image watermarking based on trimmed mean algorithm and support vector machine. J. Syst. Softw. **83**(6), 1015–1028 (2010)
3. Li, L., Yuan, X., Lu, Z., Pan, J.S.: Rotation invariant watermark embedding based on scale adapted characteristic regions. Inf. Sci. **180**(15), 2875–2888 (2010)
4. Qi, H., Zheng, D., Zhao, J.: Human visual system based adaptive digital image watermarking. Sig. Process. **88**(1), 174–188 (2008)

5. Beghdadi, A., Larabi, M.C., Bouzerdoum, A., Iftekharuddin, K.M.: A survey of perceptual image processing methods. Sig. Proc. Image Commun. **28**(8), 811–831 (2013)
6. Wolfgang, R.B., Podilchuk, C.I., Delp, E.J.: Perceptual watermarks for digital images and video. In: Proceedings of the IEEE, Special Issue on Identification and Protection of Multimedia Information, vol. 87, pp. 1108–1126 (1999)
7. Barni, M., Bartolini, F.: Watermarking Systems Engineering Enabling Digital Assets Security and Other Applications. CRC Press, Boca Raton (2004). ISBN: 0-8247-4806-9
8. Bas, P., Chassery, J.M., Macq, B.: Mthode de tatouage fonde sur le contenu. Traitement du Signal. **19**(1), 11–18 (2002)
9. Niu, Y., Kyan, M., Ma, L., Beghdadi, A., Krishnan, S.: Visual saliencys modulatory effect on just noticeable distortion profile and its application in image watermarking. Sig. Process. Image Commun. **28**(8), 917–928 (2013)
10. Chou, C.H., Li, Y.C.: A perceptually tuned subband image coderbased on the measure of Just-noticeable-distortion profile. IEEE Trans. Circ. Syst. Video Technol. **5**(6), 467–476 (1995)
11. Yang, X., Lin, W., Lu, Z., Ong, E., Yao, S.: Motion-compensated residue preprocessing in video coding based on just-noticeable-distortion profile. IEEE Trans. Circuits Syst. Video Technol. **15**(6), 742–752 (2005)
12. Watson, A.B.: Dct quantization matricies visually optimized for individual images. In: Proceedings Of the SPIE Conference on Human Vision, Visual Processing and Digital Display IV, 1913, pp. 202–216, February 1993
13. Nguyen, P.B., Beghdadi, A., Luong, M.: Perceptual watermarking using a new Just-Noticeable-Difference model. Sig. Proc. Image Commun. **28**(10), 1506–1525 (2013)
14. El Hajji, M., Douzi, H., Harba, R., Mammass, D., Ros, F.: New image watermarking algorithm based on mixed scales wavelets. J. Electron. Imaging **21**(1), 1–7 (2012)
15. Douzi, H., Mammass, D., Nouboud, F.: Faber-Schauder wavelet transform, application to edge detection and image characterization. J. Math. Imag. Vis. **14**(2), 91–101 (2001)
16. Riad, R., Ros, F., Harba, R., Douzi, H., El Hajji, M.: Pre-processing the cover image before embedding improves the watermark detection rate. In: Second World Conference on Complex Systems (WCCS), pp. 705–709. IEEE (2014)
17. Voloshynovskiy, S., Herrigel, A., Baumgaertner, N., Pun, T.: A stochastic approach to content adaptive digital image watermarking. In: Pfitzmann, A. (ed.) IH 1999. LNCS, vol. 1768, pp. 211–236. Springer, Heidelberg (2000)

A Fragile Watermarking Scheme for Image Authentication Using Wavelet Transform

Assma Azeroual[(✉)] and Karim Afdel

Computer Systems and Vision Laboratory, Faculty of Science, 80000 Agadir, Morocco
a.azeroual.ma@ieee.org, k.afdel@uiz.ac.ma

Abstract. The modification of digital content becomes easier owing to the technology development. The need of authenticating digital content is increasing. Different fragile watermarking methods have been proposed for image authentication. In some applications low complexity algorithm is required, such as real-time and video processing applications. We propose in this paper, a fragile watermarking scheme for image authentication using Faber Schauder Discrete Wavelet Transform (FSDWT) and Singular Value decomposition (SVD) where the data to be embedded is a logo. The Watermark was generated by applying XOR operation between the logo's bits and the bits of dominant blocks singular values of the image to authenticate. These dominant blocks are obtained by applying FSDWT to that image. Any image modification will result in significant change of the dominant blocks singular values, which helps the watermarking scheme to detect the authenticity of the image. Furthermore, FSDWT is composed of simple operations, hence, the algorithm. has a low complexity.

Keywords: Image authentication · Fragile watermarking · Tamper detection · Mixed scales FSDWT · Singular value decomposition

1 Introduction

The most common way to defeat tampering is to embed a fragile watermark into the image in order to identify and localize any possible image alteration [2]. A fragile watermark is a category of the exact authentication and is simply a mark likely to become undetectable after a work is modified in any way [1], thus, it provides a way to verify the integrity of an image. Confidentiality and integrity are critical in many applications of imagery and require an exact authentication.

Many techniques of spatial and frequency domain exist for authentication using watermarking [3–7]. Byun et al. [8] proposed a Singular value decomposition (SVD) based fragile watermarking scheme for image authentication. The basic idea is to extract authenticating data from the original image. The singular values are converted to the binary bits using modular arithmetic. Taheri et al. [2] based on the idea of hierarchical watermarking partitioned the image into blocks in a multilevel hierarchy, at the highest level of hierarchy, the image is divided

© Springer International Publishing Switzerland 2016
A. Mansouri et al. (Eds.): ICISP 2016, LNCS 9680, pp. 337–345, 2016.
DOI: 10.1007/978-3-319-33618-3_34

into a set of blocks, the authentication data is then constructed by computing the singular values of each level's sub-block and then incorporate them into LSBs (Least Significant Bit) of a selected pixels within the block. Unfortunately, these methods require an important time of execution, hence they can't be used in applications that require low complexity like video authenticating, due to the huge number of images that compose the video. To solve this problem, this paper proposes a new method of fragile watermarking based on SVD and Faber Schauder Discrete Wavelet Transform (FSDWT), this method requires less time of execution, hence it can be used by applications requiring low complexity and can be applied to video authentication.

The proposed algorithm starts by determining the salient zones of the image where the watermark will be inserted, this is done by selecting the salient zones as the extracted contours and textured regions that are close to those contours (CT-Regions). The contours characterize uniquely the image, thus, any modification on the image will results in a modification of CT-Regions. To find these relevant zones of the image, FSDWT is used where the transform detects the CT-Regions by using the dominant blocks of the image. The operations used by this transform are simple and have a low complexity, which results in a fast algorithm. Then the singular values of the dominant blocks are computed using SVD and combined with a logo to watermark the image. As the singular values of an image are very sensitive to their dominant blocks, any modification in the image will dramatically modify the singular values of the dominant blocks, which will lead in a more fragile algorithm and ensure the authenticity of the image. The rest of the paper is organized as follows. Section 2 describes SVD and FSDWT. Section 3 describes details of the proposed method and Sect. 4 presents the experimental results and an analysis of computational complexity. The last section concludes the paper.

2   Background and Theory

2.1   SVD

The decomposition into singular values is based on a linear algebra theorem which states that any $m \times n$ matrix A with $m \geq n$ can be factored as:

$$A = USV^T \tag{1}$$

where U is an $m \times m$ orthogonal matrix, V^T is the transposed matrix of an $n \times n$ orthogonal matrix V, and S is an $m \times n$ matrix with singular values on the diagonal. The matrix S can be presented as:

$$S = \begin{bmatrix} \sigma_1 & 0 & \dots & 0 & 0 \\ 0 & \sigma_2 & \dots & 0 & 0 \\ \vdots & \vdots & & \vdots & \vdots \\ 0 & 0 & \dots & 0 & \sigma_n \\ 0 & 0 & \dots & 0 & 0 \end{bmatrix}, \tag{2}$$

and $\sigma_1 \geq \sigma_2 \geq ... \geq \sigma_n$ For $i = 1, 2, 3, ..., n$, σ_i are called singular values of the matrix A. There are many properties of SVD from the viewpoint of image processing applications:

- Variations on the singular spectrum and on the matrix A have exactly the same level [9].
- Singular values represent intrinsic algebraic image properties [10].
- Singular values represent the image energy, and we can approximate an image by only the first few terms.
- The first term of singular values will have the largest impact on approximating image, followed by the second term, then the third term, etc.

2.2   Faber Schauder Discrete Wavelet Transform

Wavelets have been found to be extremely useful in digital watermarking. They have a growing impact in signal and image processing, mainly due to multistage and time-frequency localization of the image and their good performance in decorrelating information [11]. FSDWT is a mixed scales representation of an integer wavelet transform [12] which is based on the Lifting Scheme [13] without any boundary treatment, an example of mixed scalars representation of an image (Fig. 1) is shown in Fig. 2. The lifting Scheme of the FSDWT [12] is given by the following algorithm:

$$\begin{cases} f^0 = f_{ij} \quad for \ i, j \in Z \\ for \quad 1 \leq k \leq N \\ f_{ij}^k = f_{2i,2j}^{k-1} \\ g_{ij}^k = (g_{ij}^{k1}, g_{ij}^{k2}, g_{ij}^{k3}) \\ g_{ij}^{k1} = f_{2i+1,2j}^{k-1} - \frac{1}{2}(f_{2i,2j}^{k-1} + f_{2i+2,2j}^{k-1}) \\ g_{ij}^{k2} = f_{2i,2j+1}^{k-1} - \frac{1}{2}(f_{2i,2j}^{k-1} + f_{2i+2,2j+2}^{k-1}) \\ g_{ij}^{k3} = f_{2i+1,2j+1}^{k-1} - \frac{1}{4}(f_{2i,2j}^{k-1} + f_{2i,2j+2}^{k-1} + f_{2i+2,2j}^{k-1} + f_{2i+2,2j+2}^{k-1}) \end{cases} \quad (3)$$

CT-Regions are efficiently detected by FSDWT. It redistributes the image contained information which is mostly carried in the dominant coefficients. To facilitate the selection of these dominant coefficients in all sub-bands, we use mixed-scales representation which puts each coefficient at the point where its related basis function reaches its maximum. Therefore, a coherent image can be visually obtained with edges and textured regions [14, 15] formed by dominant coefficients. These regions are represented by a high density of dominant coefficients. They present more stability for any transformation and keep visual characteristics of the image [16].

3   Proposed Method

3.1   Watermark Embedding Procedure

Our proposed method is inspired from the one used by Taheri et al. [2] and Byun et al. [8]. In the watermark embedding procedure, the LSB planes of dominant blocks are replaced with the watermark data which is a logo combined

Fig. 1. Original Image

Fig. 2. Mixed scales representation

Fig. 3. Dominant blocks using OTSU

with the dominant blocks singular values of the image to be marked. Singular values authenticating data are used since they are sensitive to any modification [8]. Furthermore, in our method the FSDWT gives good results in the term of perceptibility.

Dominant Blocks. We use the OTSU threshold [17] of mixed scales discrete wavelet transform coefficients with a given 4×4 block as the rule to detect dominant blocks. The dominant coefficient blocks are located on the image CT-Regions. The algorithm to detect dominant coefficients blocks involves the following steps:

- Step 1: compute the image FSDWT and divide the obtained matrix into 4×4 blocks.
- Step 2: calculate the local deviation σ of each block and compare it to the OTSU threshold α of the matrix obtained in the previous step. If $\sigma \geq \alpha$, then, the block is considered dominant, thus, this block contains a big density of coefficients which are related to image CT-Regions.

The original image used is the one presented in Fig. 1, then the Fig. 3 is obtained by assigning a gray color to the positions of the image's pixels corresponding to the dominant blocks using OTSU threshold. The Table 1 shows different images OTSU threshold.

Table 1. OTSU threshold for different images

Image	Cameraman	Boat	Crowd	House
OTSU threshold	4	10	7	6

3.2 Watermark Construction

The watermark embedding process is illustrated in Fig. 4 and is discussed below:

- Step 1: Convert the image to gray scale.

- Step 2: Compute the gray scale image dominant blocks.
- Step 3: Set P selected dominant blocks LSB's plan to 0.
- Step 4: Compute SVD of each new dominant block and convert the singular values of each block to 16 bits representation and gather all the obtained bits in a vector V_{sv}.
- Step 5: Convert each logo's pixel to 8 bits representation and gather the obtained bits in a vector V_{logo}.
- Step 6: Apply XOR operation between the bits of V_{logo} and the bits of V_{sv}, if the size of V_{logo} is smaller than the size of V_{sv} we use again the bits of V_{logo} to finish the rest of V_{sv} bits.
- Step 7: Substitute the LSB's plans of the image dominant blocks with the bits obtained in the step 6.
- Step 8: Compute the inverse of FSDWT to obtain the watermarked image.

We use 8 bits representation of the logo instead of its 16 bits representation to increase the capacity of embedding.

3.3   Watermark Verification

The watermark verification is achieved by the following:

- Step 1: Compute the FSDWT of the watermarked image.
- Step 2: Calculate the dominant blocks of the matrix obtained in step 1.
- Step 3: Convert, using a key P, the dominant blocks to their 8 bits representation.
- Step 4: Repeat embedding process steps 2, 3, 4, 5 for the watermarked image.
- Step 5: Apply XOR operation between the bits obtained in step 3 and the Watermark bits.
- Step 6: Compare the bits obtained in step 5 (S') with the bits obtained in step 4 (S).

The verification algorithm is illustrated in Fig. 5. If the watermarked image is modified, the vector S will not be equal to the vector S' then we can conclude that the image is not authentic.

4   Results and Analysis

4.1   Experimental Results

The results of the proposed fragile watermarking algorithm are presented in this section. We used C++ and OpenCV library to implement the algorithm. A gray image of size 256×256 and a gray mark of size 10×10 was used to validate the proposed approach, the Fig. 8 shows this mark. The image of Fig. 1 is used as an original image. The performance evaluation of the method is done with the perceptual transparency. The image quality is measured by PSNR (Peak signal to Noise Ratio), as the PSNR is bigger, as the quality of watermarked image is better. The Table 2 shows the PSNR and MSE (Mean Squared Error)

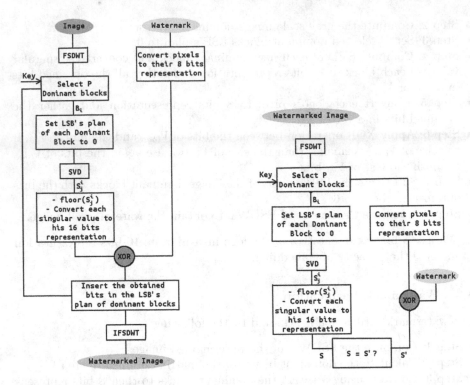

Fig. 4. The embedding algorithm   **Fig. 5.** The extraction algorithm

of the watermarked images. The Figs. 6 and 7 show the original image and the watermarked image, the difference between the two images is unnoticeable.

PSNR is measured using the formula:

$$PSNR = 10 * log_{10} \frac{255^2}{MSE} \tag{4}$$

where MSE is the mean squared error between the original image I and the watermarked image WI. Images are of size $h \times w$.

$$MSE = \frac{1}{h * w} \sum_{i=1}^{h} \sum_{j=1}^{w} (I(i,j) - WI(i,j))^2 \tag{5}$$

4.2   Computational Complexity

The computational complexity of the proposed algorithm depends on the image dimensions and the number of dominant blocks.

We put: $h \times w$ the size of the image, $hW \times wW$ the size of the logo used in watermark generation, $dim = min(h, w)$, P the number of selected dominant blocks

Fig. 6. Original Image   **Fig. 7.** Watermarked image

Fig. 8. The logo used as a mark

used in the insertion of watermark, P_v the number of selected dominant blocks used to generate the watermark vector, $lBlock$ the length of dominant block.

FSDWT complexity is of order:

$$C_{FSDWT} = \Theta(h \times w) \tag{6}$$

The dominant blocks computation complexity is of order:

$$C_{DB} = \Theta(h \times w) \tag{7}$$

In the embedding process, the pixels of watermark are converted to their 8 bits representation, so a vector of $8 \times hW \times wW$ bits is generated. Then a Xor operation is applied between this vector and the vector of 16 bits representation of singular values floored, this vector is of length $4 \times 16 \times P_v$ bits. In our case we compute the SVD of $\frac{hW \times wW}{8}$ dominant blocks of dimension $lBlock \times lBlock$, so:

$$C_{svd} = \Theta(\frac{hW \times wW}{8} \times lBlock^3) \tag{8}$$

To set LSB's plan of dominant blocks to 0, we compute their SVD and convert their singular values to 16 bits representation,then we need a complexity of:

$$C_{LSB} = \Theta(\frac{hW \times wW}{8} \times lBlock^3) \tag{9}$$

Table 2. PSNR and MSE of the water-marked images

Image	Size	MSE	PNSR
Baboon	256 × 256	0.0160	66.0837
Boat	512 × 512	0.0036	72.5665
Cameraman	256 × 256	0.0214	64.8100
House	256 × 256	0.0158	66.1300
Peppers	512 × 512	0.0029	73.4000

Table 3. Complexity comparison

Method	Complexity
Byun's method [8]	$\Theta(512^3)$
Hierarchical method [2]	$\Theta((85/64)512^3)$
Reduced method [8]	$\Theta((21/64)512^3)$
Our method	$\Theta(50 \times 512^2)$

To insert the obtained bits in the LSB's plan of dominant blocks we need a complexity of:

$$C_{inser} = \Theta(P \times h \times w) \tag{10}$$

The total running of embedding the watermark is:

$$C_{embed} = C_{FSDWT} + C_{DB} + C_{LSB} + C_{inser} \tag{11}$$
$$= \Theta(\frac{hW \times wW}{8} \times lBlock^3) + \Theta(P \times h \times w)$$

Then we can simplify C_{embed} as:

$$C_{embed} = \Theta(12 \times \frac{hW \times wW}{8}) + \Theta(\frac{hW \times wW}{2} \times h \times w) = \Theta(\frac{hW \times wW}{2} \times h \times w)$$

A comparison of the complexity of different methods with the complexity of our method using 512 × 512 and 10 × 10 mark is shown in the Table 3.

5   Conclusion

In this paper, we have presented a low complexity fragile watermarking method based on SVD and FSDWT to authenticate images. The watermarked image obtained is slightly changed and the method is fragile to any alteration attacks due to the usage of LSB's plan and singular values in the process of embedding the watermark. The method gives good results in the term of complexity and can be used in applications requiring low complexity, more works should be done to detect the tamper regions in the case of attacks. Clarke, F., Ekeland, I.: Nonlinear oscillations and boundary-value problems for Hamiltonian systems. Arch. Rat. Mech. Anal. 78, 315–333 (1982)

References

1. Cox, I., Miller, M., Bloom, J., Fridrich, J., Kalker, T.: Digital Watermarking and Steganography, 2nd edn. Morgan Kaufmann Publishers Inc., San Francisco (2008)
2. Taheri, S., Ghaemmaghami, S.: A hierarchical approach to SVD-based fragile watermarking for image authentication. In: Fifth International Conference on Information, Communications and Signal Processing, pp. 870–876 (2005)
3. Wu, M., Liu, B.: Data hiding in binary image for authentication and annotation. IEEE Trans. Multimedia 6, 528–538 (2004)
4. Kim, H.Y., de Queiroz, R.L.: Alteration-locating authentication watermarking for binary images. In: Cox, I., Kalker, T., Lee, H.-K. (eds.) IWDW 2004. LNCS, vol. 3304, pp. 125–136. Springer, Heidelberg (2005)
5. Yang, H., Kot, A.C.: Binary image authentication with tampering localization by embedding cryptographic signature and block identifier. IEEE Sign. Proc. Lett. 13, 741–744 (2006)
6. Puhan, N.B., Ho, A.T.S., Sattar, F.: Erasable authentication watermarking in binary document images. In: Proceedings of the IEEE International Conference on Innovative Computing, Information and Control, 5–7 September 2007, pp. 288–291. IEEE Xplore Press, Kumamoto (2007)
7. Rawat, S., Raman, B.: A chaotic system based fragile watermarking scheme for image tamper detection. Int. J. Electron. Commun. 65(10), 840–847 (2011)
8. Byun, S.-C., Lee, S.-K., Tewfik, A.H., Ahn, B.-H.: A SVD-based fragile watermarking scheme for image authentication. In: Petitcolas, F.A.P., Kim, H.-J. (eds.) IWDW 2002. LNCS, vol. 2613, pp. 170–178. Springer, Heidelberg (2003)
9. Vandewalle, J., De Moor, B.: A variety of applications of singular value decomposition in identification and signal processing. SVD Sig. Process, 43–91 (1988)
10. Bhagyashri, K., Joshi, M.Y.: Robust Image Watermarking Based on Singular Value Decomposition and Discrete Wavelet Transform. IEEE, Nanded (2010)
11. El Hajji, M., Ouaha, H., Afdel, K., Douzi, H.: Multiple watermark for authentication and tamper detection using mixed scales DWT. Int. J. Comput. Appl. (0975–8887) 28(6), 31–34 (2011)
12. Douzi, H., Mammass, D., Nouboud, F.: Faber-Schauder wavelet transformation application to edge detection and image characterization. J. Math. Imaging Vis. 14(2), 91–102 (2001)
13. Sweldens, W.: The lifting scheme: a construction of second generation wavelets. SIAM J. Math. Anal. 29(2), 511–546 (1998)
14. Szenasi, S.: Distributed region growing algorithm for medical image segmentation. Int. J. Circuits, Syst. Signal Process. 8(1), 173–181 (2014)
15. Canny, J.: A computational approach to edge detection. IEEE Trans. Pattern Anal. Mach. Intell. 6, 679–698 (1986)
16. El Hajji, M., Douzi, H., Mammas, D., Harba, R., Ros, F.: A new image watermarking algorithm based on mixed scales wavelets. J. Electron. Imaging. 21(1), 013003 (2012)
17. Otsu, N.: A threshold selection method from grey scale histogram. IEEE Trans. SMC 1, 62–66 (1979)

Single-Loop Architecture for JPEG 2000

David Barina[✉], Ondrej Klima, and Pavel Zemcik

Brno University of Technology, Bozetechova 1/2, 612 66 Brno, Czech Republic
{ibarina,iklima,zemcik}@fit.vutbr.cz

Abstract. We present a novel and very efficient software architecture designed for JPEG 2000 coders. The proposed method employs a strip-based data processing technique while performing a single-pass multi-scale wavelet transform. The overall compression chain is driven by incoming data while the fragments of the resulting bitstream are produced immediately after loading the corresponding data and additionally in parallel. The method is friendly to the CPU cache and nicely exploits the SIMD capabilities of the modern CPUs. Implanted into reference OpenJPEG implementation, our method has significantly better performance in terms of the execution time.

Keywords: Discrete wavelet transform · Lifting scheme · JPEG 2000

1 Introduction

The discrete wavelet transform (DWT) is a signal-processing method suitable for decomposition of a signal into several scales. It is often used as a basis for sophisticated compression algorithms. Particularly, JPEG 2000 is an image coding system based on this wavelet compression technique. The format has wide application, especially with professional use cases. For example, Digital Cinema Initiatives established uniform specifications for digital cinemas in which JPEG 2000 is the only accepted compression format. Other applications include medical imaging, meteorology, image archiving (printed books, handwritten manuscripts), or aerial documentation.

Unfortunately, several major issues exist with the efficient implementation of the JPEG 2000 codec. This is especially true for images with high resolution (4 K, 8 K, aerial imagery) decomposed into a number of scales. For high resolution data decomposed into several scales using a typical separable transform, immensely many CPU cache misses occur. These cache misses significantly slow down the overall calculation. Furthermore, by following the typical data processing, the fundamental coding units of the JPEG 2000 format (referred to as code-blocks) are generated in the order that corresponds to scales.Consequently, it is not possible to produce a bitstream fragment which corresponds to a spatial image region earlier than the complete DWT decomposition is finished. Following the decomposition procedure as defined in the standard, the coefficients of a single resolution appears all at once. Therefore, the entropy coder (EBCOT) needs to

© Springer International Publishing Switzerland 2016
A. Mansouri et al. (Eds.): ICISP 2016, LNCS 9680, pp. 346–355, 2016.
DOI: 10.1007/978-3-319-33618-3_35

once again return to the data already touched. Finally, current implementations are built using 1-D transform which is unable to fully exploit the potential of modern CPUs.

This paper presents an efficient architecture for JPEG 2000 encoders. Our approach generates multi-scale wavelet transform coefficients in a purely single pass manner and even on the code-block basis. Our fundamental processing core nicely fits contemporary SIMD instruction sets (e.g., SSE).

The rest of the paper is organized as follows. The Sect. 2 summarizes the state of the art, especially efficient software realizations. The proposed approach is presented in Sect. 3. Additionally, Sect. 4 provides a performance evaluation. Finally, Sect. 5 summarizes the paper.

2 Related Work

Many constructions of wavelets have been introduced in past three decades. As a key advance for image compression, Cohen–Daubechies–Feauveau [4] (CDF) biorthogonal wavelets provided several families of symmetric biorthogonal wavelet bases. As another important element, Mallat [7] demonstrated the orthogonal wavelet representation of images, today referred to as the 2-D DWT. It was originally computed with a pyramidal algorithm based on convolutions with quadrature mirror filters. In mid-1990s, Sweldens [5,9] presented the lifting scheme which speeded up such decomposition. He had shown how any discrete wavelet transform can be decomposed into a sequence of simple filtering steps (lifting steps). Finally, Taubman [10] proposed a new image compression algorithm – Embedded Block Coding with Optimized Truncation (EBCOT). The algorithm was quickly adopted into JPEG 2000 standard finalized in 2000.

Efficient realization of JPEG 2000 transform was outlined in [11]. The author described his implementation built with 16-bit fixed-point numbers. However, he did not provide much implementation details and he did not consider any friendliness to the CPU cache nor the SIMD set.Nevertheless, he expressed the memory requirements for multi-scale DWT as $(4 + 2S)M$ samples, where S is the number of lifting steps, and M is the width of the image. As the transform coefficients have to be arranged into code-blocks, the total memory requirements for JPEG 2000 codec are $(4+2S+3 \times 2^{c_n})M$ samples, where 2^{c_n} is the code-block height. The initial 4 term corresponds to 2 lines per one decomposition scale. This imposes that his implementation generates all code-blocks at the same time, not one after another. Here we would like to make a short comment. According to the description in [11], their implementation does not process the data in a single loop. However, for a moment, let us assume that their implementation would do so. Still, this strategy is fundamentally different from the architecture proposed in this paper which generates individual blocks sequentially while reusing the same memory area for output coefficients all the time. Regarding the input processing, we have compared these two strategies (line-based and block-based) in [1]. They were almost equally fast. However, the line-based processing does not fit the JPEG 2000 code-blocks, does not allow the parallel code-block processing, and does not allow to reuse the memory for HL, LH, and HH sub-bands. The motivation behind our work is to overcome these issues.

Many authors have tried to find an efficient schedule for 2-D DWT calculation. In [2], the authors proposed several cache-related optimizations of DWT phase. Although they still kept separated 1-D filtering, they interleaved the vertical pass of multiple columns. They also stored the LL sub-band contiguously in memory which is suitable for the next level of decomposition. Also, the authors [3] proposed several cache-related improvements and SIMD vectorization of DWT. At first, they used three specific memory layouts to improve cache locality under the multi-scale decomposition. Then, they used the same technique as the authors of [2] for interleaving the 1-D filtering on several adjacent columns. Finally, they vectorized the only the horizontal filtering using SSE instruction set. In [8], Meerwald et al. observed many cache misses especially when using large images with a width equal to a power of two. In order to overcome this problem, they have considered two improvements. Firstly, they added padding after each image row leading to a better utilization of limited set-associativity cache. Secondly, they filtered several adjacent columns concurrently as the authors of [2,3]. In [6], Kutil focused on the 2-D transform in which he merged vertical and horizontal passes into the single loop. Two nested loops (an outer vertical and an inner horizontal loop) are considered as the single loop processing all pixels of the image. His single-loop approach is line-based and vectorized using SSE set. However, they did not extend its approach to the whole multi-scale wavelet transform.

In [1], we have proposed a stand-alone unit able to transform the image in the single loop. Using this core, one can instantly produce the wavelet coefficients while the input data are visited only once. The processing of a particular scale can be suspended anytime and appropriate portions of the subsequent transform scale can be executed. In this paper, we extend this approach into a multi-scale single-loop approach on the code-block basis. This newly proposed approach is further parallelized and vectorized.

3   Single-Loop Design

In this section, we describe the single-loop core and its adaptation into the JPEG 2000 system. The established strip-based transform directly produces the code-blocks one by one. The processing of code-blocks is then chained together to progressively produce the multi-scale transform. On any level, such processing can be further parallelized in such a manner that the code-blocks are generated in parallel. As a consequence, this parallelism involves interleaving of the DWT and Tier-1 stages. Finally, the core is vectorized using the most widely used SIMD extensions.

The transform employed in JPEG 2000 decomposes the input image

$$\left(\mathrm{LL}^0_{m_0,n_0}\right)_{(0,0)\leq(m_0,n_0)<(M_0,N_0)} \tag{1}$$

of size $M_0 \times N_0$ pixels into $J > 0$ scales giving rise to the resulting wavelet bands

$$\left(\mathrm{HL}^j_{m_j,n_j} \right), \left(\mathrm{LH}^j_{m_j,n_j} \right), \left(\mathrm{HH}^j_{m_j,n_j} \right), \left(\mathrm{LL}^j_{m_j,n_j} \right), \Bigg|_{(0,0) \leq (m_j,n_j) < (M_j,N_j)} \qquad (2)$$

at scales $0 < j < J$, and the residual LL band

$$\left(\mathrm{LL}^J_{m_J,n_J} \right)_{(0,0) \leq (m_J,n_J) < (M_J,N_J)}, \qquad (3)$$

at the topmost scale J. Such decomposition is performed using the 2×2 core with a lag $F = 3$ samples in both directions proposed in [1]. For each scale $0 \leq j < J$, the core requires an access to two auxiliary buffers

$$\left({}^M\mathrm{B}^j_{m_j} \right)_{0 \leq m_j < M_j}, \left({}^N\mathrm{B}^j_{n_j} \right)_{0 \leq n_j < N_j}. \qquad (4)$$

These buffers hold intermediate results of the underlying lifting scheme. The size of the buffer can be expressed as $M \times 4$ (x-buffer) and $N \times 4$ coefficients (y-buffer), where 4 is the number of values that have to be passed between adjacent 1-D cores. Taken together, the 2×2 core needs the access to 8 values in x-buffer and 8 values in y-buffer.

In detail, the core consumes a 2×2 fragment of the input signal and immediately produces a four-tuple of coefficients (LL, HL, LH, HH). The produced coefficients have a lag of 3 samples in the vertical as well as the horizontal direction with respect to the input coordinate system. In the JPEG 2000 coordinate system, the core consumes the fragment of the input starting on odd (m, n) coordinates. Every code-block starts on even (m, n) coordinates (the LL coefficient). Note that any shorter lag is not possible due to the nature of CDF 9/7 lifting scheme. To simplify relations, we also introduce two functions

$$\Theta(m, n) = (m + F, n + F), \text{ and } \Omega(m, n) = (\lceil m/2 \rceil, \lceil n/2 \rceil). \qquad (5)$$

The function $\Theta(m, n)$ maps core output coordinates onto core input coordinates with a lag F. The function $\Omega(m, n)$ maps the coordinates at the scale j onto coordinates at the scale $j + 1$ with respect to the JPEG 2000 coordinate system. The 2×2 core transforms the fragment $I_{m,n}$ of an input signal onto the fragment $O_{m,n}$ of an input signal

$$I_{m,n} = \left(\mathrm{LL}^j_{\Theta(m,n)} \ \mathrm{LL}^j_{\Theta(m+1,n)} \ \mathrm{LL}^j_{\Theta(m,n+1)} \ \mathrm{LL}^j_{\Theta(m+1,n+1)} \right)^T, \qquad (6)$$

$$O_{m,n} = \left(\mathrm{LL}^{j+1}_{\Omega(m,n)} \ \mathrm{HL}^{j+1}_{\Omega(m+1,n)} \ \mathrm{LH}^{j+1}_{\Omega(m,n+1)} \ \mathrm{HH}^{j+1}_{\Omega(m+1,n+1)} \right)^T, \qquad (7)$$

while updating the two auxiliary buffers. Finally, operations performed inside the core can be described using a matrix C as

$$y = Cx \qquad (8)$$

with the input vector

$$x = I_{m,n} \, \| \, {}^M\mathrm{B}^j_m \, \| \, {}^M\mathrm{B}^j_{m+1} \, \| \, {}^N\mathrm{B}^j_n \, \| \, {}^N\mathrm{B}^j_{n+1} \qquad (9)$$

and the output vector

$$\boldsymbol{y} = O_{m,n} \parallel {}^M\mathrm{B}_m^j \parallel {}^M\mathrm{B}_{m+1}^j \parallel {}^N\mathrm{B}_n^j \parallel {}^N\mathrm{B}_{n+1}^j, \tag{10}$$

where $\parallel$ denotes the concatenation operator.

As a next step, we have encapsulated the processing of the code-blocks into monolithic units. These units are evaluated in horizontal "strips" due to the assumed line-oriented processing order. Inside the code-block unit, the 2×2 core can be used. Moreover, the unit requires access to two auxiliary buffers (one for each direction). The size of the buffer can be expressed as $2^{c_m} \times 4$ (for the x-buffer) and $2^{c_n} \times 4$ (for the y-buffer). As we are using the strip-based processing with a granularity of the code-block size, the y-buffer is straightly passed to the subsequent code-block processing unit. The x-buffer will be used by a strip of code-blocks lying below. At the beginning of the strip, the y-buffer contains arbitrary values. The first code-block unit initializes this buffer and passes it to the subsequent unit in x-direction. The transform of this subsequent unit is started not earlier than the EBCOT on the current unit has been finished. This allows for reusing the memory for HL, LH, and HH sub-bands.

The above-described procedure is in effect friendly to the cache hierarchy. The processing engine uses several memory regions of a different purpose. (1) The resulting code-block sub-bands occupy a few KiB of memory likely settled in the top-level cache. (2) The y-buffer occupies several hundreds of bytes. (3) The fragments of x-buffers occupy the same size as the total size of y-buffer. However, these are used only for short time and then can be evicted from all levels of the cache hierarchy. (4) The input strip can be simply streamed into the same memory region which may be in part mirrored in the cache. (5) The temporary LL bands can be partially mirrored as well. For a smaller resolution, there is a good chance that the entire working set can fit into the cache hierarchy.

The entire process can be efficiently parallelized. We have in mind the coarse-grained parallelism using the threads. The key idea is to split the strip processing into several independent regions. Thus, a single thread is responsible for several adjacent code-blocks. Each thread holds its private copy of y-buffer and the memory region for the resulting sub-bands (HL, LH, HH). Therefore, several EBCOT coders can work in parallel. Moreover, the threads are completely synchronization-free (they do not need to exchange any data). At the beginning of the strip processing, each thread initializes its y-buffer using a short prolog phase. There is only simplified core (without the vertical pass and the output phase) run in this phase. Thanks to the omission of the vertical pass, the x-buffer is not touched here and no interaction between threads is required. After the prolog, the processing continues in the usual way. Disjoint fragments of the x-buffer are accessed by all threads. In our implementation,[1] we have parallelized the wavelet decomposition as well as Tier-1 encoding. On parallel architectures, it is also possible to encode every single code-block of the strip in parallel. However, the parallelization of our implementation is constrained by

---

[1] available on demand.

the number of computing units. Note that more sophisticated implementations could parallelize almost entire compression chain.

4   Performance

In the previous section, we have described our design of wavelet transform engine with the compatibility to JPEG 2000 standard. In this section, we evaluate its performance and compare it to the competitive solutions.

Let us now focus on physical memory demands. The input image is consumed gradually using strips with height of 2×2^{c_m} lines. No more input data are required to be placed in physical memory at the same moment. For the output sub-bands, memory for only $4 \times 2^{c_m+c_n}$ coefficients is allocated (considering all four sub-bands). This memory is reused by all code-blocks in the transform (or a processing thread). Additionally, we need to allocate two auxiliary buffers of size $M_j \times 4$ and $N_j \times 4$ coefficients for each decomposition level j. Note that $M_{j+1} = \lceil M_j/2 \rceil_{c_m}$ and $N_{j+1} = \lceil N_j/2 \rceil_{c_n}$, where $\lceil . \rceil_c$ denotes ceiling to the next multiple of 2^c; initially $M_0 = M$ and $N_0 = N$. For each auxiliary LL band (excluding the input and the final one), the window of physical memory can be maintained and progressively mapped onto the right place in the virtual memory. The size of such window is roughly $3 \times 2^{c_n} \times M_{j+1}$. Note that we need 3 instead of 2 code-block strips due to the periodic symmetric extension on the image borders, additionally, a lag of $F = 3$ lines from the input to the output of the core. Roughly speaking, the code-blocks of the subsequent scales do not exactly fit each other. Taken together, our solution requires

$$(2S + 3 \times 2^{c_n})M \tag{11}$$

samples populated into the physical memory. Please note that these memory requirements are the same as outlined in [11].

Our solution was compared to C/C++ libraries listed on the official JPEG committee web pages. The OpenJPEG, FFmpeg, and JasPer libraries are distributed under the terms of open-source licences. Thus, these could be analyzed through their source code in detail. Note that OpenJPEG and JasPer are approved as reference JPEG 2000 implementations. The Kakadu implementation is a heavy optimized closed-source library. To ensure reproducible experiments, we list versions used – JasPer version 1.900.1, OpenJPEG 2.1.0, and FFmpeg 2.8. The Open-JPEG, JasPer (enforced the 32-bit type), and FFmpeg libraries implement the transform using 32-bit fixed-point format. Our implementation is based on 32-bit floating-point format.

The overview of the above described libraries is shown in Table 1. The naive approach refers to processing the entire image at once while keeping the horizontal and vertical passes as well as the transform scales separated. Furthermore, inside the horizontal and vertical passes, the lifting steps are processed sequentially. As a consequence, samples of the tile are visited many times while being over and over again evicted from the cache. Unlike the naive approach, the other two approaches use sophisticated technique where the processing of consecutive

Table 1. Software overview in terms of the transform stage.

Library	Algorithm
Our solution	Strip-based, scales interleaved
OpenJPEG	Naive
JasPer	Naive
FFmpeg	Naive
Kakadu	Line-based, scales interleaved

scales is interleaved. Moreover, in case of our strip-based processing, the horizontal and vertical passes were fused into the single loop. Regarding the strip-based processing, the input is consumed using strips, one by one. The subsequent scales are recursively processed as soon as enough data is available. For the line-based processing, no details were provided [11] about the processing of the horizontal and vertical lifting steps.

The measurements presented in this paper were obtained on Intel Core2 Quad Q9000 running at 2.0 GHz. The CPU has 32 KiB of level 1 data cache and 3 MiB of level 2 shared cache (two cores share one cache unit). The system is running on 64-bit Linux. All the algorithms below were implemented in the C language, possibly using the SIMD compiler intrinsics. In all cases, a 64-bit code compiled using GCC with `-march=native -O3` flag was used. The performance was measured using the `clock_gettime` call. We measured the average time required to produce a single transform coefficient for various range of image resolutions.

Considering our test implementation, we have vectorized our processing engine using widely spread SIMD extensions. Since we have built our implementation over the 32-bit floating point numbers, we used primarily the SSE (Streaming SIMD Extensions) instruction set. The processing inside the 2×2 core is separable into series of 1-D filtering steps. The first idea was to extend the core to fit the 4-way 128-bit SSE registers. This way, we obtained the 4×4 core inside which all of the filtering steps are performed using 4-way parallelism through the 128-bit SSE register. This case was also studied in [1]. Unfortunately, an issue appears when storing the resulting coefficients into separated memory areas. In detail, the 4×4 core produces four 2×2 fragments of the output sub-bands. This operation does not fit the SSE instruction set and consequently degrades the performance. For this reason, we decided to construct 8×8 "supercore" consisting of four adjacent 4×4 cores. The supercore does not suffer from the above-described issue and provides a slightly better performance. The 8×8 core naturally fits into 8-way 256-bit AVX registers. In this case, the storage of the resulting coefficients is performed in fragments of 4×4 coefficients which again do not fit the AVX registers. This second issue is not possible to solve because 4×4 is the smallest possible code-block size required by the standard. In other words, a theoretical 16×16 core would produce the 8×8 fragments of sub-bands which might not fit the 4×4 code-blocks. We have used the OpenMP interface to parallelize our code; however, many other implementations are possible.

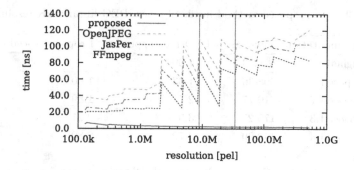

Fig. 1. Performance comparison of major libraries. Time per pixel for the transform stage only. DCI 4 K and 8 K UHD resolutions indicated by the vertical lines.

We have extracted the transform stage from the libraries described above in order to get accurate results. This stage was then subject of measurements. The results are plotted in Fig. 1. As observed also in [1,6], the single-loop processing has stable performance regardless the input resolution. The proposed implementation was measured using 4 threads and SSE extensions. However, the SSE or AVX extensions boost the performance by at most 5 %.

Table 2. Parallel processing, streaming input. 4096×2160 input, 64×64 code-blocks. The tile was decomposed into a single ($J = 1$) and multiple ($J = 8$) scales.

	Single scale		Multiple scales	
Threads	Time [ns/pel]	Speedup	Time [ns/pel]	Speedup
1	3.08	1.00	5.60	1.00
2	1.59	1.94	3.44	1.62
3	1.22	2.53	2.68	2.09
4	0.97	3.16	2.56	2.19

We have evaluated the possibility of parallel processing. The original single-loop approach [1] scaled almost linearly with the number of threads. The JPEG 2000 processing has coarser granularity (code-blocks instead of cores) and it is performed in multiple scales. Higher scales of the decomposition have, unfortunately, significantly lower resolutions in comparison with the input tile. For this reason, the parallelization is not as efficient as in case of the original approach. The results of our measurement are shown in Table 2. It can be seen that the single-scale decomposition scales slightly less than linearly with the number of threads. As it might be expected, the multi-scale decomposition is not as close to the linear relationship.

Since we have implemented only DWT stage of the JPEG 2000 codec, we have decided to implant our code into OpenJPEG library replacing the original implementation. Note that no part of OpenJPEG is optimized for the performance.

Table 3. The proposed method inside of OpenJPEG library. 4 K resolution.

Implementation	Time [ns/pel]	Original speedup	Proposed speedup
Original	528.73	1.00	—
Proposed 1	398.36	1.33	1.00
Proposed 2	210.77	2.51	1.89
Proposed 3	175.27	3.02	2.27
Proposed 4	142.09	3.72	2.80

Because our implementation is built using the floating-point format and Open-JPEG uses the fixed-point format, we have to convert the samples one by one before and after the transform. The quantization and Tier-1 stage are performed using the original OpenJPEG's code. However, these parts of the compression chain now run in parallel as these are linked to the transform of code-blocks. The rest of the code remains unmodified and runs in sequence. Eight decomposition levels, up to 4 threads, and SSE were used. As expected, the single-loop processing has stable performance regardless of the input resolution. The measurement is summarized in Table 3. It can be seen that the complete compression chain scales better than the standalone transform stage.

5   Conclusion

We have introduced a new schedule for calculation of the discrete wavelet transform with JPEG 2000 compatibility. In contrast to previously presented schemes, the newly proposed scheme: generates the code-blocks one by one while reusing the memory for the resulting coefficients; passes every single code-block to subsequent Tier-1 coding before processing any next code-block (without evicting the code-block from the cache); generates and encodes the code-blocks in parallel (fragments of Tier-1 stage run simultaneously with fragments of the transform stage); exploits SIMD capabilities of modern CPUs as the wavelet coefficients are generated using 2-D processing unit instead of a conventional 1-D vectorization.

We have integrated our test implementation into OpenJPEG library (the reference JPEG 2000 software). The performance of this implementation out-performs the original code even if no parallelization and no SIMD extensions are used. When the parallel processing is enabled, the performance increases proportionally to the input size and number of processing threads.

In future work, we would like to implement a complete JPEG 2000 compression chain.

Acknowledgements. This work was supported by the Technology Agency of the Czech Republic (TA CR) Competence Centres project V3C – Visual Computing Competence Center (no. TE01020415), the Ministry of Education, Youth and Sports from the National Programme of Sustainability (NPU II) project IT4Innovations excellence in science (no. LQ1602), and Technology Agency of the Czech Republic (TA CR) project TraumaTech (no. TA04011606).

References

1. Barina, D., Zemcik, P.: Vectorization and parallelization of 2-D wavelet lifting. J. Real Time Image Process. (in press)
2. Chatterjee, S., Brooks, C.D.: Cache-efficient wavelet lifting in JPEG 2000. In: IEEE International Conference on Multimedia and Expo, vol. 1, pp. 797–800 (2002)
3. Chaver, D., Tenllado, C., Pinuel, L., Prieto, M., Tirado, F.: Vectorization of the 2D wavelet lifting transform using SIMD extensions. In: International Parallel and Distributed Processing Symposium, p. 8 (2003)
4. Cohen, A., Daubechies, I., Feauveau, J.C.: Biorthogonal bases of compactly supported wavelets. Commun. Pure Appl. Math. **45**(5), 485–560 (1992)
5. Daubechies, I., Sweldens, W.: Factoring wavelet transforms into lifting steps. J. Fourier Anal. Appl. **4**(3), 247–269 (1998)
6. Kutil, R.: A single-loop approach to SIMD parallelization of 2-D wavelet lifting. In: Proceedings of the 14th Euromicro International Conference on Parallel, Distributed, and Network-Based Processing (PDP), pp. 413–420 (2006)
7. Mallat, S.: A theory for multiresolution signal decomposition: the wavelet representation. IEEE Trans. Pattern Anal. Mach. Intell. **11**(7), 674–693 (1989)
8. Meerwald, P., Norcen, R., Uhl, A.: Cache issues with JPEG2000 wavelet lifting. In: Visual Communications and Image Processing. In: SPIE, vol. 4671, pp. 626–634 (2002)
9. Sweldens, W.: The lifting scheme: a custom-design construction of biorthogonal wavelets. Appl. Comput. Harmonic Anal. **3**(2), 186–200 (1996)
10. Taubman, D.: High performance scalable image compression with EBCOT. IEEE Trans. Image Process. **9**(7), 1158–1170 (2000)
11. Taubman, D.: Software architectures for JPEG2000. In: Proceedings of the IEEE International Conference for Digital Signal Processing, pp. 197–200 (2002)

Robust Print-cam Image Watermarking in Fourier Domain

Khadija Gourrame[1(✉)], Hassan Douzi[1], Rachid Harba[2], Frederic Ros[2], Mohamed El Hajji[1], Rabia Riad[1,2], and Meina Amar[1,2]

[1] IRF-SIC Laboratory, Ibn Zohr University, BP 8106, Cite Dakhla, 80000 Agadir, Morocco khadija.gourrame@edu.uiz.ac.ma

[2] PRISME Laboratory, Orleans University, 12 Rue de Blois, 45067 Orleans, France

Abstract. Perspective deformation is one of the major issues in print-cam attacks for image watermarking. In this paper we adapt to print-cam process a Fourier watermarking method developed by our team, for print-scan attacks. Our aim is to resist to perspective distortions of print-cam image watermarking for ID images for industrial application. A first step consists of geometrical correction of the perspective distortions, then Fourier based watermarking is used. Experimental results of the improved method in Fourier domain show better robustness compared to existing print-cam methods.

Keywords: Print-cam · Perspective distortions · Image watermarking · Fourier transformation

1 Introduction

Developing robust watermarking method against print-cam attacks for identity images (ID) is strongly needed as industrial applications are under active development. Print-cam process produces, for the detection process of the watermark, three dimensional geometric distortions (rotation, scale changes, translation, and tilt of the optical axis). Also there are lens distortion, lighting variations including reflections, and other noises [1]. In this paper we focus on the correction of the geometric attacks called perspective distortions. While scale variation and tilt of optical axis are the main additional attacks that differentiate between print-cam and print-scan attacks Many research papers [2–5] proposed robust print-cam image watermarking methods in the spatial or Discrete Wavelet transform (DWT) domains, with the use of frame synchronization method to resist to geometric distortions. Pramila et al. [6] proposed DWT watermarking method, initially used for print-scan process [7], with a visible frame to recover the 3D synchronization. However their method can support small geometric distortion. Thongkor et al. [8,9] applied, on Thai ID cards images, a spatial domain watermarking method using perceptual vision mask. To rectify the distorted image,

© Springer International Publishing Switzerland 2016
A. Mansouri et al. (Eds.): ICISP 2016, LNCS 9680, pp. 356–365, 2016.
DOI: 10.1007/978-3-319-33618-3_36

they use feature points from both the watermarked image and the original image. Yet their method is a non-blind method. Few methods exist for print-cam image watermarking, and mostly they are done in spatial domain or DWT domain.

Discrete Fourier transform based watermarkings method is known to resist to geometric distortions (except scale and tilt of optical axis distortions) [10]. Recently Riad et al. [11,12] proposed a robust watermarking method based on Discrete Fourier Transform (DFT) for ID images. The method was developed for printed and scanned images.

In this paper we propose to adapt the DFT watermarking method, developed by Riad et al. [11], for print-cam image watermarking. In embedding process, the watermark is inserted in specific DFT frequency bands of ID images. Then, after the print-cam phase, a preprocess step is used to detect the four corners of the ID image by Hough line detector method, and an inverse projective transformation is applied to correct the perspective distortions. Finally a detection process of the watermark is accomplished by using the normalized cross-correlation function. Experimental tests will be carried out on a set of 500 ID images with random values of simulated perspective attacks. We show that the proposed method improves the detection rate compared with other existing method [6].

The paper is organized as follows: Sect. 2 reviews print-cam process and perspective distortions of the captured images, Sect. 3 presents a description of the proposed method, Sect. 4 shows the experiment results, and finally Sect. 5 presents conclusions and perspectives.

2 Perspective Attack of the Print-cam Process

2.1 Print-cam Attacks

Attacks or distortions are every deformations and actions that occur to the watermarked image and harm the mark, in other words attacks make the detection/extraction operation fails to find the mark in the image.

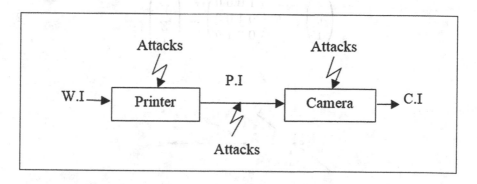

Fig. 1. Print-cam process

The Fig. 1 presents print-cam process under different attacks, where the watermarked image (W.I) is printed, and then the printed image (P.I) is captured by a camera (mobile phone's camera) to get the captured image (C.I). The attacks can be classified as attacks related to materials of the system: noise and blurring of the pixels due to quality of the printers, paper quality, lens distortions, and camera resolutions. We have also attacks related to the users, like perspective distortions caused by the camera position, and motion blur. And finally we have attacks related to the environment, as the lights, light reflection, and other noises. Attacks related to materials, can be predicted and fixed because distortion measurement still the same for each material [13]. However attacks like perspective distortions, are hard to predict and fix, because they change for each use of the system.

2.2   Perspective Transformation of the Captured Image

The operation of taking points coordinates from a 3D world (X) and map it in 2D image plan (x), is called projective transformation, as Fig. 2 shows: In a projective space where the points at infinity exist and predefined, the projective transformation become a linear transformation, and can be presented in form of a mathematical relation, as the following equation:

$$\begin{pmatrix} x \\ y \\ 1 \end{pmatrix} = H \begin{pmatrix} X \\ Y \\ Z \\ 1 \end{pmatrix} \tag{1}$$

Where $[X, Y, Z, 1]^T$ is a world coordinates, $[x, y, 1]^T$ is its corresponding image coordinates, and H is 3×4 projective matrix that describes the transformation from the 3D to 2D spaces. Similarly the capturing process of an image using a camera can be simulated by a projective transformation relation as follow:

$$\begin{pmatrix} x \\ y \\ 1 \end{pmatrix} = K \begin{pmatrix} 1 & 0 & 0 & 0 \\ 0 & 1 & 0 & 0 \\ 0 & 0 & 1 & 0 \end{pmatrix} M \begin{pmatrix} X \\ Y \\ Z \\ 1 \end{pmatrix} \tag{2}$$

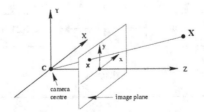

Fig. 2. Geometric projection process

Where H from Eq. (1) is replaced by the matrix multiplications showed in (2). K is 3×3 matrix, contains the intrinsic camera parameters, and M is a 3×3 matrix representing the 3D position and pose of the camera, and named as extrinsic camera parameters [14]. In particular perspective transformation is a 2D projection of 2D plan plunged in 3D world. Then the relation of the perspective transformation in our case becomes:

$$\begin{pmatrix} x \\ y \\ 1 \end{pmatrix} = H \begin{pmatrix} X \\ Y \\ 1 \end{pmatrix} \tag{3}$$

Where $[x, y, 1]^T$ is coordinates of the captured image, $[X, Y, 1]^T$ is for printed image, and M defined as the 3×3 perspective matrix.

2.3   Geometric Image Rectification

The perspective distortions come from the fact of that the camera is not in the axis of the image, and that the distance and rotation variations may be present during capturing process. Therefore the matrix M in the Eq. (3) parametrizes the perspective transformation. So from a mathematical point of view, to delete the geometric effect, we have to invert the perspective transformation. For that many mathematical methods are suggested [14]. In the following we present two useable techniques to rectify this kind of geometric deformations:

- **Four corners method:** From the Eq. (3), the projective matrix has 8 degree of freedom hence 8 unknown parameters should be assessed from the following system equation:

$$\begin{cases} x = \frac{M_{11}X + M_{12}Y + M_{13}}{M_{31}X + M_{32}Y + 1} \\ y = \frac{M_{21}X + M_{22}Y + M_{23}}{M_{31}X + M_{32}Y + 1} \end{cases} \tag{4}$$

Where $M_{ij(1 \leq i,j \leq 3)}$ are the values in i row and j column of matrix M in Eq. (3). So with corresponding four points from both printed and captured images, M can be uniquely computed [14].
- **Parallel lines method:** The projective transformation can be assumed as a product of three components similarity (H_s), affine (H_a), and projective (H_p), i.e., $M = M_s \times M_a \times M_p$. So to invert the perspective effect from the image, the method remove the projective and affine components to obtain the similarity transformed version of the original image [15].

For our adapted method, we apply the concept of frame method by using the 4 corners strategy. Parallel lines method is particularly assigned to document or text images.

3   The Proposed Method

The Fourier watermarking method used in this work gives improved results against print-scan attacks [12]. Since the big difference between the print-scan and print-cam attacks is the geometric issues, a preprocessing stage is added to correct the image geometrically. As the following figure shows (Fig. 3):

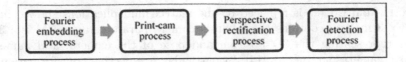

Fig. 3. Proposed method

3.1 Fourier Watermark Embedding Process

The watermark embedding is performed in the magnitude of the discrete Fourier transform (DFT) using only the luminance of the colored image (chrominance components are not modified). A symmetric watermark is inserted along a circle of radius r in the DFT magnitude.

According to [11], the application of a dedicated low-pass filtering on the embeddable coefficients of the DFT magnitude improves the detection rate. In this work, we use the same idea. The watermark W of N elements is inserted in the filtered coefficients as follows:

$$M_W = M_f + \alpha * W \tag{5}$$

where M_W is the magnitude of the watermarked DFT coefficient, M_f is the original one after filtering the embeddable coefficients using a Gaussian filter, α is the strength parameter. The parameter is determined to obtain the desired value of PSNR equal to 40dB, this value corresponds to an invisible watermark [16,17]. The final watermarked image is reconstructed by applying the inverse DFT to obtain the luminance of the watermarked image from which color image is recovered using the unmodified chrominance components.

3.2 Perspective Rectification Process

To correct the geometric effect we need to estimate the four corner positions. Therefore the steps of this process, show in Fig. 4, are as follow:

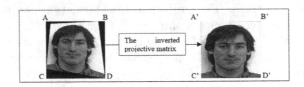

Fig. 4. Perspective rectification process

Step 1: Detect the four corners: we use Hough line to detect the frame of ID image, then we get the four points from the intersections of those lines.

Step 2: Estimate the projective matrix: with corresponding four points, we solve the system equation in (4).

Step 3: Apply the invert transformation in the whole image, to remap the rectified image.

3.3 Watermark Detection

The blind decoder needs only the captured image and watermark W. First, the DFT is applied to the luminance of the captured image. Then, image coefficients are extracted from the magnitude along the radius r. The normalized cross-correlation is computed between the extracted coefficients F and the sequence W of the watermark. As a rotation could occur during the print-and-scan process, the maximum of the normalized cross-correlation C_{Max} is to be estimated as follow:

$$C_{Max} = \max_{0 \leq j \leq 1} \left(\frac{\sum_{i=0}^{N-1}(W(i) - \overline{W})(F(i+j) - \overline{F})}{\sqrt{\sum_{i=0}^{N-1}(W(i) - \overline{W})^2 \sum_{i=0}^{N-1}(F(i+j) - \overline{F})^2}} \right) \tag{6}$$

where N is the sequence length, $\overline{W}$ and $\overline{F}$ are the mean of the watermark and extracted Fourier coefficients, respectively. The watermark is detected if the maximum value of the normalized cross-correlation exceeds a threshold t, otherwise the watermark is not detected.

4 Results

This section presents the comparison of the watermark detection between the proposed method and the method in [6], using 500 ID digital images from PICS database [18]. Perspective attacks are simulated. Both methods are implemented under the same protocols and conditions. The steps of the test are shown in the following figure (Fig. 5):

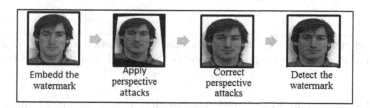

Embedd the watermark   Apply perspective attacks   Correct perspective attacks   Detect the watermark

Fig. 5. Testing process

For the perspective distortions, the simulation of 3D rotation of the image (3 rotations around x, y, and z axis) is used simultaneously with the simulation of camera position (view point position) that defines polar angles θ and φ (polar angle in the $x - y$ plane, polar angle above or below the $x - y$ plane). Those angles are measured in degrees. The following figure shows examples of simulated perspective distortions (Fig. 6):

(a)   (b)

Fig. 6. (a) - 3D rotation $(5°, -2°, 10°)$ with view-point $(0°, 90°)$. (b) - 3D rotation $(5°, -2°, 10°)$ with view-point $(10°, 60°)$

The 500 ID images are tested under random values of perspective attacks, where the rotation values around x, y, and z axis are respectively taken from intervals $[-5°, 5°]$, $[-5°, 5°]$, and $[-10°, 10°]$. And view point values of and are respectively between $[0°, 10°]$ and $[60°, 90°]$.

The detection results of both of the methods are represented in form of histograms of empirical probability density functions of correlation values.

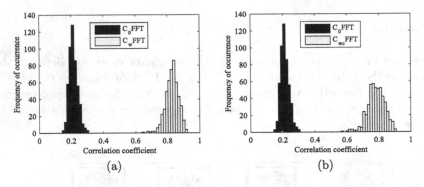

(a)   (b)

Fig. 7. Empirical probability density functions of correlation values for marked and unmarked images with our proposed method before (a) and after (b) perspective attacks

The histograms in Figs. 7 and 8 show that the detection of the proposed method is improved compared to the other method [6] after the recovery from the perspective deformations. In the same way the next figure of the probability of true positive detection shows the performance of both methods before and after the geometric attacks according to all possible threshold values (Fig. 9).

The performance of the proposed method is clearly higher than the other method, relatively to different threshold values.

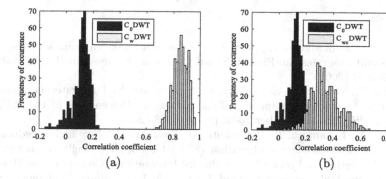

Fig. 8. Empirical probability density functions of correlation values for marked and unmarked images with method [6] before (a) and after (b) perspective attacks

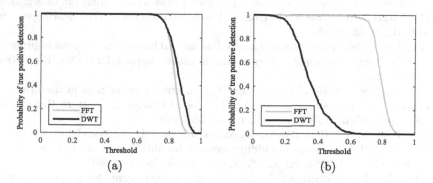

Fig. 9. Probability of true positive detection as a function of the threshold values before (a) and after (b) the perspective attacks

5   Conclusion

This paper proposes a Fourier based watermarking method for print-cam attacks. Almost all the existed few methods are done in spatial or wavelet (DWT) domains. This work shows that FFT domain resists better to the perspective distortions, compared to DWT domain. Which can be explained by the fact that Fourier transform resists the geometric attacks (except the scale and tilt of optical axis attacks) more than the wavelet transform. As future work, we intend to improve the adapted FFT method to resist print-cam attacks for real captured images.

References

1. Pramila, A., Keskinarkaus, A., Seppnen, T.: Camera based watermark extraction problems and examples. In: Finnish Signal Processing Symposium (FinSig 2007), Oulu, Finland (2007)
2. Nakamura, T., Katayama, A., Yamamuro, M., Sonehara, N.: Fast watermark detection scheme for camera-equipped cellular phone. In: Proceedings of the MUM, New York, USA, 27–29 October 2004, pp. 101–108 (2004)
3. Katayama, A., Nakamura, T., Yamamuro, M., Sonehara, N.: New high-speedframe detection method: side trace algorithm (STA) for i-appli on cellular phones to detect watermarks. In: Proceedings of the 3rd International Conference on Mobile and Ubiquitous Multimedia, Maryland, USA. ACM International Conference Proceeding Series, pp. 109–116 (2004)
4. Takeuchi, S., Kunisa, A., Tsujita, K., Inoue, Y.: Geometric distortion compensation of printed images containing imperceptible watermarks. In: International Conference on Consumer Electronics, ICCE 2005. Digest of Technical Papers, pp. 411–412. IEEE (2005)
5. Liu, J.-C., Shieh, H.-A.: Toward a two-dimensional barcode with visual information using perceptual shaping watermarking in mobile applications. Opt. Eng. **50**(1), 017002 (2011)
6. Anu, P., Keskinarkaus, A., Seppnen, T.: Watermark robustness in the print-cam process. In: Proceedings of the IASTED Signal Processing, Pattern Recognition, and Applications (SPPRA 2008), pp. 60–65 (2008)
7. Keskinarkaus, A., Pramila, A., Seppänen, T., Sauvola, J.: Wavelet domain print-scan and JPEG resilient data hiding method. In: Shi, Y.Q., Jeon, B. (eds.) IWDW 2006. LNCS, vol. 4283, pp. 82–95. Springer, Heidelberg (2006)
8. Thongkor, K., Amornraksa, T.: Digital image watermarking for photo authentication in Thai national ID card. In: 2012 9th International Conference on Electrical Engineering/Electronics, Computer, Telecommunications and Information Technology (ECTI-CON), pp. 1–4. IEEE (2012)
9. Thongkor, K., Amornraksa, T.: Robust image watermarking for camera-captured image using image registration technique. In: 2014 14th International Symposium on Communications and Information Technologies (ISCIT), pp. 479–483. IEEE (2014)
10. Pereira, S., Pun, T.: Robust template matching for affine resistant image watermarks. IEEE Trans. Image Process. **9**(6), 1123–1129 (2000)
11. Riad, R., Ros, F., Harba, R., Douzi, H., El-hajji, M.: Pre-processing the cover image before embedding improves the watermark detection rate. In: 2014 Second World Conference on Complex Systems (WCCS). IEEE (2014)
12. Riad, R., Harba, R., Douzi, H., El-hajji, M., Ros, F.: Print-and-scan counterattacks for plastic card supports Fourier watermarking. In: 2014 IEEE 23rd International Symposium on Industrial Electronics (ISIE), pp. 1036–1041. IEEE (2014)
13. Heikkila, J., Silvn, O.: A four-step camera calibration procedure with implicit image correction. In: Proceedings of the 1997 IEEE Computer Society Conference on Computer Vision and Pattern Recognition. IEEE (1997)
14. Hartley, R., Zisserman, A.: Multiple View Geometry in Computer Vision. Cambridge University Press, Cambridge (2003)
15. Jagannathan, L., Jawahar, C.V.: Perspective correction methods for camera based document analysis. In: Proceedings of the First International Workshop on Camera-Based Document Analysis and Recognition, pp. 148–154 (2005)

16. Poljicak, A., Mandic, L., Agic, D.: Discrete Fourier transform-based watermarking method with an optimal implementation radius. J. Electron. Imaging **20**(3), 033008 (2011)
17. Cheddad, A., Condell, J., Curran, K., Mc Kevitt, P.: Digital image steganography: Survey and analysis of current methods. Sig. Process. **90**(3), 727–752 (2010)
18. Database: PICS (Psychological Image Collection at Stirling), Aberdeen (2012)

3d Acquisition, Processing and Applications

No-Reference 3D Mesh Quality Assessment Based on Dihedral Angles Model and Support Vector Regression

Ilyass Abouelaziz[1]([✉]), Mohammed El Hassouni[1], and Hocine Cherifi[2]

[1] LRIT URAC 29, Mohammed V University in Rabat, Rabat, Morocco
ilyass.abouelaziz@gmail.com
[2] LE2I, UMR 6306 CNRS, University of Burgundy, Dijon, France

Abstract. 3D meshes are subject to various visual distortions during their transmission and geometrical processing. Several works have tried to evaluate the visual quality using either full reference or reduced reference approaches. However, these approaches require the presence of the reference mesh which is not available in such practical situations. In this paper, the main contribution lies in the design of a computational method to automatically predict the perceived mesh quality without reference and without knowing beforehand the distortion type. Following the no-reference (NR) quality assessment principle, the proposed method focuses only on the distorted mesh. Specifically, the dihedral angles are firstly computed as a surface roughness indexes and so a structural information descriptors. Then, a visual masking modulation is applied to this angles according to the main characteristics of the human visual system. The well known statistical Gamma model is used to fit the dihedral angles distribution. Finally, the estimated parameters of the model are learned to the support vector regression (SVR) in order to predict the quality score. Experimental results demonstrate the highly competitive performance of the proposed no-reference method relative to the most influential methods for mesh quality assessment.

Keywords: No-reference mesh quality assessment · Support vector regression · Dihedral angles · Gamma distribution · Visual masking effect

1 Introduction

With any application domain, 3D meshes are usually subject to different geometric transformations. These operations introduce slight distortions on the 3D shape of the object that may alter the visual quality of the model. The Mesh Visual Quality (MVQ) assessment tries to identify how much the original model has been distorted.

Many approaches have been used to evaluate the visual quality of a distorted mesh. Root mean squared error RMS [1] and Hausdorff distance [2] use a simple similarity between the reference mesh and the distorted one. This kind of

A. Mansouri et al. (Eds.): ICISP 2016, LNCS 9680, pp. 369–377, 2016.
DOI: 10.1007/978-3-319-33618-3_37

metrics generally fails to reflect the perceived visual quality since it computes a pure geometric distance neglecting the main operations of the human visual system (HVS) [3]. Several metrics use different perceptual principles for a better estimation of the perceived quality [4–6]. All the metrics cited above are full reference metrics, i.e. the reference content is fully available. Another type of metrics where only a part of the information is available called reduced reference. In this type, the visual quality is evaluated by comparing some features extracted from both the reference mesh and the distorted one [7–9].

Despite their suitability to several type of distortion, the main drawback of theses methods, is the non availability of the reference mesh in such practical situations. To remedy this problem, we propose a novel no-reference method for 3D mesh quality assessment. Our contribution is twofold. First, we extract features only from the distorted mesh by estimating the parameters from the dihedral angles distribution model. Then, we employ theses features in a learning framework to predict the objective quality score using the support vector regression [10].

The reminder of this paper is organized as follows. In Sect. 2, we give a brief overview of our proposed no-reference quality assessment method as well as a description of the different steps including the visual masking modulation and the feature learning. Experimental results and comparisons are provided in Sect. 3. Finally, we draw in Sect. 4 some concluding remarks and perspectives.

2   The Proposed No-Reference Quality Assessment Method

An overview of the proposed no-reference mesh quality assessment method is shown in Fig. 1. As we have already mentioned, this method focus only on the distorted mesh to predict the quality score, to put it differently, the reference mesh is not involved in any step of the processing. Given a distorted mesh, we extract in the first step the dihedral angles performed by normals of adjacent triangular faces. Afterwards, a visual masking modulation is involved in order to take into consideration the masking effect [3], which is an important characteristic of the human visual system (HVS). The next step is to estimate statistical parameters of the extracted dihedral angles using the Gamma distribution, this

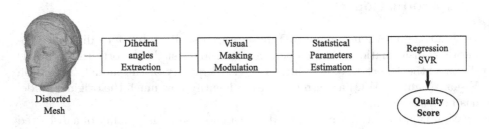

Fig. 1. Flowchart of the proposed no-reference mesh quality assessment method.

step is very crucial to deal with the time complexity. Finally, we intend to use a regression method for the constructed feature learning, we employ in our work the support vector regression with different kernels in order to predict the objective quality score.

2.1 Dihedral Angles Extraction

The first step of our processing is to extract dihedral angles representing the structural aspect of the 3D mesh. Dihedral angles were used previously by several works in the context of measuring the distortion of 3D meshes. Corsini et al. [7] behold that the dihedral angle is strongly related to the surface roughness, therefore, in that work dihedral angles are only used to construct the concept of global roughness. In our work, we avoid this assumption by taking the dihedral angle as a relevant information which can be used to extract statistical parameters. These latter are used as an input features for the regression based learning step. The dihedral angle by definition is the angle formed by two normals N_1 and N_2 of two adjacent triangular faces. The dihedral angle Φ is calculated by:

$$\Phi = acos \left(\frac{N_1 \cdot N_2}{norm(N_1) \times norm(N_2)} \right) \tag{1}$$

Where norm is the Euclidean distance. The angles vector is then obtained by concatenating all angles computed from the whole 3D mesh.

$$\Phi_i = [\Phi_1, \Phi_2, \Phi_3, ..., \Phi_n] \tag{2}$$

Where n is the number of neighborhoods in the mesh.

2.2 Visual Masking Effect Modulation

The visual masking effect is one of the most important characteristics of the human visual system HSV. In the context of 3D modeling, the concept of visual masking can be explained as the fact that the human perception cannot notice a small distortion located on a rough area, whereas human observers are able to detect distortion easily in smooth areas. To take into account the visual masking effect, we have to mask the distortion in rough regions. Using dihedral angles, roughness can be identified by extraction high magnitude dihedral angles. To reduce the high magnitude dihedral angles, we multiply the angles vector Φ_i by a roughness weight function RW_i defined as follows:

$$RW_i = \exp \left(-\frac{\Phi_i}{2 \cdot \sigma^2} \right) \tag{3}$$

where σ is the standard deviation of the dihedral angles vector. The visual masking modulation is then calculated as:

$$\Phi_{masking} = \Phi_i \cdot RW_i \tag{4}$$

2.3   Statistical Parameters Estimation

In order to restrict the amount of the learning data, and hence to keep the execution time complexity under control, we intend to use a statistical parameter estimation by a non-Gaussian statistical model which is the Gamma distribution. Figure 2 shows an example of histograms of Armadillo's and Dinosaur's angles. We observe that the estimated Gamma model fits perfectly the empirical dihedral angles distribution. Therefore, we can quite simply use the estimated parameters of the model and reduce the amount of data, and consequently optimize the computational time.

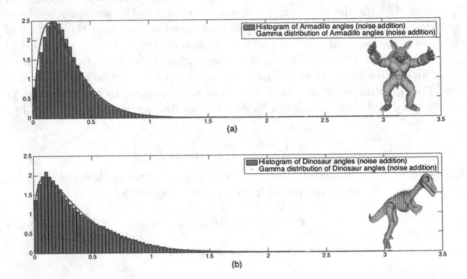

Fig. 2. Histogram of the extracted dihedral angles from Armadillo (a) and Dinosaur (b) with noise addition, with their corresponding plots of the fitted Gamma distribution.

We say that a random variable x follows Gamma law with a shape parameter b and a scale parameter θ if it admits for probability density:

$$p(x; b, \theta) = \frac{\theta^{-b} x^{b-1}}{\Gamma(b)} \exp\left(-\frac{x}{\theta}\right) \quad 0 < x < \infty \tag{5}$$

Where $\Gamma(.)$ denotes the Gamma function. We recall that parameters are estimated using the maximum likelihood ML method. The estimated parameters are then used as an input feature vectors for the support vector regression.

2.4   Feature Learning: Support Vector Regression (SVR)

Support Vector Regression (SVR) is an extension of the support vector machines (SVM) [10] for a numeric prediction. The support vector machine is a supervised classification system that finds the maximum margin hyperplane separating two classes of data. The training instances that are closest to this hyperplane are called support vectors. In order to predict the objective quality scores for distorted meshes, we use in our work the support vector regression. We denote by x_i the feature vector for a distorted mesh M_i^d with a subjective score y_i. The regression function of an observation x to classify is given as follows:

$$f_{SVR} = \sum_{x_i \in V_s} \alpha_i y_i K(x_i, x) + b, \tag{6}$$

where V_S are the support vectors, (x_i, y_i) presents the training set and α denotes the Lagrange multipliers obtained in the minimization process. Furthermore, $K(x_i, x)$ is the kernel function, in this work we compare four different kernels: linear, polynomial, radial basis function (RBF) and sigmoid. Table 1 shows the different kernels used with their mathematical equations and parameters.

Table 1. Kernels used for the support vectors regression.

Kernel	Equation	Parameters
Linear	$K(x_i, x_j) = x_i^T x_j$	-
Polynomial	$K(x_i, x_j) = (\gamma x_i^T x_j + r)^d$	γ, d, r
Radial basis function (RBF)	$K(x_i, x_j) = \exp(\gamma \|x_i - x_j\|^2)$	γ
Segmod	$K(x_i, x_j) = \tanh(\gamma x_i^T x_j + r)$	γ, r

Besides the kernel parameters cited above, SVR involves another parameter C called the penalty parameter of the error term. For each chosen kernel, it is required to select best parameters values, this selection is very crucial and strongly affect the prediction results. Discussions about the different tests as well as the experimental results are analyzed in the next section.

3 Experimental Results

In this section we evaluate the effectiveness and forcefulness of the proposed no-reference quality assessment method on two publicly available databases:

The LIRIS/EPFL General-Purpose Database[1] [4]: This database was created at the EPFL, Switzerland. It contains 4 reference meshes: Armadillo, Dyno, Venus and RockerArm, and 84 distorted models (88 models total). Two types of distortion are applied: smoothing and noise addition either locally or globally on the reference mesh Fig. 3 shows some models from the LIRIS/EPFL general-purpose database and their distorted versions. The subjective evaluation was done by 12 observers.

The LIRIS Masking Database (see footnote 1) [11]: This database was created at the Universite of Lyon, France. It contains 4 reference meshes: Armadillo, Bimba, Dyno and Lion, and 24 distorted models (28 model total). The local noise addition is the only type of distortion applied Fig. 4 shows some models

---

[1] http://liris.cnrs.fr/guillaume.lavoue/data/datasets.html.

Fig. 3. Some models from the LIRIS/EPFL general-purpose database and their distorted versions: (a) reference meshes. (b) distorted meshes, from left to right are respectively: Armadillo with global noise, Rockerarm with noise in smooth regions, Dinosaur with global smoothing, and Venus with noise in rough regions.

from the LIRIS Masking Database and their distorted versions. The specific objective of this database is to test the capability of mesh visual quality metrics in capturing the visual masking effect. The subjective evaluation was done by 11 observers.

Fig. 4. Some models from the LIRIS Masking Database and their distorted versions: (a) reference meshes. (b) distorted meshes with noise addition.

As we have mentioned before, we used in this work four different kernels for the support vector regression: Linear, polynomial, radial basis function (RBF) and sigmoid kernel, with a grid search space on the kernel parameters in order to select the best parameters values. The correlation between the perceptual distances produced by the method and the mean opinion scores (MOS) produced by subjects is used as criteria to evaluate the performance of an objective mesh visual quality MVQ metric. Usually two types of correlation coefficients are commonly used: the Pearson linear correlation coefficient which employed to measure the prediction accuracy, and the Spearman rank-order correlation coefficient which employed to measure the prediction monotonicity [12].

3.1 Comparison of Different Kernels

It is not evident beforehand which kernel to use to predict the quality score by the SVR, thus we compare four kernels: Linear, polynomial, RBF and sigmoid. The focal point is to select the adequate kernel with a selective parameters that conducts to the best SVR prediction on the two databases. Table 2 shows the tested kernels as well as the Pearson and Spearman correlation coefficients from the proposed method on the LIRIS masking database. Note that we determine the best kernel and parameters by maximizing jointly the r_s and r_p values.

Table 2. Correlation coefficients r_s (%) and r_p (%) of our proposed metric according to the tested kernels on the LIRIS masking database

	Armadillo		Lion		Bimba		Dyno		All models	
	r_s	r_p	r_s	r_p	r_s	r_p	r_s	r_p	r_s	r_p
Linear	89.2	83.4	94.4	95.3	77.8	88.5	76	89	79.7	88.6
Polynomial	77.3	83.2	77.5	97.0	77.1	95.2	94.0	88.7	88.3	91.0
RBF	**89.5**	**84.7**	**100**	**96.3**	**94.2**	**93.6**	**94.4**	**89.7**	**90.4**	**91.2**
Sigmoid	89.2	83.3	94.5	96.1	77.4	88.1	94.0	89.3	81.2	88.3

According to Table 2, the experimental tests show that the correlation scores varies from a kernel to another, although there is not a huge difference between the predicted scores by the different kernels, but it is quite noteworthy that the RBF kernel with the pair ($C = 2^{11}, \gamma = 2^{-15}$) shows a great performance and overtake the 90 % correlation threshold in term of both r_s and r_p coefficients. Similarly, we find that the RBF kernel gives the best results on the general-purpose database with a correlation scores $r_s = 81.5\%$ and $r_p = 87.5\%$ with the pair ($C = 2^{-4}, \gamma = 2^{-5}$). Accordingly, we select the RBF as the most suitable SVR kernel used for the feature learning step.

3.2 Comparison with Full Reference and Reduced Reference Methods

In this section, we compare our proposed no-reference mesh quality assessment method with several existing full reference metrics as well as reduced reference metrics. Values of r_s and r_p from the compared objective mesh visual quality metrics on the two considered databases are listed in Tables 3 and 4. The proposed no-reference metric has the highest r_s and r_p values on the LIRIS masking database (whole corpus). In fact this database is manufactured to evaluate the visual masking effect. The good results and performances provided by the proposed method confirm that the visual masking modulation used in this work is

Table 3. Correlation coefficients r_s (%) and r_p (%) of different objective metrics on LIRIS masking database.

Type	Metric	Armadillo		Lion		Bimba		Dyno		All models	
		r_s	r_p	r_s	r_p	r_s	r_p	r_s	r_p	r_s	r_p
Full reference	HD [2]	48.6	37.7	71.4	25.1	25.7	7.5	48.6	31.1	26.6	4.1
	RMS [1]	65.6	44.6	71.4	23.8	71.4	21.8	71.4	50.3	48.8	17.0
	MSDM2 [4]	81.1	88.6	93.5	94.3	96.8	100	95.6	100	87.3	89.6
	DAME [5]	96.0	94.3	99.5	100	88.0	97.7	89.4	82.9	58.6	68.1
	TPDM [6]	91.4	88.6	88.4	82.9	97.1	100	71.1	100	88.6	90.0
Reduced reference	3DWPM1 [7]	58.0	41.8	20.0	9.7	20.0	8.4	66.7	45.3	29.4	10.2
	3DWPM2 [7]	48.6	37.9	38.3	22.0	37.1	14.4	71.4	50.1	37.4	18.2
	FMPD [8]	94.2	88.6	93.5	94.3	98.9	100	96.9	94.3	80.8	80.2
	KLDGamma [9]	53.9	48.57	71.43	75.07	95.98	88.16	95.36	90.12	74.29	64.01
No-reference	Our method	89.5	84.7	100	96.3	94.2	93.6	94.4	89.7	**90.4**	**91.2**

Table 4. Correlation coefficients r_s (%) and r_p (%) of different objective metrics on LIRIS/EPFL general-purpose database.

Type	Metric	Armadillo		Dyno		Venus		Rocker		All models	
		r_s	r_p	r_s	r_p	r_s	r_p	r_s	r_p	r_s	r_p
Full reference	HD [2]	69.5	30.2	30.9	22.6	1.6	0.8	18.1	5.5	13.8	1.3
	RMS [1]	62.7	32.3	0.3	0.0	90.1	77.3	7.3	3.0	26.8	7.9
	MSDM2 [4]	81.6	85.3	85.9.4	85.7	89.3	87.5	89.6	87.2	**80.4**	**81.4**
	DAME [5]	60.3	76.3	92.8	88.9	91.0	83.9	85.0	80.1	76.6	75.2
	TPDM [6]	84.5	78.8	92.2	89.0	90.6	91.0	92.2	91.4	**89.6**	**89.2**
Reduced reference	3DWPM1 [7]	65.8	35.7	62.7	35.7	71.6	46.6	87.5	53.2	69.3	38.4
	3DWPM2 [7]	74.1	43.1	52.4	19.9	34.8	16.4	37.8	29.9	49.0	24.6
	FMPD [8]	75.4	83.2	89.6	88.9	87.5	83.9	88.8	84.7	**81.9**	**83.5**
	KLDGamma [9]	71.09	77.65	67.94	70.55	88.60	83.42	78.70	57.54	71.56	73.95
No-reference	Our method	76.8	91.5	78.6	84.1	85.7	88.6	86.2	86.6	**81.5**	**87.8**

very effective. Furthermore, the proposed method provides competitive scores on the general-purpose database (comparative scores with MSDM2 [4], TPDM [6] and FMPD [8]). These results show the effectiveness and forcefulness of the proposed no-reference quality assessment method.

4   Conclusion

We have designed and implemented an efficient and effective method for a no-reference mesh quality assessment. Given only a distorted mesh, the proposed scheme extract dihedral angles as relevant information that describe the structural information. The extracted feature vector is then modulated with a visual masking to take into consideration the visual masking effect, which is an important characteristic of the human visual system. The obtained vector is then modeled by the Gamma distribution in order to construct feature vectors with only 2 parameters instead of using whole features values. This step is very crucial to lessen the computational time. Once feature vectors are constructed, the proposed scheme predicts the numeric quality score by training features using the support vectors regression (SVR). Compared with existing full reference and reduced reference mesh quality assessment, the proposed no-reference method based on SVR provides more coherent results with subjective scores, especially on the LIRIS masking database, proving that the visual masking modulation used is very effective.

The current stage of development for the proposed method is limited to use only the visual masking effect, knowing that we can use more HVS characteristics. Extending the proposed method by using saturation effect will be a possible direction of future work. Another possible extension is to extract more relevant features that might present the visual aspect of the 3D mesh, and improve the current results.

Acknowledgment. This work has been supported the Franco-Moroccan projet STIC 02/14.

References

1. Cignoni, P., Rocchini, C., Scopigno, R.: Metro: measuring error on simplified surfaces. Comput. Graphics Forum **17**(2), 167–174 (1998). Wiley Online Library
2. Aspert, N., Santa Cruz, D., Ebrahimi, T.: Mesh: measuring errors between surfaces using the hausdorff distance. In: ICME, vol. 1, pp. 705–708 (2002)
3. Breitmeyer, B.G.: Visual masking: past accomplishments, present status, future developments. Adv. Cogn. Psychol. **3**(1–2), 9 (2007)
4. Lavoue, G., Gelasca, E.D., Dupont, F., Baskurt, A., Ebrahimi, T.: Perceptually driven 3d distance metrics with application to watermarking. In: SPIE Optics + Photonics. International Society for Optics and Photonics, p. 63120L (2006)
5. Vasa, L., Rus, J.: Dihedral angle mesh error: a fast perception correlated distortion measure for fixed connectivity triangle meshes. Comput. Graphics Forum **31**(5), 1715–1724 (2012). Wiley Online Library
6. Torkhani, F., Wang, K., Chassery, J.-M.: A curvature-tensor-based perceptual quality metric for 3D triangular meshes. Mach. Graphics Vis. **23**(1), 1–25 (2014)
7. Corsini, M., Gelasca, E.D., Ebrahimi, T., Barni, M.: Watermarked 3-d mesh quality assessment. IEEE Trans. Multimedia **9**(2), 247–256 (2007)
8. Wang, K., Torkhani, F., Montanvert, A.: A fast roughness-based approach to the assessment of 3D mesh visual quality. Comput. Graph. **36**(7), 808–818 (2012)
9. Abouelaziz, I., Omari, M., El Hassouni, M., Cherifi, H.: Reduced reference 3D mesh quality assessment based on statistical models. In: International Conference on Signal-Image Technology & Internet-Based Systems (SITIS), Bangkok, Thailand. IEEE, November 2015
10. Vapnik, V.N.: The Nature of Statistical Learning Theory. Springer-Verlag, New York (1995)
11. Lavoue, G.: A local roughness measure for 3d meshes and its application to visual masking. ACM Trans. Appl. Percept. (TAP) **5**(4), 21 (2009)
12. Wang, Z., Bovik, A.C.: Modern image quality assessment. Synth. Lect. Image Video Multimedia Process. **2**(1), 1–156 (2006)

Kinect Depth Holes Filling by Similarity and Position Constrained Sparse Representation

Jinhui Hu[1]($\boxtimes$), Zhongyuan Wang[2], and Ruolin Ruan[3]

[1] China Academy of Electronics and Information Technology, Beijing, China
cn.hjh@hotmail.com
[2] School of Computer, Wuhan University, Wuhan, China
wzy_hope@163.com
[3] School of Biomedical Engineering, Hubei University of Science and Technology, Xianning, China
rlruan@163.com

Abstract. Due to measurement errors or interference noise, Kinect depth maps exhibit severe defects of holes and noise, which significantly affect their applicability to stereo visions. Filtering and inpainting techniques have been extensively applied to hole filling. However, they either fail to fill in large holes or introduce other artifacts near depth discontinuities, such as blurring, jagging, and ringing. The emerging reconstruction-based methods employ underlying regularized representation models to obtain relatively accurate combination coefficients, leading to improved depth recovery results. Motivated by sparse representation, this paper advocates a similarity and position constrained sparse representation for Kinect depth recovery, which considers the constraints of intensity similarity and spatial distance between reference patches and target one on sparsity penalty term, as well as position constraint of centroid pixel in the target patch on data-fidelity term. Various experimental results on real-world Kinect maps and public datasets show that the proposed method outperforms state-of-the-art methods in filling effects of both flat and discontinuous regions.

Keywords: Sparse · Kinect · Depth map · Hole filling

1 Introduction

Microsoft Kinect is a representative RGB-D sensor that has achieved great success in a wide variety of vision related applications such as augmented reality, robotics, and human-computer interactions. The performance of these applications largely depends on the quality of acquired depth images. It has been observed that Kinect depth maps suffer from various defects, including holes, wrong or inaccurate depth measurements, and interference noise. Because the depth information is unavailable in holes and depth discontinuities between objects should be preserved, the recovery of Kinect depth maps has become a challenging problem.

Qi et al. [1] proposed a fusion based method using non-local filtering scheme for restoring depth maps. He et al. [2] proposed a guided filter that can preserve sharp edge

© Springer International Publishing Switzerland 2016
A. Mansouri et al. (Eds.): ICISP 2016, LNCS 9680, pp. 378–387, 2016.
DOI: 10.1007/978-3-319-33618-3_38

and avoid reversal artifacts when smoothing a depth map. Dakkak et al. [3] proposed an iterative diffusion method which utilizes both available depth values and color segmentation results to recover missing depth information, but the results are sensitive to the segmentation accuracy. In order to obtain more precise filter coefficients, Camplani et al. [4] used a joint bilateral filter to calculate the weights of available depth pixels according to collocated pixels in color image. Based on a joint histogram, Min et al. [5] instead proposed a weighted mode filter to prevent the output depth values from being blurred on the depth boundaries. However, filtering-based approaches often yield poor results near the depth discontinuities, especially around the large holes.

Inpainting techniques seem more promising in depth hole filling than filtering, interpolation and extrapolation algorithms. With an aligned color image, Liu et al. [6] proposed an extended FMM approach [7] to guide depth inpainting. Structure-based inpainting [8] fills the holes by propagating structure into the target regions via diffusion. The diffusion process makes holes blurred, and texture is thus lost. Xu et al. [9] further introduced the exemplar-based texture synthesis into structure propagation so that the blurring effects can be somewhat avoided. In order to prevent edge fatting or shrinking after hole inpainting, Miao et al. [10] used the fluctuating edge region in depth map to assist hole completion. However, the missing depth values near the object contour are directly assigned to the mean of available depth values in fluctuating edge region, which is hence inaccurate for representing the depth contours.

Reconstruction-based methods apply image synthesis techniques to predict missing depth values. Since the reconstruction coefficients are resolved in a closed-loop scheme in terms of the minimization of residuals, higher hole-filling accuracy is achievable. Chen et al. [11, 12] cast the depth recovery as an energy minimization problem, which addresses the depth hole filling and denoising simultaneously. Yang et al. [13] proposed an adaptive color-guided autoregressive (AR) model for high quality depth recovery, where the depth recovery task is converted into a minimization of AR prediction errors subject to measurement consistency.

Based on sparse representation, in this paper, we represent missing depth regions as the linear combination of the surrounding available depth values, and establish a similarity and position constrained sparse representation (SPSR) to solve the optimal weights with the help of the associated color image. SPSR comprises similarity-distance-inducing weighted $\ell 1$ sparsity penalty term and position-inducing weighted data-fidelity term, which thus not only readily grasps the salient features of depth image but also considerably promotes representation accuracy.

2 Proposed Method

2.1 Problem Setup

In reconstruction-based methods, the missing depth value is recovered from the surrounding available pixels around the target by a linear weighted combination representation. Let $D(x)$ denote the missing depth at position x and $\{D(y_m) \mid 1 \leq m \leq M\}$ denote all M known depth pixels at positions $\{y_m \mid 1 \leq m \leq M\}$ in a search window centered at x. This procedure reads

$$D(x) = \sum_{m=1}^{M} w(y_m)D(y_m) \tag{1}$$

where $w(y_m)$ is the coefficient of $D(y_m)$, reflecting the contribution of the available depth value at position y_m to the reconstruction. The key issue for successfully reconstructing $D(x)$ is to appropriately determine predictor coefficients.

Reconstruction coefficients are usually assigned by how similar surrounding pixels are to the target pixel. Gaussian smoothing filter, bilateral filter [14] and non-local means (NLM) [15] is able to obtain the coefficients.

However, the coefficients by the above mentioned methods are primarily responsible for the distance or similarity between the nearby pixels and the target pixel, but neglect the data fidelity in terms of the reconstruction error. In contrast, linear regression method can resolve the coefficients by minimizing the error between reconstructed data and observed data, whose solution is hence theoretically deduced rather than intuitively assigned. Furthermore, since the lost depth pixels cannot provide a valid observation, the objective of the linear regression is usually established on the basis of the color image instead of the depth map.

2.2 Similarity and Position Constrained Sparse Representation

In formulating the objective regression function, if only the target pixel is represented as a linear combination of surrounding pixels, the equation is too much under-determined and is thus hard to address. Inspired by the NLM, we instead perform a patch-wise regression analysis. Patches are centered on the target pixel to be recovered, where all pixels instead of the single centroid pixel attend the regression.

Figure 1 illustrates the outline of our used framework, which consists of two major phases: analysis phase and synthesis phase. The former fulfills patch-wise regression analysis to obtain the linear combination coefficients in color space, and then the latter reconstructs the missing counterpart depth with the available coefficients. To ensure that

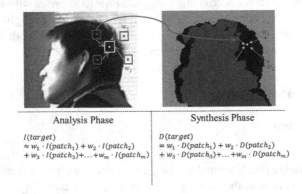

Analysis Phase	Synthesis Phase
$I(target)$	$D(target)$
$\approx w_1 \cdot I(patch_1) + w_2 \cdot I(patch_2)$	$= w_1 \cdot D(patch_1) + w_2 \cdot D(patch_2)$
$+ w_3 \cdot I(patch_3) + \ldots + w_m \cdot I(patch_m)$	$+ w_3 \cdot D(patch_3) + \ldots + w_m \cdot D(patch_m)$

Fig. 1. Outline of the analysis and synthesis framework in hole filling. Notations "I" and "D" mean the color intensity of a certain patch and the depth of a certain pixel, respectively.

the synthesis phase uses valid reference depth values, the corresponding depth pixel of the centroid pixel in a reference patch should not be located at holes.

Let $\mathbf{x} \in R^{N\times1}$ be an observed patch, stacked into a N-dimensional column vector, and $\mathbf{Y} \in R^{N\times M}$ be a training set being composed of M nearby reference patches in a window, whose m-th column consists of an individual reference patch $\mathbf{Y}_m$. Without loss of generality, the regularized linear regression reads:

$$\mathbf{w}^* = \arg\min_{\mathbf{w}} \left\{ ||\mathbf{x} - \mathbf{Yw}||_2^2 + \lambda\Omega(\mathbf{w}) \right\} \tag{2}$$

where $\mathbf{w} \in R^{M\times1}$ is an unknown coefficient vector, whose entries $\mathbf{w}_i$, $i = 1, 2, \ldots, M$ is associated with an individual basis in training set. $||\mathbf{x} - \mathbf{Yw}||_2^2$ is the so-called data-fidelity term, representing regression error (fitting error), and $\Omega(\mathbf{w})$ is a prior related penalty term. Typically, $\Omega(\mathbf{w}) = ||\mathbf{w}||_1$, corresponding to ℓ_1 norm sparse representation; or $\Omega(\mathbf{w}) = ||\mathbf{w}||_2^2$, corresponding to squared ℓ_2 norm ridge regression. The penalty term in the form of ℓ_1 norm or squared ℓ_2 norm promotes sparsity or smoothness of solution, respectively. Parameter $\lambda \geq 0$ is an appropriately chosen regularization factor, tuning the tradeoff between the regression error and the penalization.

In a deep insight, the pixels belonging the same object nearly share equal depth values, while pixels located in different objects often give quite distinct depth values. From the perspective of the reconstruction of missing depth values, the surrounding candidates in the same object should own larger weights than others. Thus, the reconstruction coefficients of depth maps are sparse in nature. In fact, sparsity priors have been extensively exploited in previous works [16–18], which approach the problem of depth inference by including a sparsity prior on local depth features. Therefore, we cast the reconstruction of lost depth values as a sparsity representation problem, thus efficiently charactering the saliency of depth maps and adapting to the structure of depth signals.

Bilateral filter considers spatial distance and intensity similarity in constructing coefficients, yet irrespective of prediction residuals. Regression analysis, on the contrary, considers fitting error, but completely ignores geometric distance and similarity. To make full use of the advantages offered by bilateral filter and regression analysis, we intend to incorporate the metrics of distance and similarity into the regularized objective function. Following this idea, one possible approach is to impose constraints onto the weight penalty term. In this paper, we take ℓ_1 norm SR and its weighted variant on penalty term is expressed as:

$$\mathbf{w}^* = \arg\min_{\mathbf{w}} \left\{ ||\mathbf{x} - \mathbf{Yw}||_2^2 + \lambda||\mathbf{h}\circ\mathbf{w}||_1 \right\} \tag{3}$$

where "$\circ$" denotes element-wise vector product and $\mathbf{h}$ is the weights preferring the desirable properties of sparse solution $\mathbf{w}$. Obviously, the large entries of $\mathbf{h}$ will result in small entries of $\mathbf{w}$. Therefore, if we specify $\mathbf{h}$ by the product of spatial distance and intensity similarity, i.e., $\mathbf{h} = \mathbf{d}\circ\mathbf{s}$, then the reference patches being close and similar to the target patch will be expected to take large coefficients. To be more precise, spatial distance $\mathbf{d}$ is patch-wisely calculated by the Euclidean measure of the centroid coordinates of target and reference patches. Suppose the target patch locates at (i, j) and the m-th reference one locates at (k, l), then the m-th entry of $\mathbf{d}$ given by:

$$\mathbf{d}_m = \sqrt{(i - k)^2 + (j - l)^2} \tag{4}$$

Intensity similarity $\mathbf{s}$ is obtained in terms of the Euclidean measure of the pixel values in target patch and individual reference one:

$$\mathbf{s}_m = ||\mathbf{x} - \mathbf{Y}_m||_2 \tag{5}$$

As illustrated in Fig. 1, although the coefficients are obtained for a whole patch centered at the target color pixel, yet they are only applied to the reconstruction of the centroid depth pixel rather than all pixels in a depth patch. Therefore, the centroid target pixel should be given higher priority than other ones in computing the regression error. In other words, the errors of centroid pixels in a patch should be overestimated while those of the faraway pixels from patch center should be underestimated. If we use weighting on errors to serve this purpose, the centroid pixels should be assigned larger weights than others. Alternatively, the weights should be in inverse proportion to the spatial intervals of the pixels to the centroid one. As usually done, weights derived from Gaussian kernel function with respect to distance could be a better choice. Let $\mathbf{p}$ denote the relative positions (in Euclidean distance) of any pixels to the centroid one, then the weights read:

$$\mathbf{k} = \exp(-\frac{\mathbf{p}^2}{2\sigma^2}) \tag{6}$$

where σ is the decay of the exponential function. Obviously, the centroid pixel owns the largest weight, namely, 1.

Incorporating the position weights $\mathbf{k}$ into the error term in Eq. (3), we have a reformulated equation as follows:

$$\mathbf{w}^* = \arg\min_{\mathbf{w}} \left\{ ||\mathbf{k} \circ (\mathbf{x} - \mathbf{Y}\mathbf{w})||_2^2 + \lambda ||\mathbf{h} \circ \mathbf{w}||_1 \right\} \tag{7}$$

which considers the spatial distance and similarity constraints on coefficients via weighting penalty term, and the position constraint on regression errors via weighting data-fidelity term.

Let $\mathbf{K}$ and $\mathbf{H}$ be diagonal weighting matrices with diagonal elements respectively being $\mathbf{k}$ and $\mathbf{h}$ and elsewhere being zeros. Equation (7) can be rewritten as:

$$\mathbf{w}^* = \arg\min_{\mathbf{w}} \left\{ ||\mathbf{K}(\mathbf{x} - \mathbf{Y}\mathbf{w})||_2^2 + \lambda ||\mathbf{H}\mathbf{w}||_1 \right\} \tag{8}$$

$||\mathbf{H}\mathbf{w}||_1$ is actually the weighted variant of ℓ_1 norm. Let $\mathbf{w}' = \mathbf{H}\mathbf{w}$, and thus $\mathbf{w} = \mathbf{H}^{-1}\mathbf{w}'$, Eq. (8) can be turned into:

$$\mathbf{w}^* = \arg\min_{\mathbf{w}} \left\{ ||\mathbf{K}(\mathbf{x} - \mathbf{Y}\mathbf{H}^{-1}\mathbf{w}')||_2^2 + \lambda ||\mathbf{w}'||_1 \right\} \tag{9}$$

which can then be conveniently solved using the popular ℓ_1 norm SR numerical algorithms. Reconstruction weights are firstly solved with Eq. (9) in the associated color image and are then used to synthesize the missing depth values with Eq. (1).

3   Experiments and Results

In this section, we conduct experiments to evaluate the overall performance of the proposed algorithm. The experimental datasets contain real-world Kinect depths acquired by ourselves in door and public datasets from Middlebury RGB-D database [19], which are respectively used for qualitative and quantitative evaluations. The captured Kinect images are in a resolution of 480×640 while Middlebury datasets enjoy a bit bigger size of 555×660. Three representative state-of-the-art methods, such as Camplani's joint bilateral filtering (JBF) [4], Liu's color-guided FMM inpainting (GFI) [6], and Yang's adaptive autoregressive reconstruction (AAR) [13], are used for comparisons on behalf of filter-based, inpainting-based and reconstruction-based methods, respectively. For parameter settings, our method sets the size of search window to 21×21, the size of patch to 5×5, and parameter λ to 0.1. The individual parameters in other methods are tuned to their best results according to [4, 6, 13].

3.1   Experiments on Real-World Kinect Depth Maps

In this subsection, our proposed similarity and position constrained $\ell1$ sparse representation is compared with the existing three methods: Camplani's JBF [4], Liu's GFI [6] and Yang's AAR [13]. To obtain real-world experimental samples, we captured indoor images under normal lighting conditions using Kinect. Because of lack of ground truth, we can only evaluate subjective effects. Two randomly selected results are shown in Figs. 2 and 4.

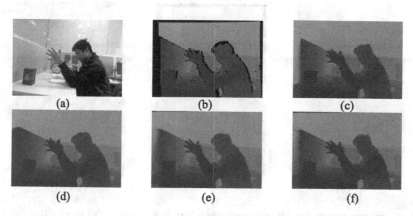

Fig. 2. Recovered results by different methods. (a) Color image; (b) Original depth map; (c) JBF; (d) GFI; (e) AAR; (f) Our method. (Color figure online)

As we can see from the recovered depth maps in Fig. 2, our method produces more reasonable recovery than anchors around the depth boundaries. Particularly, as shown in the highlighted regions, either JBF or GFI mistakes the holes between fingers in palm and incorrectly fills in them with the foreground depth values. To observe the differences more clearly, a local magnification version of the depth map in the highlighted palm region is shown in Fig. 3. As shown in the highlighted regions, either JBF or GFI mistakes the holes between fingers in palm and incorrectly fills in them with foreground depth values. AAR gives closer outcomes to our method since they are both based on reconstruction. Figure 4 shows an example where some large holes fail to be filled in due to sharp depth discontinuities, but our method produces relatively more adequate completion of the holes than anchors.

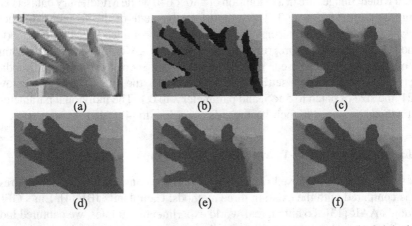

Fig. 3. A detailed comparison of marked palm area in Fig. 2. (a) Color image; (b) Original depth map; (c) JBF; (d) GFI; (e) AAR; (f) Our method. (Color figure online)

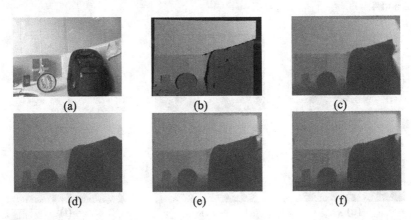

Fig. 4. Recovered results by different methods where some regions fail to be filled. (a) Color image; (b) Original depth map; (c) JBF; (d) GFI; (e) AAR; (f) Our method. (Color figure online)

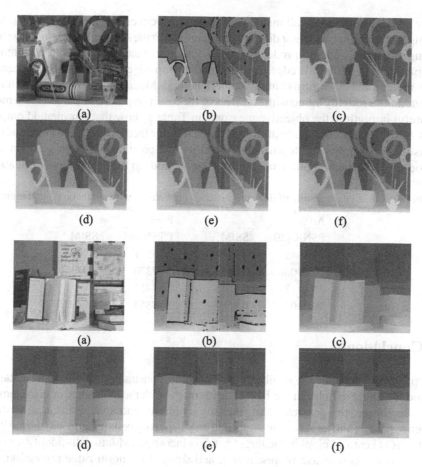

Fig. 5. Subjective results of different methods on Middlebury datasets with synthetic degradations. (a) Color image; (b) Degraded depth map; (c) JBF; (d) GFI; (e) AAR; (f) Our method. (Color figure online)

3.2 Experiments on Synthetically Degraded Datasets

In this subsection, we conduct another experiment on public datasets to comprehensively evaluate the performance of our method. In quantitative experiments, ground truth depth maps are needed to compute objective metrics, such as PSNR and SSIM (structural similarity measure). Reference [13] supplies the synthetic datasets with Kinect-like degradations from Middlebury's benchmark [19], where structural missing is created along depth discontinuities and random missing is generated in flat areas. We randomly select three groups for evaluations, referred to as Art and Book, with each consisting of a triple: a color image, an original depth map (as the ground truth), and an artificially degraded depth. Figure 5 shows the color images, degraded depths and recovered results by four methods. The quantitative results are then calculated against the ground truth and are tabulated in Table 1.

By a brief examination, all methods provide fine recovery performance for random missing in flat regions, and their differences mainly lie in the sharp discontinuities within missing areas. JBF and GFI produce annoying jaggy artifacts around depth discontinuities, particularly, at the side edge of the pot and the top edge of the book. But he results of our method and AAR turns out much more natural. Meanwhile, subjective performance variations roughly agree with statistics of the results reported in Table 1. In a more bit careful inspection, the objective measures in Table 1 show that our method outperforms AAR. This can be mainly attributed to the fact our method produces more optimal reconstruction weights due to imposed similarity and position constraints. Again, our method results in the best outcomes among four methods in the quantitative evaluation.

Table 1. Quantitative results of different methods on datasets with synthetic degradations.

	Art		Book	
	PSNR (dB)	SSIM	PSNR (dB)	SSIM
JBF	29.1845	0.9442	26.5911	0.9416
GFI	29.6900	0.9451	26.7370	0.9433
AAR	30.1118	0.9581	26.8811	0.9471
Our	30.3104	0.9587	26.8854	0.9492

4   Conclusions

This paper has presented a similarity and position constrained sparse representation method for filling in holes in the Kinect depth map. With the assistance of complementary color image, the constraints of intensity similarity and spatial distance between reference patches and target one are imposed on $\ell 1$ sparsity penalty term and the position constraint of centroid pixel in the target patch is incorporated into data-fidelity term. In contrast to standard sparse representation and squared $\ell 2$ norm ridge regression, the developed sparse representation variant considering such similarity and position constraints can provide more accurate coefficients to reliably predict lost depth pixels at sharp boundaries. The results demonstrate that our method outperforms previous approaches.

Acknowledgments. The research was supported by National Nature Science Foundation of China (61271256), the Team Plans Program of the Outstanding Young Science and Technology Innovation of Colleges and Universities in Hubei Province (T201513) and the Program of the Natural Science Foundation of Hubei Province (2015CFB452).

References

1. Qi, F., Han, J., Wang, P., Shi, G., Li, F.: Structure guided fusion for depth map inpainting. Pattern Recogn. Lett. **34**(1), 70–76 (2013)
2. He, K., Sun, J., Tang, X.: Guided image filtering. In: ECCV, pp. 1–14 (2010)
3. Dakkak, A., Husain, A.: Recovering missing depth information from Microsoft Kinect. http://www.andrew.cmu.edu/user/ammarh/projects/comp_vision.html

4. Camplani, M., Salgado, L.: Efficient spatio-temporal hole filling strategy for Kinect depth maps. In: Proceedings of SPIE, vol. 8290, p. 82900E (2012)
5. Min, D., Jiangbo, L., Do, M.N.: Depth video enhancement based on weighted mode filtering. IEEE Trans. Image Process. **21**(3), 1176–1190 (2012)
6. Liu, J., Gong, X.: Guided inpainting and filtering for Kinect depth maps. In: ICPR, pp. 1–4 (2012)
7. Telea, A.: An image inpainting technique based on the fast marching method. J. Graph. Tools **9**(1), 25–36 (2003)
8. Oliveira, M.M., Bowen, B., McKenna, R., Chang, Y.S.: Fast digital image inpainting. In: ICVIIP, pp. 261–266 (2001)
9. Xu, X., Po, L.-M., Cheung, C.-H., Feng, L., Ng, K.-H., Cheung, K.-W.: Depth-aided exemplar-based hole filling for DIBR view synthesis. In: ISCAS, pp. 2840–2843 (2013)
10. Miao, D., Fu, J., Lu, Y., Li, S., Chen, C.W.: Texture-assisted Kinect depth inpainting. In: ISCAS, pp. 604–607 (2012)
11. Chen, C., Cai, J., Zheng, J., Cham, T.-J., Shi, G.: A color-guided, region-adaptive and depth-selective unified framework for Kinect depth recovery. In: MMSP, pp. 7–12 (2013)
12. Chen, C., Cai, J., Zheng, J., Cham, T.-J., Shi, G.: Kinect depth recovery using a color-guided, region-adaptive and depth-selective unified framework. ACM Trans. Intell. Syst. Technol. http://dx.doi.org/10.1145/0000000.0000000
13. Yang, J., Ye, X., Li, K., Hou, C., Wang, Y.: Color-guided depth recovery from RGB-D data using an adaptive autoregressive model. IEEE Trans. Image Process. **23**(8), 3443–3458 (2014)
14. Tomasi, C., Manduchi, R.: Bilateral filtering for gray and color images. In: ICCV, pp. 839–846 (1998)
15. Buades, A., Coll, B.: A non-local algorithm for image denoising. In: CVPR, pp. 60–65 (2005)
16. Tosic, I., Olshausen, B.A., Culpepper, B.J.: Learning sparse representations of depth. IEEE J. Sel. Top. Sign. Process. **5**(5), 941–952 (2011)
17. Tosic, I., Drewes, S.: Learning joint intensity-depth sparse representations. IEEE Trans. Image Process. **23**(5), 2122–2132 (2014)
18. Harsha, G.N., Majumdar, A.: Disparity map computation for stereo images using compressive sampling. In: IASTED Signal and Image Processing, pp. 804–809 (2013)
19. Middlebury Datasets (2013). http://vision.middlebury.edu/stereo/data

Color Correction in 3D Digital Documentation: Case Study

Krzysztof Lech[1], Grzegorz Mączkowski[1(✉)], and Eryk Bunsch[2]

[1] Warsaw University of Technology, Boboli 8, 02-525 Warsaw, Poland
g.maczkowski@mchtr.pw.edu.pl
[2] Museum of King Jan III's Palace at Wilanów, Kostki Potockiego 10/16,
02-958 Warsaw, Poland

Abstract. Digital documentation of cultural heritage requires high quality spatial and color information. However the 3D data accuracy is already sufficiently high for many applications, the color representation of surface remains unsatisfactory. In this paper we describe issues encountered during 3D and color digitization based on a real-world case study. We focus on documentation of the King's Chinese Cabinet at Wilanów Palace (Warsaw, Poland). We show the scale of the undertaking and enumerate problems related to high resolution 3D scanning and reconstruction of the surface appearance despite object gloss, uneven illumination, limited field of view and utilization of multiple light sources and detectors. Our findings prove the complexity of cultural heritage digitization, justify the individual approach in each case and provide valuable guidelines for future applications.

Keywords: Cultural heritage documentation · Structured light projection · Color calibration · Highlights removal

1 Introduction

The technology of 3D digital documentation of shape is widely adopted in the field of cultural heritage digitization [1,2]. As the solutions mature they become easily available and offer better resolution and accuracy. However, these techniques put emphasis on the surface shape and either do not focus on the accuracy of the color reproduction or neglect it altogether. Independently, state-of-the-art multispectral and color digitization solutions exist and are also utilized in cultural heritage documentation [3,4]. They are sometimes combined with the 3D imaging in order to provide full appearance model of a documented artifact [5,6]. An important factor in capturing color of the imaged surface is its glossiness. Specular highlights affect the appearance and distort color information. Many specularity removal methods are described by Artusi et al. [7].

The presented work focuses on a combination of 3D surface digitization with color calibration and highlights removal in order to create a digital documentation of the Kings Chinese Cabinet at Wilanów Palace (Warsaw, Poland).

A. Mansouri et al. (Eds.): ICISP 2016, LNCS 9680, pp. 388–397, 2016.
DOI: 10.1007/978-3-319-33618-3_39

2   Investigated Object

King's Chinese Cabinet is a unique example of interior decorative art of the
XVIII century. Wooden panels were made using the European lacquer technique.
This work is attributed to the famous German craftsman Martin Schnell and his
workshop [8]. The original color scheme of the cabinet was much different from
its state in 2009 when a very difficult decision to remove secondary coatings
revealing the interior's original surface was made. The conservation works were
finished in 2012. The restored surface is diversified, containing lacquered matte
and glossy fragments of different colors and texture (Fig. 1a). These variations
make the digitization process challenging and enforce utilization of sophisticated
acquisition techniques.

Two scans of the whole chamber's surface with resolution 100 points per
square millimeter were made. The first measurement took place in 2009, before
the conservation work began. The second measurement was performed in
2015 [9]. The presented research is based on data collected during the second
digital documentation session.

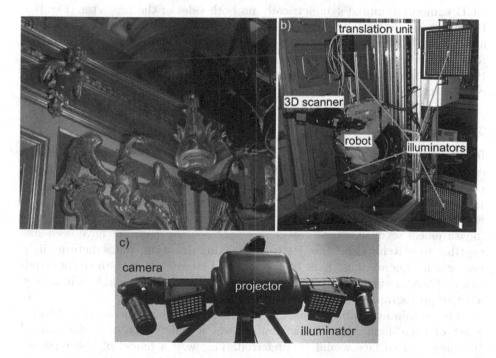

Fig. 1. The measurement setup: (a) photograph of a room corner fragment (author:
E. Bunsch). Visible part of the scanning equipment; (b) layout of the main setup
components; (c) 3D scanning head.

3   Measurement Setup

The measurement setup designed for the documentation is a dedicated device capable of simultaneous acquisition of 3D geometry and color. The main component of the setup is a structured light projection 3D scanner mounted on an industrial robot arm. Additionally, the robot is fixed on a vertical translation stage which also supports four matrix LED illuminators (Fig. 1a). In each position two series of images are captured. The first one collects data necessary for point cloud reconstruction, whereas the second series of images uses LED sources to capture texture data for color reconstruction. Because the same cameras are used for both sequences no additional texture mapping is necessary and each point in the resulting cloud features calibrated color information.

3.1   Structured Light Projection System

The structured light projection setup utilizes the well known sine fringes projection technique and Temporal Phase Shifting with Gray codes for unwrapped phase retrieval [10]. It consists of a DLP LED projector and two 9Mpix color, CCD cameras mounted symmetrically no both sides of the projector (Fig. 1b). Both cameras capture the same area of approximately 300×200 mm which gives a scanning resolution of 100 points per mm^2. The geometrical layout of the detectors is strictly related to the highly reflective properties of the scanned surface. It was important to capture the surface from two different directions in order to conveniently suppress specular highlights.

3.2   Illumination

Ideally, the illumination used for color acquisition should be diffuse, geometrically fixed and have high Color Rendering Index. However, due to specific object properties none of these assumptions could have been fully realized in practice. Because the task involved documentation of the whole room, including ceiling, it was not possible to provide fixed illumination without occlusions caused by the measurement setup itself. Moreover, the light sources must not have been susceptible to switching, because for each scanning direction, the structured light projection sequence must have been performed alternately with the color acquisition. Therefore usage of high-CRI tungsten lamps was not possible. Ultimately, a set of photographic, matrix LED illuminators was used.

The remaining problem was the distribution of the light sources. Ideally, a set of point light sources, distributed over a wide range of angles around the measured surface would be preferred. This way a model of bi-directional reflectance distribution function (BRDF) could have been estimated for each captured point. However, it was not feasible to realize in practice due to scanning time constraints and the amount of required raw data.

Using single, directional light source leads to specular highlights which are difficult to compensate for. Therefore the decision was made to use six independent lamps, switched one by one in order to capture a series of texture images.

Two sources were mounted on the measurement head, near cameras, to provide illumination from the direction close to the observation direction. Four remaining sources were fixed to the robot mount in a rectangular grid. They provide the same illumination direction, regardless of the robot's position (Fig. 1). The aim was to capture colorimetrically accurate texture of the scanned surface, without modeling the full BRDF response. Therefore the simplified light sources distribution was a compromise between appearance accuracy and real measurement conditions.

3.3   Automation of Scanning

The task of scanning the whole room with average resolution of 100 points/mm^2 required automation of the acquisition process in order to collect all data in a reasonable time. To achieve this, the robot was programmed to move along a path which spanned a grid of 25 scanning positions, distributed on a 5×5 square. Such sequence of measurements was performed automatically. Additional advantage of the automatic positions was that the 3D scanner could use the robot coordinate frame, so that point clouds within the sequence are simultaneously fitted and represented as a consistent fragment of the wall. These patches consisting of 50 clouds (for both cameras) were later positioned along each other with an ICP algorithm.

4   Color Correction Method

The aim of the color correction is to obtain trichromatic (RGB) texture, free of specular highlights and uneven illumination for each cloud. Additionally, intensity levels of color components in areas of cloud overlap should be minimized.

The proposed correction assumes a two-way approach. The first objective is to correct the texture images colorimetrically, so that differences between light sources are eliminated. Additional advantage of this procedure is that color information is obtained in independent color spaces CIE XYZ and CIE Lab for each point. This allows for future color comparison and color difference calculation. The second correction objective is the illumination uniformization and elimination of highlights. Such procedure corrects the overall model appearance and retrieves color information in places where reflections occurred.

4.1   Colorimetric Calibration

Although the utilized light sources come from the same manufacturer, they exhibit slight variations in perceived color temperature. This makes it impossible to adjust cameras white balance to fit all six sources. Therefore raw texture images show different color casts. Consequently, a linear model transforming raw camera RGB values to CIE XYZ components had to be found for each camera – source pair. Such procedure was earlier described by Hardeberg in [11].

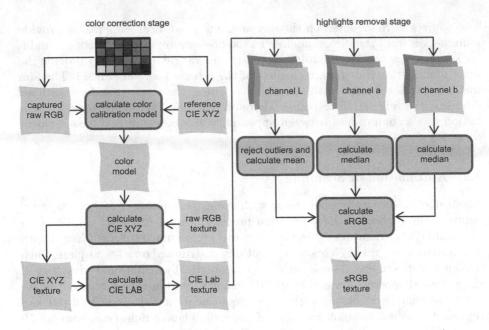

Fig. 2. Diagram of the texture correction procedure. (Color figure online)

The model relies on a linear relationship between raw camera signal in three channels (red, green and blue) and the CIE XYZ coordinates, as in Eq. 1.

$$r = q \cdot \mathcal{M} \quad \text{where: } q = \begin{bmatrix} R & G & B \end{bmatrix}, r = \begin{bmatrix} X & Y & Z \end{bmatrix} \tag{1}$$

It is justified by the fact that the CIE XYZ factors are defined as a linear function of a spectral response, with color matching functions as parameters [12]. The assumption holds as long as the camera intensity response is linear, e.g. no gamma correction is applied to the input signal.

The model can be easily established if both, the camera RGB and reference CIE XYZ values are known for a set of color samples (Fig. 2). Let $R[n \times 3]$ be the reference CIE XYZ coordinates and $Q[n \times 3]$ the RGB response of n samples. Consequently, the model can be found by inverting the response matrix with a pseudo-inverse method.

Here we use a X-Rite ColorChecker chart as a source of calibration color samples. The response matrix R is built from the average of captured RGB values of each patch of the color target. The calibration procedure is performed for each camera and light source combination yielding 12 model matrices. They are applied to appropriate texture images. Finally, for each texture image from each light source the CIE LAB color representation is calculated.

The accuracy of color calibration was evaluated in two ways. In the first approach, the absolute one, the ΔE_{00} was calculated for each patch of the ColorChecker

Table 1. Average ΔE_{00} for all patches in the ColorChecker chart, relative to the nominal CIE LAB coordinates. Numbers 1–6 indicate light source, whereas letters (A, B) distinguish cameras.

1A	1B	2A	2B	3A	3B	4A	4B	5A	5B	6A	6B
3.64	3.00	3,19	3.40	2.87	3.69	4.10	2.78	4.09	3.65	2.70	2.88

	1A	1B	2A	2B	3A	3B	4A	4B	5A	5B	6A	6B
1A	0,00	2,85	2,53	1,88	6,99	6,45	5,68	7,35	9,23	9,26	7,83	9,79
1B	2,25	0,00	2,85	3,18	6,35	7,01	6,94	6,11	7,99	8,20	6,82	8,16
2A	2,56	2,57	0,00	1,79	6,70	6,68	6,56	7,36	8,84	9,00	7,77	9,47
2B	1,77	2,97	1,33	0,00	6,39	6,07	6,10	7,10	8,44	8,48	7,20	8,98
3A	3,15	2,97	1,82	2,16	0,00	2,15	4,46	2,10	2,67	2,81	2,00	3,85
3B	2,63	3,74	2,58	2,06	1,99	0,00	2,64	3,49	4,42	4,15	2,93	5,48
4A	2,06	3,37	3,42	2,70	3,40	1,88	0,00	4,84	6,86	6,62	5,29	7,95
4B	2,78	1,71	2,80	3,00	2,11	2,98	2,60	0,00	3,14	3,34	2,20	3,20
5A	4,85	3,93	3,14	3,54	2,16	3,92	5,40	3,61	0,00	1,15	2,24	2,40
5B	4,08	3,55	2,70	2,79	1,73	3,04	4,62	3,18	1,39	0,00	1,85	2,79
6A	2,04	2,11	1,92	1,68	1,66	2,16	2,77	1,94	3,07	2,20	0,00	2,77
6B	3,30	1,85	2,72	3,15	2,13	3,44	3,96	1,70	2,52	2,43	1,73	0,00
	1A	1B	2A	2B	3A	3B	4A	4B	5A	5B	6A	6B

Fig. 3. Average ΔE_{00} for all ColorChecker patches, calculated between all combinations of light sources and cameras. Numbers 1–6 indicate light source, whereas letters (A, B) distinguish cameras. Upper triangle – before calibration; lower triangle – after calibration. (Color figure online)

chart and for each calibration model, relative to the ground truth reference CIE Lab values of the color patches. Average ΔE values are presented in Table 1.

The second, relative accuracy evaluation is considered more important because it shows differences remaining between the calibration models. Accordingly, it directly influences visible color mismatch on overlapping point clouds. In this case average ΔE_{00} from all color patches was calculated between all combinations of the calibration models. Its distribution is shown in Fig. 3. The upper triangle of the table shows ΔE_{00} calculated from the raw data, before calibration, whereas the lower triangle illustrates the outcome after calibration.

Most of the calibrated ΔE_{00} values stay in range of (1.00; 3.00), which indicates small color difference, hardly noticeable for an average observer. They are also significantly lower than the initial accuracy, before color calibration. Moreover the relative differences are generally smaller than the ones calculated with respect to the ground truth CIE LAB for the ColorChecker chart. It indicates that, although the color calibration procedure has limited accuracy, it is sufficient for suppression of relative differences between illumination conditions. This observation fulfills the color correction objective.

4.2   Illumination Non-uniformity Correction and Highlights Suppression

The goal of the second correction step is to merge data acquired with specific lights in the way that compensates unwanted effects of highlights, sharp shadows and uneven lighting. This issue has been widely studied, both with 2D images and with final 3D models. The removal of artifacts from 2D images, especially highlights removal, can be roughly classified in two main categories: the ones working on a single image, which are mainly based on the analysis of the colors of the image, and the ones using a set of images [7]. Since with our system 6 additional images are acquired with a single scan, data redundancy required for multi-images algorithms is guaranteed. 3D-space methods are more robust but complex i.e. requiring geometry analysis of measured object or additional lights position calibration [13,14].

In the discussed solution, two important requirements lead us to choose an appropriate method. Firstly, with more than 10 thousand of separate scans to process we are looking for the fastest possible method. With complex post-processing algorithms, the duration of calculation could become prohibitively long. Secondly, data must meet the expectations of art conservators. Therefore, any estimations or averaging the data from the surroundings should be omitted. Consequently, the simplified version of multi-flash algorithm described in [15] was used. After colorimetric correction CIE XYZ are converted to CIE Lab color space and splitted in separate channels. Lightness and a,b color components are analyzed separately. To preserve documentary value of the scans, all calculations are performed per pixel (Fig. 2).

For each pixel information from 6 input textures, acquired with specific lights, is taken into consideration. Lightness is calculated as a mean value after rejecting maximum and minimum outliers, which refers to specular highlights and shadows. Due to color correction performed in the first step, between-textures deviation of a and b color components is low and final a and b are calculated as median of input values. Finally, modified L, a and b textures are stacked together and converted to sRGB color space, for visualization purposes, and color information is transferred from each pixel to corresponding vertex of cloud of points. Figure 4 shows the outcome of the texture correction procedure and outcome of the final 3D model.

At the final step between-clouds averaging or segmentation and smoothing within specific segments can be performed. Each cloud is being divided into segments based on points' hue. Afterward, a small neighborhood of each point is found among the overlapping clouds and the final color value is calculated as an average of colors of points from the neighborhood. Such procedure decrease the color noise, remove local texture non-uniformity and generally improve final visual effect by guaranteeing a smooth blending between clouds. Unfortunately, neighborhood averaging makes data not useful for documentation and archiving purposes where we expect reliable data without any misrepresentations.

Fig. 4. Exemplary textures: a, b: input CIEXYZ data from 2 different light sources; c: final visualization of the L channel; d: final visualization of CIE Lab channels; e: final color-corrected 3D model of the room corner; f, g: wood panel fragment close-up artificially illuminated from two different directions. (Color figure online)

5 Conclusion

We presented a robust color correction method for 3D documentation based on an exemplary cultural heritage object. Color calibration and highlights removal steps allow for faithful texture reconstruction despite glossiness of the scanned surface and non-uniform illumination conditions. With per-point calculations results remain trustworthy and satisfactory for art conservators.

The scale of the project lead to compromises regarding distribution of the light sources. Mounting light sources both, on the 3D scanner and the robot mount may affect the illumination uniformity for different scanning directions. Additionally, highlights removal method does not take advantage of the 3D geometry of the object because of calculations complexity for a large amount of captured raw data. Nevertheless, the collected information is sufficient to develop more sophisticated data processing methods in the future research.

Acknowledgments. This work has been supported by the project "Revitalization and digitalization of Wilanów, the only Baroque royal residence in Poland" co-financed by the European Union within the European Regional Development Fund under the Infrastructure and Environment 2007–2013 Operational Programme.

References

1. Karaszewski, M., Sitnik, R., Bunsch, E.: On-line, collision-free positioning of a scanner during fully automated three-dimensional measurement of cultural heritage objects. Robot. Auton. Syst. **60**(9), 1205–1219 (2012)
2. Pieraccini, M., Guidi, G., Atzeni, C.: 3D digitizing of cultural heritage. J. Cult. Herit. **2**(1), 63–70 (2001)
3. Berns, R., Imai, F., Burns, P., Tzeng, D.Y.: Multi-spectral-based color reproduction research at the Munsell Color Science Laboratory. In: Proceedings of SPIE, Electronic Imaging: Processing, Printing, and Publishing in Color, Citeseer, pp. 14–25 (1998)
4. Cosentino, A.: Identification of pigments by multispectral imaging: a flowchart method. Herit. Sci. **2**(1), 8 (2014)
5. Simon Chane, C., Schütze, R., Boochs, F., Marzani, F.S.: Registration of 3D and multispectral data for the study of cultural heritage surfaces. Sensors **13**, 1004–1020 (2013). (Basel, Switzerland)
6. Sitnik, R., Krzesłowski, J., Mączkowski, G.: Processing paths from integrating multimodal 3D measurement of shape, color and BRDF. Int. J. Herit. Digit. Era **1**, 25–44 (2012)
7. Artusi, A., Banterle, F., Chetverikov, D.: A survey of specularity removal methods. Comput. Graph. Forum **30**(8), 2208–2230 (2011)
8. Kopplin, M., Kwiatkowska, A.: Dresdener Lackkunst in Schloss Wilanów, Münster (2005)
9. Bunsch, E., Sitnik, R., Hołowko, E., Karaszewski, M., Lech, K., Załuski, W.: In search for the perfect method of 3D documentation of cultural heritage. In: EVA Berlin, pp. 72–81 (2015)
10. Osten, W., Nadeborn, W., Andrae, P.: General hierarchical approach in absolute phase measurement. In: Proceedings of SPIE, Laser Interferometry VIII: Techniques and Analysis, vol. 2860, pp. 2–13 (1996)
11. Hardeberg, J.: Acquisition and reproduction of color images: colorimetric and multispectral approaches. Ph.D. thesis, École Nationale Supérieure des Télécommunication (2001)
12. Wyszecki, G., Stiles, W.S.: Color Science: Concepts and Methods, Quantitative Data and Formulae, pp. 4–30, 117–118, 249–253. Wiley, New York (2000)
13. Callieri, M., Cignoni, P., Corsini, M., Scopigno, R.: Mapping dense photographic data set on high-resolution sampled 3D models. Comput. Graph. **32**, 464–473 (2008)

14. Dellepiane, M., Callieri, M., Corsini, M., Cignoni, P., Scopigno, R.: Artifacts removal for color projection on 3D models using flash light. In: Proceedings of the 10th International Conference on Virtual Reality, Archaeology and Cultural Heritage, pp. 77–84 (2009)
15. Feris, R., Raskar, R., Tan, K.H., Turk, M.: Specular reflection reduction with multi-flash imaging. In: IEEE 17th Brazilian Symposium on Computer Graphics and Image Processing, pp. 316–321 (2004)

The Traveling Optical Scanner – Case Study on 3D Shape Models of Ancient Brazilian Skulls

Camilla Himmelstrup Trinderup[1], Vedrana Andersen Dahl[1],
Kristian Murphy Gregersen[2], Ludovic Antoine Alexandre Orlando[2],
and Anders Bjorholm Dahl[1(✉)]

[1] DTU Compute, Technical University of Denmark, Lyngby, Denmark
abda@dtu.dk
[2] Natural History Museum of Denmark, University of Copenhagen,
Copenhagen, Denmark

Abstract. Recovering detailed morphological information from archaeological or paleontological material requires extensive hands-on time. Creating 3D scans based on e.g. computed tomography (CT) will recover the geometry of the specimen, but can inflict bimolecular degradation. Instead, we propose a fast, inoffensive and inexpensive 3D scanning modality based on structured light, suitable for capturing the morphology and the appearance of specimens. Benefits of having 3D models are manifold. The 3D models are easy to share among researchers and can be made available to the general public. Advanced morphological modelling is possible with accurate description of the specimens provided by the models. Furthermore, performing studies on models reduces the risk of damage to the original specimen. In our work we employ a high resolution structured light scanner for digitalizing a collection of 8500 year old human skulls from Brazil. To evaluate the precision of our set-up we compare the structured light scan to micro-CT and achieve sub-millimetre difference. We analyse morphological features of the Brazilian skulls using manual landmarks, but a research goal is to automate this, fully utilize the dense 3D scans, and apply the method to many more samples.

1 Introduction

Being vital for understanding of our past, archeological specimens are a part of natural and cultural heritage which enjoys a broad professional and public interest. In this paper we discuss the benefits and challenges of scanning archeological specimens, propose a suitable data acquisition system, and demonstrate the use of our system in a small case study with a subsequent analysis of the data.

The case study involves human skulls, approximately 8500 year old, recovered from the Sumidouro cave in Brazil by the Danish scientist Peter Wilhelm Lund around 1843 [11]. These skulls are important for understanding the peopling of the Americas, and are of interest for research both now and in the future, where new technology might reveal secrets not available today. However, the skulls from

© Springer International Publishing Switzerland 2016
A. Mansouri et al. (Eds.): ICISP 2016, LNCS 9680, pp. 398–405, 2016.
DOI: 10.1007/978-3-319-33618-3_40

the Brazilian collections are fragile, and each handling of the skulls increases the risk of deterioration. Many of such handlings can be avoided by having accurate 3D models of the specimens.

Maximizing the preservation of the archeological and paleontological items, so as to make them available to future generations, is a general concern for the curators of museum collections. In this respect, one of the main advantages of 3D scanning techniques is to be compatible with objects of any size, including biological remains as well as cultural artefacts. Through 3D structured light surface scanning the shape and appearance of the artefact is documented, easily shared between researchers, and made available to the general public [4]. However, there are considerations specific for archeological specimens, which put additional requirements to the scanning system.

The first issue is accuracy. To be of use in studies of cranial morphology, the 3D skull models need to be highly accurate. The scanning system should therefore have a well documented and high precision.

Furthermore, material alteration needs to be considered when scanning archeological specimens. In case of our Brazilian skulls, it has not yet been possible to extract any DNA from the bone tissue. However, this might be made possible in the future. Despite being classified as non-destructive, scanning techniques based on electromagnetic radiation including light sources like laser scanners, but especially penetrating ionizing radiation used in e.g. CT, may potentially lead to DNA damage [3,8].

To meet these requirements we propose a setup with a structured light scanner [6]. The scanner we use is highly portable, and scanning can take place at the museums, which is important for further reducing the handling damage to specimens. As an additional advantage, our structured light scanner is assembled from of-the-shelf parts, making it a low-cost scanning modality, with a price in the range of €10,000–15,000, compared to a metrology CT scanner starting at €500,000. Furthermore, the surface appearance e.g. color is captured. The first part of this paper, Sect. 2, contains a thorough description of our scanner, and evaluates its accuracy compared to a micro CT scanner.

The second part of this paper, Sect. 3, deals with the morphological analysis of the skull data. In an investigation by Neves et al. [11] morphology of the skulls from the Brazilian collection is established by measuring certain distances following standard procedures. It is our ambition to replicate those measures on 3D models. Ideally, the measures would be automated, which requires establishing a correspondence between the skulls. This would open a possibility of constructing a unified 3D model of cranial morphology.

However, the Brazilian skulls are all incomplete in some way – an inevitable factor when dealing with ancient specimens. The most complete skull has approximately 96 % of its original mass left, whereas a big part of the collection has less than approximately 60 % left. Consequently, handling the partial data is an important concern when choosing data processing methods.

One way of addressing this issue involves building a statistical 3D model of a human skull which incorporates specific shape priors. The priors might be

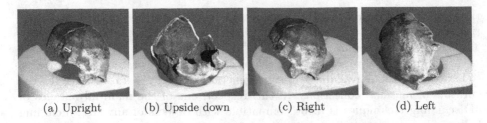

| (a) Upright | (b) Upside down | (c) Right | (d) Left |

Fig. 1. Photographs of the four different positions used while scanning. One of the less complete skulls is shown. The background is made gray to make the skull appearance clearer.

obtained from scans of complete skulls of modern man. Such a model could reconstruct the missing parts of an incomplete skull with a certain statistical significance. Our initial results, presented in this paper, are based on manually annotated landmarks, which is the typical approach for shape analysis. However, using all points in the scan would provide more information, but this requires finding corresponding points on the different scans.

In a longer-term perspective, automating data acquisition and processing of skulls would allow us to extend the model with other and diverse specimens. This leads to a statistical shape model of a skull, which can be employed for analyzing the shape variation within a set of skulls, and comparing it against variations of subgroups from the model. Furthermore, estimators for age, gender, ancestry, and race, could be provided by the model. If extended with scans of ancient skulls along the entire temporal range of human evolution, including archaic hominins, our model would be a full evolutionary model of human skull, opening for a better understanding of the phylogenetic relationship of the multiple hominin groups that existed in the last 6 million years.

2   Data Acquisition

Efficient and accurate data acquisition is essential for creating 3D models of archeological specimens, and is a prerequisite for advanced shape modeling. In this section we describe the data acquisition of the skulls from the Brazilian collection using an optical structured light scanner. The structured light scanner is based on visible light, which in practice is harmless to the specimens. In this section we also validate the accuracy of the scanner.

Scanning Skull Specimens. Our scanning setup, called SeeMaLab, is assembled at the Technical University of Denmark and is described further in [6]. It includes a rotation stage which allows for a 360° acquisition, where we chose to acquire structured light images in steps of 20°. The setup is calibrated such that it provides a single point cloud for a complete 360° scan. The cameras used are 9.1 megapixel color cameras providing highly dense point clouds. One 360° acquisition takes about 2 min and with moving the sample, a single scan can be acquired

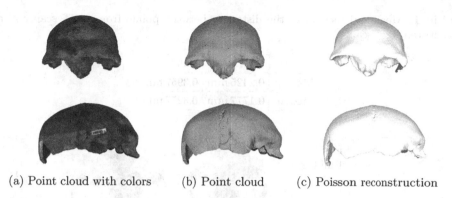

(a) Point cloud with colors   (b) Point cloud   (c) Poisson reconstruction

Fig. 2. Assembled point clouds with and without texture information and an example of a surface reconstruction of the skull presented in Fig. 1.

in about 10 min for an experienced user. We used phase shift encoding [12] with 64 projections for all scans. The texture of the objects is obtained from the captured color images. To ensure high accuracy the scanner is calibrated on a daily basis and each time it has been moved. This is possible since the calibration procedure is fully automated and easy to perform.

The scanned specimens include 24 skulls from the Brazilian collection at the Natural History Museum of Denmark in Copenhagen [11]. All skulls have missing parts, and 9 skulls are very incomplete and consists of mere bone fragments.

In order to capture their entire shape, we placed each skull in four different positions as shown in Fig. 1. The resulting point clouds were assembled using the iterative closest points (ICP) algorithm [2] implemented in the MeshLab tool.

Structured light scanning is limited to surfaces that primarily scatter light from the object surface, which rules out transparent or reflective objects. Luckily skulls have good reflective properties. However, there are some black regions that are hard to capture resulting in small holes in the point clouds.

We obtain a point cloud density of up to 300 points per mm^2 because of overlapping viewing positions giving up to 30 million points for the most complete skulls. This leaves us with excellent representation of the surface allowing us to compute an accurate and highly detailed 3D surface model using Poisson reconstruction [9] from MeshLab. An example of the point clouds obtained by the optical scanner is shown in Fig. 2 along with a Poisson reconstructed surface.

Scanning Accuracy. The standard approach for assessing the accuracy of a surface scan is established as the deviation of individual reconstructed points. In case of SeeMaLab the accuracy is down to 10 μm and it therefore meets industry standard VDI/VDE 2634 (Part 2) [1]. To investigate how the point clouds compare to a metrology scanner, we provide a distance measure between point clouds obtained using SeeMaLab and CT scans. For this experiment we used a fox and a bulldog skull.

Table 1. Mean and median of the distances between points from a CT scan and a structured light scan.

	Fox	Bulldog
Mean	0.2425 mm	0.3957 mm
Median	0.1777 mm	0.3277 mm

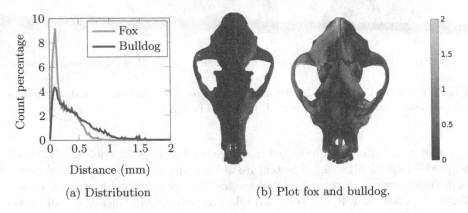

(a) Distribution   (b) Plot fox and bulldog.

Fig. 3. Left: Histogram of point-wise distances from CT to optical scan for the fox and bulldog skull. Right: Illustration of point-wise distances on the skulls.

CT scanning is valuable in metrology science [13] and had it not been for potentially harmful effects, it would be an excellent choice for scanning ancient specimens, when high accuracy is a priority. CT scanning produces volumetric data and the accuracy of a CT scanner is expressed in terms of voxel size. The scans we used have a voxel size of 190.8 μm. They are acquired for this experiment using a Nikon XT H 225 micro-CT scanner at the Imaging Center at the Technical University of Denmark[1]. The dog skull is a bulldog specimen from the Zoological Museum of Denmark at Copenhagen University and the fox skull belongs to one of the authors.

In order to compare a volumetric CT scan with the point cloud, we need to establish surface of the skull in the CT scan. This is done by thresholding voxel intensities and extracting the surface mesh using marching cubes algorithm [10] and considering the vertices of the mesh as a point cloud. The point clouds are hereafter aligned using the ICP algorithm.

There is a significant differences in the representation of the shape for the two scans. To cope with these differences we estimate a surface point cloud from the CT scans and consider point-wise distances between the scans.

The results of accuracy validation are summarized in Table 1 and Fig. 3. The larger deviations occur at the areas that are most likely to be occluded. This is e.g. seen in the inner corners of the cheekbone. Our results obtained in this

---

[1] http://www.imaging.dtu.dk/.

analysis clearly demonstrate that our optical surface scanning is an option for obtaining accurate 3D scans of fragile cultural heritage specimens. We obtain higher accuracy than reported in [7].

3 Shape Analysis

It is our ambition to use and analyze the 3D scans of ancient skulls in a statistical shape model. This would require a larger number of complete scans than we could obtain from the Brazilian collection. So, in order to initially demonstrate the use of our data we include it in a model based on the publicly available 3D-ID.org² dataset. Hence we build a model based on anatomical landmarks.

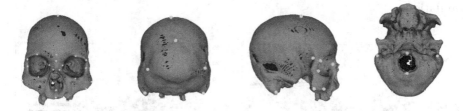

Fig. 4. Placement of the anatomical landmarks on the skull.

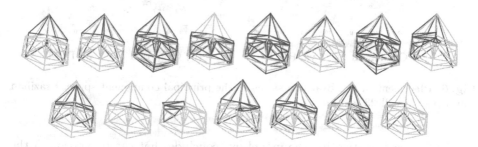

Fig. 5. Landmarks (shown as mesh vertices) for the 15 skulls from the Brazilian collections compared to the mean shape from 3D-ID.org.

Shape Model. The forensic database 3D-ID.org contains data on 889 skulls including up to 34 landmarks per skull. For building the active shape model [5] we use 759 most complete skulls and 23 landmarks. We follow the conventional approach with aligning the shapes using Procrustes analysis (translation and rotation, but not size), and preforming the principal component analysis to identify the variation within the shapes. The largest contributor to the shape variation is the size of the skull, describing nearly 30 % of the total variation.

---

² www.3d-id.org.

We chose the 15 most complete scans of Brazilian skulls to include in the shape model. We manually placed anatomical landmarks equal to those from 3D-ID.org on the skulls. The landmark setting was repeated three times, and the final positioning of the landmarks is an average of the three. In the case of the Brazilian skulls, it is not possible to locate all landmarks on every skull.

Figure 4 illustrates placement of the landmarks on a skull, while Fig. 5 shows landmarks for the 15 skulls from the Brazilian collection compared to the mean skull shape obtained from the shape model.

Modelling results. Figure 6 (a) shows the distribution of the population along the two first principle components direction (PC 1 and PC 2). The size of the skull is a chief contributor to PC 1, so PC 1 correlates largely with the gender distribution. The Brazilian skulls are not distinguishable from the general population.

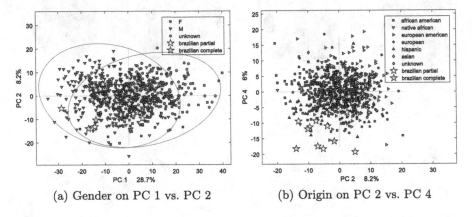

(a) Gender on PC 1 vs. PC 2   (b) Origin on PC 2 vs. PC 4

Fig. 6. Placement of the Brazilian skulls in the principal component space. Brazilian complete have all 23 landmarks.

By further investigating the model, we conclude that the separation of the Brazilian skulls from the general populations is most evident for the forth principal component (PC 4), illustrated in Fig. 6 (b) against PC 2. Investigating the forth principal component further by looking at the magnitude of the landmark contributions, we see that the three landmarks at the back of the skull have higher values. This indicates that the Brazilian skulls are distinguished from other considered populations by the shape of the posterior portion of the skull.

4   Conclusion

In this paper we suggest using optical scanning based on structured light for obtaining 3D surface models of archeological artifacts and specimens. We have demonstrated a scanning system on a collection of ancient skulls and shown that we obtain an accuracy very close to that of a micro CT scanner, using a fast, inoffensive, and inexpensive scanning modality. In addition we have shown the use of our data for shape modeling using a few landmarks. Landmark-based analysis is not ideal, because all data between landmarks are not included in the analysis. Our aim for future work is to include the full 360° point cloud, but we do see some exciting challenges for this work especially with point-to-point registration. We also wish to expand the collection of skulls obtained using our scanning system. Hereby, we will not only be documenting our cultural heritage, but potentially revealing new discoveries within evolutionary biology.

References

1. Acko, B., McCarthy, M., Haertig, F., Buchmeister, B.: Standards for testing freeform measurement capability of optical and tactile coordinate measuring machines. Measur. Sci. Technol. **23**(9), 094013 (2012)
2. Bærentzen, J.A., Gravesen, J., Anton, F., Aanæs, H.: Guide to Computational Geometry Processing: Foundations, Algorithms, and Methods. Springer, London (2012)
3. Bertrand, L., Schöeder, S., Anglos, D., Breese, M.B., Janssens, K., Moini, M., Simon, A.: Mitigation strategies for radiation damage in the analysis of ancient materials. Trends Anal. Chem. **66**, 128–145 (2015). http://www.sciencedirect.com/science/article/pii/S0165993614002490
4. Boochs, F., Trémeau, A., Murphy, O., Gerke, M., Lerma, J., Karmacharya, A., Karaszewski, M.: Towards a knowledge model bridging technologies and applications in cultural heritage documentation. ISPRS Ann. Photogrammetry, Remote Sens. Spat. Inf. Sci. **II–5**, 81–88 (2014)
5. Cootes, T., Baldock, E., Graham, J.: An introduction to active shape models. Image Processing and Analysis, pp. 223–248 (2000)
6. Eiriksson, E., Wilm, J., Aanæs, H.: Precision and accuracy parameters in structured light 3-D scanning. ISPRS. - International Archives of the Photogrammetry, Remote Sensing and Spatial Information Sciences (2016, to appear)
7. Friess, M.: Calvarial shape variation among middle pleistocene hominins: an application of surface scanning in palaeoanthropology. C.R. Palevol **9**(6), 435–443 (2010)
8. Grieshaber, B.M., Osborne, D.L., Doubleday, A.F., Kaestle, F.A.: A pilot study into the effects of X-ray and computed tomography exposure on the amplification of DNA from bone. J. Archaeol. Sci. **35**(3), 681–687 (2008)
9. Kazhdan, M., Bolitho, M., Hoppe, H.: Poisson surface reconstruction. In: Proceedings of the Fourth Eurographics Symposium on Geometry Processing, vol. 7 (2006)
10. Lorensen, W.E., Cline, H.E.: Marching cubes: a high resolution 3D surface construction algorithm. In: ACM Siggraph, vol. 21, pp. 163–169. ACM (1987)
11. Neves, W.A., Hubbe, M., Piló, L.B.: Early holocene human skeletal remains from Sumidouro cave, Lagoa Santa, Brazil: history of discoveries, geological and chronological context, and comparative cranial morphology. J. Hum. Evol. **52**(1), 16–30 (2007)
12. Salvi, J., Pages, J., Batlle, J.: Pattern codification strategies in structured light systems. Pattern Recogn. **37**(4), 827–849 (2004)
13. Suppes, A., Neuser, E.: Metrology with CT: precision challenge. In: Proceedings of the SPIE - The International Society for Optical Engineering (2008)

Author Index

Abdmouleh, Med Karim   91
Abouelaziz, Ilyass   369
Adetiba, Emmanuel   243
Afdel, Karim   337
Ahmad, M. Omair   317
Akaho, Rina   101
Alain, Chalifour   30
Aloui, Soraya   21
Amar, Meina   328, 356
Arbelo, Manuel   283
Arens, Michael   3
Azam, Muhammad   193
Azeroual, Assma   337

Barina, David   346
Becker, Stefan   3
Belaid, Ahror   12, 21
Ben Alaya, Ines   253
Benazoun, Abdeslam   40
Bougarradh, Ahlem   273
Bouguila, Nizar   193
Bouhlel, Med Salim   91
Boukerroui, Djamal   21
Bouzalim, Lahoucine   283
Bunsch, Eryk   388
Burd, Randall S.   61

Cabal-Yepez, Eduardo   71
Cherifi, Hocine   369

Dahl, Anders Bjorholm   398
Dahl, Vedrana Andersen   398
Douzi, Hassan   328, 356
Driss, Mammass   30

Eftestøl, Trygve   262
Eilevstjønn, Joar   262
El Hajji, Mohamed   328, 356
El Hassouni, Mohammed   369
El Khoury, Jessica   109
El Massi, Ismail   40
El Yassa, Mostafa   40
Elayan, M. Abdallah   317

Engan, Kjersti   262
Ersdal, Hege   262
Esmaeili Salehani, Yaser   118
Es-saady, Youssef   40

Fathallah, Nouboud   30
Firmin, David   179

Gaddour, Houda   127
Gazor, Saeed   118
Ghorbel, Faouzi   253, 273
Gourrame, Khadija   328, 356
Gregersen, Kristian Murphy   398

Hamadache, Zohra   203
Harba, Rachid   328, 356
Hasegawa, Madoka   157
Hirai, Keita   137
Hirose, Misa   101
Hofkens, Johan   79
Horiuchi, Takahiko   137
Hu, Jinhui   378
Hu, Xiaohui   304
Hübner, Wolfgang   3

Idbraim, Soufiane   283
Ishikawa, Masahiro   157

Jribi, Majdi   253

Kala, Jules Raymond   51
Kanoun, Slim   127
Kato, Shigeo   157
Keegan, Jennifer   179
Khalfallah, Ali   91
Khalid, Manchih   30
Kieritz, Hilke   3
Klima, Ondrej   346
Kobayashi, Naoki   157
Komagata, Hideki   157
Kraiem, Tarek   253

Labrador-Garca, Mauricio   283
Lakehal, Elkhamssa   148

Lech, Krzysztof   388
Li, Xinyu   61
Linde, Jørgen E.   262
Lizarraga-Morales, Rocio A.   71

Mączkowski, Grzegorz   388
Mairesse, Fabrice   79
Mammass, Driss   40, 283
Mansouri, Alamin   109
Marsic, Ivan   61
Martinez-Leon, Maricela   71
Mata-Chavez, Ruth I.   71
Mhiri, Slim   273
Mohiaddin, Raad   179
Moodley, Deshendran   51
Mostafa, El Yassa   30

Nakahata, Ryosuke   137
Ning, Liu   169

Ogawa, Shu   157
Olugbara, Oludayo O.   243
Orlando, Ludovic Antoine Alexandre   398
Ouamour, Siham   203, 213
Oudra, Moulid   283

Palit, Sarbani   293

Rahmoun, Somia   79
Riad, Rabia   328, 356
Rodriguez-Donate, Carlos   71
Roe, Paul   222, 231
Ros, Frederic   328, 356
Ruan, Ruolin   378

Sadhukhan, Payel   293
Sayoud, Halim   203, 213

Schwarzkopf, Lin   222
Shinoda, Kazuma   157
Shuang, Liang   169
Slabaugh, Greg   179
Sliwa, Tadeusz   79

Tapamo, Jules Raymond   51
Thomas, Jean-Baptiste   109
Towsey, Michael   222, 231
Trinderup, Camilla Himmelstrup   398
Tsumura, Norimichi   101

Uji-i, Hiroshi   79

Vincent, Nicole   127
Viriri, Serestina   51
Vu, Huyen   262

Wang, Qingquan   304
Wang, Yang   304
Wang, Zhongyuan   378

Xie, Jie   222, 231

Yang, Guang   179
Yarrot, Ladislaus Blacy   262
Yasumiba, Kiyomi   222
Ye, Xujiong   179
Youssef, El Habouz   30
Youssef, Es-saady   30

Zemcik, Pavel   346
Zhang, Jinfang   304
Zhang, Jinglan   222, 231
Zhang, Liang   222, 231
Zhang, Yanyi   61
Ziou, Djemel   148

Printed in the United States
By Bookmasters